THE EAST-WEST CENTER, established in Hawaii by the United States Congress in 1960, is a national educational institution with multinational programs. Its purpose is to promote better relations and understanding among the nations and peoples of Asia, the Pacific area, and the United States through their cooperative participation in research, study, and training activities.

Fundamental to the achievement of the Center's purpose are the cooperative discovery and application of knowledge and the interchange of knowledge, information, ideas, and beliefs in an intercultural atmosphere of academic freedom. In Center programs, theory and practice are combined to help current and future leaders generate, test, and share knowledge about important world problems of mutual concern to people in both East and West.

Each year about 1,500 scholars, leaders, public officials, mid-level and upper-level managers, and graduate students come to the Center to work and study together in programs concerned with seeking alternative approaches and solutions to common problems. For each participant from the United States, two come from the Asian/Pacific area. An international, interdisciplinary professional staff provides the framework, content, and continuity for programs and for cooperative relationships with universities and other institutions in the Center's area of operations.

Center programs are conducted by the East-West Communication Institute, the East-West Culture Learning Institute, the East-West Food Institute, the East-West Population Institute, and the East-West Technology and Development Institute. Each year the Center also awards a limited number of "Open Grants" for graduate degree education and research by scholars and authorities in areas not encompassed by the problem-oriented institutes.

The East-West Center is governed by the autonomous board of a public, nonprofit educational corporation—the Center for Cultural and Technical Interchange Between East and West, Inc.—established by special act of the Hawaii State Legislature. The Board of Governors is composed of distinguished individuals from the United States and countries of Asia and the Pacific area. The United States Congress provides basic funding for Center programs and for a variety of scholarships, fellowships, internships, and other awards. Because of the cooperative nature of Center programs, financial support and cost-sharing arrangements also are provided by Asian and Pacific governments, regional agencies, private enterprise, and foundations.

The Center is located in Honolulu, Hawaii, on twenty-one acres of land adjacent to the University of Hawaii's Manoa campus. Through cooperative arrangements with the University of Hawaii, the Center has access to University degree programs, libraries, computer center, and the like.

East-West Center Books are published by The University Press of Hawaii to further the Center's aims and programs.

CULTURE-BOUND SYNDROMES,

ETHNOPSYCHIATRY,

AND ALTERNATE THERAPIES

Culture-Bound Syndromes, Ethnopsychiatry, and Alternate Therapies

Volume IV of *Mental Health Research in Asia and the Pacific*

EDITED BY
WILLIAM P. LEBRA

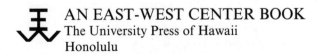

AN EAST-WEST CENTER BOOK
The University Press of Hawaii
Honolulu

Library of Congress Cataloging in Publication Data
Main entry under title:

Culture-bound syndromes, ethnopsychiatry, and alternate therapies.

(Mental health research in Asia and the Pacific; v. 4)
Rev. and enl. versions of papers originally presented at the
Fourth Conference on Culture and Mental Health in Asia and the
Pacific held Mar. 20–24, 1972 at the East-West Center.
"An East-West Center book."
Includes bibliographies and index.
1. Psychiatry, Transcultural—Congresses. 2. Folk
medicine—Congresses. 3. Ethnopsychology—Congresses.

I. Lebra, William P. II. Conference on Culture and Mental Health
Research in Asia and the Pacific, 4th, East-West Center, 1972.
III. Series. [DNLM: 1. Culture—Congresses. 2. Mental disorders
—Congresses. 3. Ethnopsychology—Congresses. 4. Mental
disorders—Therapy—Congresses. 5. Psychotherapy—Congresses.
W3 C587 1972c / WM20 C744 1972c]
RC455.4.E8C84   616.8'9   74-78860
ISBN 0-8248-0339-6

Composition by Asco Trade Typesetting Limited, Hong Kong
Manufactured in the United States of America

Contents

Preface

THE FOURTH CONFERENCE on Culture and Mental Health in Asia and the Pacific was held during the week of March 20–24, 1972, at the East-West Center, University of Hawaii. The conference was a part of the Culture and Mental Health Program, which has been sustained by the East-West Center, the University of Hawaii, and the National Institute of Mental Health (Grant #MH09243). The origins and principal objectives of that program were described in some detail by William Caudill and Tsung Yi Lin in the first volume of this series (*Mental Health Research in Asia and the Pacific*, edited by W. Caudill and T. Y. Lin, Honolulu, East-West Center Press, 1969). Essentially, the program stimulated and facilitated contact between researchers in the field of culture and mental health in the Asia and Pacific regions. Asian and American researchers in anthropology, psychiatry, and psychology were brought together in Honolulu for periods varying from several months to a year to participate in a weekly seminar with Hawaii faculty, to conduct research, and to write. In a period of over seven years more than sixty individuals took part. Week-long conferences, held in 1966, 1969, 1971, and 1972, drew upon those who had been in residence in the program as well as selected colleagues engaged in research relevant to the program goals.

The papers contained in this volume represent a majority of those presented at the fourth conference. The theme, Culture-Bound Syndromes, Ethnopsychiatry, and Alternate Therapies, seemed to us a natural outgrowth or culmination of our accumulated experience in the program. There are several factors which have led us to this opinion. For one thing, it is abundantly clear that the overwhelming majority of people in the Asia and Pacific area do not have access to modern psychotherapy for the treatment of mental health problems. Moreover, given continuing population explosion and rising economic cost factors, it is apparent that the bulk of these people will not enjoy such services in the foreseeable future. Obviously, the folk therapist and folk therapy, as well as other nonmedical modes of healing and curing, will prevail for some time to come. Therefore, at least minimally it behooves all of us to understand the nature of folk therapy and its effects. In Malaya, for example, there were in 1970 eight psychiatrists available for 9 million people; Dr. Eng-Seong Tan and his colleagues have studied the phenomena of traditional healing and curing among the various ethnic groups comprising the citizenry of their country and have refrained from public (or private) diatribes, rather they have quietly investigated the prospects for cooperation and/or coexistence.

There is yet another conclusion which has emerged and that is the undeniable fact that even where there are relatively adequate and readily available modern psychotherapeutic staffs and facilities, a significant segment of the population nonetheless will preferably select a nonmedical course of healing and another large segment may elect to pursue both simultaneously. Japan is one of the top three industrial nations, and its rates for literacy and life expectancy exceed those of the United States; yet, in Tokyo, the world's largest city, Dr. Yuji Sasaki and his coworkers found that a majority of the patients being treated at their clinic were also actively involved, for health reasons, in one of the so-called new religions. It is obviously erroneous then, if Japan is any guide for the rest of mankind, and I think it likely, to expect that the passing of the traditional therapist and the increasing accessibility of modern psychiatry will automatically result in the triumph of the latter. For one thing, as already noted, the early passing of the traditional therapist appears highly improbable, for even in intensively industrialized and urbanized Japan, the traditional folk therapist may still be found. And it is only recently that Japanese researchers have turned to the new religions since these now attract, for health purposes, a larger percentage of the population than do the more traditional therapists, many of whom nonetheless are still thriving.

Equally as significant as the persistence of traditional psychotherapy and/or the concurrent employment of modern psychotherapy with new religious cults is the evidence compiled by Sasaki and others indicating that markedly favorable responses can be attained with neurotics through participation in the programs of some of the magico-religious cults; even epileptics suffering grand mal attacks felt themselves to be improved and confidently anticipated further progress. This indeed raises a challenge of considerable magnitude for contemporary psychotherapy and is urgently demanding of further research.

A common occurrence in this program has been the repeated contention of virtually every Asian participant who obtained all or a portion of his or her clinical training in North America or Western Europe that so much had to be "unlearned" after returning home if their therapeutic efforts were to be effective. This did not refer to minor nuances of style but to fundamental issues of therapeutic procedure and implicitly to the whole theoretical basis, especially of psychoanalysis, of Western psychotherapy. We have only recently, and painfully, learned that our political system and ideology are not as easily exportable to Asia as we once believed (somehow we seemed unmindful of the earlier failure of our religious proselytizing). So it should come as no great surprise that much of the theory and practice of Western psychotherapy is not instantly exportable in unmodified form to the various cultures of Asia, for, as Dr. Kyoichi Kondo writes, psychotherapy is closely related to the cultural milieu of society. In fact, we may note, as a parallel, that the recent rapid proliferation of "off-beat" therapies and healing cults in contemporary United States probably reflects the need for a "better fit" of therapies and subcultures comprising the various ethnic, class, and religico-ideological commitments making up our pluralistic society.

The critical linkage of culture and mental illness is highlighted by the so-called culture-bound syndromes or culture-specific disorders. Not only are there marked cultural variations in the frequency of mental disorders, but also there are vast differences in behavior content and culturally ascribed meanings. In the first volume of this series Caudill and Schooler delineated the symptom patterns of hospitalized Japanese patients giving particular attention to *shinkeishitsu* which is commonly encountered in Japan and which is a distinctly Japanese disorder. Not surprisingly, a distinctly Japanese psychotherapy, Morita Therapy, has been developed for the treatment of *shinkeishitsu*. The literatures of psychological anthropology and of transcultural psychiatry are replete with descriptions of culture-bound ("exotic") syndromes, frequently with accompanying accounts of traditional folk therapy for the treatment of these. Morita Therapy, however, is not the practice of a traditional folk-healer or shaman, but the creation of a psychiatrist who obviously found limitations in the application of Western-derived psychotherapy to certain Japanese disorders. Similarly, Japanese Naikan Therapy has been fashioned by a contemporary Buddhist priest, and while visiting his clinic my wife and I observed the admission of a patient who had been referred by a psychiatrist at a major medical school. The essential point is that in modern Japan we are witnessing the emergence of new or alternate therapies which probably will not be applicable for all of mankind but which are effective for treating certain types of disorders within this culture and possibly in some others. Undoubtedly the coming decades will witness the emergence of many additional alternate therapies in the cultures of Asia as well as elsewhere in the non-Western world.

In the foregoing paragraph I mentioned behavior and culturally ascribed meaning, a simple fact of which we are mostly unaware. Recently I witnessed a large meeting dominated by Western psychotherapists in which Chinese and Japanese colleagues argued, persuasively I thought, that East Asians can handle dependency more openly and confidently than their Western counterparts. Their illustrative examples, rather than successfully underscoring their points, seemed to elicit amusement and mirth from some segments of the audience. Given the nonstatic nature of culture and the fact that all cultures are continually changing and evolving, it would seem expedient, minimally in terms of survival, to urge the need for tolerance, flexibility, and adaptability. A true transcultural psychotherapy can only stand on the combined truths and universalities in all ethnopsychotherapies, and this can be facilitated through transcultural research and interchange, as we have attempted here.

Most of the papers were received in advance of the sessions permitting duplication and distribution to all of those taking part. An oral presentation, limited to twenty minutes, was followed in each case by a discussion period of approximately twenty or more minutes. Most of the papers were extensively revised, and frequently lengthened, after the conference. Several of the papers could not be included here, usually because of space limitations or lack of relevance. Although the discussion sessions were taped and transcribed, they unfortunately could not be added to this volume, but where real disagreement or argument was engendered, copies were given the authors concerned for their consideration when rewriting. In keeping with the precedent established by Caudill and Lin in the first volume of this series, I have refrained from adding my personal comments or interpretations.

Many individuals contributed to the success of the conference. My colleague and coprincipal investigator Dr. Thomas W. Maretzki offered useful advice regarding selection of participants. In addition to those whose papers are included here, Dr. Ruth Finney, University of Hawaii; Dr. Ah-Leng Gwee, General Hospital, Singapore; Dr. Alan Howard, University of Hawaii; Dr. Anthony Marsella, University of Hawaii; Dr. Koichi Ogino, Kanazawa University; Dr. Bou-Yong Rhi, Seoul National University; and Dr. Richard Williams, National Institute of Mental Health, played active roles and were valued participants. Special thanks are also due to Miss Kathleen Kay who handled the logistics and to Mrs. Laura Felix, Mrs. Freda Hellinger, and Miss Phyllis Watanabe who typed and retyped the papers and portions of the manuscript. The assistance of all of the foregoing as well as that of the National Institute of Mental Health in funding the conference and program is gratefully acknowledged.

On March 24, 1972, the final day of the conference, we were all saddened to learn of the untimely death of our colleague, William Caudill, who played an instrumental role in establishing the conference series and who was in the forefront of culture and mental health research. This volume is respectfully dedicated to his memory.

William P. Lebra

Honolulu, Hawaii
August, 1973

CULTURE-BOUND SYNDROMES

1. Notes for a Theory on *Latah*

H.B.M. MURPHY, M.D.

Department of Psychiatry
McGill University
Montreal, Canada

CULTURE-BOUND SYNDROMES can be likened to rare genetic defects, attracting attention through their unusual features but causing comparatively little damage to humanity, and hence are of importance to medicine mainly for the light that they cast on little-understood aspects of human functioning. They must, of course, be properly described and differentiated, but beyond that our interest should be not so much in the syndrome per se as in the relation it bears to current theories of mental functioning and structure. Sometimes that relationship seems fairly simple, the syndrome having arisen merely through an unusual conjunction of otherwise familiar factors: the conjunction, for instance, of certain beliefs about spirit possession with a specific environmental stress and the normal reactions to that stress, as in the case of the Windigo psychosis (Fogelson, 1965). With other culture-bound syndromes, however, there are no obvious links to be found between the cultural beliefs, the environmental stressors, and the symptomatology; and these invite closer examination. Studying them could just possibly lead to the discovery of some process that was previously unrecognized or at least poorly understood.

 Latah is one of these more interesting syndromes, for there is no obvious connection between its manifestations and the beliefs of the peoples among whom it mainly occurs, and although in one form it seems to be linked to the well-known "startle reaction," in its other main form such a connection is missing. Because my time is limited I am going to assume that the reader of this volume, interested in culture-bound syndromes, knows of the condition and has read some descriptions of it. However, since descriptions have varied, it can be useful to recall its main features.

Its distribution, or at least the distribution of related syndromes, is quite wide, from Africa to Siberia and the northeastern coast of America (Pfeiffer, 1971; Yap, 1952); yet, cases have been very rare except in one cultural region, the Malaysian, where it is sometimes quite common (Murphy, 1972). Its manifestations take two main forms, a startle reaction often accompanied by coprolalia, and a compulsive mimicry, persisting despite the victim's conscious desire to stop. There is no obvious environmental stressor with which it is associated, but the precipitating circumstance is usually an unexpected noise, touch, or gesture experienced in the presence of persons whom the victim views as superior or desires to please. It has been labeled variously as an anxiety reaction, a fright neurosis, a state of hyper-suggestibility, and a psychosis, but my concern here is not with how to label it but with how to explain its various features. As the title of this paper suggests, I do not think that we know enough at present to explain it fully, but I believe there are a number of overlooked clues that lead us closer to a comprehensive theory for the syndrome than previous writers on the subject have realized.

The Startle Pattern

In their simplest form, *latah*-type disorders appear to be little more than exaggerated startle reactions and it is appropriate, therefore, to commence by reviewing what we know about the latter. Startle reactions are found in all normal men and animals (Landis and Hunt, 1939). Their intensity can be increased by placing animals in conflictual or frustrating situations (Bachmann and Armus, 1970), and under these conditions repetition of the startle stimulus may lead not to habituation, which is to say a reduction in the amount of startle shown, but to a more complicated type of "conditioned frustration" (Wagner, 1963). In man habituation is not consistent (Gogan, 1970), but if subjects are divided into rapid and slow reactors, the latter tend to show both the less habituation and the greater signs of a momentary loss of consciousness, something which is to be distinguished from momentary loss of control (Sternbach, 1960). The classic studies of Landis and Hunt (1939) have shown that after the invariable primary reaction there comes a secondary conscious or conditioned one that can indicate curiosity, fear, or annoyance but that can also suggest an "overflow" of emotion or temporary release of repressed drives into the motor system. In infants the startle pattern can sometimes include penile tumescence (Landis and Hunt, 1939; Greenacre, 1952), and in some psychotics it includes protection of the genitals (Landis and Hunt, 1939), suggesting that the reaction can have sexual associations.

Exaggerated secondary reactions are particularly marked in catatonic schizophrenics, but not in schizophrenic patients with a different type or phase of the disorder. Brain-damaged individuals tend to give the most exaggerated reactions of all, those which Goldstein (1939) called "catastrophic" and which he interpreted as being due mainly to loss of a sense of wholeness. However, swearing or the repetition of a purposeless phrase can occur in startled normal persons, and the startle stimulus can be a sudden realization of a social situation instead of a pistol shot. Bleuler, for instance, cites the case of a healthy man who, meeting a lady on the staircase and realizing that his fly was undone, caught himself murmuring "oil immersion, oil immersion, oil immersion," that being a topic he had stopped discussing half an hour earlier (1950). The main difference between such a person and the mild *latah* victim is that the former will react only if the stimulus is a genuine surprise and will recover almost immediately, while the latter is likely to react even when forewarned, and his recovery takes much longer. The literature on startle reactions tells us under what conditions the reactions are likely to be exaggerated, but it does not tell us how they can be repeatedly elicited even after all element of surprise is past, which is the case with many *latah* victims. In the further search for clues, therefore, it seems obvious to turn to some other disorder in which such explosive reactions repeatedly occur despite the subject's desire to stop them. The most suitable example of such a disorder is the *maladie des tics*, or Gilles de la Tourette's syndrome.

Gilles de la Tourette's Syndrome

This syndrome was once thought to be the same as *latah* (Gilles de la Tourette, 1884), but the two are quite distinguishable. Gilles de la Tourette's syndrome starts in childhood with motor tics and unstructured verbal explosions, the coprolalia and echopraxia appearing only later, whereas *latah* is a condition of adult life, starting immediately with coprolalia or echopraxia and rarely associated with motor tics. Also, the eponymous syndrome requires no startle stimulus or social setting, whereas *latah* usually does. However, in both conditions one gets coprolalia, echolalia, and echopraxia, and in both the victim is usually (though not invariably) unable to prevent the behavior by forewarning or will power.

The primary lesion in Gilles de la Tourette's syndrome is thought to be a fault in the corpus striatum or striopallidal connections between the basal motor centers and the higher cortical inhibitory ones (Balthasar, 1957; Mahler and Rangell, 1943), something which led to a neurological lesion being suspected in *latah* also. However, this neurological lesion is not thought by most authorities to be sufficient to bring on the full picture; rather, it "renders the individual defenseless against overwhelming emotional and psychodynamic forces ..." (Mahler and Rangell, 1943) aroused by a disturbed family milieu (Lucas, 1970). Not all children with the syndrome have a disturbed family milieu, but those who show the larger verbal component usually do; and when one meets a similar condition, resulting from the absorption of a poison such as manganese, in an adult then the coprolalia and echopraxia are nearly always absent (Korbin, 1970). Conversely, if the verbal symptoms are a major component, they can sometimes be relieved by psychotherapy (Carluccio et al., 1964; Clark, 1970), the psychodynamics of their development being quite apparent.

The evidence from Gilles de la Tourette's syndrome suggests that the tendency to coprolalia found in many cases of *latah* may have its roots in a disturbed relationship with the milieu (which accords with our earlier observation of the relationship between startle intensity and current frustrations) but that is not likely to receive more than very occasional expression unless there is interference with inhibitory functions. The interference could be neurological, but no one has turned up evidence of a neurological disorder in *latah*, and the epidemiological picture, which I will report later, argues against the idea. Therefore it seems desirable to search for evidence of other disinhibitory influences in *latah*, and since drugs have never been implicated the most seriously considered factor has been hypnotism or suggestion. Back in the 1890s Clifford (1898) remarked that *latah* resembles hypnosis in many respects, and although he went on to note that "it differed from it in the important respect that it (*latah*) in no way depends on an original voluntary surrender of will-power (1. 189)," the resemblance between some *latah* states and hypnotic states is sufficiently strong for the matter to invite further attention.

Hyper-suggestibility

When one thinks of hyper-suggestibility in most non-Western peoples, one tends to think of possession states and shamanism. At first thought this association appears unhelpful for the present problem, since such possession states are much less common among Malaysians as a whole than among some other peoples in whom *latah* does not occur, for instance the Haitians. Also, the two groups of Malaysians among whom possession and trance are most common, the Peninsular Aborigines and the Balinese, seem to have virtually no cases of the syndrome. (I cannot remember having read of a single Balinese case, and there were none among the 144 case records collected by Van Loon [1924].) However, since we are dealing here not with a conventional entry into a trance state but rather a psychiatric syndrome that psychoanalytic teaching would view (like most other syndromes) as a form of regression to an earlier developmental phase, the subject should not be left without enquiring into possible hyper-suggestibility states in children, and when we do this we come upon an interesting fact. Although no other major Malaysian people now continues the deliberate encouragement of trance states in children that one still finds in Bali, there is evidence that such states have been tolerated as part of a children's game over a much wider geographic area.

In his monograph on Malay amusements, Wilkinson (1925) tells us that there were four such games known in Perak, that girls as well as boys played them, and that adults tended to disapprove. Here is how he describes one:

> In the game known as *main hantu musang* [the polecat spirit
> game] the principal player goes on hands and knees, is covered
> by a white sheet, and is said to be hypnotized into unconscious-
> ness by the others who march round and round him, stroking

and patting him and repeating the following words [words omitted]. After this the player is said to be possessed and is quite unconscious of his humanity. He chases the others, climbs up trees, leaps from branch to branch and so far forgets himself as to run the risk of injury by venturing on boughs too frail to bear his weight. In the end he is called to his senses by being addressed repeatedly by his name. (P.14)

Such games, he says, are distinguishable from others where an animal is merely being imitated. Others who have described similar activities by children are Hurgronje (1906) for the Sundanese, Koentjaraningrat (1957) for the Javanese, and McHugh (1955) for other parts of Malaya. Still (1940) has referred to a related game in Burma, and those who knew Belo's *Trance in Bali* (1960) will recognize the quotation above as being, apart from the method of induction, completely applicable to the adult folk trance *Sangyangs* found in East Bali. Almost certainly the relegation of such possession states to the status of a game is the result of the conversion to Mohammedanism (Alkema and Bessemer, 1950), but what is important for my argument is not their origin but the fact that they existed, persisting even against adult opposition and hence presumably without adult instruction.

Are such children's games found in other cultures, and if so is *latah* or a *latah*-like syndrome also found there? I have searched the Human Relations Area Files and other anthropological sources of information regarding children's games, and I have found only one doubtful report of children in another culture employing trance for their own amusement. That other culture is the Burmese, as cited above, and in the locations where the practice is found one also finds a *latah*-like condition called *Yaung de Hte* (Still, 1940). There is no evidence that this type of game is found in cultures where trance states are common among the adults but where *latah* is rare or unknown. In the latter societies children may play at being possessed, as Bourguignon has described (1965), just as they play at all other adult activities, but there is no evidence that the children actually go into a trance. On the other hand, there are instances of *latah* victims (Swettenham, 1898) and other mentally disturbed adults (Van Loon, 1922) in Malaysian cultures imitating animal behavior in the same fashion as in the children's games.

A connection between such children's games and the *latah* syndrome thus seems probable, but at the same time it is unlikely that this connection is a direct one and that *latah* victims are persons who played such games when they were young. If that had been the case one would expect it to be mentioned some-times in clinical histories of *latah* subjects, and this is not so. Moreover, with at least one of the *latah*-like syndromes found in other parts of the world, namely the "jumper" syndrome in Eastern Canada and the United States, it is virtually certain that an experience of trance states in childhood does not occur, even though with another *latah*-like syndrome, that found in North Africa, it may sometimes happen.[1] It seems preferable, therefore, to hypothesize not that such games predispose one to a *latah* state later (though this may happen) but that genetics or upbringing predisposes one to hyper-suggestibility, which then shows itself in the games, in *latah*, and in the ease with which Malaysians seem able to enter into trance states when the social setting encourages them to do so. Given that hypothesis, we can start looking for ways in which this predisposition or susceptibility could have been brought about.

Child Rearing

Evidence for a genetic predisposition to *latah* and to the related Jumper syndrome in America is wholly lacking, but if one takes the literature on hypnotizability as a guide there are certain aspects of child rearing in parts of the Malaysian culture sphere which do seem significant.

In Western populations hypnotizability has been found to be linked to one definite aspect of child rearing and to a personality trait that in turn seems likely to have been acquired in childhood. Furthermore, there is another personality trait that has not been researched in normal Western populations, since it is very rare among them, but that is common in some Malaysian peoples and that would theoretically seem relevant. The definite link concerns the type of parental contact. Many researchers of hypnotism have noted that subjects who were positively oriented toward their parents tended to be more easily hypnotizable than those who were negatively oriented, and this had usually been assumed to mean merely that the former were thus less distrustful of the hypnotist, but Long (1968) found that the explanation goes further. Studying college students, he found hypnotizability to be positively associated with a history of intimate physical contact with parents, with a tendency for the mother to use verbal rather than physical punishment, and with the father's religious involvement. Hence a predominance of such features among the relevant Malaysian peoples would lead us to expect that the children would be hyper-suggestive.

The researched personality characteristic concerns the mode of reacting to frustration. Rosenzweig, testing some aspects of a personality theory he had been developing in association with Henry Murray, discovered that "hypnotizability as a personality trait is to be found in positive association with repression as a preferred mechanism of defense and with impunitiveness as a characteristic type of immediate reaction to frustration" (Rosenzweig and Sarason, 1942). (Impunitiveness means denying that a real frustration exists, and it is contrasted in this theory—and in the Picture-Frustration Study that derived from it—with both extrapunitiveness and intrapunitiveness, the commoner reactions in Western subjects.)

Finally, the unresearched trait is the tendency to dissociation, whether this be dissociation of body from will, of thought from appearance, or of part from whole. Since all Western child training makes virtues of the opposites to these—a virtue of honesty in showing one's feelings, for instance—normal individuals showing a dissociative tendency are rare in the West, and we tend to think of it as a pathological trait. In some cultures, however, it is not so unusual, and theory would lead us to expect that since hypnosis is in a sense a dissociation of one's will from the body and part of the mind, any tendency to the latter would include a tendency to hyper-suggestibility as well. Certainly most of the dissociated hysterics studied by Pierre Janet (1889) proved to be easily hypnotizable.

These observations suggest that where we find a culture practicing strong parent-child affection, much body contact between parent and infant, a detachment of feeling from behavior, the surrender of one's body to guidance by others, repression as the main method of handling intrapsychic conflict, and evasion or denial as the way of handling interpersonal conflict we should also have a culture whose members are easily hypnotizable or, to speak more generally, easily led to put aside some inhibitory controls under suitably suggestive conditions. The question now is whether those Malaysian peoples in which one meets *latah*, child trance states, or other signs of hyper-suggestibility follow the foregoing practices to a greater degree than peoples within the Malaysian culture sphere or elsewhere who do not show as great an apparent tendency to hyper-suggestibility.

To answer this it seems best to search out the child-rearing practices common to Java, Sumatra, Bali, the Malay Peninsula, and perhaps Celebes, and then to contrast them with the practices described for such groups as the Alorese and Filipinos.[2] If differences exist in the expected direction, then it seems reasonable to suspect that child-rearing practices and hyper-suggestibility are associated.

Most professional and many other observers have commented on the remarkably close and warm relationships that young Malaysian children have with their parents. Geertz remarks that children are much wanted and enjoyed (Geertz, 1961:83), and Djamour (1955) notes that the Singapore Malays believe a child will pine and die if away from his mother, so close is their bond. Physical punishment is very rare in both societies and when it occurs often results in parental strife. In Bali the relationship is a little more complex, with the mother sometimes not following through with a caress, but the relationship is still close, with feeding given on demand. In Alor, however, the infant may be left at home when the mother goes to the fields, and among the Bisayan it is not long before the child begins to hear harsh words from the father. In Java, Bali, Celebes, and much of the Peninsula the young child is in almost constant physical contact with the parents, being carried in a relaxed fashion in a cloth sling at the mother's side, a practice which is not as common in Alor and the Philippines. One of the consequences of this body-sling contact is that body tonus is low and passivity is high. Mothers throughout the region encourage the passive molding of the child's body to their own, and proceed from this to a manipulation of the child's body as if it were an extension of their own. In part this may be due to the cultural demand that the small child make certain religious and social gestures long before he is able to understand what he is doing. Whatever the reason, the result is that the child learns many body movements passively and in a dissociated fashion. Mead writes of the Balinese that virtually all motor learning, whether it be walking, eating, or something more complex, is "accomplished with the teacher behind the pupil, conveying directly by pressure ... the gesture to be performed. Under such a system of learning, one can only learn if one is completely relaxed and *if will and consciousness as we understand those terms are almost in abeyance* (Bateson and

Mead, 1942:15; italics added). Geertz writes similarly that "the kind of learning by being pushed and pulled through a simple pattern of motion" (1961:100) covers much of the Javanese child's first motor and linguistic development. As a result, one sees quite early in the Balinese photographs something that Mead and Macgregor call "dissociated body parts" (Mead and Macgregor, 1951, pl. 55 and 56), which continues into adult life, both under normal conditions and in trance (Belo, 1960). "Where an American or a New Guinea native will involve almost every muscle in his body to pick up a pin, the Balinese merely uses the muscles immediately relevant to the act, leaving the rest of the body undisturbed" (Bateson and Mead, 1942:17). The same has been noted to a lesser degree in the Javanese but not in the Filipino and Alorese.

That apparent dissociation of body parts is accompanied, as the child grows older, by a dissociation between conventional gesture and real feeling. The renowned politeness and propriety of the Malay and Javanese are learned early, with the performance of the correct gestures or attitudes of respect being valued far ahead of the actual feeling of respect. "In fact, a significant aspect of all Javanese (and Malay) social relationships is that the important thing is not the sincerity of the action but the successful concealment of all dissonant aspects of the relationship" (Geertz, 1961:111). This both strengthens the dissociative tendency and promotes an "impunitive" reaction to immediate frustrations. For instance, if a conflict arises, the traditional Malay reaction is not to thrash out the matter openly or to wait for one of the parties to take responsibility on himself but to avoid the topic or perhaps avoid social contact, even repressing one's feelings in private. There are numerous instances in Malayan epics of a hero swallowing some insult but exploding with wrath a considerable time later, often to do much greater damage than the original insult merited; that is char-acteristic of inflexible repression as a defense.

There is thus ample evidence suggesting that the child-rearing practices of some Malaysian peoples are likely to predispose one to hyper-suggestibility and to the suspension of inhibiting ego controls under suitable circumstances. If *latah* were merely a sign of hyper-suggestibility and if a startle stimulus could throw hyper-suggestive individuals into a hypnotic state, the problem of the syndrome's origin would be solved. But easily hypnotized persons in Western populations do not become *latah* when startled, and among the Malaysians the group that shows the greatest inclination to enter trance states, the Balinese, do not become *latah* either. Hence, while it seems probable that a predisposition to hyper-suggestibility is one factor in *latah*, there must be others that come into play before the syndrome can manifest itself. These have still to be tracked down.

One fairly obvious factor is the pressure of repressed libido drives, and it is easy to imagine that when the concealment of strong feelings is demanded, as with the Javanese, repressed drives will be stronger than when such feelings are expected to be expressed, as in many Western societies. Another factor is the availability of alternative outlets for such repressed drives, and here it is easy to imagine that the socially approved trance states of the Balinese offer such an ample outlet that the relatively unsatisfactory mode of expression offered by *latah* would not be used. But these factors by themselves do not permit us to account for the remaining elements in the *latah* story. Of these remaining elements the most initially puzzling is the change in incidence which the condition has shown through time and space, and it is to this which I now wish to turn.

Epidemiology

The changes in the incidence of *latah* since its first description are not well known, but are quite striking when one looks for them. Since I have described them in detail and with full references in a previous paper (Murphy, 1972), I propose only to summarize them here, directing the reader who wishes more information to that earlier review.

Latah was first described by Europeans in the middle of the nineteenth century, and although there are at least two prior references to a condition called *latah* in earlier Malay texts (Wilkinson, 1901–1903; Hervey, 1885), it is my opinion that these earlier references concern a simple startle reaction or ticklishness and not the syndrome later called *latah*. (In the one earlier source I have been able to trace, a wife accidentally stabs her husband with a needle when he tickles her.) Until about 1890 it seems to have remained quite uncommon or at least unobserved, but around that time a series of reports came out from both Malaya and Java suggesting that cases could be found in every village or city street, a couple of authors suggesting that the condition had almost an epidemic character. At that time it was occurring almost as often in men as in women, as much in the educated upper classes as in the lower, and in the young adult as well as the old. In location it was definitely concentrated around the centers of European settlement. Over the next three decades the picture changed, *latah* becoming rarer in the centers of European influence, rarer in the young, almost unknown in males, and concentrating now in female servants. Whereas cases had been described as occurring in almost every street at the turn of the century, a survey of physicians in the early 1920s revealed that few had seen more than a single case.

Another three decades and the picture has changed again. Now, as Yap found (1952), cases are almost impossible to find in the main centers of European influence and are then atypical, but quite typical ones are still to be found in smaller towns, and the condition is extending into a population that seems previously to have been free of it, namely the Iban of Borneo. It still occurs almost wholly in women of little education, but these women are now not merely servants, and few of them have had contact with Europeans. Among the Iban, cases were found in the new urban and suburban settlements where Malay culture dominates, for instance around Kuching, but not in the traditional communities. Once again the condition is almost wholly a female one and in Java seems mainly to affect older women, but in Borneo young women are affected as well.

Some of these changes might be interpreted as the result of an infection—a mild encephalitis, for instance—brought in by Europeans and spreading outward like the wave in a pond from a dropped stone, leaving immune populations in its wake. There are many details of the picture which do not fit this interpretation, however, notably the sex distributions, the absence of the syndrome in populations such as the Batak, among whom Europeans were quite active, and the fact that some of the earliest cases occurred in people who had no prior contact with Europeans. It seems preferable, therefore, to think of the Europeans not as bearing some infection but as creating or precipitating a new social problem, and when one approaches the problem from this angle the obvious key is rapid social change. By the mid-nineteenth century Europeans had changed from bizarre transients to people whom it could be profitable to copy or to serve, but the learning of their outlandish ways and the changed behavior they demanded could have posed a severe problem, one that might be relevant to the *latah* story.

As was noted earlier, children in the relevant Malaysian peoples learn by submitting passively to the guidance and suggestions of their teachers, and by this means they acquire certain skills and behaviors much more rapidly than a Western child would, even though they have not yet grasped the meaning of such behaviors. It seems very possible, therefore, that when these children become adults and are faced with the need for the rapid learning of some little-understood social behavior, they would revert to the same method of learning, i.e., submitting themselves to the guidance and suggestions of others, assuming a passive and hyper-suggestive state. Only relatively small numbers within the population would feel called on to take this stance, of course, and of them only a very few would develop *latah* as a side-effect, but one can imagine that for a time the numbers of hyper-suggestive persons would have increased, with the numbers of *latah*-prone individuals increasing as a result. Moreover, although it was mainly the Europeans who evoked such a learning state, any other demand for adaptive acquisition of the customs of a higher-prestige group could do the same.

On the other hand, such evoked hyper-suggestibility is not likely to have remained for long in normal individuals. The passive mode of learning, though rapid, has the disadvantage that the principles underlying the learned behavior are not grasped, and hence the learning cannot be easily adapted to changed circumstances. As soon as the new behavior becomes less incomprehensible or the pressures to learn it are reduced, one would expect the style of learning to change, with the middle-class male making the change much more rapidly than the lower-class female, since the former is much the more likely to want to adapt his new knowledge to his own purposes. But one could imagine that for a time the relevant Malaysian peoples would exploit their capacity for hyper-suggestibility in order to master strange new behaviors or demands as quickly as possible, and the changing distribution of *latah* might reflect, as a side-effect, the prevalence of this hyper-suggestive adaptability.

Such a theory, if acceptable, would account for the spread of *latah* among Clifford's male servants (1898) once they had learned the advantages of pleasing him; the initial occurrence but rapid disappearance of the syndrome in educated Malays (Fletcher, 1908); its occurrence in lower-class women finding themselves in more refined middle-class society (Geertz, 1968); its appearance in Iban women adjusting to Malay suburban life at a time when it was absent in Iban women still living in their own bush communities (Chiu et al., in press); and its disappearance from many more urban locations where it had formerly been common (Yap, 1952). Moreover, it accords well with the presence of echopraxia as a symptom, if we take Stengel's view (1947) of that behavior as being in part an effort at identification in the psychoanalytic sense.

But it does not account for the whole syndrome. The person who experiences an embarrassing or painful episode under hypnotism will usually guard against recurrences or, if he cannot, will usually show signs of neurosis or other mental disturbance. Some *latah* victims do manage to rid themselves of the abnormality once it has become embarrassing, and others are clearly suffering from a chronic mental disturbance quite apart from their *latah*. The majority of victims, however, neither guard adequately against the episodes nor show any sign of mental abnormality outside of these. The coprolalia is clearly embarrassing to most female victims of *latah* (this symptom is much commoner in the females than in the males), and one would normally say that it could gain such expression only if it were a manifestation of a severe neurosis linked to sexual anxiety. Yet outside of their *latah* episodes, which may be few, such women usually show no signs of such a neurosis. There would thus seem to be still another factor beyond the startle, the hyper-suggestibility, and the presence of unconscious sexual anxieties, and this we have still to look for, making use of overlooked clues.

Tickling and the Generalization of Erotic Arousal

One of these clues, I suggest, lies in the name of the syndrome, which in Malay also means simply "ticklish" (Wilkinson, 1901–1903). In Thailand the related syndrome, *bah xi*, is reported to mean "tickling madness" (Rasch, 1895), and some of the other *latah*-like syndromes around the world are reported to be precipitated particularly by tickling. It seems worthwhile, therefore, to look at what we know about tickling in relation to psychopathology and in relation to Malaysian child rearing or culture.

For Malaysian children, tickling and physical teasing are not as infrequent and as trivial a matter as they are for Western children, judging by the literature. Mead writes of the Balinese that a baby is for a woman "something to play with, to toy with, to titillate and to tease, ... to stroke and to tickle" (Bateson and Mead, 1942:24). Moreover, this is not done solely by the mother; "... on a crowded occasion a popular baby may change arms forty times in an afternoon. People tickle them and tease them ... making them cry ..." (Mead and Macgregor, 1951:38). In consequence, "as the children grow older they withdraw into themselves, away from the overstimulating and unrewarding teasing" (Bateson and Mead, 1942:26). In other Malaysian peoples the overstimulation may be less, but Djamour (1955) comments on the teasing of almost a sexual nature that children receive from their mothers. Similarly, Geertz notes that patting and ruffling of an infant's penis by mothers is common, with any resultant erection being "received with pleasure and more ruffling" (1961:102). All this does not imply tickling in the most limited sense but it does imply a teasing and sexually oriented stimulation of the skin, which is what tickling mainly is. Finally,

Wilkinson reports that among the very first formal games played by children with each other are two tickling games. "One infant tickles the other. The child that stands the tickling longest is the winner" (1925:7). This sounds like a more mutual and invited process than the tickling that older children elsewhere impose on some victim, and I have been able to locate only one other culture (in New Guinea) where tickling has also been noted to be a regular children's game. It is justifiable, therefore, to infer that such tickling plays a larger role in the lives of some Malaysian children than one would expect to find in many other cultures. From other clues one may guess that the practice was favored as a means of teaching children a repressive mode of self-control.

Turning to the relationship between tickling and psychopathology the picture is less clear, for this is a subject that most psychiatrists appear to have ignored. However, there seems to be general agreement that tickling, maternal seduction, and other methods of tactile and sexual stimulation in the pregenital phase carry the risk of stimulus generalization and libidinous overflow, features which were earlier noted to occur sometimes in the startle pattern. These features can in turn lead to a masochistic tendency to seek pleasure in the passive role or in a state of denied discharge (Orchinik, 1958), and this seems possibly relevant, since masochism is a recognized feature in many *latah* histories, with the subject being passive and implicitly inviting attack. Another consequence, this time of the stimulus generalization, is that nonsexual stimuli are taken as sexual ones or are responded to not through a single appropriate channel but through many channels simultaneously. Greenacre (1952) had a patient with a history of over-stimulation in the pregenital phase who responded to stress situations by "an unexpected bowel movement, involuntary urination, an unexpected vomiting, a genital orgasm or a severe menstrual flooding." This is strikingly similar to Ellis' (1897) *latah* subject who, when admonished, "stands trembling for a few seconds, micturates and passes flatus, and then as if startled by the sound she loudly utters a filthy word and promptly apologizes for her conduct." A third connection between tickling and psychopathology has been proposed as respects the symptom of stuttering, a symptom which also finds an echo in the blurting echolalia and coprolalia of *latah*. It has been theorized that because direct motor and sexual reactions are denied the tickled victim, laughing and panting being the expected responses, there develops a displacement of the genital reaction toward the mouth and a tendency to take the word for the deed (Orchinik, 1958). This is not the orthodox psychoanalytic theory respecting stuttering, but Orchinik found a history of being persistently tickled in a high proportion of stutterers, and therefore the point deserves attention.

These observations suggest that the Malays' use of the word for ticklish to describe the syndrome may have a deeper significance than has been realized, and tickling was apparently the precipitating cause in one of Yap's male cases (1952). The strongest evidence for a deeper connection between childhood tickling and adult *latah,* however, comes from the most recent firsthand study of *latah* to be published (Chiu et al., in press). Following up a lead suggested by Van Loon (1924), Chiu asked a group of *latah* victims about dreams, both recent and at the time the *latah* started. Twelve of his Malay cases reported having had a disturbing dream prior to the start of the condition; most of these dreams had frankly sexual imagery; two of the twelve mentioned being tickled by or in association with male genitalia![3] I therefore suggest that the Malay *latah* victim's failure to defend herself adequately against recurrences may be related to being tickled or sexually stimulated in the pregenital phase, with a consequent masochism and stimulus generalization. Because of that generalization, the *latah* stimulus or startle is interpreted as a sexual attack; because of the masochistic tendency there is an acceptance or inviting of such attacks; because of the hyper-suggestibility and reduced inhibitions the expression of sexual feelings is permitted in a fashion that is at other times repressed; and because of the learned displacement of sexual reactions toward the mouth this sexuality shows itself more in coprolalia than in other ways.

Dreams and Dream Censorship

The final feature of *latah* that I feel calls for explanation is the frankly sexual dream that often precipitates it. According to Freud and Jones, the more forbidden or anxiety-provoking the wish which a dream has sought to fulfill, the more disguised will be its manifest content. If we assume that in many female *latah* subjects there is an underlying, masochistic sexual desire that has been forbidden direct expression, then the apparent lack of disguise in these *latah*-precipitating dreams would seem to indicate either that the repressed desire provokes very little anxiety or that the Malaysian *latah* subjects do not have a normal dream censor as part of their ego. The first of these alternatives could harmonize well with the fact that most *latah* subjects are apparently quite healthy and free of neurosis outside of their attacks, but it accords poorly with the fact that some of the women recall the dreams as being accompanied by considerable anxiety. The second alternative would be in accordance with the statements of some earlier writers concerning the primitive nature of the Malaysian psyche, but does not accord with the rest of the evidence. If one considers the dream topics reported by Van Loon (1924) and Chiu et al. (in press), then it is clear that symbolization does occur. Moreover, where it does not and where the penis is frankly represented, then it is difficult to think of the remembered dream—for instance, a dish of wriggling penises prepared for eating—as being an adult's simple wish-fulfillment. On the contrary, the disgusting nature of these dream fragments suggests quite strongly that censorship and counter-cathexis has been at work. There was less anxiety provoked when the penis was symbolized as a worm, and so forth, than when it was undisguised. Yet if censorship had occurred, what was there to censor?

The answer becomes clear if we compare the more openly erotic nightmares cited by Jones (1951) for European subjects with the frankly sexual semi-nightmares in the Malays. The European woman dreams of a man lying heavily on her but with no genitals seen; the Malaysian dreams of the genitals attacking her, but usually with no man seen. In both types of dream there is a separation of person and genitals and hence an obstruction to the repressed wish to be sexually attacked by a specific person. In Europe, where male genitals were concealed even in small boys, it was that half of the complete wish that was removed from the manifest dream; in Malaysia, where the small boy's penis is displayed and fondled by his mother and sisters but where incest taboos are no less strong, the genitals can be allowed representation but the identity of the desired seducer cannot. Moreover, whereas in Europe it is rare to think of a body part without the whole unless death is implied, to the relevant Malaysian peoples the dissociation of bodily parts which can retain a life of their own is not at all a strange idea. Graveyard spirits can be represented in the Javanese shadow plays as personified limbs; legendary spirits can be described by the Peninsular Malays as comprising only part of the body (McHugh, 1955). Mead, writing of Balinese children's toys (often live ones) refers to them as symbolizing the "idea of a separated and animated phallus" (Bateson and Mead, 1942:25), a strikingly pertinent insight in view of the present dream evidence.

There are good reasons, therefore, for thinking that in the cases reporting such dreams the *latah* is precipitated not merely by a repressed sexual hunger but by a reawakening of, or a regression to, the childhood desire for incorporation of the father's penis. That it is a reawakened childhood desire is evidenced by the symbolic incorporation through the mouth that a few of these dreams depict.[4] That the *latah* episodes have relieved the tension can be inferred from the fact that dreams experienced after the condition has started do not have the same content (Chiu et al., in press).

It would be unwise to go further with the interpretation of the limited evidence and say that it is penis envy or desire to be a male rather than a simple seduction wish that sparked the dreams. But it does not seem too much to suggest that if a return to a hyper-suggestive state had occurred, as has been hypothesized here, then this would facilitate regression of other types as well, including regression to a desire for the loving, powerful father in place of the comparatively powerless husbands that these women are sometimes described as having (Geertz, 1968). Or alternatively, one can envisage the old desire for incorporation of the father's power as likely to contribute to the readiness with which such subjects would submit themselves to the suggestions and demands of superiors, whether they be white colonials, the higher or more sophisticated strata of their own society, or merely the more forceful members of their own villages.

Conclusion

The foregoing exposition suggests that there are seven main factors contributing to the development of a typical case of *latah* in a Malaysian female, although whether all are necessary for its development is another matter. The seven factors are:

1. *Repressed wishes* probably of an infantile sexual character, adequately cathected and seeking an outlet.

2. *Stimulus generalization* leading to nonsexual stimuli being misinterpreted as sexual.

3. *A masochistic tendency* resulting in a failure to defend against the provocative stimuli and perhaps provoking such stimuli instead.

4. *Dissociative child-rearing practices* conducing to hyper-suggestibility.

5. *The rewarding of hyper-suggestibility in adults*, as by the introduction of beneficial but little-understood knowledge that could most rapidly be mastered by rote learning.

6. *Suppression of lengthier dissociations* or trance states through which the repressed wishes could obtain fuller expression.

7. *An inflexibility of impulse control* that leads to exaggerated startle reactions (such as occur also in catatonia) and thence to temporary suspension of inhibitions when startle occurs.

The first three of these are such as could be expected to produce a neurosis in a Western subject, or at least some sexual perversion, the patient probably being quite handicapped by the continuous conflict between the upsurging wishes and the ego controls. The *latah* subjects show no sign of such a continuous conflict. Instead, the inhibitory ego controls usually appear quite sufficient to prevent the forbidden wishes from penetrating consciousness or affecting behavior until they are tricked by suggestion or by a startle stimulus into releasing their hold briefly. One can say that this is due to the repressed wishes being relatively weak and easy to control, and there is some support for this in the fact that all the main investigators of the syndrome report some subjects to be more seriously affected, either going into a *latah* state many times a day on the slightest provocation or showing signs of another form of mental disturbance. However, one can also interpret the evidence as suggesting that the milder cases of *latah* illustrate a different type of ego-id relationship from that which seems to exist in the milder varieties of Western neurosis. It is this, in my opinion, which makes the quite rare and otherwise unimportant condition of *latah* worthy of attention by psychiatric theorists.

The factors which I have cited here as probably contributing to the development of the *latah* state have nearly all been mentioned at one time or another by other students of the subject, notably by Yap, whose monographic study of the subject was far ahead of its time. What has been added here has mainly been an attempt to account for all instead of for only some of the features of the syndrome, and to relate the different factors to each other. That a complete theory for *latah* has now been proposed is too much to say, however, for the question of the ego-id relationships in this condition need further exploration, and it is not at all clear how many of the suggested factors are absolutely necessary for the development of the syndrome. That they all contribute to most of the cases described from Malaysia is in my opinion highly likely, but it is equally clear that some must have been absent from the histories of patients with *latah*-like syndromes in other cultures. What has been done here for the Malaysian cases therefore still needs to be done for some other group such as the "jumpers" of Maine. Some of the suggested factors are sufficiently related for the presence of one to make the presence of another probable—numbers 2 and 3, and 4 and 7, for instance. But if so many factors are truly necessary, then this could explain the peculiarly transient character of the group of syndromes around the world. They have been described in many places, but usually we have only one or two reports and then the condition seems to disappear from view again. The regrettable fact is that outside of Malaysia the reports which we have had on these transient states and on the peoples that harbor them have usually been too slight to permit much deduction.

NOTES

1. The Aissaoua sect, with members from Morocco to Ethiopia, regularly employs trance in its ceremonies and has "clans," with each clan being possessed by its own animal spirit. When a clan's animal is nimble rather than fierce, children are recruited to be possessed by it (Wavell et al., 1966: 142). The reports of *latah* from that region do not mention the victims as belonging to this sect, but the concurrence of the two states in the same people is suggestive.

2. The main sources used for this comparison are the incomparable series of photographs collected by Bateson and Mead (1942) and Mead and Macgregor (1951); the books of Geertz (1961), Guthrie and Jacobs (1966), Jocano (1969), DuBois (1944), and Koentjaraningrat (1957); and the theses of Chabot (1954), Djamour (1955)—whose thesis is better than her book for this purpose—and Mahmud (1967). However, there are others, like Hurgronje (1906), who deal with childhood less thoroughly but corroborate or cast additional light on the observations of the first-named group. Regarding the Filipinos, it can be argued on the basis of Jocano's description of their frequent hallucinations, delusions, or illusions that they must be highly suggestible (1970), but the type of suggestibility is different from the hyper-suggestibility being discussed in this section insofar as the ego appears to be easily deceived but not easily displaced. See Gill and Brenman's discussion of ego states (1961).

3. The content of the twelve dreams is as follows: "... male genitalia hanging on a tree, eating eggs and sleeping with boyfriend and male and female genitalia, giving birth, being tickled and male genitalia, basketful of steamed male genitalia, ghosts and worms, snakes, monkey and snakes and crocodiles, male genitalia and death of a friend, being tickled by enlarging male genitalia, basketful of genitalia and snakes, a man physically resembling a child." The comparable dreams of 4 Ibans concern: "the souls of the dead, being chased by snakes, snakes crawling, bathing and pounding rice."

4. Van Loon (1924) reports of his cases that "the one dreamt that she was in the marketplace buying a big basket full of wriggling penises which were still alive and moving. The old woman told her that she should take them home, bake them in oil and eat them." This is similar to the "basketful of steamed male genitalia" recalled by Chiu's subject.

REFERENCES

Alkema, B., and T. J. Bessemer. 1950. Concise handbook of the Dutch East Indies. New Haven, Human Relations Area Files.

Bachmann, R. F., and H. L. Armus. 1970. Effect of avoidance-avoidance conflict on startle magnitude. Psychological Reports 26:363–67.

Balthasar, K. 1957. Über das anatomische Substrat der generalisierten Tic-Krankheit. Archives of Psychiatry 195:531–37.

Bateson, G., and M. Mead. 1942. Balinese character: a photographic analysis. New York, New York Academy of Sciences.

Belo, J. 1960. Trance in Bali. New York, Columbia University Press.

Bleuler, E. 1950. Dementia praecox or the group of schizophrenias. New York, International Universities Press.

Bourguignon, E. 1965. The self, the behavioral environment and the theory of spirit possession. *In* Context and meaning in cultural anthropology. M. E. Spiro, ed. New York, Free Press of Glencoe.

Carluccio, C., et al. 1964. Psychodynamics of echo-reactions. Archives of General Psychiatry 10:623–29.

Chabot, H. T. 1954. Kinship, social status and sex in the South Celebes. New Haven, Human Relations Area Files.

Chiu, T. L., J. E. Tong, and K.E. Schmidt. In Press. A clinical and survey study of *latah* in Sarawak, Malaysia. Psychological Medicine.

Clark, D. F. 1970. Behavioral approach to treatment of Gilles de la Tourette's syndrome. New York State Journal of Medicine 70:2205–10.

Clifford, H. 1898. Studies in brown humanity. London.

Djamour, J. 1955. The Malay family in Singapore. Ph. D. thesis, London School of Economics.

DuBois, C. 1944. The people of Alor. Minneapolis, University of Minnesota Press.

Ellis, W. G. 1897. *Latah*, a mental malady of the Malays. Journal of Mental Sciences 43:33–40.

Firth, R. 1943. Housekeeping among Malay peasants. London School of Economics, Monographs on Social Anthropology 7.

Fletcher, W. 1908. Latah and crime. Lancet 2:254–55.

Fogelson, R. D. 1965. Psychological theories of Windigo "psychosis" and a preliminary application of a models approach. *In* Context and meaning in cultural anthropology. M. E. Spiro, ed. New York, Free Press.

Geertz, H. 1961. The Javanese family. Glencoe, Illinois, Free Press.

———. 1968. *Latah* in Java; a theoretical paradox. Indonesia 5:93–104.

Gill, M. M., and M. Brenman. 1961. Hypnosis and related states. New York, International Universities Press.

Gilles de la Tourette, H. 1884. Jumping, *latah*, myriachit. Archives of Neurology 8:68–73.

Gogan, P. 1970. The startle and orienting reactions in man. Brain Research 18:117–35.

Goldstein, K. 1939. The organism. New York, American Book Company.

Greenacre, P. 1952. Pregenital patterning. International Journal of Psychoanalysis 33:410–15.

Guthrie, G., and P. J. Jacobs. 1966. Child rearing and personality development in the Philippines. Philadelphia, Pennsylvania State University Press.

Hervey, D. F. A. 1885. Malacca legends of Nakhoda Ragam. Journal of the Straits Branch of the Royal Asiatic Society 15(26) (Notes & Queries Suppl. no. 2).

Hurgronje, C. S. 1906. The Achehnese. London.

Janet, P. 1889. L'Automatisme psychologique. Paris, Alcan.

Jocano, F. L. 1969. Growing up in a Philippine barrio. New York, Holt, Rinehart and Winston.

──────. 1970. Varieties of supernatural experiences among Filipino peasants: hallucination or the idiom of cultural cognition. Paper presented at the reconvened Annual Meeting of the American Psychiatric Association, Honolulu.

Jones, E. 1951. On the nightmare. New York, Liveright.

Koentjaraningrat, R. M. 1957. A preliminary description of the Javanese kinship system. New Haven, Yale University Southeast Asia Studies Series.

Korbin, K. B. 1970. Gilles de la Tourette's syndrome; common neurophysiological facts reported in literature. New York State Journal of Medicine 70:2193–97.

Landis, C., and W. A. Hunt. 1939. The startle pattern. New York, Farrar and Rinehart.

Long, T. E. 1968. Some early-life stimulus correlates of hypnotizability. International Journal of Clinical and Experimental Hypnosis 16:61–67.

Lucas, A. R. 1970. Gilles de la Tourette's disease; an overview. New York State Journal of Medicine 70:2197–2200.

McHugh, J. N. 1955. Hantu-hantu: an account of ghost belief in modern Malaya. Singapore, Donald Moore.

Mahler, M. S., and L. Rangell. 1943. A psychosomatic study of maladie des tics (Gilles de la Tourette's disease). Psychiatric Quarterly 17:579–91.

Mead, M., and F. C. Macgregor. 1951. Growth and culture; a photographic study of Balinese childhood. New York, Putnam.

Mahmud, Mohammed Hassan bin Ngah. 1967. Patterns of child-rearing practices among the Malays. Thesis, Department of Social Work and Social Administration, University of Singapore.

Murphy, H. B. M. 1972. History and the evolution of syndromes: the striking case of *latah* and *amok*. *In* Psychopathology: contributions from the biological, behavioral and social sciences. M. Hammer, K. Salzinger, and S. Sutton, eds. New York, John Wiley & Sons.

Orchinik, C. W. 1958. On tickling and stuttering. Psychoanalysis and Psychoanalytic Review 45:25–29.

Pfeiffer, W. M. 1971. Transkulturelle psychiatrie. Stuttgart, Georg Thieme Verlag.

Rasch, C. 1895. Über die Amok-Krankheit der Malayen. Neurologica Zentralblatt 14:856–59.

Rosenzweig, S., and S. Sarason. 1942. An experimental study of the triadic hypothesis. Character and Personality 11:1–19, 150–65.

Stengel, E. 1947. A clinical and psychological study of echo-reactions. Journal of Mental Sciences 93:598–612.

Sternbach, R. A. 1960. Correlates of differences in time to recover from startle. Psychosomatic Medicine 22:143–48.

Still, R. M. L. 1940. Remarks on the aetiology and symptoms of "Yaung de Hte." Indian Medical Gazette 75:88–91.

Swettenham, F. A. 1898. Malay sketches. London.

Van Loon, F. G. H. 1922. Acute confusional insanity in the Dutch East Indies. Geneesk. Dienst Nederlands-Indie (no vol. no.): 100–20.

──────. 1924. Lattah, eene Psychoneurose der Maleische Rassen. Geneesk. Tijds. Nederlands-Indie 64:59–82.

Wagner, A. R. 1963. Conditioned frustration as a learned drive. Journal of Experimental Psychology 66:142–48.

Wavell, S., A. Butt, and N. Epton. 1966. Trances. London, Allen and Unwin.
Wilkinson, R. G. 1901–1903. A Malay-English dictionary. Singapore, Kelly and Walsh.
———. 1925. Papers on Malay subjects. Life and customs—Part III; Malay amusements. Kuala Lumpur.
Yap, P. M. 1952. The *latah* reaction: its pathodynamics and nosological position. Journal of Mental Science 98:515–64.

2. *Malgri*: A Culture-Bound Syndrome

JOHN E. CAWTE, M.D.

The University of New South Wales
Little Bay, N.S.W., Australia

ARE THE MENTAL DISORDERS of preagricultural "primitives" different from those found in modern society, or are they variants of the familiar Western diagnostic categories? This paper presents an account of a previously unreported but superbly interesting culture-bound syndrome, *malgri*, which sheds light upon this question and upon other questions commonly asked about such syndromes. Some of the issues involved in a study of culture-bound syndromes should be outlined (with reference in this case to *malgri*), at the outset. The reader may consider how far these issues pertain to the well-publicized culture-bound disorders or "ethnic psychoses," including *latah* (in Malaysia), *koro* (in Malaysian Chinese), *witiko* (in Indian cultures of northeast America), and *amok* (in Malaysia).

1. *Malgri* describes a pattern of symptoms and behaviors specially characteristic of the culture in which it appears.

2. The culture exerts both a causal and a shaping influence in cases of *malgri*.

3. There is no one-to-one correspondence between cases of *malgri* and Western psychiatric categories—*malgri* cases cover a range of Western diagnoses.

4. Not all cases of *malgri* are psychopathological. Some are; others represent culturally acceptable expressions of anxiety or other discomfort, not amounting to psychiatric disorder.

5. Individual differences in susceptibility to *malgri* are traceable to variations in personality and experience.

6. *Malgri* serves the functional purpose of social regulation in the culture (by contributing to the maintenance of territorial boundaries). *Malgri* is found only in the Wellesley Islands of the Gulf of Carpentaria. Focal distribution of such sicknesses is to be expected in view of the comparatively restricted diffusion between the various cultural blocs of Australia, probably associated with marked ecological differences. (Details of the culture are to be found in *Cruel, Poor and Brutal Nations,* 1972.) The disorder might perhaps be termed culture-specific rather than merely culture-bound.

Malgri was encountered, in a typical sequence, through children's games. Two of my children, a girl of seven years and her brother, six, were visiting Mornington Island with me; they spent much of their time playing with a Lardil girl. During a ramble near "Picnic Place" a mile or more from the settlement, the Aboriginal girl found, exuding from a tree, some resin that was good to chew. After chewing a while, the European children ran toward the beach. The Aboriginal child called out to them to stop; they must wash their hands and mouth in a freshwater hole before going to the sea. Otherwise the rainbow snake would come out of the sea and make them sick or even kill them. My daughter, impressed with this warning, complied; her brother was skeptical but washed his hands and mouth just the same. He was not going to be the one who got *malgri* and died. An event of the next day showed how justified the precautions were. A Lardil man came to the Mission carrying his small son in his arms. The boy was very distressed and complained of pains in the legs and stomach. He kept moaning and asking his father to "Rub me guts." The Missionary gave him a sedative and he gradually recovered. The story came out that despite warnings about poisonous jellyfish, he had been bathing in the sea. But it was not a jellyfish that had stung him; his grandfather, Jacob, a tribal practitioner, comfirmed that it was *malgri.* The boy was lucky to recover, said his grandfather, who was irritated that he had not been called on to treat it. He did, however, demonstrate how he would have treated it, using his grown son for the subject, in a posed demonstration for the camera.

It was ascertained from Jacob and from other Lardil men and women that *malgri* is a prominent disorder in the Lardil medical system at Mornington Island. It appears to be a spirit-intrusion syndrome linked with the totemic organization of the people and their territory. All seemed agreed on the phenomenology.

The central theme in *malgri* is the mutual antipathy between land and sea. A person who enters the sea without washing his hands after handling land food runs the risk of succumbing to *malgri.* Traces of land food are dangerous in the sea and must first be rubbed off with sand and water; even body paint and grease must be removed. If these precautions are neglected, the totemic spirit that is guardian of that particular littoral is believed to invade the belly "like a bullet." The *malgri* victim grows sick, tired and drowsy. His head aches, his belly distends, he writhes and groans in pain, and may vomit. The pain is described as constant rather than colicky, although the precise symptoms depend on the nature of the possessing spirit. The distended abdomen might result from diaphragmatic fixation coupled with air swallowing, as in the pattern of pseudocyesis, or false pregnancy; some uncertainty exists as to the accuracy of this description of distension. Most islanders seemed to have some anxiety about contracting the illness.

To appreciate this disorder one must know that a feature of Lardil cosmology is the division of the coastline of Mornington Island into upwards of thirty littorals, each the sea frontage for a particular subsection of the tribe or class of totemites, and each with its distinctive totem. In many cases the totems, such as the shark, stingray, coolibah tree, and rock cod, are obvious local natural species; in other instances (such as totems of the moon and sea serpent) the legendary associations of the site are represented. *Malgri* spirits can also operate in the reverse direction—from the land: for example, when a person who has been fishing in the sea uses a freshwater rockpool or lagoon without first cleansing his hands of all traces of salt-water food. With the aid of several islanders, and later, map-makers, I spent a good deal of time making a chart of Mornington Island as the people saw it. Understanding the territorial scheme is essential to an accurate appreciation of the disorder.

Malgri is a sickness of intruders. The social group occupying the estate enjoys some immunity in its home range. The Lardil elder, Gully Peters, described this feature. "Me boss belong that Sandalwood River country. Yarragarra [sea eagle] is boss of the sea around that part. I can eat swamp turtle belong to that land and I can go down to that sea and I can't *malgri*. I say: 'It's me, I'm boss of this country, don't *malgri* me, Yarragarra.' If somebody doesn't belong to my country, he will *malgri* there. If I go to South Side, Sydney Island way, I can *malgri* there—not my country. If people walkabout a long time at my place, like Fred, they're all right—the sea gets their smell and knows them. It's strangers that *malgri* all the time."

When the cry goes out that somebody has fallen victim to *malgri*, everybody runs to help. A fire is made near the prostrate victim. From the throng emerges a native practitioner or other elder with knowledge. Kneeling, he massages his axillary sweat into the victim's body. A grass or hair belt is unraveled to provide a long cord which is tied by one end to the victim's foot while the other end is run down to the water, to point the way home for the intruding spirit. The healer commences the song of exorcism, which is sung through the night, with innumerable verses, while the assembled people scan the sky for a shooting star. The star is *malgri's* eye personified, at last diving from the sky to indicate the spirit's dispossession and banishment. The string is then snapped. The victim recovers. So runs the procedure for treatment.

In that part of the Appel Channel at the mouth of the Dugong River, where the island's population now congregates, the strand totem is Thuwathu, the sea (rainbow) serpent. A song for his exorcism in cases of *malgri* runs:

> *Shu! Damudaia, damudma.*
> *Gangulmaia, gangulma.*
> *Worramaia, worrama.*
> *Budgerunguru nalma.*
> *Gidilingini djuwadju wadju.*

Mudjinbi djinbi baladma.
Budjimarana, budjimaran.
Yalkamalara bingula.

Stop biting, unloose your teeth.
Unclench your jaws.
Open wide your mouth.
Move your head from this body.
Crack, break your backbone.
Relax your tail and go.
Begone you rainbow belly.
Fall back in the home you come from.

The song goes at a slow rhythmic pace with repetitions. *Djiri djiri* ("make him cold with water") can be added to any of the lines to help the exorcism or to cool the fever.

Histories were collected of cases of *malgri* occurring around the time of my visit. Various sickness and behavioral patterns were represented.

Pattern 1

A middle-aged woman contracted *malgri* shortly after our expedition arrived on the island. She had been on a picnic with two friends and had eaten some dugong meat before washing her hands in the river. A truck had to be sent to fetch her, since she insisted she could not move because of *malgri*. On arrival at the Mission hospital she complained of prostration and severe abdominal pain. No physical abnormality was detected, and she was reassured. After a few hours she recovered and was discharged. Her hospital record showed frequent attendances for complaints of pain in the head and in the chest, probably psychogenic. Medical interviews with her revealed deep dissatisfaction with her family life. Her husband had left her to take a job on the mainland, and she had to look after her boy aged two and an adopted son of seven. Her various complaints of headache, "angina," and *malgri* had to be evaluated in this context.

Pattern 2

A party of five children was taken to nearby Denham Island in charge of an intelligent and literate Aboriginal matron. *Malgri* spoiled the picnic. She subsequently reported: "The children ate bread and tinned meat. Then they went in swimming in the channel. Two of the children got pain in the stomach in that water. It could not be a jellyfish sting, because only the stomach got sore. It was tight and bulging. I took them to Sister—she only given them aspirin, she didn't know what to do. So I took them down to the camp, and an old woman said, 'See Kitchener Steele.' He treated those children. He used body sweat and that *malgri* song." The nursing Sister reported: "Both children were rolling all over the hospital verandah, clutching their stomachs and yelling. I examined them.

Maybe their stomachs were distended but they were soft to palpation. They seemed healthy apart from all the screaming, so I didn't admit them. They were better that night." Further discussion with the Aboriginal woman in charge of the picnic revealed a transactional situation of possible relevance. She was envious of the Mission nursing sister and lost few opportunities of disparaging her in an indirect way. She seemed gratified at being the central figure in an illness context that the nurse was not competent to handle. It is not suggested here that the situation was consciously engineered with this in mind, but, having once arisen, it was exploited in this way.

Pattern 3

A middle-aged man is reporting a hunting trip that was interrupted by *malgri*.

> That morning we got a sea turtle and had it for breakfast. Then
> we split up and D.B. went along the north side and he went into
> a freshwater hole. He should know better than that. He should
> have gone home. You can't take sea turtle into freshwater; this
> would *malgri*. You should eat it on the beach and then wash
> your hands. D.B. had to turn back and come to our camp. We
> helped him in; stomach was all blown up. We got hair string
> from a belt and put it from a toe to a spear under a tree. We
> sang him till five in the morning. I saw a star traveling over the
> sky from the east like a white cloud, very slow. It disappeared at
> five o'clock and that man got better. People said it was the rat
> spirit, Dowa—it was rat country—you see these rats at Birri and
> Rocky Island. We could see light all along the beach, in the
> water.

It was hard to discover the transactional background of this incident, and I was left speculating why the party of four had split up before the isolated member committed his error and contracted *malgri*.

The traditional illnesses of the Kaiadilt group from Bentinck Island were less closely studied than those of the Lardil because of the greater difficulty in communication. From discussions in the village it appeared that Kaiadilt intrusion syndromes were also common and involved the spirits of the soldier crab, reef octopus, and particularly, the mangrove rat called Wadn't by the Kaiadilt. There was no evidence that these syndromes achieved the complexity of *malgri*, though their generic name, *malgudj*, is similar. They illustrate the confluence between the two cultures and languages that developed in spite of the geographical separation and biological divergence (see *Cruel, Poor and Brutal Nations*).

Pattern 4

An old Kaiadilt woman was in the habit of talking excitedly to herself a good deal, and was generally morose to others. Routine physical examination revealed a number of highly cheloidal cicatrices on the front and back of her chest. She said that the scar in the fold under her right breast was made by her mother with a firestick during her childhood on Bentinck Island, presumably as a decoration. The wounds on her back were made by her father when she was sick as a child, to remove Wadn't, the sea rat, who was making *malgudj* inside her. The old woman volunteered this information separately from my *malgri* enquiry.

Analysis

The significance of the *malgri* syndrome was the subject of much discussion by the sociomedical team. In fact it sparked off a flurry of conjecture, which—even if we did not arrive at a full understanding of the condition—illustrates the fascination of applying modern interpretations to traditional patterns. Small wonder that exotic culture-bound syndromes provide a happy hunting ground for speculative interpretation. For example, *malgri* might be viewed, from a functionalist perspective, as a part of the total belief structure maintaining social institutions and organization, and ultimately, adaptation. From the psychiatric viewpoint it is necessary to scrutinize the pathogenic and conflictual elements of the pattern. In doing so, several elements attract comment: the antipathy expressed between land and sea, the handwashing ritual, the violated taboo, the possibility of a corresponding Western diagnosis, and the widespread phobia of the condition.

In classical psychoanalytic idiom, the preoccupation of the islanders with the sea-land antipathy would suggest to the analyst a displacement of a family antipathy, for example that between father and son, as emphasized in the Oedipal theorizing of Freud's *Totem and Taboo* (1946), or Roheim's *The Eternal Ones of the Dream* (1945). This would represent a case of the lesser fear displacing the greater terror, as suggested by Freud. In terms of neoanalytic interpersonal theory, the displacement might rather be from the individual's current family and social transactions. Some support for these interpretations could be found in day-to-day observations of the islanders' behavior, in which displacement was a common feature. It had been observed that displacement of hostility is part of the ethos of Mornington Island, an ethos that values the "happy" man, the peacemaker who is consistently generous and congenial, who avoids confrontation, and who constantly looks for ways to attribute village quarrels and fights to forces beyond anyone's control.

From the phenomenological viewpoint, the displacement might not represent an antipathy having reference to the family tensions, but refer rather to the essential difference, for the individual, between the land-sea elements. The conflict between the land and the sea is real and earnest to the islander of the Gulf. Sometimes the sea yields its food, sometimes the land. A hunting-gathering people is in a condition of sustained competition with nature and with its own members for survival. From the phenomenological perspective, the syndrome is more specifically "totem and trespass" than "totem and taboo." It is part of the network of ecological relationships evolved to prevent trespassing and to conserve proper distances between human groups. It exemplifies the ethological concept that "territory" of a social group is a pertinent consideration in behavior; indeed, often a mainspring of motivation and social interaction. What ethologists call reaction distance has been described in psychiatric patients as the "body buffer zone" (Horowitz, 1965). *Malgri* is perhaps the most specific instance in medicine of an illness associated with the concept of territoriality. While it cannot be said to represent simple extrapolation of animal territoriality to human behavior, it offers a striking example of the universal fear of leaving one's own territory and of the danger inherent in breaking the rules on foreign ground.

Some details of the *malgri* syndrome, especially the handwashing and/or contaminatory themes, do not at first sight possess a clear association with the territory theme. The handwashing pattern might be interpreted psychoanalytically as a ritual cleansing of blood after killing the land animal (symbolically father), but phenomenological examination of the situation suggests another interpretation. The injunction underlying the *malgri* taboo is not directed against killing and eating land food, but reflects the need to propitiate the sea by refraining from mixing spirits from land and sea. The sea, like the mother, is the main food-giving element for the Lardil. Offending it could lead to engulfment, failure of the food supply, or attack by its contained objects. This interpretation does not deny a possible historical origin of the handwashing precaution in terms of an actual event; the sea does periodically enter these islands in the form of an exceptionally high spring tide. Where might the contaminatory theme come from? Enquiries revealed that the traditional Lardil toilet training schedule differs from the pattern in Western culture, where weaning precedes bowel control. On Mornington Island the child is taught to hide his excreta around the age of weaning, roughly when he is four years old, and he is taught by his peers rather than by his parents. This coincides with the time of the first major developmental crisis of the Lardil child: weaning or displacement at the breast by the newborn sibling, a time of tantrums and distress. It may be inferred that oral-dependent needs are frustrated and aggressive drives provoked at the same time that control of anal drives is developing. Under these cirumstances, a man's desire to invade the sea to take fish might symbolize the repressed urge to enter and take food from mother, an urge that was controlled contemporaneously with the desire to soil, and might provoke projective fantasies of being entered, in retaliation.

We found that in the discussion of *malgri* among our expedition members, "wild" psychoanalytic interpretations were heady stuff, not always palatable to those reared in the more pedantic biological traditions. Observers of the latter type pointed out that the act of handwashing itself contains biological advantages that possibly operate outside of conscious awareness to reinforce it. The advantages of handwashing might, for example, reside in more successful fishing with clean hands, or in better health from removal of hand-borne pathogens of conditions such as dysentery. But it has to be conceded that if biological advantage underlies the ritual of handwashing, it does so at an unconscious level; the explanation is one that would occur to a biologically trained team of doctors rather than to primitive fishermen.

Functional explanations of culture-bound syndromes, of whatever doctrinal origin, are not completely satisfying. Room must be reserved to account for the finding that some individuals are susceptible to *malgri* while others are not, a difference traceable to individual variations in personality and to individual experience of interpersonal or ecological transactions. Because of these individual variations, exact correlations need not be expected between modern medical syndromes and culture-bound disorders. In my casebook, *malgri* corresponds most frequently to a gastrointestinal disturbance (often with constipation) over-laid with a psychogenic, culturally determined superstructure. In other cases it corresponds to a conversion reaction, and in yet others to a paranoid development. In most instances, the "spirit intrusion" explanation is applied *post hoc* to various entities by the Lardil. Interpretation has to be made individually in each case in the light of all the circumstances, especially considering the social inter-action pattern in which the patient is enmeshed.

The implications that an awareness of ethology may have for the *malgri* syndrome call for further comment. Some readers may interpret the syndrome as an extrapolation to man of the phenomenon of territoriality that occurs through-out the animal kingdom. But territoriality is not universal throughout the animal kingdom, especially among nonhuman primates. It would be facile to relate the territorial behavior that occurs in some lower animals directly to man, as a biolo-gical justification of property rights. Klopfer (1969) points out that territoriality is in fact subject to great diversity, and represents not one but many different adaptations serving different purposes for various animals. Thus, it would be misleading to extrapolate from birds to men without attempting to account for all relevant evolutionary and ecological factors. Nevertheless, without resorting to the possible analogies with animal behavior, it is likely that *malgri* may have something to teach about the composition of the horde in hunter-gatherer society, and about the horde's territorial rights.

The aspect of the *malgri* sickness that should not be overlooked in concentrating upon its intricacies is that the Lardil's fear is directed toward the intruding spirits that ring the island, rather than toward the illness itself. The fear is thus a policing agent in Lardil society. In any definition of medicine and the law, a limited correspondence between these institutions in primitive and modern society may be pointed out. The law of real property may be cited as an example, it being assumed that primitive hunting-gathering society has no comparable con-cept. Yet we find the island home of the Lardil seemingly legally partitioned (by a fear of local spirits producing sickness) as distinctly as hereditary estates partition an English county.

Malgri therefore provides a source of material for social anthropology in its task of evaluating the nature of the relationship between local group organi-zation and the geographical territory that it occupies. As described by Hearne (1970), the current debate on this issue concerns several interrelated questions of both social organization and territory, including:

1. The composition and stability of local group membership.
2. The distinctiveness or exclusiveness of the local group's territorial boundaries.

3. The availability and variety, as well as the utilization patterns, of the food and water resources to which the local group has access rights or ownership claims.

4. The nature of the social, economic, and political ties that may bind local groups to one another.

We are reminded by Hearne that Radcliffe-Brown in the 1930s proposed that "the horde" was the residential unit in the social organization of Australian Aborigines. The horde was composed of males and unmarried females who were members by birth, and the wives of the male members. It was thus an exogamous unit, patrivirilocal in residence, owning and occupying a territorial area containing the horde's totemic sites and the food and water resources necessary for subsistence. Radcliffe-Brown's model has been subject to question. Hiatt (1962) argues that local groups failed to form autonomous, separate, and self-sustaining economic units opposed, in a structural sense, to similar units.

The apparent distinctiveness and exclusiveness of the Lardil estates may be attributable to the fact that the Lardil occupy an island, limited in resources and capable of supporting only a limited population, so that territorial rights might be jealously safeguarded. The *malgri* syndrome itself appears connected with the fact that the territory is an island; it is not encountered among mainland tribes. But there are ways in which the "ideal" territorial scheme elaborated by the Lardil might be modified or relaxed. One is that the littorals are not guarded by spirits equally dangerous in terms of *malgri*, suggesting that some littorals are better fishing sites and therefore need stronger policing. "Burned serpent" and "moon" are reputed to be particularly dangerous spirit guardians, and even today the littorals of which they are totems are prolific sources of food. Thus, ecological factors, as well as structural factors, enter into the determination of the territorial units or estates. The "ideal" scheme is relaxed in another way, by the practice of admitting outsiders to live with the local social unit. Gully Peters, boss of the sea-eagle country, had Fred, from the other side of the island, in his social unit. This was possible, according to Gully, because the sea-eagle spirit eventually came to know Fred's smell and accepted him as a resident.

It seems reasonable to infer that ecological or subsistence tensions were factors leading to the modification of the composition of island social units. The composition of the social units, after fifty years of European contact, is not known with any precision, although, with the help of the islanders, I have made an approximation to begin with. It is in any case more a task for the social anthropologist than for the psychiatric anthropologist.

Malgri illustrates problems of crowding, stranger contact, and aggressive behavior, to which attention has been directed by Hamburg (1971). Hamburg reviewed the information available on these relationships in primates and in man. He suggests that millions of years of vertebrate and primate evolution may have left us with many legacies, one of which is a readiness to react fearfully and aggressively toward strangers, especially if we are crowded in with them, competing for valued resources. Whether or not this tendency is part of our biological inheritance, *malgri* shows how a group of preagricultural, pretechnological men appreciated it, and regulated it by means of "medical" theory and practice.

This quest for regulation of aggression has become an acknowledged aim of modern medicine. Hamburg points out that hostility between human groups represents one of the great dangers of our era, perhaps even greater than most diseases. It may well be that it was regarded as a greater danger in a preagricultural era. The quest is certainly not new, as our subjects show.

The technical question with which we began, concerning the correspondence between culture-bound syndromes and Western diagnostic categories, can be answered with respect to *malgri*. There is no simple relationship, because the social dimensions of illness are different in the two cultures. We conclude that crowding and stranger contact are connected with illness in each culture. But we would need to hold to too narrow a "medical model" of disease to expect to find a direct relationship between individual cases of *malgri* and modern Western diagnoses.

ACKNOWLEDGMENTS

The Institute of Aboriginal Studies, Canberra, provided funds for my expeditions to the Gulf of Carpentaria. I am deeply indebted to my Aboriginal hosts and informants, and to their Missions. The Social Science Research Institute (under NIMH GRANT #MH09243) and the East-West Center at the University of Hawaii invited me to utilize their facilities in the preparation of this and related manuscripts.

This paper was published in slightly different form in *Medicine Is the Law*, The University Press of Hawaii, 1974.

REFERENCES

Cawte, J.E. 1972. Cruel, poor and brutal nations. Honolulu, The University Press of Hawaii.
————. 1974. Medicine is the law: studies in psychiatric anthropology in Australian tribal societies. Honolulu, The University Press of Hawaii.
Freud, S. 1946. Totem and taboo. New York, Random House.
Hamburg, D.A. 1971. Crowding, stranger contact, and aggressive behavior in society, stress and disease. Vol. 1. L. Levi, ed. London, Oxford University Press.
Hearne, T. 1970. Ecology and affinal ties among Kung bushmen and coast Salish. Mankind 7:199–204.
Hiatt, L. 1962. Local organization among the Australian aborigines. Oceania 32:267–86.
Horowitz, M.J. 1965. The body buffer zone: an aspect of the body image. Paper presented at the Western Divisional Meeting of the American Psychiatric Association, Honolulu.
Klopfer, P.H. 1969. Habitats and territories: a study of the use of space by animals. New York, Basic Books.
Roheim, G. 1945. The eternal ones of the dream. New York, International Universities Press.

3. An Outbreak of Epidemic Hysteria in West Malaysia

JIN-INN TEOH, M.B.B.S., D.P.M.

Department of Psychological Medicine
University of Malaysia
Kuala Lumpur, Malaysia

ENG-SEONG TAN, M.B.B.S., M.R.C.

Department of Psychological Medicine
University of Malaysia
Kuala Lumpur, Malaysia

EPIDEMIC HYSTERIA is increasingly becoming a rarity in medical and psychiatric literature, although it does still make its appearance from time to time as a social phenomenon. This phenomenon was nothing unusual or spectacular during the Middle Ages and the nineteenth century where mass outbreaks were a fairly common occurrence. These outbreaks were then attributed to evil spirits possessing young women. Ignorance, insecurity, and anxiety were among the important factors (Madden, 1964) generating epidemics of hysteria that disturbed society. Then, "people did not think clearly and fell into a way of viewing remarkable outbursts of frenzy like those of the Reign of Terror of the French Revolution, the Spanish Inquisition or the witch hunts of Salem" (Veith, 1965).

Mass epidemics were noted by Hecker (1844) in convents and nunneries, by Huxley (1952) at Loudun, by Schutte (1906) in Meissen, by St. Clare at Oxford (Hunter and MacAlpine, 1964), by Davenport (1906) at John Wesley's revival meetings, and by Stone (1934) during the height of the Millerite Second Adventist movement in New England. In more recent times, Johnson (1945) described the "Phantom Anesthetist of Mattoon"; Schuler and Parenton (1943) reported an epidemic of involuntary twitchings in a high school in Louisiana; and Cantril (1940) documented the mass panic resulting from Orson Welles' broadcast of "War of the Worlds." Ikeda (1966) reported an epidemic of somatic symptoms with paranoid delusions among nurses in a Japanese leprosarium.

In Britain, McEvedy and others (Moss and McEvedy, 1966; McEvedy et al., 1966; McEvedy and Beard, 1970a; McEvedy and Beard, 1970b) observed epidemics of fainting among schoolgirls at Blackburn, England. They also postulated that the Royal Free Disease of encephalomyelitis could have been an outbreak of epidemic hysteria among the hospital staff.

Recent Outbreaks of Epidemic Hysteria in Schools in West Malaysia

The Federation of Malaysia consists of East and West Malaysia. The Malay Peninsula constitutes West Malaysia and has a population of eight million people of diverse cultures; thus it is a multiracial and plural society. The indigenous peoples consist of the Malays and the aboriginal tribes who reside mainly in the rural regions. There are also the immigrant communities consisting of the Chinese, Indians, Pakistanis, Eurasians, and others who make their residence in the urban areas of Malaysia. The Malays form 51 percent of the population, and common ties of history, race, and culture (the Malay language and Islamic faith) have made the Malay group the most structured and socially cohesive in the country. New educational policies attempting to restructure society and to bring the more economically backward Malays to the same level as the more affluent non-Malay have caused many new schools and hostels to be built in rural areas. This rapid expansion resulted in a makeshift administration in the hands of personnel who were not necessarily the best trained or qualified.

It is in these Malay schools and hostels that a spate of epidemic hysteria has occurred, mostly among Malay adolescent schoolgirls. Tan (1963) reported an outbreak of hysteria in a Malay religious school and vividly described the pattern of behavior that still exists unchanged. In 1970 and 1971, 27 Malay medium schools in mainly rural regions of Malaya were affected by outbreaks of epidemic hysteria—almost all among young adolescent Malay girls. The manifestation throughout all the 27 schools was monotonously similar. The affected teenage girls hyperventilated, screamed, complained that they saw ghosts and devils (practically all descriptions of objects perceived fitted with the description of figures in Malay mythology recorded by Skeat [1900]), and either went into a trancelike state or fainted. Practically all claimed amnesia during the outbreaks. traditionally all outbreaks were handled by the *bomoh* or *pawang* (Malay magician or native healer), and supernatural explanations were given for the outbreaks.

One of these outbreaks was investigated by the authors in depth. All parties involved in the outbreak were interviewed immediately after the episodes. The affected girls were psychologically tested, and the headmaster of the school was given ten sessions of psychotherapy for both diagnostic and therapeutic purposes. This paper deals with that outbreak, its native interpretations and anthropological implications, the personalities involved and their social interactions, and the psychodynamic factors causing the outbreak of hysteria. The names of places and people are disguised.

Epidemic Hysteria at Helang

Comfortably nestled among the mountains of the Central Range of the Malay Peninsula is the small, secluded township of Helang, some 40 miles from the capital city of Kuala Lumpur. One has to traverse narrow, winding roads over mountains and across tropical jungle to reach this township. As is typical of the region, the town is inhabited by Chinese while the Malays dwell in the neighboring *kampong*s ("villages") in the suburbs, earning a sparse living by rubber tapping, *padi* planting, and vegetable gardening.

The Murai Malay Lower Secondary School and Girls' Hostel, where the outbreak of epidemic hysteria occurred, is three miles east of Helang. It is one of the many new schools constructed by the government to bring universal education to rural Malays. The girls' hostel, adjacent to the school, was opened in June 1970. At the time of the hysteria it accommodated fifty rural Malay girls, who came from all over the state. It had no electricity, and recreational facilities were almost nonexistent. The hostel was managed by the headmaster of Murai School, who had made no serious attempt to replace the first hostel mistress after she resigned over his interference in her administration.

Onset and course of Epidemic Hysteria.   In the beginning of January 1971, devastating floods occurred in West Malaysia. The headmaster was reluctant to evacuate the girls to higher ground, much to the annoyance of the district officer. The Ministry of Education subsequently issued a directive to all heads of schools to issue flood relief financial subsidies to affected pupils without undue investigation or delay. The headmaster of Murai School felt unable to deal with this open-ended order and delayed the handing out of the money, bringing on a rash of petitions from the parents against him.

On Sunday, February 21, six weeks after the floods, AS, a hostel resident, became depressed, complained of difficulty in breathing, and went into a state of tetany. She was revived when the *bomoh* was called in to pacify the offended spirits which had possessed her. During the next fortnight, she was affected on two more occasions. Later on, two more hostel residents, NZ and JL, became possessed. NZ, in a state of possession, spoke out for the first time in the stylized manner of Malay royalty, saying that the place was dirty and that there was enmity and jealousy among the hostel residents. She complained to the *bomoh* that the girls had thrown their soiled sanitary napkins into a disused mining pool behind the hostel and had thus dirtied the possessing spirits' territory. (The girls had indeed done so, on the instruction of the headmaster, to avoid clogging the sewer.) She further ventilated the grievances and ill feelings of the hostel residents. The next day, another resident, ZK, became possessed, and NZ was again affected. The following day three girls, ZK, NM, and NZ, were possessed. Only NZ spoke out. Similar episodes of possession occurred almost daily until eventually five girls (NZ, ZK, NM, AW, SA) would become possessed together several times daily. Sometime during this period, the head prefect of the hostel, BN, claimed to have been possessed once, but this was vehemently discounted by the five girls as a fake possession. Another young girl, MR, was possessed once near the end of the outbreak.

During possession, only NZ spoke out in a trancelike state, making wrongdoers among the girls apologize in public, demanding that all stolen articles be returned or burned, and castigating the headmaster whenever he interfered with her wishes.

The climax of these episodes occurred on the morning of April 28, when the chief education officer of the state and some high-ranking officials visited the school to investigate the outbreak. All five girls went into hysteria together and chaos reigned. The important community leaders of Helang—the district officer, the *penghulu* (the traditional Malay headman of the area), the chairman of the school board of governors—all witnessed the dramatic scene of NZ holding court in a trancelike state. She demanded a blood sacrifice, bargained with the *bomoh*, the headmaster, and eventually with the *penghulu*, who won the day by obtaining her agreement to the sacrifice of a white cockerel instead of a goat as was originally demanded. NZ spoke in extremely fluent, regal Malay, almost poetic and very imperious. All the onlookers agreed that her vocabulary was beyond her educational status.

Three days later, a Friday (the Muslim sabbath), a *pawang* (native magician who claims powers over vast regions) performed a ritual ceremony in the school before 300 witnesses to placate the offended spirit. The ritual was as old as mythology and after reciting verses from the Koran, spraying *tepong tawar* (watery rice paste), and scattering *beras beteh* (parched burnt rice) all over the area, he assured the offended spirit, on behalf of the community, that no one would transgress his territory again. He then instituted a three-day *pantang* (period of abstinence), during which the whole community had to refrain from (1) saying or thinking bad thoughts, (2) destroying any insect, animal, leaf, or flower, and (3) going outdoors if possible. If the *pantang* rules were violated, the offended spirits might return. Following this ritual, the hysteria stopped except for two further minor episodes by NZ.

Native interpretation. The native interpretation of the outbreak was subscribed to by almost all members of the Malay community in Helang. The hysterical episodes were due to possession by offended spirits called *jin*s ("free spirits"), probably a good Muslim *jin*. The *jin*s were believed to dwell in the territory behind the hostel. They were offended by the disposal of the girls' soiled sanitary napkins in their territory. When they could no longer tolerate the pollution, they decided to attack the girls when their *semangat* ("life force," "vital energy") was at its lowest ebb.

The *bomoh* and *pawang* claimed that they were in contact with the *jin*s, who communicated with them in dreams and gave them instructions to follow. It was believed that the school and hostel were constructed on territory inhabited by a family of *jin*s for many generations. Had the elders in the Malay community been consulted, they would have advised against constructing the building, "as the living place of spirits was no fit place for human habitation."

It is interesting that all these episodes of epidemic hysteria were controlled by native methods. It was believed by those involved that when the *semangat* within each individual was low, the person was more vulnerable to spirit possession. The *semangat* is alleged to be reduced by sickness, old age, and fatigue and augmented by good health, keeping one's proper station in life, and the maintenance of a harmonious relationship with nature (Endicott, 1970). When *jins* attack people, the *bomoh* or *pawang* is invariably called to be an intermediary between the supernatural world of spirits and the world of man (McHugh, 1955).

Jins are believed to be inferior to human beings and of a lower intelligence and can therefore be deluded by transparent lies and meager offerings. Since they can be very demanding, it was only correct for the *penghulu* in this case to bargain with them over the sacrifice, so that they would not become masters of man. The paradox was that the *penghulu* felt that his status had risen as he had contact with the supernatural, while NZ's parents were pleased with her possession because they thought she would take on the qualities of a *bomoh* herself. Jane Murphy (1964) has noted that shamanism and possession were definite factors in elevating the status of the possessed. This was borne out when NZ was promoted to head prefect by the headmaster when (the existing head prefect) BN left the hostel at the end of the school year.

Headmaster's relationship with the hostel residents.   The headmaster of Murai School undertook the management of the hostel when the original hostel mistress left due to his gross interference with the affairs of the hostel. He made no efforts to find a new hostel mistress. He would spend much of his time making unannounced rounds at the hostel at odd hours of the day and night. The girls resented and were embarrassed by that practice. He rationalized that since he treated the girls like daughters, he was free to transgress the strong Malay social taboo against walking into the living quarters of adolescent girls. It became a universal unspoken fear among the girls that he might suddenly appear while they were undressed.

It was universally felt by the Malay community at Helang that it was incorrect and improper for a man to be in charge of a girls' hostel. In Malay society the social taboo of a Malay male entering the living quarters of a Malay female is very strong and the sexes are separated at an early age (Fraser, 1962; Wilder, 1970). The open secret of the headmaster's voyeuristic behavior was regarded with apprehension, and some community leaders even suspected that he had sexually molested the girls, although there was no evidence of it.

The girls' attitude toward the headmaster seems to have been rather ambivalent. Though they resented his "prowling," his nagging about untidiness, and his not respecting their confidences, they saw him as a father figure, and he pampered them when they were ill.

How the community solved its problems.   After the hysteria subsided, there was mounting community pressure to have the headmaster transferred. The following were the main claims of dissatisfaction and causes of tension within the community: (1) the maladministration of the school and poor relationships between the headmaster and the teachers, (2) the rumors that the headmaster was molesting the hostel girls, and the general impropriety of a man being in charge of a hostel, (3) the administrative inefficiency in not obtaining a supply of electricity for the school, (4) the crisis during the January floods, when the head-master endangered the lives of the girls by refusing to evacuate the hostel, (5) the mass petition by parents over the delay in the distribution of flood-relief money, and (6) the low standard of education at Murai School.

The district officer, *penghulu*, and chairman of the school board of governors, initially put political pressure on the chief education officer of the state to transfer the headmaster out of the school. Although the chief education officer agreed to the transfer and demotion to another neighboring school, before the order could take effect, the headmaster rushed to Kuala Lumpur, where, with the aid of high-level Ministry of Education officials, he managed to retain his post. The chief education officer's deputy visited the school and re-primanded all the teachers, especially the senior assistant (the headmaster's main antagonist), for insubordination.

Owing to the deputy chief education officer's efforts, a new hostel mistress was eventually appointed, and the headmaster was indirectly warned to stay away from the girls' hostel. The chairman and *penghulu* felt that the com-munity had solved part of its problem by obtaining a hostel mistress. However, the headmaster of a neighboring school (a Eurasian) commented that no one actually understood the message of epidemic hysteria and thus no real change was brought about.

Nevertheless, it was agreed that the crisis had produced some form of social change in the community, although no one consciously comprehended the message of epidemic hysteria except for the abreactive retaliation of the frustra-tions of the hostel girls. The community, including the *bomoh* and *pawang*, refused to interpret the outbreak on any level other than that of spirit possession. Interestingly enough, no one in the community cited the epidemic hysteria as a reason for removing the headmaster. All attributed the phenomenon to super-natural causes. The indirect form of communication within the cultural system did not endanger anybody. Since change had to take place within the existing social system, and the introduction of alien concepts into the subculture was immediately rejected, items most familiar were accepted and easily implemented.

Thus, the Helang community took two steps forward and one step back. The social change that was needed was concrete in nature, i.e., to obtain a mistress for the girls' hostel and to prevent the headmaster from interfering with the girls.

Analysis

The personalities involved. The following is an account of the personali-ties and social characteristics of the persons playing key roles in this epidemic of hysteria. Seven of the eight girls affected were psychologically tested using the Raven's Progressive Matrices, the TAT, and the Draw a Man Test in the Malay language. From the findings of these tests and from their interrelationships, we constructed a sociogram demonstrating the psychodynamic constellations of attitudes, affiliations, and antipathies leading to the outbreak of hysteria. The sociogram showed that the individuals can be grouped into clusters.

The headmaster. The headmaster, a 41-year-old Malay, a short, nervous person, had been managing the school since its inception in 1966. In personality type he was inadequate and very limited, obsessional and conflict-ridden.

The insiders—girls affected by hysteria:

1. NZ, 13 years old, appeared to be the leader competing for the attention of the headmaster. She had formed a clique of five girls (who went into possession with her) to oppose BN. Of average intelligence, she tended to express her ill feelings easily. She was emotional and harbored aggressive feelings that she had difficulty controlling. She was a rather immature and superficial girl and demanded immediate gratification of her needs. Her identification with the headmaster was ambivalent.

2. AW, aged 15 years, had a pleasing, very seductive, and hysterical personality. She was also manipulative, demanding excessive attention, and tended to be narcissistic. Her mood was labile and ranged from sentimentality to self-confidence. She expressed her anger easily and suffered from very severe depression, usually amounting to self-punishment. She had very poor self-identity, and there were suggestions of latent homosexuality in her tests. She was the first girl to experience the hysteria.

3. SA, 13 years old, was of above-average intelligence and presented herself as being rather poised but tended to be hostile and aggressive, with emotional lability. Obsessional, she harbored guilt feelings: she came from a broken family and identified negatively with her father for remarrying. Her feelings for the headmaster were ambivalent, but her hostility overshadowed her admiration for him.

4. NM was 14 years old and of average intelligence. She experienced severe separation anxiety from home. She was most embarrassed by the headmaster's unannounced appearance in the hostel.

The outsiders—girls affected peripherally:

1. BN, 17 years old, was the chief hostel prefect and a favorite of the headmaster. Although the girls tended to identify BN as a mother figure, they projected their hostile feelings toward the headmaster onto her. She could be hostile when provoked. Her main problems centered around difficulties with identification. She did not have much control over her feelings and behavior and as a result was very preoccupied with death and morbid fears of murder. Her mother died when she was very young and her father had remarried. BN thus looked up to the headmaster as a father figure and was jealously protective and loyal to the headmaster although she was also embarrassed by his misdemeanors.

2. JL, 13 years old, was an unattractive girl of borderline intelligence. She was the most superficial, suggestible, and irresponsible of the lot, being unable to form a stable relationship with anyone. Her one episode of possession appeared to owe to her suggestibility as an onlooker.

3. MR was 13 years old and of above-average intelligence. Being a close

friend and classmate of SA, she had one episode of possession following her good friend's possession.

The teachers. The senior assistant harbored negative feelings for the headmaster and actively stirred up the community leaders and teachers against him. He was known to be a manipulator and a politician, and in fact had been demoted for alleged corruption. The other teachers were also supporters of the senior assistant but played a passive role.

The parents. The parents of the hostel girls lived mostly outside Helang and were much troubled by the headmaster's behavior.

The community leaders:

1. The district officer had had a confrontation with the headmaster during the flood crisis, and had been working actively since then to remove him.

2. The *penghulu*, who was also a member of the school board of governors, was involved only after his negotiations with the offended spirit over the nature of the sacrifice.

3. The chairman of the school board of governors was also a strong political figure of the community and was responsible for negotiating with the chief education officer for the headmaster's transfer.

The headmaster of a neighboring school, a Eurasian, was involved only because some of the affected girls attended his school.

The native healers. The *bomoh* was called in for all episodes of the hysteria. The *pawang* came in only to perform the final propitiating ritual, since he claimed greater power than the *bomoh* over land spirits.

The educational authorities. The chief education officer, the deputy chief education officer, and Ministry of Education officials in Kuala Lumpur.

Social interactions in the outbreak. The social interactions of the girls were based upon expressed feelings or preferences for each other. Relationships at the time of the outbreak were rated as positive, ambivalent, and negative.

The parents of the pupils received the most positive feelings because all of them sympathized with their daughters who became possessed. The five girls affected together (NZ, SA, AW, NM, and ZK) elicited more positive feelings than did those who were incidentally affected (BN, JL, and MR) because they were more directly involved with the tensions and conflicts in the hostel. The five affected girls were united under NZ's leadership.

The headmaster was the most important personality in the outbreak for he was the only person who knew everyone connected with it. Yet he had positive interaction with only three persons, the outsiders who were his distant administrative superiors. He interacted ambivalently or negatively with the rest. This suggests that almost no one at Helang thought well of him despite his importance to the town.

The senior assistant, a recent arrival in the community, had positive interaction with more groups than the headmaster and was held in high esteem by the girls and the community leaders. However, he interacted negatively with the outsiders, who were better informed of his dubious past.

The *bomoh* interacted most positively with all parties but he was there only to calm the hysterical girls. Ever the true outsider, while others became involved in the tensions and conflicts of the school, he maintained the esteemed, natural position of a healer. Almost every Malay involved believed in spirit possession, and the numerous positive feelings he evoked could be related to this cultural belief.

Though the headmaster and the *bomoh* were at opposite poles in community regard, the headmaster relied heavily on the *bomoh*, who adhered to his professional healing role and refused to become involved in the politics of the situation. The *pawang* interacted less positively, only entering in at the end, to perform the final ceremony. The *penghulu* was intimately involved as a neighbor of the ambitious senior assistant and tried to help him achieve his aspiration to head the school. He took a more intense interest only after negotiating with the offended spirit.

While the *penghulu*'s contact was more direct and personal, the school board chairman's role was official and formal. He appeared to be the only Malay who did not believe in spirit possession, and from this position he was able to effectively bring about the required social changes in the community.

The sociogram therefore showed that the *bomoh*, who was actually an outsider, interacted most positively, while the headmaster, despite his key position in the community, was disliked by almost all he interacted with. Something obviously was wrong with the interpersonal relations of the headmaster.

Psychodynamics in the outbreak.   One of the authors (J.I.T.) conducted ten weekly psychiatric interviews with the headmaster for both diagnostic and therapeutic purposes, from October 1971 to February 1972. It was felt that these interviews might allay his anxiety and depression (from which he had been suffering for the previous three years), a view that was shared by his general practitioner, who had been treating him symptomatically. The headmaster came eagerly and promptly to these sessions though they entailed a drive of about 80 miles round trip. For the author, the sessions extended his understanding of the character structure and neurotic conflicts of the headmaster.

His lifelong character pattern was that of an obsessive-compulsive personality. He was rigid, stubborn, overly dutiful and overly conscientious. As headmaster, he felt he was "a servant of the people" and "could not shirk his duty." When subjected to stress, as he was at the time of the floods and the epidemic hysteria, his defenses became even more intense. He clung to rules and regulations even when they violated common sense. The more threatened he felt, the more stubborn he became.

His object relations had been ambivalent since early childhood, when he felt "lonely and isolated." Characteristically, he needed his wife but also hated her for being aggressive and nagging. His Rorschach and TAT responses showed that he harbored strong death wishes against her. He blamed her for his father's death and enjoyed only physical relations with her. He struggled to take the lead in their relationship but was constantly tempted to relinquish it to her. When his passive wishes surfaced, he became anxious and depressed and allowed his wife to run his school, hostel, and his life. He resisted all pressures from authorities and the community during the episode of epidemic hysteria for similar reasons. He was incapable of yielding to pressure because of the imperative need to combat his inner passivity. His compulsive defenses also served this purpose.

He blamed all the problems of his school on his senior assistant. There was considerable evidence that he saw the senior assistant as a competitive, extroverted younger brother whom he resented and yet had an unconscious homosexual attachment to. The latter provoked passivity, which in turn brought out an instantaneous defensive response of fear and suspicion of almost delusional proportions.

Just as he dealt with his passive wishes by reactive activity and stubbornness, he dealt with his sexual impulse toward his students by reaction formation. He spied on them constantly, particularly when they were undressing or sleeping, under the guise of protecting them. There was evidence that his unconscious purpose in becoming the girls' hostel master and his reluctance to relinquish the post were, at least in part, an effort to relive earlier years when he frequented young prostitutes, even after many years of marriage. He was sexually impotent with his wife, and psychological tests showed that his sexual impulse had a strong voyeuristic component with a need to obtain stimulation to satisfy his wife. Finally, there was some regressive degradation of his sexuality to a more primitive level and a connection with dirt and anality. This was seen in his concern over the disposal of students' sanitary napkins and his preoccupation with honesty.

It should be noted that the students who were possessed with seizures indicated in diverse ways that they were responding to the sexual nature of his nocturnal visits, his peeping, his interest in dirt and cleanliness, his honesty and stealing. His concern thus became the students' concern as well, although in a somewhat distorted form.

His relationship with BN, the chief hostel prefect, appeared to cause a polarization of feelings among the students. BN developed strong sexual feelings for him by positive identification, which was perceived with jealousy by the other girls of the hostel. In turn, NZ and her clique, who were also unconsciously vying for the headmaster's affection and attention, expressed their repressed frustrations in the socially sanctioned pattern of an epidemic hysteria. BN was under considerable pressure, and in a culturally sanctioned manner had one episode of hysteria. Two other girls, JL and MR, were affected as suggestible outsiders.

Summary

An episode of epidemic hysteria in a residential school for adolescent Malay girls of the Islamic faith was described. The school is located near the secluded town of Helang in West Malaysia.

The authors conducted interviews with the many individuals involved, including the students, teachers, parents, the headmaster, and members of the Helang community. Special emphasis was placed on the psychopathology of the headmaster, whose personal limitations and psychological conflicts appeared to play a key role in the outbreak. His personal problems interlocked with those of the students afflicted.

Factors contributing to the epidemic included the personality of the headmaster, religious, social, and political pressures, the character of the student body, and the community matrix.

Two specific events contributed to the outbreak: the resignation of the hostel mistress and a severe flood.

A sociogram was constructed of the interactions among all concerned in the outbreak. The headmaster turned out to be the most disliked, although he was the most important person in the social constellation. The *bomoh,* the real outsider, was most liked because he kept to his neutral professional role as healer and appeared on the scene when he was most urgently needed. Malay superstition and magical belief and the roles of the *bomoh* and *pawang* played special parts.

ACKNOWLEDGMENTS

The authors are grateful to the following people and institutions without whose help this work would not have been possible. The Minister of Education, the Honorable Inche Hussein Onn, gave permission for this study to be conducted. The Ministry of Education, Malaysia, gave its cooperation. Mrs. S. Soewondo and Mrs. M. Sidharta, psychologists, tested the girls and headmaster. Dr. Ernest Kahn, M.D., Instructor in Psychiatry, Harvard Medical School, gave advice about the psychodynamic formulations. Dr. Kahar Bador, anthropologist and Dean, Faculty of Arts, University of Malaya, provided an anthropological perspective on the outbreak of hysteria. Research Assistants Phyllis Xavier, Chan Lay Lan, and Ranjan Ariyapala analyzed many tedious hours of audiotapes and processed and helped refine the data.

REFERENCES

Cantril, H. 1940. The invasion from Mars. Princeton, Princeton University Press.
Davenport, F.M. 1906. Primitive traits in religious revival. New York, Macmillan.
Endicott, K.M. 1970. An analysis of Malay magic. Oxford, Clarendon Press.
Fraser, T.M. 1962. Rusembilan: a Malay fishing village in southern Thailand. Ithaca, New
        York, Cornell University Press.
Hecker, J.F.C. 1844. The epidemics of the middle ages. London, Sydenham Society.
Hunter, R. and I. MacAlpine, eds. 1964. Three hundred years of psychiatry. London,
        Oxford University Press.
Huxley, A. 1952. The devils of Loudun. London, Chatto & Windus.
Ikeda, Y. 1966. An epidemic of emotional disturbance among leprosarium nurses in a
        setting of low morale and social change. Psychiatry 23:152–64.
Johnson, D.M. 1945. The phantom anesthetist of Mattoon: a field study of mass hysteria.
        Journal of Abnormal and Social Psychology 40:175–84.
Madden, R.R. 1964. 1798–1886. Epidemic insanity and mass psychology. *In* Three hundred

years of psychiatry. R. Hunter and I. MacAlpine, eds. London, Oxford University Press.

McEvedy, C.P., A. Griffiths, and T. Hill. 1966. Two school epidemics. British Medical Journal 2:1300–1302.

McEvedy, C.P., and A.W. Beard. 1970a. Royal free epidemic of 1955:a reconsideration. British Medical Journal 1:7–11.

———. 1970b. Concept of benign myalgic encephalitis. British Medical Journal 1:11–15.

McHugh, J.N. 1955. Hantu-hantu:an account of ghost belief in modern Malaya. Singapore, Donald Moore.

Mead, M. 1943. Coming of age in Samoa. Harmondsworth, Pelican Books.

Moss, P.D., and C.P. McEvedy. 1966. An epidemic of overbreathing among school girls. British Medical Journal 2:1295–1300.

Murphy, J.M. 1964. Psychotherapeutic aspects of shamanism on St. Lawrence Island, Alaska. *In* Magic, faith and healing. A. Kiev, ed. London, Free Press of Glencoe.

Schuler, E.A., and V.J. Parenton. 1943. A recent epidemic of hysteria in a Louisiana high school. Journal of Social Psychology 17:221–35.

Schutte, P. 1906. Eine neue Forme hysterischer Zustande bei Schulkindern. Muenchener Medizinische Wochenschrift 53:1763–64.

Skeat, W.W. 1900. Malay magic. London, Macmillan & Co.

Stone, S. 1934. The Millerite delusion: a comparative study in mass psychology. American Journal of Psychiatry 91:593–623.

Tan, E.S. 1963. Epidemic hysteria. Medical Journal of Malaya 28:72–76.

Veith, I. 1965. Hysteria: the history of a disease. Chicago and London, University of Chicago Press.

Wilder, W. 1970. Socialization and social structure in a Malay village. *In* Socialization: the approach from social anthropology. P. Mayer, ed. London, Tavistock.

POSSESSION

4. Possession and Trance in Cross-Cultural Studies of Mental Health

ERIKA BOURGUIGNON, Ph.D.

Department of Anthropology
Ohio State University
Columbus, Ohio

THE TERMS "possession" and "trance" are relevant to the subject of this conference in that on the one hand possession is sometimes considered to be one of a variety of culture-bound syndromes, and on the other, its relation to trance is not always made explicit. Furthermore, trance itself is often considered a pathological phenomenon. I may best begin with a definition of terms as I shall use them in this paper. I distinguish between two orders of admittedly interrelated phenomena: (1) psychophysiological states, which we may refer to as states of consciousness, and (2) culturally constituted beliefs and practices relating to these states. It should be noted that it is often difficult to separate these beliefs and practices from the states to which they refer, for the beliefs affect the states; the interpretations tend to pattern the behavior.

The states with which we are particularly concerned here are those frequently referred to as altered states of consciousness. They are a category of psychophysiological phenomena amenable to observation and other objective methods of study. They may be intentionally induced and terminated by a variety of methods, including psychoactive drugs, psychological means such as hypnosis, suggestion, sensory deprivation, and physiological causes such as high fever and so forth.

They may occur spontaneously as dissociation, hallucination, catalepsy. In psychiatric terms, they may or may not be pathological. Thus, dissociation induced by means of suggestion or hypnosis or driving should not necessarily be considered hysteria. Furthermore, though the rather imprecise term "trance" is frequently used in the literature and in the study on which I am reporting I have kept it intentionally because of its broad and vague sense. The data required for a statistical study must be culled from the broad ethnographic literature and lack the detail necessary for a more refined classification and analysis. However, it should not be assumed that all trances or all states of altered consciousness are necessarily dissociational states.

In contrast to altered states of consciousness, spirit possession, soul loss, etcetera, are culture-bound concepts used to explain these states. These folk concepts cannot be discovered by direct observation, EEGs, or studies of heart rate and blood pressure. They can be discovered only by interviewing informants and by studying the sociocultural settings in which the states so explained are observed and experienced. In traditional societies, altered states of consciousness are most often interpreted and dealt with in a sacred context, although this is not always the case. In our research we have found it useful to distinguish between altered states interpreted as possession and those given some other explanation. We have termed the former "possession trance" (PT) and the latter simply "trance" (T). (The latter category could, of course, be subdivided into instances explained as soul loss, or travels of the soul, and those given other explanations, but at this stage of our work we have not done so.) It should also be noted that there may also be belief in a type of possession by spiritual entities that is not linked to an altered state. We have termed this simply "possession" (P).

Let me illustrate these concepts with examples from the Pacific area. For instance, Lieban (1967) tells us that among the Sugbuhanon of the Philippines, certain types of illness are believed to be caused by possession by insects or animals. These are thought to be sent into the body of the victim by a sorcerer and the victim feels them to be crawling about inside of him and biting him. There is no indication in this report of an altered state of consciousness. While possession is not by spirits in a narrow sense, there is of course supernatural or extraordinary power involved in the sorcerer's ability to cause illness by such means. Among other Filipino groups, too, such as the Ifugao, Bontok, and Kalinga, illness is explained as due to possession, this time by evil spirits. On the other hand, possession trance also exists in the Philippines. Kroeber (1919:85) writes of the Ifugao: "The medium becomes possessed by a god during the public and open-air conduct of a ceremony and speaks as the god." Assuming that no conscious play-acting is involved here and that the medium does temporarily lose his or her ordinary sense of identity, such impersonation is indeed one of the hallmarks of possession trance, which is characterized most often by such "otherness." However, when the Sugbuhanon sorcerer obtains diagnosis and cures in visions (as well as in dreams) from his spiritual mentors, indeed when he receives in a vision a call to become a curer (Lieban, 1962, 1967), we have an example of visionary trance, without any reference to a notion of possession. There is no obvious reason in any of these examples to raise the issue of mental illness. However, Rin and Lin (1962) tell us that among the Atayal of Taiwan, the mentally ill see or hear *utox*, the local evil spirit. That is, they experience auditory or visual hallucinations.

Before confronting the difficult issue of psychopathology with reference to possession, possession trance, and trance as defined above, it may be helpful to consider some statistics.

For our statistical studies (Bourguignon, ed., 1972) we drew a worldwide sample of 488 societies from Murdock's *Ethnographic Atlas* (1967). It should be noted here that, although we took our sample from the *Atlas*, as well as various types of data on social organization coded there, our data on institutionalized sacred altered states and related belief systems derive from a separate search of the literature. Those topics are not coded in the *Atlas,* nor did the categories of the Human Relations Area Files make them readily accessible, so we turned to the original sources for the information which we required. We found that 437, or 90 percent, of these societies had institutionalized some form of altered state (trance or possession trance or both). For the Insular Pacific, this was true of 81 of the 86 societies in our sample, or 94 percent. It should be noted that our sample was weighted toward traditional societies, as is indeed the *Atlas*, and that "institutionalized altered states" meant almost exclusively institutionalized in a sacred context. While we would have to consider, for example, alcohol intoxication to be an altered state and one that takes on an institutionalized form in most societies where it appears, we rather arbitrarily did not include it in our coding. Nor did we include addictive narcotics, such as opium, which are entirely secular in nature. Kava and betel pose an interesting problem here, since they do not clearly appear to alter consciousness (or at least, the literature is not clear on this point) but rather, under certain circumstances, appear to facilitate an altered state. This seems to be the case, for example, with betel as it is currently used by mediums and diviners in Palau (Leonard, 1972). On the other hand, we did of course include those societies in which the primary induction agent in a ritual context is a psychotomimetic drug, such as datura, peyote, *banisteriopsis*, and tobacco in the Americas and *Amanita muscaria* in parts of Asia.

These remarks are meant to indicate that we were rather conservative in our coding, yet we found a remarkably high percentage of societies having institutionalized forms of altered states. It should also be noted that absence of a trait is notoriously difficult to ascertain from the anthropological literature, and we may very well find that additional sources may tell us that some societies coded in the "absent" column do in fact exhibit the pattern. So our figures may be said to underrepresent the phenomenon rather than overrepresent it.

The widespread nature of such insitutionalization of altered states is a phenomenon of note. It suggests strongly that such states are institutionalized not only in societies that are "peculiar" or aberrant in some way, that they are particular only to societies undergoing certain kinds of stresses, and so forth. Rather, it appears that we are dealing with a human potential that is utilized by the vast majority of societies but utilized in ways that are perhaps characteristic of certain types of societies or are revealing with reference to certain other aspects of the societies in which they occur. I stress this because with respect to the part of the world with which I am most familiar, the Caribbean area, it has often been suggested that possession trance, as it occurs in the context of the Haitian *vodou* cult, is a sign of a particular psychological lability, of a characteristic tendency to neurosis and hysteria. The figures I have cited would suggest the need for some caution in establishing such generalizations.

However, the mere fact that cultural institutionalization of altered states is widespread does not tell us anything about the incidence or epidemiology of such states in any given society. This is a subject about which very little hard information is available and even impressions concerning it can be gained from the literature for only a relatively few societies. Nor do the figures I have cited tell us anything about the particular interpretations given to altered states in particular societies, the forms they take, or the uses to which they are put. Here, however, we do have some additional information.

Of our worldwide sample of 488 societies, 52 percent had possession trance, either as the only form of altered state or together with trance; 62 percent had trance alone or with possession trance. (Of this total, 24 percent had both types of states.) Only 10 percent had neither. Each of the six major world areas into which Murdock's *Ethnographic Atlas* is divided clearly appears to have its own profile in respect to this classification. For example, although the Insular Pacific does not deviate widely from the world averages, it does show a somewhat larger percentage (65 percent) of societies having possession trance, either alone or in combination with trance, and it has somewhat fewer societies (6 percent) without altered states. Great differences appear, however, between the four "Old World" areas (Sub-Saharan Africa, Circum-Mediterranean, East Eurasia and Insular Pacific) on the one hand and the Americas on the other, particularly North America. In North America, 92 percent of the societies have trance, 25 percent have possession trance, and only 3 percent have neither.

These differences, the unique profiles of the areas, and the great contrast between the Americas and the Old World, suggest that we may be dealing in part with results of cultural diffusion. This is obviously true even on superficial inspection. In North America, the aboriginal vision quest and guardian spirit complex is clearly reflected in the figures. We can trace the continuous diffusion of the peyote cult during the last century. In the Far East, widespread beliefs in fox possession surely indicate diffusion also. However, diffusion is not the whole story. Our statistical tests on the worldwide sample indicate convincingly that there is a relationship between types of altered states and societal characteristics reflecting variations in complexity. Complexity here refers to such matters as size of population, size of local community, jurisdictional hierarchy, settlement patterns, stratification, and the existence of slavery in the recent past. The more complex the society, along these lines, the more likely it is to have possession trance; the least complex, the more likely it is to have only trance. Societies having both of these types of states tend to fall between the other two groups with reference to the dimensions listed. Of course, this is a statement of probabilities and does not mean that we may not find exceptions. The Eskimos, for example, have possession trance, as do some Australian aborigine groups. The generalization we have made is only a statement of statistically significant associations found in a large sample of societies.

One might ask how to account for our findings. A number of comments as well as hypotheses might be suggested. One: societies which do not utilize these states clearly are historical exceptions which need to be explained, rather than the vast majority of societies that do use these states. Two: the specific beliefs associated with altered states are cultural inventions. They are, as noted, subject to diffusion. On the other hand, the specific beliefs, and attendant practices that have taken root and survived over a period of time may be said to have coherence with other aspects of the culture, and with other aspects of the behavioral environment in which the people of a given society live. This has been beautifully documented by Spiro (1967) for Burmese supernaturalism. Here the analysis is carried through on the level of individual life experiences, on the level of historical and political reality and on the level of coherence with a broader (and at first blush contradictory) world view, that of Buddhism. Altered states among Burmese villagers may involve hallucinatory trance states and possession trance states, and these may be thought to require a cure (exorcism). Or, possession trance may involve a coming to terms with the spirits, as in the "marriage" of the shaman with her *nat*. Such an arrangement gives the shaman power. It also serves as a cure from the illness by means of which, it is thought, the spirit tried to compel the reluctant candidate. Three: the specific behavior of altered states and the beliefs with which they are linked may be said to reflect certain types of social realities. The content of the possession-trance dramas and the roles that are played mirror some of the patterned relationships of societies. The groups that carry out these activities tend to represent social microcosms. The relationship between the supernaturals and the participants reflects cultural patterns of relationship. Four: the institution of one or another or both of our types of altered states of consciousness may be said to "do" something on the one hand for the participating individual, the trancer or possession trancer, and on the other hand to "do" something, to fulfill a function, for the society. I. M. Lewis (1971) has suggested that his category of "peripheral cults" provides means of supernatural vengeance for the downtrodden. My associate, Lenora Greenbaum (1972), has suggested on the basis of African data that mediumistic possession trance is more likely to exist in more rigid societies than in more flexible ones. That is to say, the medium acting as the spirit may make it possible for the individual, for the client, to be provided with solutions to some of his problems in ways that circumvent the rigid demands of his society. And yet, one might add, he follows the social constraints in that he relies on an external authority, a spirit speaking through the medium, to get authorization for his actions. I have suggested elsewhere (1965) that possession trance may involve what I have termed "regression in the service of the self." By playing the roles of spirits, the individual may be able to modify social constraints and the behavior of others and thus enlarge the scope of actions open to himself.

We have noted the association between trance and simpler societies and possession trance and more complex ones. The reasons for these differential associations may be clarified by spelling out in greater detail the differences between trance and possession trance. We may do so by treating them for the moment as opposite types of behaviors, knowing as we do so that we are in fact setting up prototypical models, not a concrete representation of the actual cultural realities, which are much more complex. Indeed, for some other purposes trance and possession trance may better be thought of as ranged along a continuum between the two contrasting types established here for analytic purposes. In fact, in another context, I have suggested (1972) a continuum that includes the type of sleep in which dreams occur.

Trance, which often involves hallucinations (or visions, in a sacred context) is an intrapersonal event. It is a private experience of the individual that others can know about only from the individual's report, as he remembers the experience. Possession trance, on the other hand, involves the impersonation of another being on an occasion when there are withnesses. As such it is an interpersonal event, for the witnesses, the audience, have a crucial role to play in the event. The Okinawan potential shaman is likely to have hallucinatory experiences (Lebra, 1966), and these may be considered indicative of her calling. An actual or imitated possession trance before an audience, however, is a way of bringing the spirit into direct contact with that audience. Firth (1967), following the lead of Jane Harrison, has shown in a most illuminating article the relationship between possession-trance ritual and drama in Malay curing and exorcism. The development of theater has gone a step further in Bali, where the kris dancers no longer go into possession trance but imitate that behavior (Mead, 1970). Possession trance, in other words, involves role playing, taking roles not otherwise available to the actor and demonstrating one's performance of these roles to others. To separate the performer from the everyday self, possession trance is frequently followed, or expected to be followed, by amnesia.

Because it is a playing of roles before an audience, possession trance is indeed the prototype of theater. It is acting out and as such may be cathartic for the actor and provide catharsis for the audience as well. In its scenario, which may vary from familiar and repetitive to spontaneous and innovative, the ritual drama gives a symbolic rendition of some aspect of the society. The intrapsychic state of the visionary, in the contrasting pattern of trance, hardly fits any portion of this description, except to the extent that the trancer may be recounting his visions dramatically to others. Since trance is a private state, it tends to stress the individual and his separation from others. He may act for the group but he does so as himself and not as another. The spirit deals with the visionary, not with the group as in possession trance, where the actor is believed to be merely the more or less involuntary vehicle of the supernatural presence.

It is interesting that this picture is consistent with that developed by D'Andrade (1961) with respect to the use of dreams to seek and control supernatural power. D'Andrade found that it is the nonagricultural societies of his worldwide sample (i.e., the "simpler societies") that are more likely to use dreams in this way. These societies have also been found to be essentially those that use trance rather than possession trance (Bourguignon, 1972). The nonagricultural societies are also those that are more likely to train their children for assertiveness rather than compliance (Barry et al., 1959). And note furthermore that in all types of societies boys are trained for assertiveness more than are girls. Possession trance seems to involve dependence and compliance to a much greater extent than trance. Again, data on sex distribution are hard to come by, but there is an impression generated from the literature that possession trance is often more widespread among women and trance more likely to occur among men. But the supporting hard data are still needed to test such a hypothesis.

What, now, does all this have to do with pathology? It seems to me that the anthropologist had best report observable behavior, cultural meanings, and cultural norms. What is pathological in local terms may well be different from what is pathological in a supracultural psychiatric context. Pfeiffer (1971), working in Java, has insisted that not all types of dissociation he has had occasion to observe should automatically and necessarily be viewed as pathological, It may well be that some types of possession trance are indeed frankly pathological; while others are therapeutic with respect to existing disturbances; and still others are neither. Perhaps the difference has to do with the distinction made long ago by Oesterreich (1922) between voluntary and nonvoluntary possession. Where the spirit invades the personality and takes over, this may be felt as a disturbance and the spirit must be brought under control or driven out. Where the spirit is invited, there may be less reason to suspect an uncontrolled, disruptive takeover of unconscious forces. Yet while such a distinction is persuasive, it may not be as simple as that after all, as an example will indicate. In Haiti, a frightening situation, such as an encounter with a suspected zombi or a highway accident, may bring on spontaneous possession trance. And it is believed to be a defense of the individual by the possessing spirit.

With respect to the differences between such types of possession trance, I am fascinated by the contrast between two: the *zar* cult of Ethiopia, Somalia, and neighboring areas on the one hand and spirit possession in India on the other. In Ethiopia (Messing, 1959) and Somalia (Lewis, 1971), women who exhibit disturbances ranging from infertility to psychosomatic symptoms to, apparently, boredom may be diagnosed by a specialist as being possessed by a *zar* spirit. This spirit must be feasted, induced to appear in the form of a possession trance, and then questioned as to his desires. These as a rule involve periodic feasting, membership in the cult group, and the acquisition of bangles and other gifts for the spirit from the sufferer's husband and family. By such means the spirit is said to be kept under control. Messing likens such cult practices to group psychotherapy; Lewis considers that the women, a dependent group, are getting supernatural vengeance. Whatever view one takes, the system appears to work. It gives relief to the sufferer and presents a safety valve for the society. In the Indian system, no accommodation with the spirit seems to be attempted. Rather, various attempts are made to exorcise the possessing spirit (Freed and Freed, 1964; Teja et al., 1970). If they fail, the patient may be brought to a psychiatric hospital if one is within reach. Teja et al. report on fifteen cases, thirteen women and two men. They consider that of these fifteen, seven were cases of hysteria, six schizophrenia, and two mania.

One wonders what the difference may be between the Indian and the East African situations. What is it about the Indian family and the larger society that disrupting psychic forces—for so we may consider the spirits—must be exorcised or the patient must be extruded, if only temporarily, from the family, whereas the Ethiopians and Somalis can work out an accommodation with the spirits, a compromise in domestic relationships, a safety valve for society? However, it is true that temporary extrusion, such as sending an Indian bride home to mother, may be a short-term accommodation to the harsh realities of life under a mother-in-law's rule, and the secondary gains available to the young woman should not be overlooked. Nonetheless, if we are dealing with cases of hysteria in the classic sense, secondary gains are surely not the whole story. And deaths from attempted exorcisms in India are reported periodically in the press. It is obviously easier to raise such a question than to offer an answer.

The question itself, however, suggests a number of issues. First, possession trance is a highly differentiated phenomenon, utilized differently in different societies. Our category of possession trance, contrasted with trance, represents a first, crude attempt at classification. It sheds, I believe, some light, it creates some order, but it does not claim to be more than a first step. Second, because possession trance is a highly differentiated phenomenon, even where we can speak of a possession trance syndrome, the societal contexts may vary so widely that in fact we may be talking not about one but about several such syndromes. In his contrast between findings in France and Hong Kong, Dr. Yap (1960) said this in effect. Third, even if we can talk of possession syndromes, what are the limits of variation? And the variations in the severity and types of pathology? Fourth, what are the social factors that shape such syndromes, and what are the types of societies in which they are likely to occur?

I have touched very lightly on a large number of points. I note with interest that the titles of other papers in this conference suggest that others will talk of similar matters. The concern with the great variety of forms that institutionalized altered states may take on, will, I believe be amply illustrated in this conference. It is my own principal aim to stress the virtual universality among human societies not only of states of altered consciousness but of their social utilization. I wish to stress both the variety of these states and the order liness of their relationship to other social and cultural variables, as well as to purely psychological ones.

ACKNOWLEDGMENTS
The statistical findings on altered states of consciousness presented here are part of a larger investigation supported by Research Grant MH07463 from the National Institute of Mental Health.

REFERENCES
Barry, H., I. Child, and M. Bacon. 1959. Relation of child training to subsistence economy. American Anthropologist 61:51–63.
Bourguignon, E. 1965. The self, the behavioral environment and the theory of spirit possession. *In* Context and meaning in cultural anthropology. M.E. Spiro, ed. New York, Free Press of Glencoe.

————. 1972. Dreams and altered states of consciousness in anthropological research. *In* Psychological anthropology, new edition. F.L.K. Hsu, ed. Cambridge, Massachusetts, Schenkman.

————,ed. 1972. Religion, altered states of consciousness and social change. Columbus, Ohio State University Press.

D'Andrade, R. 1961. Anthropological studies of dreams. *In* Psychological anthropology. F.L.K. Hsu, ed. Homewood, Illinois, Dorsey Press.

Firth, R. 1967. Ritual and drama in Malay spirit mediumship. Comparative Studies in Society and History 9:190–207.

Freed, S.A., and R.S. Freed. 1964. Spirit possession as illness in a North Indian village. Ethnology 3:152–71.

Greenbaum, L. 1972. Possession trance in Sub-Saharan Africa: a descriptive analysis of fourteen societies. *In* Religion, altered states of consciousness and social change. E. Bourguignon, ed. Columbus, Ohio State University Press.

Kroeber, A.L. 1919. Peoples of the Philippines. New York, American Museum Press.

Lebra, W.P. 1966. Okinawan religion: belief, ritual and social structure. Honolulu, University of Hawaii Press.

Leonard, A.P. 1972. Spirit mediums in Palau: transformations in a traditional system. *In* Religion, altered states of consciousness and social change. E. Bourguignon, ed. Columbus, Ohio State University Press.

Lewis, I.M. 1971. Ecstatic religion: an anthropological study of spirit possession. Baltimore, Penguin Books.

Lieban, R.W. 1967. Cebuano sorcery. Berkeley, University of California Press.

————. 1962. The dangerous Ingkantos: illness and social control in a Philippine community. American Anthropologist 64:306–12.

Mead, M. 1970. The art and science of fieldwork. *In* A handbook of method in cultural anthropology. R. Narroll and R. Cohen, eds. Garden City, New York, Natural History Press.

Messing, S.D. 1959. Group therapy and social status in the Zar cult of Ethiopia. *In* Culture and mental health. M.K. Opler, ed. New York, Macmillan.

Murdock, G.P. 1967. Ethnographic atlas. Pittsburgh, University of Pittsburgh Press.

Oesterreich, T.K. 1922. Die Bessessenheit. Langensalzach, Wendt und Klauwell.

Pfeiffer, W.M. 1971. Transkulturelle psychiatrie. Stuttgart, Georg Thieme Verlag.

Rin, H., and T.Y. Lin. 1962. Mental illness among Formosan Aborigines as compared with the Chinese in Taiwan. Journal of Mental Science 108:141–45.

Spiro, M.E. 1967. Burmese supernaturalism. Englewood Cliffs, New Jersey, Prentice-Hall.

Teja, J.S., et al. 1970. "Possession states" in Indian patients. Indian Journal of Psychiatry 12:71–87.

Yap, P.H. 1960. The possession syndrome: a comparison of Hong Kong and French findings. Journal of Mental Science 106:114–37.

5. Hysterical Psychoses and Possessions

LEWIS LANGNESS, Ph.D.

Department of Anthropology
University of Washington
Seattle, Washington

I DELIBERATELY CHOSE the terms "hysterical psychoses" and "possessions" partly because there are no suitable alternative terms for the phenomena I wish to classify and partly to dramatize that fact. What I wish to say should be accepted merely as a series of linked suggestions about what seems to be involved in this oversight, not as a definitive account of finished research.

A number of "esoteric," "culture-bound," or "exotic" syndromes have been reported from around the world. These are here labeled hysterical psychoses.[1] The best-known of these are *amok* (Arieti & Meth, 1959; Burton-Bradley, 1968; Van Loon, 1927), *latah* (Yap, 1952), *imu* (Winiariz and Wielawski, 1936), *pibloktoq* (Gussow, 1960; Wallace, 1961), *wiitiko* (Parker, 1960; Teicher, 1960), *koro* (Yap, 1965), and *susto* (Rubel, 1964). There are others, less well known or described, that may also fit this designation: *negi negi* (Langness, 1965), the Puerto Rican syndrome (Fernandez-Marina, 1961), malignant anxiety (Lambo, 1962), *boxi* (Sharma, 1966), *zar* (Pavicevic, 1966), and undoubtedly several more. Please notice that these appear here as if they belong together. Indeed, it has been pointed out elsewhere that perhaps they do represent a single phenomenon (Kennedy, n.d.; Langness, 1967; Weidman and Sussex, 1969), although this remains an assertion rather than a fact. My first suggestion is that for purposes of further study, we should assume that these do represent a single class, which we will refer to here as hysterical psychoses. We should also heed the recent statement by Weidman and Sussex (1969:1):

Little attention has yet been directed to the possibility that
these syndromes, however much they may differ clinically from
one another or from syndromes which merit specific labels in
the standard psychiatric nosology, may share basic psychological
mechanisms and processes.

In addition to these hysterical psychoses there are other forms of behavior
that have often been described as "possessions" or "possession syndromes"
(Bourguignon, 1968; Eliade, 1964; Lewis, 1971). No one, to my knowledge, has
attempted to compare hysterical psychoses with possessions. This is due, in part
at least, to the failure to separate the various behaviors involved into categories
that satisfactorily enable such a comparison to be attempted.

Erika Bourguignon and a group at Ohio State University, primarily
interested in dissociational states and the explanatory systems to which they are
linked, have done a worldwide survey of possession states. They indicate that at
least two important varieties of possession occur: possession associated with
trance, and possession not so associated. They also make clear that trance can
occur without being linked to possession beliefs at all (1968:3). If I understand
them correctly, possession with trance would be best exemplified by shamanistic
performances in which the shaman deliberately invokes a spirit to possess him
and subsequently falls into a seizure of some sort (Eliade, 1964; Lewis, 1971;
Murphy, 1964; Nadel, 1946). *Negi negi*, as I have described it previously (1965),
would be an example, in Bourguignon's categories, of possession without trance.
In *negi negi*, possession by a ghost is offered as an explanation for the behavior
only after it has occurred, and trance is not associated with it. Trance without
possession, according to Bourguignon (1968:6), is illustrated by the Samburu
(Spencer, 1965), who apparently believe that trances occurring in their young men
are due to "peculiarities of their status and tensions associated with it." There
are elaborations on both types of possession, these elaborations being mainly
classified as either positive (desired) or negative (undesired) (Bourguignon,
1968:12–13).

Though this system of classification may be useful for those interested
in indigenous explanations of illness and trance, it is of no use if one wishes to
compare possessions with hysterical psychoses. This is an obvious conclusion, as
Bourguignon's category of possession includes at least some of the hysterical
psychoses. *Negi negi* is one case in point; a more important one, perhaps, is the
wiitiko phenomenon. But unless, like Bourguignon, one is specifically interested
in local explanations, the term possession is simply inappropriate for the purposes
of transcultural psychiatry. It is fundamentally an emic unit rather than an etic
one (Pike, 1954–1960). That is, it is not a descriptive or classificatory term in our
own universe of discourse. It is one of a class of local explanations—nothing
more.[2] For example, that the Bena Bena explain *negi negi* in terms of possession
by a ghost could potentially help explain it someday, but if so, it will be because
there will turn out to be some kind of psychophysiological link between their
specific possession belief and the emergence of the individual behavior, not

because their explanation, as such, is correct. We do not employ terms in our scientific or medical laguage that mean "witchcraft-induced states," or "soul-loss-induced states," which would be the direct equivalents of "possession." These terms are the explanations of others, and even if one of them were somehow correct, it would still have to be converted into our own terminology. Consider what Marvin Harris has said of this (1964:139):

> Pike himself admits that all emic analysis must begin with etic description. He also proposes that once the emic units have been discovered, they can be "listed for comparative purposes with the similar emic units from other languages (and cultures) so studied" (p. 12). But what shall be the grounds of communication, what the standards of similarity and difference, if one can be certain neither to begin with nor in final statement of the etic content of the sought-after emic units? An emic description, in short, can be no better than the etic units in which it must unavoidably be expressed.

Thus, for example, for Richard Salisbury to assert that what I described in the Bena Bena as a hysterical psychosis is not that, but is, rather, a possession (Salisbury, 1966), is to shift from one universe of discourse to another. This is true independently of whether hysterical psychosis is itself the proper term. But in addition to being an emic unit, "possession," as we have used the term in the past, has also been notoriously ill-defined.[3] My second suggestion, then, is that we deliberately incorporate the term "possession" into our terminology, but restrict it to include only a state that demonstrably results from the conscious intent of the affected individual to induce it. Although there might still be controversy over whether or not "x" behavior was consciously sought or induced, the argument would not be exacerbated by an imprecise terminology, and the answer could be empirically determined (Langness, 1965, 1967b, 1969; Salisbury, 1966, 1967, 1969). Thus, the most typical shamanistic performance, involving deliberately induced altered states of consciousness, would be considered possessions; but altered states of consciousness such as those observed in *negi negi, wiitiko, latah* and so on, would be considered hysterical psychoses. Trances, depending upon the definition, could potentially be associated with either of these behavioral syndromes, and could be examined separately. Local classifications and explanations for any of these behaviors, although remaining of interest, would be considered irrelevant (unless there are cases similar to the classifications or explanations derived from the investigator's own categories and which are subject to the same rules of adequacy and verification). This would necessitate some reclassification at first, but that would not be particularly difficult, and the rewards in analytical precision would be considerable.

What, then, are the distinguishing features of hysterical psychoses and possessions? What are the similarities and differences? I would suggest that episodes of both hysterical psychoses and possessions, although they may be recurrent, are temporary and of relatively brief duration. They last from only a few minutes to a few days and disappear quickly. Also, all examples of both syndromes are similar in that they are predictable in form. That is, the behavior of the victim of *wiitiko*, of *latah*, of *imu*, and the like is stereotyped, and can be described in advance in fair detail by members of the culture. The same is true of shamanistic performances and many other induced altered states of consciousness. There is, then, only slight variation around known, recurrent themes. Hysterical psychoses and possessions are also similar in that, in any given culture, the particular behavior will occur primarily in only one segment of the population—that is, not all ages will have such episodes, and there may be a gender limitation as well. Thus, *negi negi* occurs only in young men (Langness, 1965); *saka*, in Kenya, occurs almost exclusively in females (Harris, 1957); Samburu trances, also in East Africa, occur in young men (Spencer, 1965); *amok* is usually considered a male disorder, whereas *latah* is female (Linton, 1956); and among !Kung Bushmen, where trance is exceedingly common, it occurs far more importantly in adult males (Lee, 1968). Shamanism is predominantly a male activity in most of the societies where it occurs, but there are, of course, exceptions (Eliade, 1964; Lewis, 1971). Little systematic attention has been paid to this unequal distribution of possession behaviors or hysterical psychoses although it would seem to be a factor of considerable importance. Finally, although it is less obviously the case for hysterical psychoses than for possessions, both of these categories of behavior are similar in that they are learned and extragenetically transmitted from one generation to the next.

When we consider differences between hysterical psychoses and possessions, the heuristic value of these categories becomes more apparent. The most fundamental and important difference, implicit in the above, is that possessions are actively sought and induced, whereas hysterical psychoses are not. Possessions can be induced by various means: the eating of mushrooms, the taking of drugs, smoking, dancing, singing, drumming, fasting, and no doubt, many others. But always, on the part of the individual, there is a conscious, deliberate intent and attempt to bring about the experience. However, the victim of a hysterical psychosis is innocent of such intent, at least at the level of consciousness. There is no apparent attempt to bring it about. Although this would appear to be a psychological difference of absolutely crucial significance, in most studies of these phenomena it is either unrecognized or mentioned only in passing (Bourguignon, 1968; Eliade, 1964; Lewis, 1971; Ludwig, 1968; Yap, 1967).

The failure to make this distinction has led to a fair amount of confusion, much of which has to do with the place of hysterical psychoses and possessions in the cultural milieu in which they occur. Thus, investigators have often claimed that episodes of hysterical psychosis are considered "legitimate" or "normal" in their cultural context because they are recurrent, learned, predictable in form, and accepted (Hirsch and Hollender, 1969). I suggest, however, that hysterical psychoses are usually considered abnormal, both by the members of the culture and by the investigator. To believe otherwise is to confuse the term "normal" with other terms—like "recognized," "recurrent," "predictable," "tolerated," or, perhaps, "statistically rare but known about." The Bena Bena, for example, certainly know about *negi negi*; and they can tell you what the behavior will be like when you see it, as well as what causes it, and roughly how often it occurs. They also do not censure those who have it, nor do they regard it as a significant social problem. But, I would argue, they do regard it as abnormal in much the same way I regard it as abnormal. As a form of behavior it is considered undesirable from a personal standpoint. People do not consciously want to experience it themselves; they know that the person who has it does not want to have it, and they regard the behavior as inappropriate, uncontrolled, nonordinary, disruptive, and extreme. Although they explain it as the result of the action of ghosts, they apparently do not understand it any more than we understand schizophrenia (because we believe it is caused by genetics, or social factors, or both). The same thing must be true of *amok, wiitiko, pibloktoq, koro,* and other hysterical psychoses.

But how can such syndromes as *negi negi* be considered abnormal if they are learned, patterned, recurrent, and culturally transmitted? This paradox can be reconciled, I think, through the concept of the "ethnic unconscious" (Devereux, 1956). People have unconscious conflicts which, stemming from the ethnic unconscious, are similar to those their parents and peers have. As these conflicts are part of the ongoing but unrecognized cultural tradition, they recur, and the "proper" reactions can become stereotyped and are unconsciously learned by everyone. Those individuals less able to cope, for whatever reason, can react, then, in terms of what Linton called the cultural "patterns for misconduct" (1936:433). But, as the conflicts are unconscious, and the learned responses are likewise unconscious, the ensuing behavior can be regarded by all concerned as abnormal. Hysterical psychoses then, in Spiro's terms, are behaviors having "intended but unrecognized functions" (1961).

Although this point of view enables us to understand hysterical psychoses as intended but unrecognized patterns of behavior, it does not distinguish between hysterical psychoses and possessions. There is no necessary difference between the two syndromes because one is related to the ethnic unconscious and the other is not. Unconscious motives may well be involved in shamanism also; indeed, it was in a discussion of shamanism that Devereux first invoked the notion of the ethnic unconscious (1956). A crucial difference does result, however, from the institutionalization or noninstitutionalization of the behavior patterns involved. Possessions are institutionalized; hysterical psychoses are not, even though they may result from the same conflicts and be learned in the same ways. I see no reason why a *negi negi* victim, if he happened to be in the proper cultural context, could not be selected for the role of shaman on the basis of his abnormal episode. But, for whatever reason, the Bena Bena have not developed such a tradition. Ioan Lewis, in his recent book, appears to hold a similar view (1971:54):

> Among the Tungus, then, possession by pathogenic spirits is a
> common explanation of illness (though not the only one), and
> at the same time the normal road to the assumption of the
> shaman's calling. The stock indication of a person's initial
> seizure by a spirit is culturally stereotyped "hysterical"

behavior (although such behavior, as we have seen, may also be interpreted non-mystically). The signs of this "Arctic hysteria," as it is usually known in the literature are: hiding from the light, hysterically exaggerated crying and singing, sitting passively in a withdrawn state on a bed or on the ground, racing off hysterically (inviting pursuit), hiding in rocks, climbing up trees, etc. Unless there are contraindications, people who exhibit these symptoms of hysterical flight are likely to be regarded as possessed by a spirit, and may, or may not, be encouraged to become shamans. If they do receive support and encouragement, they quickly learn to cultivate the power of experiencing demonstrable ecstasy.

In this view, hysterical psychoses and possessions can be seen as functional equivalents. But as in one case the behavior becomes institutionalized, it is, in Glick's terms, a "sociocultural experience" (1968) and, as such, is considered normal by the members of the culture (but not necessarily by the investigator). In the other case, remaining noninstitutionalized, the episodes occupy an ill-defined middle ground between what could be considered full-blown psychotic episodes, understood by no one at all, and the unusual but fully (locally) understood performances of shamans, trance dancers, and the like. Silverman (1967) has argued that the only essential difference between certain kinds of shamans and schizophrenics is that the former are culturally accepted while the latter are not, and this is not such an unusual view. Rabkin has also suggested that hysteria may be learned (1964), and there is a growing literature suggesting similar relationships between mental illnesses, particular institutions, and community reactions in general (Spiro, 1965; Sullivan, 1953; Szasz, 1961). The institutionalization or noninstitutionalization of such behavior, however, must be kept apart from the question of normality or abnormality, as Yap has suggested (1967:175):

> The psychogenic reactions (psychoses) of severe degree are obviously abnormal, and are recognized as such in their own cultures; they require psychiatric treatment, if this were available. If they are of moderate degree like possession states, and, less obviously, *latah* (cf. Yap, 1952), they can sometimes serve certain socially desirable purposes. However, even if some cases of psychogenic reactions are capitalized upon by society, this by itself cannot argue against their abnormality. In the realm of somatic disease the same kind of social exploitation can be found (e.g., midgets, giants, or siamese twins in circuses, etc.)

Nonetheless, it is the fact of institutionalization that allows local judgment of normality to possessions and denies it to hysterical psychoses. In the first instance, the judgment of the outside observer is usually at variance with the local opinion; in the latter, there is agreement.

Finally, I would suggest that hysterical psychoses are profane, whereas possessions are sacred (Durkheim, 1915). This results in part from the nature of the experience (what Ludwig describes as the "eureka experience, during which feelings of profound insight, illumination, and truth frequently occur"); and in part from the probably related fact of institutionalization. Thus *pibloktoq, wiitiko, negi negi, koro,* and so on, however else they are described, are not usually viewed as having any sacred or religious character. Possessions, on the other hand, are typically so described. This is particularly true of shamanistic performances (Bogoras, 1907; Eliade, 1964; Lewis, 1971; Lowie, 1954; Nadel, 1946; Rasmussen, 1929), but it is also true even of the Bushmen performances described by Lee, and in spite of the fact that "the Bushman trance performer derives his power from within the social body" (1968:50). It is not strange, then, as Spiro has observed, that religions can serve as "culturally constituted defense mechanisms" (1965). What is strange, perhaps, is that this seemingly obvious and potentially important point has been so often overlooked or ignored. Thus we find Lewis arguing that as "possession is a culturally normative [religious] experience" (1971:65), hysterical psychosis (Langness, 1967a) and culture-bound reactive syndromes (Yap, 1969) cannot properly be seen as abnormal (Lewis, 1971:181–82), even though the latter experiences are not members of the same class of religious behaviors as the former. Lewis makes the same mistake that Salisbury makes (1966) in assuming that there is only a single class of behavior involved— that is, possession.

To summarize, I have suggested that for heuristic purposes (if for no others): (1) we should consider *wiitiko, latah, imu, negi negi, koro,* and the like, all as members of the same class of behavior, labeled, for want of another term, hysterical psychoses, (2) we should accept the term "possession," for want of a better term, fully into our own language, but restrict its use only to behavioral syndromes in which there is a conscious attempt to induce the experience, (3) we should carefully separate etic and emic categories, (4) we should consider trance as a phenomenon apart from either hysterical psychoses or possessions, (5) we should likewise consider the question of normal-abnormal independent of the two suggested classifications (if we consider this question at all), (6) we should consider hysterical psychoses and possessions similar in that (a) the episodes of both are of brief duration (though there can be recurrent episodes), (b) they are predictable in form, (c) they occur only in limited segments of populations, (d) they are learned, and (e) they can both be seen as stemming from conflicts in the ethnic unconscious, (7) we differentiate between hysterical psychoses and possessions in that (a) the former are seen as abnormal by both the people themselves and the investigator, whereas the latter are regarded as abnormal only by the investigator, (b) possessions are institutionalized whereas hysterical psychoses are not, and (c) hysterical psychoses are profane whereas possessions are sacred, (8) hysterical psychoses and possessions are functional equivalents that, in Nadel's words, both "exploit and at the same time canalize existing neurotic leanings and relieve mental stresses" (1946:36).

In addition to aiding "the clarification of concepts and terminology" called for by Bourguignon (1965), my suggestions here expose certain errors in our current view of the phenomena in question, allow a new look at old problems, and suggest several avenues for further investigation. This view allows comparison of two distinct forms of behavior not previously compared. It suggests that the underlying causes of individual episodes might be the same for both hysterical psychoses and possession syndromes, and that these probably have to do with universal human reactions to stress and anxiety. It suggests that hysterical psychoses and possessions are sociocultural as well as individual phenomena and must be examined in context.

If hysterical psychoses and possessions are functional equivalents, the presence of one in a culture would be related to the absence of the other—that is, where you found a hysterical psychosis, like *wiitiko*, you would tend not to find a possession syndrome. Clearly you would not expect to find both behavioral syndromes simultaneously in the same individual; and if you found both hysterical psychoses and possessions in the same culture, different classes of individuals would be expected to exhibit them (that is, only males would have one and females the other, or only those of a certain age would experience one, and so on). It is also possible that some societies would have neither of these syndromes, replacing them instead with certain kinds of institutions, particularly religious, but perhaps others as well. Ifaluk may well be an example of this (Spiro, 1950, 1953, 1959). Also, contact with other societies would affect the behaviors in question somewhat differently. All other things being equal, hysterical psychoses would probably disappear faster than either possessions or other institutionalized patterns.

Finally, may I suggest that if this view is correct, the controversy over whether or not any of these are culture-bound syndromes (Langness, 1971; Yap, 1969) is fruitless. If the emphasis is shifted, as suggested here, to the social responses to unconscious conflicts and to the cultural contexts in which the behaviors appear, all such behaviors (indeed, all mental illnesses) can be seen as culture-bound. In the past it has been simply that the more exotic the culture, the more culture-bound the syndrome was claimed to be, thus ignoring the basic questions in favor of novelty and sensationalism.

ACKNOWLEDGMENTS
I have been assisted at various times in studying these phenomena by grants from the University of Washington School of Business and the Social Science Research Institute of the University of Hawaii (under NIMH Grant # MH09243). This assistance is gratefully acknowledged.

NOTES

1.   Contrary to Lewis' assertion (1971:181), I do not wish to "vehemently maintain" that these are (absolutely, positively, certainly, obviously, irrevocably, or what-

ever) hysterical psychoses. I do maintain that they stem from no known organic cause (and in that sense might be considered "hysterical"); that the observed behavior can be on the "psychotic" end of a normal-neurotic-psychotic continuum (provided one wishes to speak in those terms in the first place); and that they are not possession syndromes as those are understood by either Salisbury (1966) or Lewis (1971). I believe the actual labels attached to the two categories involved should not be a matter of such vital concern. Further, I would like to make clear that hysterical psychosis is a classification as well as a diagnosis, and I use it here for classificatory purposes.

2.   That we sometimes use the term "possession" in English, as in "possessed by the devil," "possessed by spirits," "possessed by God," and in others does not invalidate this statement as these usages are, themselves, folk explanations rather than part of a system of medical science terminology.

3.   I am indebted to William P. Lebra for calling my attention to Anthony F.C. Wallace's earlier discussion of this. Wallace makes the point very clear indeed (1959:59–60):

> A second major problem . . . is that perennial flower of confusion, the word "possession." Casual observers and many anthropologists alike use this word in two very different senses: as a label for some person's overtly observable behavior, and as a label for a native theory to explain this behavior. These two uses are, unhappily, often confused. It may be best to state flatly, at the outset, that I shall use the word "possession" to denote any native theory which explains some event of human behavior as being the result of the physical presence, in a human body, of an alien spirit which takes over certain or all of the host's executive functions, most frequently speech and control of the skeletal musculature. A phenomenon of possession does not, therefore, for me exist; the word merely labels a theory.
>
> Now the possession theory happens to be frequently applied, in folk beliefs, to three very different classes of phenomena, for each of which other terms exist. One of these is hallucination; the second is hysterical dissociation (including multiple personality, fugues, somnambulism, conversion hysterias, and hypnotic states); the third is obsessive ideation and compulsive action. Clinically, these are distinguishable phenomena. But any one, or group of them can be, in folk theory, explained by the mechanism of possession. Unfortunately, some observers have, in their eagerness to empathize with their subjects, used the word possession to denote not only a type of folk theory but also whatever phenomenon their folk happen to use the theory to explain. In other words, if a people use the concept of "possession" to explain certain hysterical dissociations (such as the stereotyped fugues which are so commonly induced in many religious rituals), the anthropologist tends to say that the dancers in the ritual are "possessed"; similarly, if a people use the theory to explain hallucination (which is, incidentally, a less common use of the concept), the anthropologist may refer to hallucinators as "possessed" persons. Even more confusingly, the ethnographer may use the word to denote any person who is thought to be persistently influenced by a super-natural being, whether located inside or outside the person's body.

REFERENCES

Arieti, S., and J.M. Meth. 1959. Rare, unclassifiable, collective, and exotic psychotic syndromes. *In* An American handbook of psychiatry. S. Arieti, ed. New York, Basic Books.

Bogoras, W. 1907. The Chukchee. Memoirs of the American Museum of Natural History, vol. 2.

Bourguignon, E. 1965. The self, the behavioral environment, and the theory of spirit possession. *In* Context and meaning in cultural anthropology. M.E. Spiro, ed. New York, Free Press of Glencoe.

————. 1968. World distribution and patterns of possession states. *In* Trance and possession states. R.M. Prince, ed. Montreal, R.M. Bucke Memorial Society.

Burton-Bradley, B.G. 1968. The amok syndrome in Papua and New Guinea. The Medical Journal of Australia 1:252–56.

Devereux, G. 1956. Normal and abnormal: the key problem in psychiatric anthropology. *In* Some uses of anthropology: theoretical and applied. J.B. Casagrande and T. Gladwin, eds. Washington, D.C., Anthropological Society of Washington.

Durkheim, E. 1915. The elementary forms of the religious life. Joseph Ward Swain, trans. London, Allen and Unwin.

Eliade, M. 1964. Shamanism: archaic techniques of ecstasy. Princeton, Princeton University Press.

Fernandez-Marina, R. 1961. The Puerto Rican syndrome: its dynamics and cultural determinants. Psychiatry 4:47–82.

Glick, L. 1968. Possession on the New Guinea Highlands. Transcultural Psychiatric Research 5:200–05.

Gussow, Z. 1960. Pibloktoq (hysteria) among the polar Eskimo: an ethnopsychiatric study. *In* Psychoanalysis and the social sciences. W. Muernsterberger, ed. New York, International Universities Press.

Harris, G. 1957. Possession "hysteria" in a Kenya tribe. American Anthropologist 59:1046–66.

Harris, M. 1964. The nature of cultural things. New York, Random House.

Hirsch, S.J., and M.H. Hollender. 1969. Hysterical psychosis: clarification of the concept. American Journal of Psychiatry 125:909–15.

Kennedy, J. N.d. Cultural psychiatry. Manuscript.

Lambo, T.A. 1962. Malignant anxiety. Journal of Mental Science 108:256–64.

Langness, L.L. 1965. Hysterical psychosis in the New Guinea Highlands: a Bena Bena example. Psychiatry 28:258–77.

————. 1967a. Hysterical psychosis: the cross-cultural evidence. American Journal of Psychiatry 124:47–56.

————. 1967b. Rejoinder to Salisbury. Journal of Transcultural Psychiatry 4:125–30.

————. 1969. Possession on the New Guinea Highlands. Transcultural Psychiatric Research 6:95–100.

————. 1971. Culture-bound syndromes: yes or no? Culture and Mental Health in Asia and the Pacific. Working Paper, Social Science Research Institute, University of Hawaii.

Lee, R.B. 1968. The sociology of !Kung bushmen trance performances. *In* Trance and possession states. R. Prince, ed. Montreal, R.M. Bucke Memorial Society.

Lewis, I.M. 1971. Ecstatic religion: an anthropological study of spirit possession. Baltimore, Penguin Books.

Linton, R. 1936. The study of man. New York, Appleton-Century-Crofts.

————. 1956. Culture and mental disorders. Springfield, Illinois, Charles C. Thomas.

Lowie, R.H. 1954. Indians of the plains. New York, McGraw-Hill.

Ludwig, A.M. 1968. Altered states of consciousness. *In* Trance and possession states. R. Prince, ed. Montreal, R.M. Bucke Memorial Society.

Murphy, J.M. 1964. Psychotherapeutic aspects of shamanism on St. Lawrence Island, Alaska. *In* Magic, faith and healing. A. Kiev, ed. London, Free Press of Glencoe.

Nadel, S.F. 1946. A study of shamanism in the Nuba mountains. Journal of the Royal Anthropological Institute 76:25–37.

Parker, S. 1960. The Wiitiko psychosis in the context of Ojibwa personality. American Anthropologist 62:603–23.

Pavicevic, M.B. 1966. Psychoses in Ethiopia. Transcultural Psychiatric Research 3:152–54.

Pike, K. 1954–1960. Language in relation to a unified theory of the structure of human behavior. Vols. 1–3. Glendale, Summer Institute of Linguistics.

Rabkin, R. 1964. Conversion hysteria as social maladaptation. Psychiatry 27:349–63.

Rasmussen, K. 1929. Intellectual culture of the Iglulik Eskimo. Copenhagen, Gyldendalske Boghandel, Nordisk Forlag.

Rubel, A.J. 1964. The epidemiology of a folk illness, *susto*, in Hispanic America. Ethnology 3:268–83.

Salisbury, R. 1966. On possession in the New Guinea Highlands. Transcultural Psychiatric Research 3:103–16.

————. 1967. Possession on the New Guinea Highlands. Transcultural Psychiatric Research 4:130–34.

————. 1969. Possession on the New Guinea Highlands. Transcultural Psychiatric Research 6:100–102.

Sharma, D.P. 1966. Report from Dr. D.P. Sharma, Kathmandu, Nepal. Transcultural Psychiatric Research 3:132–33.

Silverman, J. 1967. Shamans and acute schizophrenia. American Anthropologist 69:21–31.

Spencer, P. 1965. The Samburu. Berkeley, University of California Press.

Spiro, M.E. 1950. A psychotic personality in the South Seas. Psychiatry 13:189–204.

————. 1953. Ghosts: A anthropological inquiry into learning and perception. Journal of Abnormal and Social Psychology 48:376–82.

————. 1959. Cultural heritage, personal tensions and mental illness in a South Seas culture. *In* Culture and mental health. M.K. Opler, ed. New York, Macmillan Co.

————. 1961. Social systems, personality and functional analysis. *In* Studying personality cross-culturally. B. Kaplan, ed. Evanston, Illinois, Row, Peterson and Co.

————. 1965. Religious systems as culturally constituted defense mechanisms. *In* Context and meaning in cultural anthropology. M.E. Spiro, ed. New York, Free Press of Glencoe.

Sullivan, H.S. 1953. The interpersonal theory of psychiatry. New York, Norton.

Szasz, T.S. 1961. The myth of mental illness. New York, Harper & Row.

Teicher, M.I. 1960. Windigo psychosis. *In* Proceedings of the 1960 annual spring meeting of the American Ethnological Society. V. Ray, ed. Seattle, American Ethnological Society.

Van Loon, F.H.G. 1927. Amok and latah. Journal of Abnormal and Social Psychology 21:434–44.

Wallace, A.F.C. 1959. Cultural determinants of response to hallucinatory experience. Archives of General Psychiatry 1:58–69.

————. 1961. Mental illness, biology and culture. *In* Psychological anthropology. F.L.K. Hsu, ed. Homewood, Illinois, Dorsey Press.

Weidman, H.H., and J.N. Sussex. 1969. Cultural values and ego functioning in relation to the atypical culture-bound reactive syndromes. Typescript. 38 pp.

Winiariz, W., and J. Wielawski. 1936. Imu: a psychoneurosis occurring among Ainus. Psychoanalytic Review 23:181–86.

Yap, P.M. 1952. The *latah* reaction: its pathodynamics and nosological position. Journal of Mental Science 98:515–64.

———. 1965. Koro—a culture-bound depersonalization syndrome. British Journal of Psychiatry 111:43–50.

———. 1967. Classification of the culture-bound reactive syndromes. Australian and New Zealand Journal of Psychiatry 1:172–79.

———. 1969. The culture-bound reactive syndrome. *In* Mental health research in Asia and the Pacific. W. Caudill and T.Y. Lin, eds. Honolulu, East-West Center Press.

6.   *Phii Pob*: Spirit Possession in Rural Thailand

SANGUN SUWANLERT, M.D.

Srithunya Hospital
Nondhaburi, Thailand

Introduction

In Thailand, as in all other countries, there are many people who seem to believe in spirits and ghosts. The Thais refer to the spirits and ghosts in general as *phii*. From my experience in treating psychiatric patients, I have found that the patients and their relatives are very much concerned with spirits and ghosts. *Phii* (evil spirit) possession is often found to be a basic cause in mental disease, both functional and organic, and we can divide them into three types:

- Ghosts of the dead: *phii* of grandparents, father, mother, ancestors, or spirits of important and respected people.
- Spirits of sacred things, not emanating from human beings.
- Spirits of the living, such as *phii pong, phii pob, phii ka,* and *phii krasu.*

My paper will be on the spirits of the living, the third type, or *phii pob*, with special emphasis on the psychiatric study of the *phii pob*. The first two kinds of *phii* mentioned above, those that originate from the dead and sacred things, are found to possess people more often than the third kind. Reports of spirits originating from the dead and sacred things in Asia were given previously by Lin (1953), Yap (1960), Sasaki (1963), and Spiro (1969), but none have touched on the spirits of the living.

Phii pob or *phii ka* is a common spirit in the northeast, north, and some provinces of the central plain of Thailand. Some say that *phii pob* is nonsubstantial;

that nobody can definitely describe its shape. Some say that it is in the shape of a black dog; others say it is shaped more like a monkey. I have been unable to find any data about its origin. Villagers simply say that it has been in existence since "olden days."

Phii pob originates in a living person, conceals itself in the body of that person, who is called the originating host, and comes and goes at any time. There are three ways in which a person can become a source of *phii pob*: it may originate in the person himself; he may inherit it from his ancestors; or he may possess an object said to bring good fortune to its owner, and the *phii pob* dwelling in this object may transfer itself to the owner.

Origination within the host. *Phii pob* seems to originate in people who study magic arts and spells, such as the spell for prosperous trading, the spell enabling one to talk cleverly, and the magical love arts, to make a person desire sexual intercourse with the opposite sex or to make one's sexual organs attractive. After a person completes his study, he becomes a teacher in his special field of magic. Almost every teacher of magic observes certain restrictions against doing certain things (called *kalum*). These restrictions may proscribe eating certain kinds of food, accepting fees for treatment and teaching, or going underneath a clothesline. As time passes and such a person forgets these restrictions, the *phii pob* originates automatically within him, although the host may not be aware of it. Since it is believed that the *phii pob* hiding within a person can leave the body of that person to possess another, the new possessed host can discover and make known who the originating host of the *phii pob* is. Usually a person hosts only one *phii pob* of the same sex as himself, but many informants confirm that it is possible for a person to host many and possess both males and females.

Inherited from the host's ancestors. Although the host grows old and eventually dies, the *phii pob* does not. It goes on hiding in the children of the host, usually the eldest child of the same sex; that is, the father's *phii pob* will transfer to the eldest son and the mother's to the eldest daughter. If the host has no children, the *phii pob* will hide in a close relative and is called *pob chue*.

Origination in objects. One can become host of *phii pob* by possessing commodities such as *wan krachai* and *wan phii pob,* a tuberous plant, or *see poeng sanei,* a wax charm, which are said to bring good fortune to the possessor. Some believe that *phii pob* dwell in these things and may transfer themselves to the owner.

A person will be possessed by a *phii pob* when he has had an argument with its host, but this is not necessarily the only time. A person or animal can be possessed in four ways:

1. Possession can occur in time of sickness, causing complications, during menopause or at the age of involution, or during the transition from adolescence to adulthood. It is believed that the spirit will eat away at the viscera (kidney, intestines, liver, et cetera) until the individual finally dies.

2. A *phii pob* can possess a boy or a girl under ten years of age and make the child talk irrelevantly. It is believed that most children thus possessed will eventually die.

3. Large domestic animals such as cows, buffalo, and horses can be possessed and die suddenly.

4. A *phii pob* can enter people who have had no previous symptoms, generally women between the ages of 18 and 40, men, less frequently. The possessed host will usually identify the originating host; this is called *ook pak* ("to speak out") in Northeastern Thai.

The Study

At various times from 1967 to 1971, I conducted a study of *phii pob* possession in north and northeast Thailand. My research had the following aims:

• To study the nature of *phii pob* in the upper regions of Thailand, where people believe that *phii pob* is the cause of some illness.

• To study the relationship between the possession syndrome and the environment, the local culture, and the reaction of the people toward this syndrome.

• To determine whether this is a psychiatric syndrome and, if so, how to classify it.

• To study folk treatment for the possessed host and originating host.

This paper reports on sixty-two cases of possessed hosts; six cases of originating hosts; and ten cases of possessed hosts whose *phii pob* refused to leave them.

Methodology

In 1967, I worked as a member of the Medical Services Department's Mobile Unit for three months, covering the area of Amphour District, Amnatcharoen, Phana, and Lerngnoktha, in Changwad Province, Ubol-rajathani. In 1968, I had an opportunity to work for the Mobile Medical Unit in the Dhat Panom District of Nakorn Panom Province for one month. In 1971, I went to the northeast a few times to get more information.

I spent the first month interviewing inpatients and outpatients at the health station in Amnatcharoen, the main station of the mobile medical unit, and villagers when the mobile unit went out to the outlying villages. A questionnaire of twenty questions was made up. Preference was given to people who had no physical disease at the time of being possessed.

In 1967 in Ubol-rajathani I selected and interviewed fifty possessed hosts, two males (ages 20 and 25) and forty-eight females. The informants at the health station had just been possessed and were in for treatment. The ones in the villages were introduced to me by the heads of the villages, by teachers, and by village doctors. I interviewed these people myself in Northeastern dialect for 15 to 45 minutes, depending on the circumstances, since I was able to spend more time with those at the health station than with those in the villages.

In 1968 in Nakorn Panom Province, with the assistance of a Buddhist monk, I interviewed six originating hosts in the vicinity of Pra Dhat Panom, a Buddhist pagoda where Buddha's *urungkardhat* ("chest bone") is kept. Originating hosts often come to Buddhist monks to have the spirits expelled by the sacredness of the pagoda and the power of holy water. I also interviewed twelve possessed female hosts in the villages and questioned lawyers and judges regarding litigation involving originating hosts of *phii pob* because one often hears of suits of bodily assault and defamatory statements made against originating hosts.

In 1969–1971, I studied in detail ten cases of possessed women whom *phii pob* refused to leave after more than 48 hours. The women were admitted to the Srithunya psychiatric hospital as psychotics, having been brought by relatives after shamans had not been able to drive off the spirits. After one week of treatment, they felt much better.

There are many ways in which *phii pob* can enter a person, but I am told there are five most frequent points of entry: arms and hands, especially the fingers; feet; eyes; nose; and nipples.

Symptoms of Possession

The earliest sign of the onset of possession is a numbness of limbs, followed by falling, with or without convulsions. Most who are possessed become unconscious; some become rigid, clench their fists, and must be forced to lie down or sit. After being in this condition for a while, some can answer questions, although somewhat confusedly. There are five categories of symptoms that appear after a person has been possessed:

1. Making noises like "*phii*," shouting out, screaming, weeping.
2. Tensing, clenched fists, or short spasms.
3. Shaking following spasms, (not in all cases).
4. Timidity or shyness, manifested by an inability to speak to or face others. Sometimes facial expressions are similar to those of the originating host.
5. Identifying or speaking out the host's name (*ook pak*).

The fifth is the most important symptom, for it reveals not only the host's name but also the purpose of the possession, whether it is good or bad and whether it is merely passing through the village. Whether this symptom appears depends largely on the ability of the shaman; if he is skillful, he will have the victim talking relevantly.

Possessed Host: Case Illustrations

For illustration, I would like to describe the two cases of possession occurring at the health station that I was able to observe from the onset. I will compare them with a representative case from the ten patients whom *phii pob* refused to leave. I will also give an account of my interview with a shaman.

Case 1. A young, unmarried girl, 16 years of age, a Buddhist, with a primary-school education, from the Amnatcharoen District, and of low economic status was admitted to the Class I health station complaining of abdominal pain in the umbilical region. A physical examination revealed no abnormality, and she was referred to me for observation.

In an interview with the girl's mother, it was learned that, although she was very cooperative, the mother knew very little about her daughter because since the age of two the girl had been under her grandmother's care and had lived in another district. When the mother was in her sixth month of pregnancy, the girl's father left home and never returned. After the birth of the child, the mother struggled to make a living for both of them; when the girl was two, the mother remarried, and the child was sent off to her grandmother's. At the age of 15 the girl went to Bangkok with relatives and worked as a servant for six months, but she was unable to cope with her job so went back to live with her mother and stepfather.

Two days after witnessing her drunken stepfather slap her mother during an argument, the girl was possessed by a *phii pob*. The possession, according to the mother, lasted for about an hour. The originating host seemed to be one of the stepfather's friends who lived in the next village, because during possession the girl's general bearing was masculine when she described the kind of husband her stepfather was and when she threatened him with punishment by his ancestors' spirits.

The patient, with decorative cotton strings tied around her neck and wrists, was an attractive girl with sad eyes and a low, soft manner of speaking. During the interview she repeatedly said, "I don't know what my problem is, but I'm anxious about it." Crying, she complained of severe abdominal pain while continually asking her stepfather to do things for her.

The second night after being admitted, about 11:00 P.M., the patient was again possessed by a *phii pob*. When I went to the ward, the relatives, fearful of her falling off the bed, had her lying on the floor, and her mother was massaging her legs. I spoke to her but there was no recognition on her part. However, when she heard me, she sat up immediately in a cross-legged position. Her face became flushed and her eyes widened but did not focus. She raised her hand and said coherently, "I'm Mr. ——— (stepfather's friend). I was angry when I heard that my friend did something wrong in the village. I'm here for a visit only." The mother cried out, "Please, go." "No," replied the girl. To the other relatives' suggestion of calling a shaman, the possessed girl answered, "I don't care." Then a relative asked, "Why don't you? This is a government office." (It is a common belief that *phii pob* are afraid of government offices.) The reply was, "I want my friend to behave. I want to let him know that if he doesn't, the ancestors' spirits will break his neck." After the stepfather promised that he would behave, the other relatives asked many questions; an hour later the spirit departed via the mouth, without the help of a shaman.

The patient was treated for ten days with a mild tranquilizer and superficial psychotherapy. She was discharged when she stopped complaining of abdominal pain, and she returned home to her grandmother.

Case 2. A 32-year-old Buddhist woman, wife of a peasant, with a primary-school education, and of low-income status, was admitted to the health station because of manifest muscle twitching in both arms, insomnia, and loss of appetite. A physical examination did not reveal any abnormality.

According to her husband, they had been married for several years. Before their marriage he had been a bachelor and she a divorcée with no children.

About a year before admission, the wife was informed that the husband had had a long talk with a girl. Subsequently she began to nag, asking about his relationship with the girl. The more he denied, the more she nagged. A few days later the woman was possessed twice in one day. Ten days before her hospitalization, the husband went to see the girl in question on a business matter. When the wife learned of it she became hysterical, swore at her husband, cried, and ultimately fell into depression. Two days later the muscles in her arms began to twitch.

I visited the patient an hour every morning during her hospitalization because she was on a mild tranquilizer and superficial psychotherapy under my care. Whenever I started talking to her, her husband had to hold on to her arms to prevent them from twitching. Although the patient was pale, she looked younger than her years. She seemed to understand me well enough to make me think that she was not confused. However, she often said, "I'm quite worried about my future."

On the fourth night after admission, she became possessed by a female *phii pob*. The spirit claimed that it had come for a visit and asked the husband how things were going at home and how he had been behaving lately. Approximately fifteen minutes later the patient became silent and fell into depression, indicating that the spirit had departed. After ten days at the health station, the patient felt much better and the muscle twitching disappeared; she was discharged.

I consider the two cases cited above simple cases, but only when the precipitating cause of possession is taken into consideration. The cause was a kind of wish-fulfillment for people living in a noncomplex society.

For comparison with the foregoing cases from 1967–1968, let us examine one of the ten cases of *phii pob* that refused to leave their hosts, which I studied in 1969–1971.

Case 3. Mrs. T., 56 years of age, married, a Buddhist, farmer, born and raised in Uthaithanii Province in the central plain, of middle economic status, educated through the fourth grade, was admitted to Srithunya Hospital in 1970 with the chief complaint of insomnia.

A few days prior to admission, she screamed without reason, alternated between talking and laughing, and her body shook. She kept saying that she was possessed by the spirit of a dead woman and *phii pob*, and seemed to understand few questions asked by her relatives.

The day before admission she would not speak to anyone, except to say, "the spirit prohibits me from saying anything." Her relatives repeatedly asked what kind of spirit she had but she did not answer; she only shook her head. About 3:00 A.M., her whole body became completely stiff, and both eyes stared for an hour. Then she began to talk coherently, and made up questions and answers by herself.

On admission, she was shaking and seemed afraid of someone, and then she asked for her husband to stand behind her. She stated that she was a spirit, and her memory and orientation were poor. The diagnosis was senile psychosis.

The patient was born and brought up in a village, the fifth child in her family. Her parents both died twenty years ago. At the age of 18 she married a man whom she had not met before. Her eldest sister had advised her to marry him because he was a good man. She was the mother of seven children, 5 males and 2 females, ranging in age from 12 to 34. About seven years before the 1970 admission, she went to visit her eldest sister, who lived in another village. During their conversation, the patient developed numbness and palpitation when the topic turned to her aunt, who had died many years ago. Later on she entered a state of spirit possession. Her husband took her to a shaman. After a week's treatment she recovered.

One year before the 1970 admission, she was very anxious over the death of her buffalo. (Buffalo are very important to Thai farmers.) A few days later she was possessed by the spirit of a dead woman. Symptoms were similar to those of the previous occasion, and she received treatment at the provincial hospital. Her symptoms lasted for two weeks and then she recovered.

To me, she looked younger than her stated years, and was well dressed. She preferred to be interviewed lying in bed. During the conversation, both legs started to shake and jerk, and she raised them up. She experienced a hallucination about the spirit, which seemed to say to her, "I will take your soul away." She thought that one of the hospital attendants was her daughter. Sometimes she became confused and stopped talking.

She had difficulty walking about the ward, but she wanted to walk, so the attendant supported her by holding her hands. Her behavior was dramatic. She could walk slowly within three days' time, but the "voice" still persisted. Several times during the night the spirit possessed her.

She felt much better within a week, after receiving strong tranquilizers. Her speech became normal and associations coherent. She stated that she was disappointed about her fifth son, who had married before being ordained a Buddhist monk. She wanted to see him in the yellow robes of the Buddhist priest before she died. Her son had brought his wife to visit her, but she refused to welcome them. Then she changed the subject and cried. She complained about her different feelings and believed that *phii pob* was a cause of her illness. The "voice" still persisted.

This off-and-on condition lasted for a week, and at the beginning of the third week her delusions and hallucinations disappeared. As it turned out, her son divorced his wife and promised to be ordained. She was very happy, and was discharged within one month, apparently symptom-free.

This was one of ten cases in the mental hospital about which our staff agreed that the diagnosis was hysterical psychosis but that the underlying cause was *phii pob* possession.

Folk treatment of the possessed host.   The shaman uses many kinds of medicinal herbs and rattan canes for driving out the spirit. He also uses Gatha, sacred verses or spells, derived from Buddhist texts in Pali or Sanskrit. The first thing the shaman does when he meets the patient is to perform a spell by blowing. The natives call these probing spells which are carried out by blowing three times onto the top or crown of the head of the possessed to see how strongly the spirit is imbedded. Then the shaman pricks parts of the patient's body, especially the bifurcations of the body, such as between the fingers or toes, the armpits, groin, breasts, or the sexual organs. All the while the shaman continues with the spell. When he comes to the area where the spirit is located, the patient will cry or moan out loud, expressing his pain. Then the shaman questions the possessed and his relatives and neighbors.

Many kinds of spirits commonly possess people (See Table 1). A skillful shaman is able to differentiate each type.

When it is known that a person has been possessed by a spirit, the villagers gather around as though they are attending a spectacle. In some cases, they try to help drive it out before the shaman appears. They may burn chili peppers in front of the possessed, so that the smoke will get in his eyes and drive out the spirit. The villagers are not afraid to witness the possession because they believe a spirit does not possess two people at the same time. The villagers are also interested in learning who the originating host is so that they can be watchful for themselves and their families.

The person who is accused of being the originating host denies it and quarrels with the villagers when accused. At times in these quarrels the villagers turn to physical violence in their zest to drive out the spirit. On the other hand, if the accused offers no denials but tries to help by blowing a spell on a lump of sticky rice and placing it near the mouth of the possessed to lure the spirit, he will receive sympathy from the villagers and can live happily in that village.

A shaman.   Going hand in hand with their belief in Buddhism is the people's belief in spirits, which plays an important role in Thai daily life. In the rural areas, one who is ill has several choices of whom to consult: the modern medical doctor in town, the herb doctor, the shaman (for *phii pob*), and the priest. Many people consult a fortuneteller for advice on which is the best.

The *thaw jam* I interviewed was a dignified, neatly dressed man of 45, married, a peasant, a Buddhist with a primary-school education, and of average economic status. He said that he was appointed *thaw jam* by the villagers for ten years since he had to look after the *puu ta*, the guardian spirit of a village (*puu* means paternal grandfather and *ta*, maternal grandmother). It is enshrined in a wooden structure, three by five meters, called the spirit house, which is built under the direction of heaven when a village is established. It is usually located on a hillock in a quiet and peaceful place or near the entrance to the village.

The duties of a *thaw jam* are several: looking after the *puu ta* and the

Table 1:   Types of Spirits and Effect on Possessed Host

Spirit Type	Effect on Possessed Host
Phii pob	Smiles shyly, looks folk therapist *(maw)* straight in the face.
Phii tai or *than* (spirit from heaven)	Loves to have fun, sings and dances.
Phii ban pha burut (ancestor spirit)	Acts defiant, is afraid of no one, and never turns away when stared at.
Phii cak sing saksit (spirit of sacred things)	Displays quiet superiority.

spirit house; arranging for the annual ceremony with shaman and village representative to make offerings for expulsion of evil spirits, including *phii pob*; and preservation of traditions and customs of the village. The *thaw jam*'s role is as important as that of the head of the village, who is appointed by the government. To qualify, one must be mature in age, a shaman or otherwise interested in spirits, honest, articulate, of average economic status, and one must have finished a study of magical arts.

For the ritual to expel evil spirits (called *kawat khaw*), the *thaw jam* asks the afflicted to make bundles consisting of five pairs each of flowers, candles, and joss sticks, and another consisting of eight pairs each of the same. Then he mixes them up and places them on a tray-table. On the same tray-table is placed an egg-sized, molded ball of glutinous rice. The patient takes the tray and lifts it above his head and hands it to the *thaw jam*. Then the patient lies down with his head toward the north and feet toward the south. The *thaw jam* lights a pair of candles and joss sticks, blows spells on the rice, and bows three times. He takes the riceball off the tray and places the tray above the patient's head. He then places the riceball on various parts of the patient's body, starting from the tips of the toes and working upward to the top of the head, while calling the names of spirits and asking the patient to pray with him. The riceball is then thrown away, indicating that the spirits have departed. The tray-table is left at the ritual spot until the patient recovers. Later it is placed in a temple or the spirit house of the village. The ritual for expulsion of *phii pob*, the spirit that eats away at the viscera, is a modification of the foregoing one performed by a *thaw jam*.

In 1968, I again had an opportunity to work for the Mobile Medical Unit in Dhat Panom district of Nakorn Panom Province, and thus a chance to continue my study on *phii pob*, of both possessed and originating hosts. Twelve females of possessed hosts were studied. The characteristics of them before, during, and after possession are similar to those studied in 1967. Their habits and outlooks are also similar; there is not much difference between the two samples. The difference, if any, is only slight, due mainly to local customs. My study in this area was concentrated on originating hosts.

Originating Hosts

Tables 2 and 3 give brief background information on the *phii pob*s interviewed. For further details, two cases are described below.

Case 1. Mrs. S., age 65, was from Amphur Wapee Patum, Mahasarakam Province. She looked slightly younger than her age, was dressed neatly in a long-sleeved blouse and a local type of skirt and wore the Northeastern type of earrings. Throughout the interview she sat properly and was very cooperative.

According to her, about five years ago in 1963, one of her sons who was working at Amphur Barn Pai in Kohnkaen Province befriended a man who had fallen off a car and broken his leg. The man had run out of money and wanted to sell a box containing a small image of Buddha on one side and a closely knitted gold fabric on the other. The man wanted 100 baht (US$5) for it but took the

Table 2:   Characteristics of Originating Hosts

Case	Sex	Age	Marital Status	Education	Profession
1	F	65	Widow	Illiterate	Farmer
2	F	40	Married	Illiterate	Farmer
3	M	36	Married	4 yrs. of primary school	Farmer
4	M	70	Married	Illiterate	Farmer
5	F	65	Married	Illiterate	Farmer
6	M	66	Married	Religious	Merchant

Table 3:   Origin, Duration, and Effect of Role as Originating Host

Case	Cause	Duration (yr)	Number of Possessed Hosts Affected
1	Unknowingly possessed a sacred commodity, or "*pob* agent"	1	3
2	Possessed or inherited a *pob* agent	1	0
3	Possessed a wax charm	3	Several
4	Invoked a magic spell for a better plantation	1	1 (dead)
5	Possessed a *pob* agent	1	1
6	Possessed a *pob* agent	5	Several

20 baht offered. The man told him to take good care of it since it was valuable. When her son returned home, he placed the object on the shelf for worship. About a month later Mrs. S. began to have headaches and insomnia, so she consulted a shaman. He advised her that the object was the cause of the ailment and to get rid of it. One neighbor suggested that she throw it away but another asked for it so she gave it to the latter. Her headaches and insomnia soon disappeared.

After she disposed of the object in 1967, three of her neighbors, girls aged 14–15, were entered by *phii pob*. All of them claimed that it was a *phii pob* from Mrs. S. Mrs. S. felt very uneasy and asked the head of the village to find an expert who could expel the *phii pob* from her. She was referred to someone and paid over 1,000 baht (US$50) for his service. Because she feared that she might not be completely cured, she continued to receive a treatment of "holy water" at least once a month.

When asked how she felt after the shaman had beaten her with a stick and the *phii pob* had supposedly left, although the neighbors still accused her of being a *phii pob*, Mrs. S. said that she felt no pain nor anything else but shame and worry. She did not want to see anybody. She was worried about her seven sons who would have to bear the accusation for a long time. This is why she made her way to Wat Dhat Panom for the expulsion of *phii pob* from her. The person she consulted told her that if she would gather together a small Buddhist image, holy thread, and a fallen fragment of a pagoda, she would be protected from *phii pob*. She replied that she had spent all her money and could not purchase the necessary articles. I bought and gave them to her, and it seemed to lift up her spirits.

Case 2. A 36-year-old man, Mr. B., married and living in Amphur Boor Kaw, Kalasinthu Province, came to Wat Dhat Panom to have *phii pob* driven out of his body. He was told that he had two *phii pob*, both in the shape of monkeys, perched on his shoulder. In our interview, Mr. B. reported that about five years before, when he was unmarried, he bought a wax charm to attract women and make them fall in love with him. He did not think much more about it until he discovered that his *phii pob* was going around possessing the neighborhood women.

When asked how he felt when the *phii pob* left his body to enter into another, he said that he trembled with no apparent cause, but did not feel anything leave his body. He was not concerned that his neighbors would do any harm to him. Whenever he thought about it, he said, he felt sad and worried, but he strongly denied having any illness.

I then asked him about his wife's and children's reaction to his being called the host. He said they were all ashamed and worried about it, especially when one of his children overheard the villagers talking about him.

About a month before he came for treatment at Wat Pra Dhat, someone in the village became possessed again. At that time a villager fired a shot into the sky, and Mr. B. began to fear for his life. Until then, he was sad and worried about the situation he was in, but he never thought anyone would do him any harm. (The probable reason for this was that he had a relative in a monastery who was highly respected by the villagers.) After this incident, he was unable to sleep well and often dreamed of monkeys and black dogs. Finally he decided to seek help at Wat Pra Dhat since the two spirit doctors who had treated him did not help him feel better.

I studied the symptoms of depression in the six cases of originating hosts to see whether illness such as depression existed in the distant villages. A questionnaire based on Cleghorn and Curtis' depression study (1959) was used. Results suggested that the patients came for treatment out of worry over bodily harm that they might receive and out of depression manifested by the symptoms such as sadness, insomnia, and loss of appetite. These symptoms lead one to conclude that villagers do become depressed and try to avoid other people when they are accused of being a *phii pob*.

Methods of treating originating host. The first type of treatment is by holy water. When originating-host *phii pob* came to Wat Dhat Panom for treatment, they first registered their names and announced that they were *phii pob*. The monk in charge recorded their names, listed their symptoms, arranged them in groups of 100 (300 to 400 came daily), and set up appointments (early evening or morning) for treatment. The treatment began with an explanation of the use of holy water. Then each person was called by name but several grouped themselves together and crawled out to the monk so that they could be seen by all. They sat with both legs tucked to one side and both hands in the position of salutation. The medium called to the spirits and informed the monk of the number of *phii pob* in the hosts' bodies and the number of days required for the holy water treatment. The monk took out a whip made of bamboo and poured holy water over the head and body of each *phii pob* while uttering a magic incantation. He used the whip lightly but repeatedly for five to ten minutes to expel the spirits and stopped only when he was certain that they had left. Finally, the monk told each one to take home some holy water to bathe with and to drink.

To observe another method of treatment, that by shaman, I went to Tolo, a village in Roi-Et Province, which is known as the "village of *phii pob*s." At the time, the village had about 400 households, but the population was increasing constantly, mainly owing to the reputation of a highly respected and widely known shaman, Mr. R. Five to ten families came to see him for treatment during a year. The treatment was successful, so they remained in Tolo, never possessing anyone else in the village.

I observed Mr. R.'s treatment of Mrs. M., the *phii pob*'s host. Mrs. M. was brought to a cemetery. The ceremony area was surrounded by two circles of holy thread; the outer circle covered an area of 2,024 square meters and the inner circle about 25 square meters. The equipment used was one medium-sized earthen pot, a piece of white cloth to cover the top of the pot, and holy thread as specified by the shaman. A small shrine in the shape of a house for the spirit was put in the inner circle. The host's head was shaved and she was dressed like a nun. The shaman brought the woman into the inner circle and she sat under the shrine and meditated. During this time no one was allowed to enter the outer circle.

When Mrs. M. felt ready for the ceremony, the shaman meditated and ordered all the *phii pob* to gather around her (it was known she had nine of them). Only seven of them gathered, two being with her brother who was away. They waited for several hours until the brother returned, and his two *phii pob* were included. When all nine *phii pob* were present, the shaman told Mrs. M. to write down on a piece of paper all the incantations that she had learned. He placed the paper in the pot, ordered all nine *phii pob* to go into the pot, and covered it up with the white cloth. He placed the pot into a square pit in the inner circle and buried it deeply. Mrs. M. was told not to dig up the pot because if she did the *phii pob* might possess her again. She agreed to comply. The ceremony was then completed.

Three or four days later I went to inquire about Mrs. M. She said that she did not feel well, for she kept thinking about the *phii pob* and could not sleep. About three months later she was not able to stand it and she dug up the pot. The *phii pob* repossessed her and her condition became worse; the *phii pob* went out to possess others in the village.

Some time later I inquired about Mrs. M. I was told that she had recovered after her relatives took her to Tolo for treatment. She did not return home and later was ordained to become a nun at Wat Tolo. The shaman has since died, and his children are successfully carrying on his art of healing.

Villagers' Attitude toward *Phii Pob*

Belief in spirits has become a part of village tradition. The spirits, both good and bad, are perceived as superhuman beings, so good spirits are worshipped or respected and the bad ones are driven away as quickly as possible. The modernization introduced by education and communication has not changed these beliefs much. The villagers justify their belief in spirits by declaring that it is not harmful to anyone.

Actually there are three groups of people with respect to belief in spirits. (1) Nonbelievers include persons who have had some training in Buddhism, those who have been educated in cities or towns, and those whose families were troubled by spirits and have become good Buddhists. (2) Partial believers usually have a little more formal education than the average villager and often talk about true and false spirit possession and have tried to prove it. (3) Full believers include those who have lived only in the village, those who have experienced spirit possession, and those persuaded by others to believe in spirits. In actual number there are more full believers than nonbelievers and partial believers put together.

One may conclude that *phii pob* are considered suprahuman but bad spirits that should not be dwelling inside a human being. The method of driving out the bad spirit is either by physical punishment, beating the possessed with a cane, or by luring the bad spirits with the good because if the spirit is in a person too long the person can die or become mentally ill (*phii ba'*). Once a person's spirit has been expelled, he is considered cured and can continue to live in the village without prejudice.

Court Cases

I interviewed two lawyers in Nakorn Panom Province who had represented both plaintiffs and defendants in cases concerning *phii pob*. The last case that one of them could remember was a case of bodily assault with a knife, in which the person accused of being a host incurred stab wounds on the head. The attacker was imprisoned—the lawyer could not remember for how many years.

Both lawyers stated that most cases were usually settled prior to trial upon the advice of the police or the public prosecutor. (I was unable to meet or talk with them.)

Although I was unable to investigate any court cases firsthand, I would like to report on one case that led to Supreme Court Decision No. 200 based on the Criminal Law Code, Section 326, proscribing slander.

Mrs. L.P., the plaintiff, brought action against Mrs. T.P., the defendant, alleging that the defendant accused the plaintiff, before a third party, of being a *phii pob*. Such accusations, claimed the plaintiff, subjected her to dishonor and ostracism, causing her mental suffering; therefore the defendant should be punished in accordance with Section 326 of the Criminal Law Code.

The District Court, after preliminary cross-examination of the plaintiff's witnesses, concluded that the word *phii pob* may sound offensive and hurt the feelings of the accused, but it would not bring about dishonor or ostracism. According to the witnesses, the plaintiff was still respected by the villagers and was invited to all religious functions. Furthermore, the Court declared that it was impossible for anyone to be a *phii pob*; the defendant was judged not guilty.

The plaintiff was dissatisfied and took the case to the Court of Appeals. The District Court's decision was upheld; the case was then petitioned before the Supreme Court.

The Supreme Court's adjudication was like the two lower courts'. The Court reiterated that in order to be guilty of slander under Section 326 of the Criminal Law Code, the accusation must be detrimental to the accused's honor or character; the Court was certain that Mrs. L.P., the plaintiff, did not suffer dishonor or defamation of character by Mrs. T.P.'s calling her a *phii pob* because as far as the Court could determine there was no such thing as a *phit pob*.

The interesting point here is whether *phii pob* do exist or not. At present very few people are interested in or mention them, so it has no significance now, but the lasting effects of the courts' decision remain to be seen.

Analysis

Possessed host group 1. Working in the health station and in the villages, I was soon able to recognize a person who had been possessed by a *phii pob*. A possessed woman was usually distinguished in her beauty, dramatic in manner, and charmingly seductive. It was common to see her with cotton strings tied around her neck and wrists. While being interviewed, I noted, the possessed hosts were sensitive and easily stimulated, quick-tempered, self-centered, and susceptible to suggestions. These characteristics may be classified as belonging to a "hysterical personality," which is generally found more in women than in men. Perhaps this could be one of the reasons for the predominance of women among the 50 possessed hosts whom I studied in 1967 (see Table 4). Fully 96 per cent of them were women, and only 4 per cent were men; 38 per cent were 21–30 years old; 76 per cent were married. They may have had problems before being possessed. It seems that the mechanism of *phii pob* possession is a socially accepted way of solving social and internal conflicts.

The feeling of numbness prior to possession experienced by 42 per cent of the possessed was, I feel, a result of emotional tension rather than malnutrition, because most of the possessed hosts were physically healthy (see Table 5). After exhibiting other symptoms, such as depression and visual and auditory hallucinations, they went through a state of which they had no recollection. This syndrome should without question be considered psychiatric, although there was not much content to their hallucination. Mainly they saw round objects, monkeys, cats,

Table 4: Characteristics of Possessed Hosts (Group 1, 1967: N = 50)

Characteristic	Number	Percent
Sex:		
Male	2	4
Female	48	96
Age at Possession		
10-20	13	26
21-30	19	38
31-40	12	24
41-50	6	12
Marital Status		
Married	38	76
Single	9	18
Widowed	2	4
Divorced	1	2

Table 5: Pre- and Post-Possession Symptoms (ranked by frequency)

Pre-Possession Symptoms (frequency rate = 42-2)*	Post-Possession Symptoms (frequency rate = 41-2)**
1. Felt numbness throughout the body and limbs.	1. Felt quite well.
2. Felt like crying.	2. Felt aches and pains all over the body.
3. Felt dizzy.	3. Felt weary.
4. Had vision of round shapes.	4. Became frightened and worried.
5. Felt sick at heart.	5. Developed insomnia.
6. Had headaches and chills.	6. Felt heart palpitations.
7. Had vision of a monkey.	7. Became groggy and befuddled.
8. Had vision of a man.	
9. Had vision of a dog or a cat.	
10. Heard voices calling.	
11. Felt stiffness in chest.	
12. Had vision of a chicken.	
13. Heard a dog barking.	
14. None.	

*Some symptoms appeared in combination, e.g., numbness and having vision of a monkey, but here they are listed separately.

**Most of the possessed could not remember what they said or did while being possessed, but some felt pains as though beaten with a cane, although very vaguely. Their gestures were similar to those of the originating host.

men, or dogs, suggesting toxic psychosis. But the symptom that makes it different from toxic psychosis is the state of trance, during which the patients could talk relevantly.

While being possessed, the patients seemed to take on a "double personality" for a short period, not more than an hour (see Table 6). At this time the possessed seemed to be in a state of trance as if hypnotized, which I would classify as "dissociative reaction" (Freedman and Harold, 1967). *Phii pob* possession may be a type of hysteria, but I feel that it is a kind of "dissociative reaction" that occurs only in specific Thai cultural groups but has not yet been geographically localized or classified, unlike *amok* or *latah* (Freedman and Harold, 1967; Yap, 1969).

An originating host is considered a clever person who practices many kinds of spells and is respected by the villagers. Because he is considered a clever person, the possessed identifies with the host and does not feel that any harm will come about. Identification is said to be an important mental mechanism in hysteria (Arieti, 1959) and it occurs in people who have had a previous relationship with each other (Table 7). Characterization appears to be on the conscious level.

The villagers feel that *phii pob* possession is a genuine occurrence— everyone in my investigation believed in it. They might be smiling and giggling, but when asked about *phii pob*, their facial expression at once becomes solemn.

Table 6:   Characteristics of Possession Episode (Group 1, 1957: N = 50)

Characteristic	Number	Percent
Duration:		
Momentary	13	26
1 hour	16	32
2 hours	7	14
3 hours	5	10
8 hours	2	4
48 hours	1	2
Undetermined	6	12
Departure Point:		
Unknown	16	32
Mouth (vomiting)	9	18
Bladder (urinating)	7	14
Another part of the body	18	36
Number of times Possessed:		
1	22	44
2	6	12
3	10	20
> 3	12	24

Table 7:   Characteristics of Originating Hosts

Characteristic	Number	Percent
Sex:		
Male	25	50
Female	13	26
Unknown	9	18
Either Male or Female	3	6
Reason for Possession:		
Unknown	21	42
To visit	14	28
To satisfy desire; to eat rice and betel	7	14
To do harm	5	10
To satisfy desire to love	3	6
Magical arts studied:		
Unknown	15	30
None: inherited from parent or close relative	9	18
Casting love spells	7	14
Casting spells to become better-liked	7	14
Casting protective spells to make people invulnerable	6	12
Casting spells for prosperity and good fortune	3	6
Casting spells to cause abortion	3	6
Relationship between possessed and originating host:		
Acquainted	31	62
Unknown	11	22
Known by name only	8	16

They also believe that the *phii pob* or the hosts have their central location in Baan Chyak, Tambon Nacik, which perhaps accounts for the fact that more patients come from south of Amnat Charoen than from north of it.

Possessed host group 2.   Group 2 includes ten possessed hosts, whose *phii pob* refused to depart after 48 hours, whom I studied in 1969–1971. After receiving treatment at the hospital for about a week, these persons felt much better. In their case, the diagnosis might be hysterical psychosis and the mechanism of *phii pob* is more complicated and difficult to generalize than for group 1 (Suwanlert, 1969; Hollender and Hirsch, 1964, 1969; Langness, 1967).

Originating hosts.   It was very difficult to get information from originating hosts at the beginning of the study, because I presumed that my clients would resent inquiries from a total stranger. In addition, there were always others around when I conducted the interviews, and I felt that harm might result. However, through the cooperation of the Buddhist monks, I was able to interview six originating hosts (*phii pob*).

Through the interviews it was established that one could become a *phii pob* by three means: through inheritance, incantation study, and possession of "sacred" things. Although the *phii pob* accepted the causes, they could not see how the spirits in their bodies could go and possess others. They admitted to worrying and feeling depressed and ashamed about what had happened, but they had no other feelings or reactions.

Being a *phii pob* seemed to last from one to five years. All of those affected earnestly sought to expel the spirits in them. I felt that the only time the villagers noticed that one of them was a *phii pob* was when the *pob* possessed another and "spoke." On the other hand, such identification could have been a vindictive fabrication. Once identified, though, the only way out for the accused was to announce that he was going to have treatments to expel the *phii pob*.

Judging from the six cases I studied, the mental health of the accused was poor, affecting the immediate family members and other relatives. I often wonder what was the basic cause of the one case where the healing process was completed and the *phii pob* was supposedly buried only to have the woman go and dig it up. Was it the power over others that she enjoyed, or was she really overpowered by the spirits, as claimed? These questions still remain unanswered.

Some people are sympathetic toward *phii pob* but will not live under the same roof with them and will try to exile them. Tolo Village in Roi-Et Province seemed to accept the exiles; no one in that village seemed possessed, although the majority of the villagers were known to be *phii pob*s.

Phii pob possession is both good and bad. It may be a socially acceptable way of solving social and interpersonal conflicts. On the other hand, it is quite simple for a person to falsely accuse another of being *phii pob*, with disastrous consequences. Usually the only way out for the accused is to admit that he is a *phii pob* and to promise to undergo treatment to drive out the spirit, or move to another place. I believe that public reaction profoundly affects a person's mental health.

Conclusion

Phii pob is a common spirit in Northeast Thailand. It originates in a living person, conceals itself in the body of that person (called the originating host), and comes and goes at will. It is said that *phii pob* is nonsubstantial; nobody can concretely describe it. Some say that it is in the shape of a black dog, while others say it is shaped more like a monkey. It is believed that the *phii pob* can leave the body of its host to possess another. When this happens the possessed host can identify who is the original host of the *phii pob*. Usually a person becomes a host of only one *phii pob* of the same sex, but it is possible for a person to become a host of many and possess both males and females. There are two ways in which a person can become a source of *phii pob*: it may originate in the person himself or he may inherit it from his ancestors.

Sixty-two cases of possessed hosts were studied in the villages of two provinces in Northeast Thailand; ten were admitted by relatives for treatment at Srithunya Hospital, Nondhaburi, because shamans could not drive the spirits off. With group 1, 50 cases studied in 1967, *phii pob* possession occurred in the village, and the duration of possession was momentary to 48 hours. After the spirit was driven off, the possessed hosts became their former selves and felt quite well. The personalities of hosts who were repeatedly possessed were hysterical, precipitating various kinds of causes for illness. During the period of possession, the symptoms were similar to hysterical trance or a dissociative phenomenon. The diagnosis might be a hysterical neurosis that occurs only in specific Thai cultural groups. It seemed that the mechanism of *phii pob* possession was a socially accepted way of solving social and internal conflicts.

Group 2, studied in 1969–1971, comprised ten cases of *phii pob* who refused to depart from their possessed hosts within 48 hours. The possessed hosts were brought into the psychiatric hospital as psychotics. After receiving treatment for about a week, they felt much better. The diagnosis might be hysterical psychosis. The mechanism of *phii pob* possession for this group is more complicated than for group 1.

Once identified, it is difficult for an originating host, whom the people call *phii pob*, to live in the community because the villagers believe that the originating host is the cause of illness, and they try to exile him.

ACKNOWLEDGMENTS

The author is deeply indebted to the Social Science Research Institute (NIMH Grant # MH09243), the Open Grants Program at the East-West Center, University of Hawaii, and Professor Phon Sangsingkeo for assistance in the preparation of this paper.

REFERENCES

American Psychiatric Association. 1952. Diagnostic and statistical manual. Committee on Nomenclature and Statistics.

Arieti, S., ed. 1959. An American handbook of psychiatry. New York, Basic Books.

Cleghorn, R.A., and G.C. Curtis. 1959. Psychosomatic accompaniments of latent and manifest depressive affect. Journal of the Canadian Psychiatric Association 4, Special Supplement.

Freedman, M.A., and I.K. Harold, eds. 1967. Comprehensive textbook of psychiatry. Baltimore, Williams & Wilkins.

Hollender, M.H., and S.J. Hirsch. 1964. Hysterical psychosis. American Journal of Psychiatry 120:1066–74.

———. 1969. Hysterical psychosis. American Journal of Psychiatry 125:909–15.

Langness, L.L. 1967. Hysterical psychosis: the cross-cultural evidence. American Journal of Psychiatry 124:143–52.

Lin, T. 1953. A study of the incidence of mental disorder in Chinese and other cultures. Psychiatry 16, 4:313–36.

Sasaki, Y. 1963. Social psychiatric study of shaman ("Miko") in Japan. Proceedings of the joint meeting of the Japanese Society of Psychiatrists and Neurologists and the American Psychiatric Association, May 13–17, Tokyo.

Spiro, M.E. 1969. The psychological function of witchcraft belief: the Burmese case. *In* Mental health research in Asia and the Pacific. W. Caudill and T.Y. Lin, eds. Honolulu, East-West Center Press.

Suwanlert, S. 1969. Possession syndromes. Journal of Psychiatric Association of Thailand 14:273–287.

Yap, P.M. 1960. The possession syndrome: a comparison of Hong Kong and French findings. Journal of Mental Science 106:114–37.

———. 1969. The culture-bound reactive syndromes. *In* Mental health research in Asia and the Pacific. W. Caudill and T.Y. Lin, eds. Honolulu, East-West Center Press.

7.   Taking the Role of Supernatural "Other": Spirit
       Possession in a Japanese Healing Cult

TAKIE SUGIYAMA LEBRA, Ph.D.

University of Hawaii
Honolulu, Hawaii

Theoretical Considerations Regarding Spirit Possession

It is not uncommon to interpret the phenomenon of spirit possession not only in light of pathology but also in terms of sociological implications. Kiev (1961) noted that spirit possession among voodoo devotees in Haiti "provides legitimized public roles for private repressed impulses and needs." This view was seconded by Bourguignon (1965), who saw in this "temporary substitution of other 'selves' the opportunity for acting out certain positively evaluated social roles." *Saka* attacks, as observed by Harris in a Kenya tribe, allow women to demonstrate and execute their "rights" vis-à-vis their husbands—"the rights of dependents" (1957). The sociological implication of possession is evident from the use of such terms as "legitimized," "roles," and "rights."

Insofar as possession is viewed in terms of the supernatural "role" taken by the possessed, we must recognize that the possessed has some degree of self-awareness of "playing" that role. Without such awareness one would be incapable of assuming a role. This suggests the theory of self developed by G.H. Mead (1967) that the individual is not a self unless he is an object to himself. Such a reflexive self develops through one's taking the role of other individuals and responding to it. The role of other persons, thus vicariously assumed, becomes internalized and constitutes "me" as distinct from "I," the subjective side of self. "I" and "me" together make up the whole self.

Mead's concept of self fits the phenomenon of spirit possession remarkably well. Indeed, Yap used it for his interpretation of the possession syndrome. He attributed possession to "a disturbance in the balance of what Mead calls the 'I' and the 'me;'" to "the unusual predominance, temporarily, of one phase of the Self at the expense of the other; of a certain portion of the 'Me' at the expense of the 'I'" (1960).

I shall take Yap's position as my point of departure. While Yap stressed the pathological imbalance of "I" and "me" in possession, I would like to delineate the sociological implication, as set forth in the first paragraph. Yap may be right in emphasizing the pathological aspect of possession, first because the role taken in possession is not that of social others, as Mead would expect, but that of the supernatural, and secondly because the "me" (the role of the supernatural other) is externally acted out instead of being internalized as should be in Mead's self. However, we can look at the same phenomenon from the standpoint of the variety of roles that can be taken voluntarily by the possessed. We can further assume that taking the role of a supernatural other enables one to overcome, however temporarily, the role deprivation being suffered in the social world, which may trigger a change in the behavior system, including that of curing.

A role that is part of a social system can be taken and played only if other roles in the same system are complementarily played. The "central role" to be played by Ego must be complemented by a "counter-role" played by Alter. This requirement of "complementarity" (Bateson, 1935, 1971; Watzlawick et al., 1967) is no less compelling in the assumption of a supernatural role, no matter how arbitrary that role may appear. The complementary role may be played by Ego himself or by other persons. The satisfactory performance of a supernatural role by the possessed requires Ego or other persons to accept the complementary role willingly. This means that the complementary role should be as desirable as the supernatural role. This is a major constraint on the repertoire of supernatural roles, and it precludes the randomness of possession behavior. In actuality, however, there seems to be no special problem since internalization of a role through socialization entails internalization of its complementary role; to learn how to play a dominant role, for instance, one must simultaneously learn how to play a submissive role.

I shall apply these assumptions to the possession behavior observed in a healing-oriented Japanese cult. The sociological interpretation of possession in the sense above, seems particularly relevant to the Japanese subject because Japanese culture sensitizes the individual to role gratification and role frustration as the primary source of his pleasure and pain. My objective in this paper is twofold: generally to validate the theoretical assumptions advanced above, and particularly to show how the selection of role types in "Japanese" possession is culturally biased.

The Cult, Field, and Data

The Salvation Cult[1] was established in 1929 and has continued to flourish since its founder's death in 1948, under the postwar freedom of religion in Japan.

The membership of the cult as of 1969 is claimed to have reached more than 168,000 (Bunkachō, 1970). Doctrinally, the Salvation Cult traces its ancestry to Shugendō, the mystic mountain sect, which was the earliest attempt to amalgamate the indigenous Shinto with imported Buddhism and Taoism. This syncretism is at the heart of the Salvation Cult, which reveres all deities and spirits without discrimination, although it recognizes some loose, partial rank orders among them. The Shinto pantheon consisting of *kami* ("gods") is worshipped side by side with Buddhas of Hindu origin, and supernatural status is conferred on the ancestors and the departed as well. While "qualified" members study abstract doctrines that were developed by the founder and his successors and that typically involve interpretations of Chinese characters, the rank and file are led to believe in the ubiquity of supernatural beings, including animal spirits.

The difference between leading members and rank and file is not limited to beliefs; the difference is also apparent in places for action. Important members operate primarily in the two centers of the cult. One is the "spiritual" center, a shrine complex, which is the most sacred place for members to visit as pilgrims or as religious trainees; the other is the cult's "headquarters" which administratively controls the whole organization. These centers not only take leadership in religious teaching but run "health schools," treating sick members "medically" and prescribing "natural foods," which can be purchased at the cult's store. Ordinary members engage in cult activities most regularly in local branches controlled by local leaders. There were over 300 local branches as of 1971.

Fieldwork was conducted during the summers of 1970 and 1971, covering, intensively, two ward branches in a provincial city—let it be called Eastern City—and, more superficially, three other branches, located in central Japan. Activities at the two cult centers were also observed. This paper is based on information collected primarily in Eastern City.

The two ward branches together comprise roughly 200 members, although the number of regularly active members is much smaller. Each branch is headed by a woman in her seventies, one a widow, the other a divorcée. While in formal membership the sex ratio is about 2 to 1 in favor of female members, active members are overwhelmingly female, the ratio being approximately 5 to 1. (This gap between the formal and active membership owes partly to the Japanese inclination to register in the name of the head of the household.) In age the members were concentrated in the forties through the sixties.

Cult activites in local branches vary from regular, collective services to more private, informal ones. Collectively, periodic ceremonies are conducted at the branch leader's residence, involving a long, standardized ritual in front of an altar and a lecture by a teacher sent from the headquarters. Group visits to local shrines, cemeteries, and other supernaturally affected places are also regular activities. The branch is also always open to casual visitors (both registered and prospective members) for personal consultation and informal religious services. It is during such casual visits that interaction between a member and the leader is maximally intensified.

The information on which this analysis is based was obtained, first, from interviews with two male and fourteen female members conducted mostly in their homes, and secondly from direct observations of rituals and personal religious services at the branches. The latter were always followed by relaxed conversation and sharing of the food retrieved from the altar. These post-service social gatherings, immensely enjoyed by the participants, also provided valuable information. The sixteen informants ranged in age from thirty-eight to seventy-eight, a few of them having been members for more than thirty years. The following tabulation is a rough indicator of the socioeconomic status of the informants.

Occupation	*Number of Informants*
Storekeeper	5
Restaurant- entertainment business	3
Schoolteacher	2
Entertainer	1
Office worker	1
Candymaker	1
Hairdresser	1
Hotel maid	1
Fisherwoman	1
Total	16

In this list there are no special characteristics that would distinguish this group from other residents of Eastern City. Entertainer and hotel maid are not unusual occupations, since the city is a resort.

Situations and Behavior Patterns of Possession

Possession takes place in different situations. The most "sacred" possession is associated with a particular ritual, called "Five Laws," that is deliberately performed to induce supernatural visitation. The leader takes the role of *chūkaisha* ("mediator") between the visiting spirit and the human host. The host, presented as *bontai* ("temporal body") for the spirit to enter, is a member who is suffering from illness, family friction, or the like and who seeks a supernatural message that will explain this suffering. Note that the mediator and the host of the spirit are different persons, and that the receiver of the supernatural message is the same as the giver of the message. The *chūkaisha* and *bontai* sit side by side in front of the altar and go through a spirit-inviting ritual, invoking the names of deities and Buddhas and repeatedly bowing toward the altar. The spirit's arrival is signaled by the sudden rapid movement of the *bontai*'s folded hands, in which a special charm is held. Unless unusually resistant, the spirit identifies itself and conveys its message through the *bontai*'s mouth or hands (tracing letters on the floor) in response to requests and questions by the *chūkaisha*. The spirit is identified at least by sex and, if an ancestral spirit, by the number of generations it is separated from its descendant, the *bontai*. Beginners are said to be poor hosts "because their souls are still polluted"; sometimes they are only able to cry or shake. It takes six months, I was told, for a convert to become qualified. During this time the convert is supposed to work at self-purification by means of a meditation ritual called "Secret Law." However, there are devices by which almost anyone can generate some information about the spirit and thus perform a supernatural role. The commonly observed resistance to verbalization is overcome by the ritually directed sign communication: the *bontai* indicates the sex of the spirit, for instance, by pointing to the left or right side of his own body; he indicates the number of ancestral generations by hitting his knee a certain number of times. Whenever the question-and-answer communication becomes deadlocked, the *chūkaisha* gives a binary choice of a yes or no answer. She will ask, "Are you an ancestor or a *kami*? If you are an ancestor, please stretch your hands straight forward. Otherwise, raise your hands over your head." After giving its message, the spirit is thanked and asked to return to where it belongs. The spirit that refuses to leave the *bontai* invites reproach from the *chūkaisha*. The whole possession performance is observed by any other members who happen to be present, unless the *bontai* demands privacy. I observed five instances of this possession ritual, one of which was performed especially for my benefit. In addition, one of the branches kept a written record of the possession ritual for a time, including sixty-five cases, which I was permitted to read.

While members consider such ritualized possession which tends to be a dramaturgical performance, the most important and legitimate form, a more spontaneous, unstructured possession also takes place. Some informants have experienced "unexpected" possession during the purifying meditation or while chanting a sutra in front of the altar, praying at a local shrine, and the like. Some claimed that spirits had taken control of them while they were sleeping or talking to a neighbor. Spontaneous possession usually does not manifest itself vocally but through gestural simulation of the possessing spirit. If the spirit was a fox, the possessed might jump around like a fox. The snake spirit might be simulated by crawling and wriggling. Walking with a limp would show possession by the spirit of a person who was lame. These experiences were not observed directly but were described in interviews or at branch gatherings.

Supernatural Roles

The supernatural visitors relate to the human host, the *bontai*, in a number of ways. Both my observations and the branch's record of possession rituals indicate that the visitor is most likely to be an ancestor or departed kin with a strong bias for patrilineality in the case of remote ancestors. Not only ascending generations but descending generations are recognized as supernatural: a living mother may be visited by her dead child or miscarried fetus.

If the spirit is of human origin but is not Ego's kin, it is likely to be the spirit of a person who committed suicide, was killed in warfare, or whose death was otherwise disastrous, in the place where Ego currently resides. A number of informants identified their residential lots as former battlefields where thousands of samurai were buried and whose spirits were disturbing the welfare of the current residents. These are called land-related spirits.

Different from these is the animal spirit. The spirit of a fox, for example, is recognized either as the deity who was worshipped by Ego's ancestors over many generations as the house protector, or as Ego's own guardian deity.

The other spirits mentioned are more or less miscellaneous, but I am tempted to group some of them into another class called sex-related spirits. Examples are the spirits of Ego's former fiancée, of a divorced husband, or of the raped maidservant of Ego's ancestor.

Now let us look at the supernatural roles that the *bontai* takes in possession through identification with one of these spirits.

The supplicant role. In an overwhelming number of possession cases the spirit is dependent and supplicant. The spirit which is most responsive to the ritual invitation turns out to be a sufferer from pain, floating around helplessly, and solicitous of human help for its salvation. The *bontai* discovers that it was this spirit that was causing trouble, most typically sickness, to himself or his family; that the spirit did so only to remind the *bontai* of its suffering and to appeal for sympathy.

The suffering of the spirit usually owes to some *tsumi* ("sin" or "pollution") committed when it was alive in the world. Most often mentioned are *tsumi* of suicide, homicide, adultery, rape, abortion, and miscarriage. These are all considered *tsumi* because a moral standard was violated or because the sanctity of life was breached. They are *tsumi* also because they involve pollution with blood at the site where the action took place. Being killed or dying in a natural disaster is as sinful, in the polluting sense, as killing. Commission of such *tsumi* infuriates the deity governing or residing in that particular location, and the deity punishes the spirit by preventing its salvation. My informants frequently referred to "strange deaths" (*henshi*) by hanging or drowning.

The suffering of the spirit is compounded by its isolation from other spirits; thus, most suffering spirits soliciting human help are also identified as *muen* ("lonely, affinity-less") spirits. A spirit is *muen* not only because of its *tsumi* but because it has been neglected or abandoned by human survivors. For this reason, too, the *muen* spirit must notify an appropriate living person of its loneliness by causing trouble. Salvation for the *muen* spirit means finding its proper place by joining a group of its own kind: an ancestral *muen* spirit is anxious to join its own group of ancestors; a *muen* fox spirit should have a shrine specially built for it or be placed in an existing shrine dedicated to the fox spirit.

The supplicant role of the suffering spirit must be complemented by a nurturant, indulgent role. The latter role is expected to be performed by the *bontai* after the possession. It is believed that the spirit is not indiscriminate in choosing the target of its possession. The spirit prefers a person who will be responsive, helpful, dependable, and experienced enough to solve its problem. Informants generally believe that blood ties are the strongest attraction for the spirit, and one male informant stressed that the spirit chooses its descendant in the direct line. The *bontai* promises to do his best to relieve the spirit's suffering, to gratify and please the spirit.

The relationship between the supplicant spirit and the nurturant human is acted out in two ritual forms. One is *kuyō*, a propitiatory service offered to the spirit. An ancestral spirit, for instance, would ask the *bontai*, through the latter's mouth, to indulge it with *kuyō*. The *kuyō* takes several forms: the repeated incantation of sutras and prayers in front of a tablet that has the spirit's name on it; the repeated pouring of (hydrangea tea, believed to be sacred and purifying, over the tablet or any other spot where the spirit resides; and the offering of food and drink that the spirit likes. The last form accentuates the maternal, nurturant role of the human feeder for the hungry, infantlike spirit. Indeed, the spirit quite often is a *muen* infant who solicits maternal help from the *bontai*, for example, by causing pain in the breast. Milk and baby food are then considered the most appropriate *kuyō* offering. Sometimes the spirit, in response to the *chūkaisha*'s question, specifies what it wants to eat and where the food should be placed.

The other form of the nurturant role performed by the *bontai* for the sake of the spirit is *owabi* ("apology") made to redeem the spirit's *tsumi*. The *bontai* is asked by the spirit to present *owabi* on its behalf, since the spirit is incapable of doing so, in front of the shrine of the deity against whom the *tsumi* was committed. The spirit tells which shrine is to be visited, how many visits must be made (sometimes every day for thirty days), the kind of offering that should be taken, and so on. Usually *owabi* is presented at a local Shinto shrine, but if the *tsumi* had to do with water pollution, for example, the *bontai* will have to visit the shrine of a water deity. A standard statement of apology is given "on behalf of such-and-such spirit." Many informants told me that they had to go to shrines to present *owabi* before dawn every morning even in winter. Presentation of *owabi* includes a ritual endurance walk back and forth a hundred times in front of the shrine. This is supposedly to prove the sincerity of the one making the apology.

Owabi thus involves a substantial sacrifice made by the human helper for the sake of the sinful spirit. Informants agreed that without the completion of *owabi* the spirit is not permitted to receive *kuyō* and that *owabi* must precede everything else to save the spirit. Nurturance in the performance of *owabi* may involve role substitution: the human helper apologizes to the deity as a substitute for the sinful spirit. We are again reminded of a motherly role of the human complementary to an infantlike role of the spirit. Indeed, in one recorded case, the spirit of a suffering girl begged its young female *bontai* to search for her missing mother and, if the mother could not be found, for the *bontai* herself to become a surrogate mother.

The two mutually complementary roles, supplicant and nurturant, are taken sequentially by Ego—the succorant role during possession, and the nurturant role after possession. During possession, the nurturant role is being played by the *chūkaisha*, leader-mediator, in communicating with the spirit. The *chūkaisha*'s role thus involves temporary substitution for the *bontai*, who is busy playing the supernatural role. It is the *chūkaisha* who asks the spirit what it wants and promises to carry out *kuyō* and *owabi* so that the spirit will be perfectly satisfied; the spirit demands rice cake, *miso*-soup, and so forth, as if from the *chūkaisha*. Being fully aware of this role substitution, the spirit sometimes openly addresses itself to the *chūkaisha*, asking her to do something for it. In one of the ward branches the *chūkaisha*, the branch leader, is a grandmotherly woman whom the members indeed call Grandma as well as Teacher and Branch Head. She takes a nurturant, indulgent role vis-à-vis a member during possession. Even after possession, she helps the member offer *kuyō* and *owabi*, often accompanying the member to a shrine.

Whether the complementary role is performed by the *bontai* or the *chūkaisha*, it is evident that both the nurturant and supplicant roles are well cathected by my informants.

The reciprocal role.   While the supernatural role is predominantly of the supplicant type, other role types are seen.

When the suffering of the spirit has been relieved through *kuyō* and *owabi* offered by the human helper, the spirit is obligated to return the favor. The spirit that appears in possession after the *bontai* has performed such services typically expresses gratitude and promises to repay the debt. Let this be called the reciprocal role. If the *bontai* is ill, a cure is promised; a bankrupt man can expect to recover his losses and prosper in business; a single girl is guaranteed to meet a good prospect for a husband.

Complementary to the reciprocally obligated role is the role of a benefactor—obviously a desirable role. Not only the *bontai* but also the *chūkaisha* and the audience at the possession ritual often receive the spirit's gratitude and promises of repayment since they have helped the *bontai*. General gratitude is expressed to "every member" of the branch and to the cult as a whole.

A widow said that when she was possessed it was always by her deceased mother-in-law. One day the mother-in-law appeared to tell the daughter-in-law, "You are troubled with your husband the spirit's son, so I shall take him with me." Shortly after this, the informant found her good-for-nothing husband dead, which she seemed to take as a clear indication of her mother-in-law's gratitude.

The disciplinarian role.   Some ancestors and personal guardian spirits scold the *bontai* harshly. Here the supernatural other assumes a dominant, disciplinarian role. In a commanding tone using a masculine style of speech, the spirit berates the *bontai*, expressing displeasure with his lack of discipline, sincerity, and devotion. Such a punitive role may be played not merely verbally but also physically: in one of the cases I observed, a woman possessed by an ancestor kept saying "I am displeased," shaking her head disapprovingly and striking her chest violently.

The complementary role taken by the *chūkaisha* during possession is dual. On one hand, she serves as an arbiter, trying to restore harmony between the spirit and the *bontai*. She tries to appease the spirit by assuring it that she will transmit its message to the *bontai* and oversee the latter's self-improvement. On the other hand, the *chūkaisha* occasionally slips into the complementary role to be played by the *bontai*, namely, an apologetic, self-accusatory, docile role. What takes place then is a temporary status reversal between leader and follower, the latter playing an authoritarian role and the former a submissive role. Status normalization follows as soon as possession is over, when the *chūkaisha*, now as the leader, reproves the *bontai* for displeasing the spirit. Comparing the two cult branches, the spirit's assumption of a disciplinarian role took place more often in one branch that is headed by a woman of a more disciplinarian character. (The other branch, headed by the indulgent "grandmother," shows a stronger inclination toward the supplicant role.)

Possession can thus gratify the wish to be both dominant and submissive. Also implied in this role is a disguised confession of guilt on the part of the *bontai* for neglecting his spiritual and social obligations. Finally, this role provides an opportunity for a member to demonstrate to others that he has a rigorous standard for religious devotion that keeps him discontented with what he is.

The retaliatory role. Similar to the disciplinarian role is the retaliatory role. The difference between the two is that, while the disciplinarian role is motivated by a benevolent intention, the retaliatory role is activated by a male-volent one. Malevolence is, in the vernacular of my informants, "anger," "curse," or, most commonly, "grudge."

Many instances of possession by animal spirits involved assumption of the retaliatory role. A fox spirit would be angry with the *bontai*'s ancestors for having abandoned it though they owed it so much for protecting their house. Usually these ancestors were samurai who moved from one battlefield to another, not taking the time to serve the house-protecting fox deity. Their worst offense was to destroy a shrine dedicated to the fox spirit. A woman discovered through possession the reason for her husband's neurosis: the fox spirit, angry at having been neglected by his ancestors, decided to punish the descendants of the house.

Spirits of human origin also play a retaliatory role. A divorcée informant was possessed by the spirit of a maid who had served one of her ancestors. The master apparently had raped the maid, said the informant, for she became pregnant and was discharged. In despair, the maid drowned herself in a well, cursing all the descendants of the family.

The retaliatory role calls forth its complementary role, that of the accused—not a desirable one. The difficulty is resolved by expanding the dyadic role system into a triad. The *bontai* does not take the role of the accused but of the innocent victim of the spirit's malevolence. The role of the accused is attributed to an ancestor of the *bontai* or of the *bontai*'s spouse. An ancestor angers a spirit, which takes revenge by punishing the wrongdoer's offspring. Such a triadic repercussion in punitive reciprocity is a common theme in the Japanese belief system: it reinforces the "lineal" focus of self-identity, coupled with the Buddhist idea of karma.

In this triad, the *bontai* is able to identify with the spirit to form an alliance against the sinful ancestor, who has caused trouble for the spirit and the *bontai* alike. One might speculate that the aforementioned divorcée (who once was a *geisha*) perceived a parallel between the rapist ancestor and her former husband (or men in general) and between the raped maid and herself.

There are some exceptions to this rule of triadic interchange. The retalia-tory spirit sometimes is against the *bontai*, as in possession by a former fiancée or a divorced husband who is still attached to the *bontai*. In such a case, however, the retaliatory role is softened into a more supplicant role, which elicits a nurturant response from the *bontai*.

The retaliatory role merges with the supplicant role whenever the spirit faces the problem of its own salvation. However malevolent it is, a suffering and *muen* spirit depends upon the very person it is cursing for its salvation, evoking a nurturant role in the *bontai*. A fox spirit will ask the *bontai* to restore its *kami* status by enshrining it, in addition to making *kuyō* offerings.

In triadic retaliation, the *bontai* performs two kinds of *owabi*. First, he assumes the role of the ancestor who was responsible for the spirit's malevolence and apologizes on his behalf to the angry spirit as well as to the deity of a local shrine; he then apologizes to the deity for the sin committed by the retaliatory spirit, the sin of holding a grudge.

The status-demonstrative role. The ancestral spirit tends to hold prestigious status, typically samurai status. A male informant was possessed many times by Taira Kiyomori, the first warrior-ruler of the country in the early twelfth century, who identified himself as an ancestor of the *bontai* eighteen generations removed. This motivated the *bontai* to study his genealogical background.

The *bontai* can elevate his status through being possessed by distinguished ancestors. In this case, the main complementary role is played by the audience, who may be impressed by the disclosure of such eminent ancestry. Many members do not question the credibility of such information and talk about it admiringly. Some individuals are singled out by leaders or fellow members as coming from a formerly distinguished house that has declined.

Ancestors of high status are uniformly sinful, since there is perfect correlation in the members' eyes between power and moral deficiency. Such ancestors killed people, exploited poor commoners to enrich their own coffers, engaged in political trickery, indulged in sexual promiscuity, even seducing a reluctant virgin, and the like.

The *tsumi* committed by a high-status ancestor is certain to activate a retaliatory drive in its victim. This means that the status-demonstrative role and the retaliatory role are mutually complementary and reinforcing. Such complementarity may be responsible for the intimacy observed between a woman once possessed by a victim of her ancestor and a man possessed by his distinguished and sinful ancestor.

The status-demonstrative role also becomes a supplicant role. The ancestor will ask the *bontai* to do *kuyō* and *owabi* for his sake and for the sake of the victims of his *tsumi*. Taira Kiyomori, in the case mentioned above, asked the *bontai*, the direct descendant of the Taira family, to apologize for his *tsumi* to the guardian deity of the family, and to save the spirits of those killed in warfare between Taira and Minamoto clans, the two most powerful warrior clans of the time.

There is a variant type of status-demonstrative role. An animal spirit occasionally appears in possession to signify its wish to receive *shugyō* (religious discipline) at the spiritual center of the cult. The *bontai* grants that wish of the spirit by sending the spirit to the center "via" a local ward shrine, which means that the *bontai* goes to the shrine with offerings and "sees the spirit off." The *bontai* is accompanied by the leader and some fellow members as helpers and witnesses. After several weeks of *shugyō*, the spirit returns again via the local shrine, and the homecoming is marked by the ritual of "receiving" the returning spirit. During the absence of the spirit, the *bontai* is supposed to undergo the same *shugyō*, as if he were accompanying the spirit. *Shugyō* involves the routine disciplines which a volunteer trainee would receive at the spiritual center, such as getting up early, keeping the house clean, performing religious services regularly, and avoiding meat.

It is believed that the spirit raises its status to that of *kami* after the completion of *shugyō*. The status elevation of the guardian spirit seems reflected in the status elevation of the *bontai*. Several months after joining the cult, many a member thus gets possessed by a guardian spirit who wants to undergo *shugyō* at the center.

Neither the role of *shugyō* candidate nor that of *shugyō* graduate can be played well unless fellow cult members play a complementary role. The *bontai* must be confident that fellow members would recognize his qualifications for playing such roles. In an observed case of possession, the *bontai* was informed that her guardian spirit wanted to go to the spiritual center. Instead of willingly accepting its wish, the *bontai* let the spirit decide to postpone the *shugyō* because it did not yet qualify. After possession, when the *chūkaisha* reprimanded her for not complying with the spirit's wish, the *bontai* confessed that there was criticism among fellow members about her being jealous of those who had already sent their spirits away for *shugyō*.

The informant role.   Finally, the supernatural role can be identified as that of an informant. Unlike the roles above, to which the role players are attached as an end, the informant role is an instrumental one used to facilitate communication. A person is able to express himself more freely by taking a supernatural role than by representing himself. The informant role, in other words, allows its player to make a statement to others that would be too embarrassing or audacious to make outside that role.

First, the spirit possessing the *bontai* praises and thanks the *bontai* for his sincerity, devotion, and religious accomplishment. A whole list of ancestors may be named as having been saved by the *bontai*. The spirit sometimes describes in detail what the *bontai* has done for his own self-discipline and for the salvation of many spirits. A young girl had the spirit of her kin praise her and declare that everyone was talking about her favorably.

Along with such self-praise, the *bontai* can express disapproval and hostility toward others. The spirit of a male cousin criticized many relatives of the *bontai*, including the mother, grandmother, and aunt, clearly indicating the *bontai*'s displeasure with them. Criticism is directed against selfishness, greediness, stubbornness, lack of faith, resistance to the cult, and so forth. The spirit goes as far as to threaten that, if the person continues this behavior, misfortune would follow.

The *bontai*'s wish is sometimes expressed in the form of a command by the spirit. If the *bontai* wants to have a new house built for his family, the spirit commands the family to start construction on a certain date. That command was effective in one instance, despite strong resistance by the head of the household.

A credulous audience is a necessary complement to the informant role. The credulous person will be frightened if he is accused in this manner; even if the accused is skeptical, other credulous branch members may apply pressure to make him comply with the spirit's commands.

Reviewing the supernatural role types and their complementary roles, I am tempted to propose that many of the cult members, although they do not form a separate group in socioeconomic status, were (or are) deprived in the social roles available to them; and that through possession they are able to overcome such role deprivation, at least temporarily.

Conclusion

Spirit possession in a Japanese cult was analyzed from the sociological point of view of "taking the role of supernatural other," derived from Mead's concept of self. It was suggested that possession provides an opportunity to temporarily remedy role deprivation by assuming a supernatural role. Satisfactory performance of a supernatural role, the proposition goes, presupposes a complementary role. Field work in local branches of the cult revealed six types of supernatural role played by the possessed: suppliant, reciprocal, disciplinarian, retaliatory, status-demonstrative, and informant. These are paired, respectively, with the nurturant role, the role of recipient of gratitude, a submissive role, the role of a victim of retaliation, an admirer's role, and the role of a credulous listener. These complementary roles are played by the possessed person himself after possession, or by the leader-mediator, who converses with the spirit (the spirit host), and by fellow members, who constitute a congenial or supportive audience.

What stands out in this variety of role pairs is the suppliant-nurturant pair, which appeared with overwhelming frequency, either singly or in combination with other roles. It might be argued that this pair predominates because the majority of the cult members are women of middle age and older. I believe, however, that Japanese in general, regardless of age and sex, tend to find gratification in playing a suppliant or nurturant role, or, more likely, both. The main support for this position comes from Doi's (1971) theory of *amae* as a key to Japanese culture and personality. I deviate from Doi's point of view only in my stress upon role complementarity, which requires both *amaeru* (to be dependent) and *amayakasu* (to indulge Alter's wish for dependency) to be desirable and satisfying.

The concluding hypothesis is that role gratification, temporarily facilitated through spirit possession, is likely to bring relief from illness.

ACKNOWLEDGMENTS
I wish to acknowledge with gratitude the support of NIMH (Grant # MH09243) in carrying out this research. The Social Science Research Institute, University of Hawaii, rendered technical assistance in the preparation of this paper.

NOTE

1.　　This cult was reported upon in previous papers (Lebra 1971, n.d.). While those and the present paper differ in focus, there is partial overlap in descriptive information.

REFERENCES

Bateson, G. 1971. The cybernetics of "self": a theory of alcoholism. Psychiatry 34:1–18.

————. 1935. Culture contact and schizmogenesis. Man 35:178–83.

Bourguignon, E. 1965. The self, the behavioral environment and the theory of spirit possession. *In* Context and meaning in cultural anthropology. M. E. Spiro, ed. New York, Free Press of Glencoe.

Bunkachō [Japanese National Agency of Culture]. 1970. Shūkyō nenkan [Religion yearbook]. [In Japanese].

Doi, T. 1971. Amae no kōzō (The structure of *amae*). Tokyo, Kobundo. [In Japanese].

Harris, G. 1957. Possession "hysteria" in a Kenya tribe. American Anthropologist 59:1046–66.

Kiev, A. 1961. Spirit possession in Haiti. American Journal of Psychiatry 118:133–38.

Lebra, T.S. 1971. Social ecology of a healing cult. Paper presented at the thirtieth annual meeting of the Society for Applied Anthropology, April 14–18, Miami, Florida.

————. In press. The interactional perspective of suffering and curing in a Japanese cult. The International Journal of Social Psychiatry.

Mead, G.H. 1967. Mind, self and society. Chicago, University of Chicago Press, Phoenix books.

Watzlawick, P., J.H. Beavin, and D.D. Jackson. 1967. Pragmatics of human communication: a study of interactional patterns, pathologies, and paradoxes. New York, Norton.

Yap, P.M. 1960. The possession syndrome. Journal of Mental Science 106:151–56.

SHAMANS AND OTHER FOLK THERAPISTS

8.   Shamans, Curers, and Personality: Suggestions toward a Theoretical Model

ARTHUR E. HIPPLER, Ph.D.

University of Alaska
College, Alaska

THE EXISTENCE of shamans or curers (individuals who gain special healing and religious powers through a "spirit guide" of some type) is a characteristic of many non-Western societies. Because of apparent gross differences between shamanistic behavior and Western European "scientific" healing models or Judeo-Christian religious beliefs, such behavior has been of interest to many Western anthropologists. This original interest, based on the somewhat ethnocentric notions of nineteenth-century anthropologists, has been buttressed and changed by more contemporary interests in the relationships of such behavior to other aspects of culture and social structure and, by some investigators, in its relationship to personality dimensions as well.

Shamanism in Cross-Cultural Perspective

The presently extensive cross-cultural literature on shamans and curers can be sorted into a paradigm in which essentially polar positions have been taken. Based in part upon notions of the integrative function and integrated aspects of culture, in part viewed in terms of psychoanalytic theory and its psychiatric derivatives, and finally investigated in the perspective of social structural theory, shamans have been seen by some as deviants and abnormals (Ackerknecht, 1943; Billig et al., 1948; Devereux, 1956, 1957; Nadel, 1946; Pfeiffer, 1966;

Silverman, 1967 [who finds no difference between shamans and acute schizo-phrenics]), and by others as well-integrated personalities (Billig et al., 1948; Boyer, 1964a; 1964b; Boyer et al., 1964 [with reservations]; Nadel, 1946; Romano, 1965; Sasaki, 1963 [also with reservations]). The interesting overlap in views—many investigators at one and the same time see the shaman as "abnormal" yet somehow "integrated"—suggests the need for an interpretation of these viewpoints.

If shamans as individuals have been viewed so divergently in terms of personality, the shamanistic role itself has been seen in an equally diverse manner. The role of shaman has been viewed by some as a haven for the disoriented (Billig et al., 1948; Devereux, 1956, 1957; Turner, 1964) as well as a cultural niche for the owner of an ethnopsychiatric technique who might thus be permitted to function, though badly disturbed, and/or as a culturally necessary quasi-psychiatric role providing the very best kind of "therapy" (often more effective than Western insight therapy) that "primitives," peasant societies or even the underclasses of modern industrial nations can offer (Amiel, 1966; Hes, 1964; Kiev, 1968; Madsen, 1964; Murphy, 1964; Pfister, 1932).

There have also been other less theoretically oriented cross-cultural studies of shamanism. Bennett and Zingg (1935) describe shamanism among the Tarahumara, as does Parsons (1936) among the inhabitants of Mitla, Mexico, but they do so in a traditionalist anthropological fashion; that is, they stress the functional aspects of shamanism, yet still note that it is one of the socially inte-grative institutions in society.

Others, such as Amiel (1966), have simply described shamanistic curer practices (on the Ivory Coast) that are quite similar to those reported elsewhere. Such studies generally stress that the shaman is an "odd bird," but they also stress that he serves a useful social function, essentially an ethnopsychiatric one, even if it is not spelled out as such.

The techniques used by those inhabiting the role of shaman have been described as "charlatanism" by some (Murphy, 1964; Nadel, 1946; Opler, 1936; Roheim, 1951) and as insightful by others, a discussion paralleled by the notion advanced by some writers that some shamans are "true shamans" and others not (Balikci, 1963; Boyer, 1962, 1964b; Posinsky, 1965; Sasaki, 1969).

The adequate versus inadequate continuum of attitudes concerning shamanism is further complicated by a cross-cutting dimension whose polar ends stress culturalogical versus psychological explanations of the phenomenon. For example, some see cultural content reflected in shamanistic practice (Boyer, 1964b; Boyer et al., 1964; Kiev, 1968), while others, such as Silverman (1967), have stressed only the psychological dimension.

As an example of the culturalogical end of this spectrum, Devereux (1956) suggests that the shamanistic role is one way in which various cultures can provide prestigious roles to deviants. This position is generally accepted by the "cultural relativist" wing in anthropology. Adherents to this position (though Devereux cannot be characterized in this fashion, and accepts absolute standards for judging normality) tend to be less concerned with the internal psychic process and individual meaning in shamanistic behavior than with the broader cultural validation of the behavior. Also in this camp are those who propose quasi-functionalist arguments ordinarily not phrased in personality terms. Balikci (1963), in a variant of this position, finds that shamanistic client behavior reflects the relationships between men and their gods. Using data gathered from the Netsilik Eskimos, he suggests that shamans are always viewed ambivalently. He proposes that the potential for danger from the shaman is what really gives him his power: that is, if one can control the universe or its objects for good purposes, one can use that power for evil as well.

An example of ideas from the more psychoanalytic end of the cross-cutting dimension is Boyer (1964a), who suggests that the real power of shamans lies in their ability to use primary-process thinking to create transference. According to Boyer, the shaman never resolves this transference but uses it to create a social conformity in his patient and to channel the patient's dependency needs. This particular technique, Boyer continues, introducing a cultural perspective, matches the needs of the Mescalero Apaches. In his studies, he found that their "favorite" character disorder includes elements of hysteria and impulsiveness with a variety of schizophrenic tendencies and shows specific problems in the area of orality and dependency.

A parallel but not precisely similar point is made by Nadel (1946), who stresses that shamans among the Nupa, while having a high incidence of "insanity," seem to be able to "absorb" the mental problems of others. Moreover, Nadel attempted to relate Nuba shamanism to the incidence of mental disease. He tried to correlate the low incidence of insanity in a culture to a high incidence of shamanism. Failing in this, he alternatively suggested that shamanism was a preventive measure for mental health.

Despite these imprecise though interesting formulations, Nadel also notes, as has Boyer, the variety of shamanism from fake to sincere, and the fact that shamans themselves rely on trance states, which is at least partially indicative of some disturbance. He finally suggests that shamans can cope with psychological disturbances in acculturation without the collapse that others show, which is reminiscent of the formulations of Kris (1952) in which he talks about the ability that some people, such as artists, have to regress in the service of the ego.

Bourguignon (1965), Bourguignon and Pettay (1965), and Boyer (1962), however, suggest that shamans may be very well integrated indeed, which also seems to support Nadel's work. Pfeiffer (1966), taking an approach related to Boyer's also sees shamans as reflecting the "favorite" disorder of their community, thereby personally integrating the modal pathology of the group.

Even so, some writers have found limits to the ability of even the "adequate shaman." Murphy (1964), using a psychiatric approach similar to that of Boyer, while noting the value of shamanism in treating mental illness, also suggests that it is limited-objective therapy relying essentially on dependency and integration into the group. His findings also seem to imply that, while some degree of personal integration is present for the shaman, he does not resolve the transference he elicits.

Other writers have suggested still other levels of theories in shamanistic studies that are at times supportive of those using psychological models but are couched in cultural or social structural terms. Turner (1964), for example, notes the great ability of the native witch doctor in Rhodesia to comprehend social relationships involved in emotional upset. Obviously, if the witch doctor can do so, this provides him with a special tool for refining his analysis of the inter-personal problem that may be at the root of the psychic disorder, and therefore permits some kind of directed therapy to solve the problem.

Billig et al., (1948) have investigated the personality of the curer in Guatemala, using yet another approach. Though they find *curanderos* have psychotic tendencies, they have also noted that *curanderos* are less rigid than the rest of the society and have a greater potentiality for creativity. This also seems to reflect Boyer's (1962) findings.

Some writers have attempted to view changing shamanistic styles using a variety of both cultural and psychiatric approaches. Redfield and Tax (1951), for example, note the ubiquity of *curanderos* in Mexico's American Indian society and detail some of the changes in *curandero* techniques which come about as the result of internalizing selected aspects of modern medical theory. Along these same lines, Sasaki (1963) has described syncretic aspects of shamanistic religion in Japan. Both Bloom (1964) and Hes (1964) have also indicated the changing roles of native healers in two different cultures under acculturation. Bloom finds rural curers among the Zulus to be more conservative and traditional, reflecting pressure against cultural change. Hes finds that the Yemenite *mori* (shaman), upon coming to Israel, tends to change specifically from a physical folk healer to a kind of folk psychiatrist. These studies seem to suggest that shamans change their tactics with their cultural milieu.

Others who have discussed the tactics of shamanism have noted the instrumental competence of shamans and their general personal shrewdness. Kiev (1966), for example, notes that the *hungman* (shaman) in Haiti becomes rich by exploiting the poor. The goat sacrifice that he performs from time to time seems to act as symbolic murder to channel some of the aggressions directed at him toward an object representing him. Thus, it would seem that his instru-mentality is integrated with a sophisticated expressive activity. Madsen (1964) also notes the reality-testing ability of the Mexican-American *curanderos*, who will not take terminal cases, and who demand that the client believe in them before they undertake his case. Such realism no doubt promotes the cure rate for the *curandero* and in turn increases local belief in his power. Opler (1936), like Madsen, however, has suggested that the successes of Apache shamans were enhanced by their shrewdness in picking patients in that they avoided those who were skeptical of their ability and treated only those who had high expectations of relief. Opler's findings then also suggest that either the shaman possesses no special psychiatric ability, or is at best merely a clever manipulator.

The issue of adequate versus inadequate is further complicated by the fact that some authors have recognized that both aspects may be present in the same shaman. Posinsky (1965), for example, specifically suggests the essentially ethnopsychiatric function of shamanism among the Yurok and notes the high incidence of transvestism among shamans. In Western cultures such behavior would be taken as a clear indication of personality disorder, yet the case does not seem so simple in analyzing shamans. Posinsky and Boyer also note that there is a wide variety of levels of competence in shamanistic behavior, which further complicates the problem of a simple discussion of shamanism. Posinsky describes ritual fasting and dreaming as part of shamanistic training, as does Dundes (1963), who relates ritual fasting to oral dependency needs. Such behavior suggests the possibility of personal pathology among shamans that would be difficult to relate to the personal competence that these authors also ascribe to shamans.

A clue to this complex relationship of apparent pathology and apparent competence is offered by Romano (1965), who, in a study of folk healing among Mexican-Americans in Texas, corroborates this emphasis on oral organization by noting the need for the male to abandon male role directives if he is to be nurturant enough to be a healer. Romano's work implies that what would otherwise be considered as pathic cross-sex anxiety (which is common for Mexicans [Hippler, 1969]), is creatively integrated into nurturant, nearly feminine behavior. Such behavior, however, is apparently both personally and socially integrative.

Pfister (1932), along the same lines and similarly to Boyer's formulations, suggests that the access the Navaho shaman has to the unconscious of his patient as well as to his own is one of his chief abilities that permits him to heal. This finding of Pfister's tends further to support the theory that shamans may in fact have some real ability and not be merely lucky charlatans.

Exactly what psychiatric function the shaman performs and how he performs it has been discussed in some detail by several authors. Roheim (1951), in a discussion of Hungarian shamanism, suggests that the shaman defends people against phallic women and that, in the process, oral aggression is defended against in a phallic manner. The material he presents in the form of folk tales suggests shamanistic regression to infantile omnipotence states as well. If this is so and if it is done effectively and creatively, it would seem that shamans can regress in the service of the ego.

Devereux (1957) takes the position that the shaman (who, among the Mohave, creates his "spirit songs" from myths he has reworked in his dreams) essentially offers in his behavior an explanation of, and a social sanction for, what are called, in Western society, psychoses and border psychoses—thereby reducing anxiety about them. This tends to suggest that shamans offer an ego-supportive role; however, the reworking of myths in dreams to provide a spirit guide also suggests true creative ability.

Rogler and Hollingshead (1961), noting the use of trance states by shamans in Puerto Rico, suggest that the social function of shamanism is to offer a culturally acceptable, nonstigmatized role for the deviant. Once again this suggests that the shaman is simply not psychically healthy. Kiev (1962c) sees the shamanistic behavior of the cult leader as a way of handling reelicited, ambivalent affects concerning god as protector, rival, and punisher. The *hungman* (shaman) in Haiti focuses the aggressions and instinctual urges of the group and permits them an acceptable outlet. Kiev's formulations suggest much more strongly the creative aspects of shamanism.

Even identifying the shaman has been a problem. Boyer (1962) suggests that there is much confusion as to who is a shaman and what level of competence various shamans occupy. In discussing how to identify a shaman as well as how to understand him, he investigates Devereux's (1956) feelings that all shamans must be judged by absolute standards of genitality, comparing this to Acker-knecht's (1943) suggestion that shamans and other deviants be judged only in terms of their own community and its attitudes. Thus, he focuses once more on the key problem we have noted—that of adequacy versus inadequacy, sick versus well, charlatan versus honest healer—as descriptive aspects of shamanism.

Since Boyer feels that the typical Apache is neurotic, this would mean the statistically normal Apache is "abnormal" in Western psychiatric terms. Boyer, who is inclined toward absolute standards in judging personal integration, finds the shamanistic personality to be much the same everywhere. Moreover, he suggests that the true shamanistic integration is nonetheless a healthy one. In this sense we may see the statistically "abnormal" Apache as approaching psychiatric normality of a type.

Finally, Kiev (1962d), in discussing the origin of shamanism, uses an economic and social structural argument. He suggests that it is the food surplus existing in hunting and gathering societies that allows shamans to specialize in folk medicine. Since there are no societies in which there is no surplus, it is difficult to assess such an argument. Further, since shamanism is ubiquitous, it does not appear to assess its meaning on this basis.

An Integrative Approach to Shamanism

Basically, the literature on shamanism suggests the following: shamanism is variously a method of working out individual psychological problems, a role that permits the deviant some degree of comfort, an ethnopsychiatric healing technique that in the absence of insight therapy permits some degree of personal reorganization with group support, and a mature, integrated life-style of a special creativity.

The literature further suggests that shamans are viewed ambivalently and may or may not be to some extent conscious fakers. The shaman is felt to owe his success to his ability to deal with unconscious materials, the faith of his clients, and to the generally higher tolerance for deviance (his own as well as that of his patients) which tends to exist in primitive cultures. He is seen as shrewd and competent, conservative and adaptable, and highly disorganized.

Some aspects of these positions appear to be in obvious conflict with each other, though many may be true at the same time. My own observations and study of the literature on Eskimo shamanism suggest that there is an integrated perspective that may help to order some of these diverse comments.

Shamans traditionally among the Eskimo and to the extent that they still operate, appear to have certain characteristics, to fill certain roles, and to have a special cultural meaning. I suggest that it is difficult to discuss shamanism apart from these three interdependent dimensions of culture, social structure, and personality.

Two aspects of Eskimo shamanism stand out immediately in any observation. First, shamanism and shamans are covert, not openly discussed, and surrounded by an aura of positive respect and negative fear or dislike. Second, present-day reputed shamans apparently do have significant contact with and tolerance of personal emotional chaos. Whether or not they have ever used "psychedelic mushrooms" such as *Amanita muscaria* (abundant in Alaska), Eskimo shamans are familiar with and responsive to such notions as "bad trips," oceanic feelings, a sense of merging with the universe, and the meaningfulness and meaninglessness of all actions and ideas—all of which are common in the dissociative reaction that accompanies psychedelic agent use. Shamans, however, tend to view this dissociative state, whether natural or drug-induced, tolerantly. That is, "true shamans" tend to exhibit a sense of personal security without the need for massive support from obsessive-compulsive or phobic behaviors, as would be needed by many other people who experienced such psychotomimetic or protopsychotic episodes as the shaman.

The Eskimo shamanistic ideation, which I have observed and also noted in the literature, seems to include very strong oral aspects such as incorporation, nurturant support by the universe, and body destruction fantasies. These aspects are also true of certain dissociative states. Such feelings, however, tend to be handled by the shaman with an optimistic fatalism rather than in a pessimistic or frightened fashion. That is, the shaman does not appear to feel bedeviled but at least partly in control of or, more accurately, integrated with the powers he uses. This is probably related in part to Eskimo "basic personality," and in part to something common to shamans everywhere.

Eskimos tend to be oral optimists in that lenient child rearing provides a basic security that is not easily undone by the vicissitudes of life. That disposition is complicated, however, by the cultural need to train against aggression and selfishness, and by the apparently paradoxical cultural value of permitting any person to do what he wishes. This is more easily understood if we note that the infrequency of early childhood frustration does not help the Eskimo develop a tolerance for frustration. Frustration in childhood as well as in adulthood in the past was apparently viewed magically as talion punishment for some unknown transgression. That is, the universe was and is invested with generally optimistic and nurturant but unpredictable qualities. In the past, failures of any sort were attributed to taboo breaking, and taboos were too numerous to avoid.

I suspect that this belief has its genesis at least in part in the infrequent, apparently inexplicable, but harsh teasing that the infant receives from its parents. The teasing usually concerns the child's desire for the breast, and ends as inexplicably as it begins. This, I feel, must confuse the child and convince him that the universe can be arbitrary even though nurturant. The child, by the way, responds to the teasing with rage, which is usually thought humorous by his parents.

If nothing ever overtly displeased the parent, something inexplicable (to the infant) must cause the occasional frustration of nurturance. It is probable that part of the genesis of the adult fear of frustrating someone and intolerance for frustration is also talion anxiety for oedipal urges strongly elicited by the close sleeping quarters of Eskimo households. In any event, phobic and counter-phobic acts were invented, I believe, both to explain and to deter these lapses in the maternal (universe) nurturance and to reduce anxiety over oedipal urges, and these acts often took the form of taboos.

The shaman traditionally suggested which taboos had been broken when difficulties occurred, and acted to overcome the effects. He provided, through a form of confession, an instrument for explicating taboo violation and provided new counterphobic magic for that which had failed. This form of shamanistic behavior reflects rather well the passive oral, optimistic but fatalistic, Eskimo value system. Childhood fantasies of omnipotence and powerlessness become intertwined and both projected and introjected. The omnipotent, nonfrustrated child, when faced with frustration, can find no reason for it. As an adult he is also dependent upon magical techniques for rescue from his fate, but again, he has no control over these techniques. This tends to suggest that Kiev's (1966) formulations which state that ethnopsychiatric tactics will probably reflect socialization patterns might well be extended to shamanism.

The shaman also embodies this optimistic, fatalistic, and passive ethic, but has been able to (1) introject more of the omnipotent parental imago and (2) has been able to fuse with projected power and work in concert with it. Thus, while not "owning" the technique (control of the universe), he nonetheless may operate with it.

This power is, of course, viewed with awe and fear by nonshamans and results in ambivalence toward the shaman as toward the occasional inevitably, incomprehensibly frustrating mother. This is further complicated by the fact that in aboriginal times the expansive, touchy ego of the adult Eskimo often brought him into violent confrontation with others of a similar emotional organization. Though a complex system of conflict avoidance existed, murder was common. The "bully-like" attitude that some persons could develop from this kind of socialization meant that, if they were strong enough, they could take what they wanted (including wives) from other men. Since there was little in the way of organized social control in the form of a legal system, the only alternatives open to the victim were avoidance, submission, or murder.

The continual fears of Eskimos, realistically based both upon their recognition of their own carefully buttressed aggressiveness and upon the fact that the animals they hunted disappeared at times, were often solved by shamanistic intervention. The shaman, at one with all life in his oceanic expansiveness, could not only securely bring back missing game but also serve as a threat to the local bully, whom he could kill by magic. Thus, the "true" shaman served a social integrative purpose.

On the other hand, some shamans themselves became bullies and terrorized communities until they were killed. All shamans appear to have been equally feared. You could never tell when the "socially useful" shaman would become the local bully. It would seem that the "true" shaman had the power to regress in the service of the ego, deal with difficult objects, and serve socially useful purposes. However, "bad" shamans might also have some of this power, all of it, or a simulacrum of it. Further, a "good" shaman could become "bad," and vice versa.

We suggest that, in this particular phenomenon of variance in shamanistic form, social need and individual psychology can be applied more universally than simply for Eskimos, and we suggest the following general propositions for the study of shamanism.

> Regardless of the core modal emotional organization of the group, we hypothesize that the "true" shaman would show unusual ability to organize unconscious needs and concerns whether they were anal, phallic, or oral.

> We further hyothesize that the form of his shamanistic acts would be directed toward precisely those unconscious needs which were dominant in the group and would clearly reflect them.

Thus, primarily anal concerns might well be responded to by shamanism, stressing sadistic or retentive elements directly related to identification with the aggressor or body-protection devices. Such a formulation has in part already been proposed by Kiev (1966), as noted above, in which he discusses research that has shown strong correlations between socialization practices and the form of "pre-scientific" psychiatry; he also integrates Boyer's (1962) notions on shamanistic ability. It would be most instructive to view the results of research directed in the same fashion toward shamanistic behavior itself.

Such hypotheses as we are proposing would suggest why shamanism inevitably would not be insight therapy but essentially counterphobic. They also suggest that the shaman needs power more overwhelming than the incipient (unconsciously derived) danger, and therefore explains the commonly noted cross-cultural need for massive social involvement in the process of healing. Another aspect of such a model would be an attempted explanation of the variety among shamans—that is, why there may be differences between shamans and pseudo-shamans and how they can be distingushed, at least by other shamans. This attempt would support Boyer, et al. (1964) in their discussion of true and pseudo-shamans.

> We further hypothesize that true shamans would very likely not be seriously disturbed as some have suggested, but fairly well integrated, and with a high tolerance for unconscious material and primary-process thinking. "Pseudo-shamans" and those less capable of success would be those for whom the role provided a haven and an explanation for their personal disorganization.

> Finally, we hypothesize that the distribution of such individuals might well be on a continuum and, in fact, individuals might grow from one state of emotional integration to another (or, conversely, regress).

In fact, if such a model is used, it might offer a degree of explanation for how some individuals grow easily into the role (the better-organized shamans) and others feel it thrust upon them, and are frightened by it (those less well organized).

Thus, it is possible that "shamanism" in the broadest sense, can be both a refuge role for the seriously disturbed deviant, and a role for the more maturely integrated, emotionally labile, and unfrightened "normal." It could provide a life-style for the insightful observer of his own community who could act easily within its cultural limits and still, on the other hand, provide a necessary identity to the individual who is almost schizophrenic.

The content of the shaman's acts would then reflect dominant psychosexual concerns, but such concerns would be creatively integrated, though their content would differ from culture to culture and according to the degree of ability to "regress in the service of the ego" of the individual shaman.

Hopefully, an approach similar to this would have power for more than the study of shamanism. It may provide some elements of a framework for an integrated view of culturally shaped, expressive emotional life in a much broader sense.

REFERENCES

Ackerknecht, E.H. 1943. Psychopathology, primitive medicine and culture. Medicine and culture. Bulletin of Historical Medicine 14:30–67.

Amiel, R. 1966. Hygiène mentale en côte d'ivoire. Transcultural Psychiatric Research (Review) April:34–35.

Balikci, A. 1963. Shamanistic behavior among the Netsilik Eskimos. Southwestern Journal of Anthropology 19:380–96.

Bennett, W.C., and R.M. Zingg. 1935. The Tarahumara: an Indian tribe of Northern Mexico. Chicago, University of Chicago Press.

Billig, O., J. Gillin, and W. Davidson. 1948. Aspects of personality and culture in a Guatemalan community: ethnological and Rorschach approaches. Part 2. Journal of Personality 16:326–68.

Bloom, L. 1964. Some psychological concepts of urban Africans. Ethnology 3:66–95.

Bourguignon, E. 1965. The self, the behavioral environment and the theory of spirit possession. In Context and meaning in cultural anthropology. M.E. Spiro, ed. New York, Free Press of Glencoe.

Bourguignon, E., and L. Pettay. 1965. Spirit possession and cross-cultural research. Transcultural Psychiatric Research (Review) April:13–14.

Boyer, L.B. 1962. Remarks on the personality of shamans. In The psychoanalytic study of society. Vol. 2. W. Muensterberger and S. Axelrad, eds. New York, International Universities Press.

————. 1964a. Folk psychiatry of the Apaches of the Mescalero Indian reservation. *In* Magic, faith and healing. A. Kiev, ed. New York, Free Press of Glencoe.

————. 1964b. Further remarks concerning shamans and shamanism. The Israel Annals of Psychiatry 2:235–57.

Boyer, L.B., et al. 1964. Comparisons of the shamans and pseudo-shamans of the Apaches of the Mescalero Indian reservation: a Rorschach study. Journal of Projective Techniques and Personality Assessment 28:173–80.

Devereux, G. 1956. Normal and abnormal: the key problem in psychiatric anthropology. *In* Some uses of anthropology: theoretical and applied. J.B. Casagrande and T. Gladwin, eds. Washington, D.C. Anthropological Society of Washington.

————. 1957. Dream learning and individual ritual differences in Mohave shamanism. American Anthropologist 59:1036.

Dundes, A. 1963. Summoning the deity through ritual fasting. American Imago 20:213–20.

Hes, J. 1964. The changing social role of the Yemenite *mori*. *In* Magic, faith and healing. A. Kiev, ed. New York, Free Press of Glencoe.

Hippler, A.E. 1969. Popular art styles in mariachi festivals. American Imago 26:167–81.

Kiev, A. 1960. Primitive therapy: a cross-cultural study of the relationship between child training and therapeutic practices related to illness. *In* The psychoanalytic study of society. Vol. 1. W. Muensterberger and S. Axelrad, eds. New York, International Universities Press.

————. 1962a. Psychotherapy in Haitian voodoo. American Journal of Psychotherapy 26:469–76.

————. 1962b. Brief note: primitive holistic medicine. International Journal of Social Psychiatry 8:58–61.

————. 1962c. Ritual goat sacrifice in Haiti. American Imago 19:349–59.

————. 1962d. The psychotherapeutic aspects of primitive medicine. Human Organization 21:25–29.

————. 1964. The study of folk psychiatry. *In* Magic, faith and healing. A. Kiev, ed. New York, Free Press of Glencoe.

————. 1966. Pre-scientific psychiatry. *In* An American handbook of psychiatry. Vol. 3. S. Arieti, ed. New York, Basic Books.

————. 1968. Curanderismo—Mexican-American folk psychiatry. New York, Free Press of Glencoe.

Kris, E. 1952. Psychoanalytic explorations in art. New York, International Universities Press.

Madsen, W. 1964. Value conflicts and folk psychotherapy in South Texas. *In* Magic, faith and healing. A. Kiev, ed. New York, Free Press of Glencoe.

Murphy, J.M. 1964. Psychotherapeutic aspects of shamanism on St. Lawrence Island, Alaska. *In* Magic, faith and healing. A. Kiev, ed. New York, Free Press of Glencoe.

Nadel, S.F. 1946. A study of shamanism in the Nuba Mountains. Journal of the Royal Anthropological Institute 76:25–37.

Opler, M.E. 1936. Some points of comparison between the treatment of functional disorders by Apache shamans and modern psychiatric practice. American Journal of Psychiatry 92:1371–87.

————. 1941. An Apache life way: the economic, social and religious institutions of the Chiricahus Indians. Chicago, University of Chicago Press.

Parsons, E.C. 1936. Mitla, town of the souls. Chicago, University of Chicago Press.

Pfister, O. 1932. Instinctive psychoanalysis among the Navajos. Journal of Nervous and Mental Disease 66:234–54.

Pfeiffer, W. 1966. Psychiatrische besonderheiten im Indonesien. Transcultural Psychiatric Research 3:116–19.

Posinsky, S.H. 1965. Yurok shamanism. Psychiatric Quarterly 39:227–43.

Redfield, R., and S. Tax. 1951. General characteristics of present-day Meso-American Indian society. *In* Heritage of conquest. S. Tax, ed. Free Press of Glencoe.

Rogler, L.H., and A.B. Hollingshead. 1961. The Puerto Rican spiritualist as psychiatrist. American Journal of Psychology 6:17–21.

Roheim, G. 1951. Hungarian shamanism. *In* Psychoanalysis and the social sciences. Vol. 3. G. Roheim, ed. New York, International Universities Press.

Romano, O. 1965. Charismatic medicine, folk healing and folk sainthood. American Anthropologist 67:1151–73.

Sasaki, Y. 1963. Social psychiatric study of shaman ("Miko") in Japan. Proceedings of the joint meeting of the Japanese Society of Psychiatrists and Neurologists and the American Psychiatric Association, May 13–17, Tokyo.

———. 1969. Psychiatric study of the shaman in Japan. *In* Mental health research in Asia and the Pacific. W. Caudill and T.Y. Lin, eds. Honolulu, East-West Center Press.

Silverman, J. 1967. Shamans and acute schizophrenia. American Anthropologist 69:21–31.

Turner, V. 1964. An Ndembu doctor in practice. *In* Magic, faith and healing. A. Kiev, ed. New York, Free Press of Glencoe.

9. *Vai Laaqau* and *Aitu*: Healing in a West Polynesian Village

JOSEPH FINNEY, M.D., Ph.D.

Department of Educational Psychology and Counseling
University of Kentucky
Lexington, Kentucky

THIS PAPER is based on a six-month study on a small island, having a population of less than 600, in the Gilbert and Ellice Islands, a British crown colony northwest of Samoa. To protect the informants, all names of persons and places have been changed. The actual name of the village will be released to anthropologists and other scientists with a need to know.

On Expectation Island (pseudonym), healing practices of all kinds are known as *vai laaqau*, a phrase meaning water of trees. The traditional medicines are crushed leaves dissolved in coconut oil. The leaf preparations can be taken by mouth but are usually applied by anointing. *Vai laaqau* is also the word used for Western medicines; by extension, the term has come to include all forms of traditional healing practices (such as massage) and all forms of Western medical treatment.

The island is pervaded by a belief in *aitu*, ghosts that are believed to have the power of harming people. Most islanders are afraid to walk alone after dark lest they be grabbed and eaten by the ghosts. Some are even afraid to go into the wilderness alone in the daytime. (In point of fact, the island is a safe place to walk around, by day or night, because of the absence of violent crime.)

The older language had two words for supernatural beings, *aitu* and *atua*. In modern Tuvalu (the dialect of the islanders), as in Samoan, *atua* is the word used for the Christian God, while *aitu* refers to ghosts and harmful spirits.

Catholic Rotumans use the same terms, but for Protestant Rotumans the meanings are just the opposite: *aitu* means God, and *atua* means ghost. A few of the old men on Expectation Island remember traditional stories of the old Polynesian gods, called *aitu*, and they distinguish such spirits from the spirits of dead people who are also called *aitu*. But most people on the island have forgotten such traditions, and even the names of the *aitu*. Today the people of the island keep talking fearfully about *aitu*, but not as identifiable individual spirits; rather, as a vague group of harmful spirits.

There are two systems of health care on the island. When someone is believed to be physically sick from organic causes he goes to the Health Department. On the island the Health Department is represented not by a physician but by a first-aid man or medical assistant who has been trained to practice medicine in a limited way. He is authorized to give penicillin injections at his discretion. Though he does not give physical examinations, he administers medicine for everything from pneumonia to indigestion, based on the symptoms described. Because much of his work is dressing wounds, he is called "the dresser" (*tulesa*).

On the other hand, when a person speaks unrealistically (from either an organic delirium or schizophrenia), or when his bodily symptoms are unusual and unresponsive to treatment, the local folk conclude that his troubles come from the *aitu* and he is sent to one of the traditional cult practitioners. The traditional way of healing, which is now called bush medicine, was of several kinds. Massage was widely used, and the healers are said to have been highly successful in setting bones, though some bad treatments of fractures have been reported. Even today, the cult healers are the ones to whom people go for physical therapy, especially massage.

The herb preparations (*vai laaqau*, literally "tree juice") are the means by which the spirits are made to enter the body, and are also the means by which the spirits are made to depart from it. Hence the term *vai laaqau* is extended to include the system of dealing with ghosts or evil spirits. When the people speak English, they translate *vai laaqau* either as "medicine" or "magic," according to the context. As used in this paper, magic means an extraordinary event that fulfills either a desire or a requirement of conscience, and that can neither be explained nor controlled through natural science, but only by some supposed power of a mysterious and awesome nature.

The cult practitioners see no conflict between their practices and those of the Health Department. When people have wounds that need dressing, they go to the *tulesa* in the Health Department. The *tulesa*, so far as is known, never went to the cult practitioners for treatment, but neither has he ever spoken ill of them.

Against this background, let us examine some incidents of healing that I observed on the island.

Incidents of Treatment

On the afternoon of March 14, the *tulesa* told me about Lauto, a forty-year-old patient with a temperature of 102; he had diagnosed the case as meningococcus meningitis and had begun a course of penicillin injections and sulfa tablets. As did nearly all seriously sick people, the man stayed at home, lying on the floor. The *tulesa* visited him daily. I began to visit him, at first thrice daily. He was febrile and had some limitation of forward motion of the head at the neck. I concluded that he had some form of meningoencephalitis, possibly a bacterial one that might respond to penicillin, but more likely a viral one that would not respond.

On the afternoon of March 15, two men were treating Lauto, while fourteen adults sat around the house watching. (The presence of an audience is required for all activities on the island, including medical treatment. It is assumed that privacy or secrecy signifies evil intent, and an audience assures good behavior.) Lauto was kneeling. The older man, a kinsman, knelt behind him, hand on his shoulder, and massaged his back with oil. The younger man, Measano, a healer, faced Lauto from the front, grasped the patient's hand in his right hand and shook it, with his left hand on the patient's forehead, he moved the head around from time to time. He kept asking Lauto questions, insistently; Lauto sat back on his heels, his arms occasionally jerking. He seemed dazed and did not answer. The young healer kept asking "Who is that?" evidently to test Lauto's reality testing. The patient moved his lips but no sound came forth. The young healer told him to speak louder. The patient's wife wiped his skin with a cloth. I took his pulse and found it to be 92. Ignoring me, the healer massaged Lauto's neck muscles and asked him if he could bite the healer's hand. He seemed to be trying, persistently and patiently, to establish some communication with Lauto, who was out of contact, in a quiet delirium or daze. The wife now took the patient's hand and talked to him. The healer again began asking, "Who is that?" pointing to the patient's sister who sat nearby. She and the healer gave her name. They repeated the question, and gave the answer each time. Then they lay him on his back to sleep. His eyes stayed open, and he kept moving his lips soundlessly.

When the healer left, a young male schoolteacher, Hame, stayed with Lauto's wife and another woman. They held the patient's head, jaw, and hands, and massaged them. The patient passed gas loudly. The audience laughed briefly.

After leaving Lauto's house, I passed by the house of a young girl I knew. She told me that the villagers regarded Lauto as *masaqi mai aitu*, sick from evil spirits.

Early the next morning, the *tulesa*, who had already visited Lauto and given him a penicillin injection, reported normal temperature. Not trusting the patient not to bite the thermometer, he had taken the temperature underarm. In doubt that the temperature had fallen so soon, I decided to take rectal temperatures several times a day for a few days. (The *tulesa* never took rectal temperatures, even of men, because, not being a medical man, he did his prescribing without physical examinations, and because the people have a strong *tapu* (prohibition) against the exposure of private parts of anyone past puberty.)

At this point, not knowing what was happening in the indigenous healing cult, I sought information from two young adults: a man, Pimou, and a woman, Teaa. Both were twenty-four years old; both were natives of the island and from prominent local families; both had been away from the island for some years, attending high school in the colonial capital and then working there; and both happened to be taking several months' vacation on their home island. Teaa was a registered nurse. Since they both spoke English fluently, and I was far from fluent in the island tongue, I came to rely on them for information. Teaa told me: "On the evening of March 8, Lauto was walking home from the jungle, carrying a long stick. Suddenly an evil spirit came and broke the stick. The next day he fell sick." That was all she knew or would tell at the time.

In the afternoon I called on Lauto again. He lay supine, saying his name repeatedly, and other things, keeping his eyes shut. A young woman, Fune, talked with him, and he answered her. I did not know yet that this woman, aged twenty-four, was one of the leading magic-makers on the island. She was the only female prominent in this field, and she had a larger band of devoted followers than any other practitioner, with one possible exception. I beckoned Teaa aside, and she explained, "He's talking nonsense. The people think that a ghost is in Lauto, and that the ghost is doing the talking, not Lauto. They believe it because lots of people have suffered like this before. They believe that some man who has been angry with him has caused the trouble. These people are trying to get rid of the ghost. They went to the jungle to get some medicine. And their talking is to make the ghost go away. By touching the man and talking, they are trying to find out in which part of his body the ghost is staying. If they find that the ghost is in his foot, they will treat it by massaging it with their medicated oil."

While Teaa, the nurse, professed her disbelief in evil spirits, the equally well educated young man, Pimou, frankly admitted his belief and his fear. Twelve days earlier, March 4, he had told me: "My mother could do some bush medicine, though only for boils. She would crush the leaves of the *talialia* tree, dissolve them in oil, and rub the oil around the edges of a boil, to relieve the pain. Other people know other kinds of medicine or magic. If someone who knows how is angry, he can put some medicine onto the other person and make him sick. Or he can hide the medicine, bury it in the ground, and affect the other person. Such a condition can be cured by another person who also knows that kind of medicine. Such people can make a ghost come or go away. I myself won't walk alone at night, outside the village, for fear of the ghosts." Now, on March 16, he explained, "If such people wish to poison somebody, they hide their medicine in his house. Do you believe in this?" [I said, "No, do you?"] "Yes, I believe. The ghosts are now inside this man, Lauto." ["By ghosts, do you mean the spirits of dead people?"] "I think maybe so. It's the ghosts inside that make Lauto murmur. Some experts can help people who are under the influence of magic. I think even the pastor believes it."

On the morning of March 17, I found that blankets had been hung around Lauto, shielding him from view. (His house, like many others, had no walls and was open to public view.) As I approached, his wife said, "*Tapu*," and motioned me to sit down between her and Lauto. I asked whether his speech was good, or still addled. She said it was good. I felt his forehead, which was cool, and counted his pulse at 96. I asked him how he felt. He answered, "Thanks to God, I'm recovering." At the health station, a few minutes later, I learned from the *tulesa* that he had discontinued the twice-daily penicillin injections after the first one the day before. Though without any authority to direct him, I requested him to resume the injections, as a precaution, and he agreed to do so.

That afternoon, I found the young teacher, Hame, aged seventeen, seated crosslegged at the patient's head. For the first time, it struck me that Hame was an apprentice magic-maker. The thought came as a shock. Hame was a bright young man, and though not a trained teacher nor even a high school graduate, he had recently been hired as an extra teacher at the Island Council School, for which the Council paid him five dollars a month. He had been accepted as a student at the Marine Training School. As a Scout Leader, he had also been attending a course in which I taught first aid and elements of human physiology and physical diagnosis. Only two days before, I had taught him how to use a stethoscope and listen to the heart beat. In the class, studying the rudiments of Western medicine, he had been an apt and respectful pupil. But that day he was in his element, and he directed me. I had sat down on the floor, resting one hand on the floor mat on which Hame and the patient were seated. Hame informed me quietly that I was not allowed on that mat. "That's only for us." I pulled my hand back but after a minute reached over and felt the patient's forehead. Hame asked me about the temperature, and I told him it was okay. Then I asked him, "What about the mat?" He answered, "Only the people who are working to cure his troubles can sit on this mat." I said, "I am working to cure his troubles." Hame insisted, "Only the people who are working to cure his mental troubles." As a psychiatrist and clinical psychologist, I felt constrained to say, "I am working to cure his mental troubles." Hame answered tolerantly, "In a different way."

Pimou was still afraid to give me the name of the wicked magician, but I prevailed on him to give me a list of all the magic-makers in the village, and then to point to the name of the evil one without speaking the name aloud. The name was Malevole.

An election was two days off. I interviewed both candidates about their platforms, and asked both men if they believed that Lauto was sick from evil spirits. One said he believed it and added that there was a law against casting spells; the other, who was an ordained minister, refused to say.

The next morning, March 18, the *tulesa* asked me to see a patient with food poisoning, not caused by evil spirits. When a sickness appears with common symptoms and signs or seems to belong to a known type, it is not ascribed to evil spirits.

That afternoon, ten women, six men, and several children gathered at Lauto's house. Measano was present, but Fune was in charge of the treatment. She was staring intently, with a faint smile, puffing on a cigarette. To my greeting she gave no answer but held one finger up, filled her lungs with cigarette smoke, held it a long minute, and blew it out. She shook her head at me, held a finger up again, and then tapped on the mat as if spelling out a message. The patient's sister replied by tapping and looked at me as if expecting me to do the same. Fune kept her left eye shut. The patient's sister said to me in the local language, "Malevole is the bad person. He kills people."

A little girl came into the house and stood shyly in the background. I recognized her as Pilaamou, a sweet, shy eleven-year-old, one of a class of eighteen children I had been teaching for over three weeks. Suddenly it dawned on me that the sick man, Lauto, was her father.

The patient's sister, perched on a high chest, droned rhythmically, then sang, then chanted. She opened a Bible and read a passage. I grasped only an occasional word, just enough to tell that it was Samoan, and not the Tuvalu dialect of the island. She threw combs down and jumped down to retrieve one. Fune kept watching me with her left eye shut. Now she lay on the floor near me and opened both eyes. Her left eye was pink with infection.

Lauto recovered gradually over the next few days. For a while, Teaa, the nurse, reported that she still considered him mentally sick: he did not always talk sense. But even that sign disappeared and he was soon about his business. The people of the village ascribed his cure to Fune's magical powers in exorcising the evil spirits. Had his troubles been psychogenic, I might have agreed that the cult treatment had done the job. But not for meningoencephalitis. The *tulesa* believed that he had cured meningococcus meningitis with penicillin. I believed that a virus disease had spontaneously remitted.

On the night of March 25, the women of the Meifama tribe held a traditional dance. Hame and three other musicians and I were the only men present. Fune tapped me to dance with her. Her face was stern. She kept snapping commands at me as I helplessly tried to follow her lead.

On March 29, Fune dropped in for lunch at the home of the family with whom I regularly ate. She chattered at me in rapid speech that I could not understand and ended with an English phrase, "All right, darling?" I replied in Tuvalu, greeting her as my friend. She answered in English, "Not friend." Asked why, she made another incomprehensible speech, put her finger to her lips (as she had done when treating Lauto), mentioned Lauto's name, and touched her rump (objecting to my having taken Lauto's temperature or to my sitting on her mat?). At length she agreed to be my friend, and we shook hands.

On April 4, word came to me that a five-month-old baby boy had died. A few minutes later, the messenger reported, "He lives again!" Fune had been called to recall the baby from the dead by magic. But still later, word came that Fune had tried and failed.

On the night of April 12, an eleven-year-old boy pupil of mine came with his father, the village policeman, to summon me to Fune's party. It was in celebration of Lauto's recovery, but I had been invited as an afterthought, and by the time I got there most of the people had eaten and were leaving. As I ate, Fune kept chattering to me in pidgin English and Tuvalu. Someone translated, "She says you may go now." As I had been there only fifteen minutes, I did not go. Fune brought forth a perfumed handkerchief and stuffed it into my pocket. She put a wreath of flowers on my head. She asked for a twenty-cent coin, and gave it back. She brought out delicious cakes made of grated coconut and coconut toddy molasses; I stayed an hour altogether.

The nurse told me, "Fune has been telling people that you are a great magician and that you have powerful magic."

The following day, Fune volunteered to take some census papers and help me do the village census. Then she spoke slowly, and I could tell that she was speaking neither English nor Tuvalu. Teaa commented, "She is talking nonsense." It came out that Fune often spoke in nonsense syllables. Some people in the village considered her *faqavalevale* (out of her mind), but most did not. When Fune returned the census papers to me, they had only scribblings on them.

Within a week, Fune began to hold nightly dances, Western style, at the home of a teacher on the school grounds. An older woman in that family was getting treatment by Fune for chronic indigestion. The dances were held even on Sunday nights, much to the dismay of the Congregational pastor and some of the villagers. Perhaps the reason nobody interfered was that the house was not within the village proper. On April 28 I attended one of these dances. The night was dark and stormy, the room dimly lit by kerosene lamp. There was some lively dancing to jazz music until the school's battery-powered record player quit. Fune stormed angrily over to me and dragged me off to repair it. When I could not, she screamed, kicked me in the shins, and tried to hit me. I tossed her sharp palm stick out the window, as a precaution. She ordered me to dance the twist with her, without music. After humoring her thus a few times, I refused to go on and sat down again. She sat beside me, scolding me angrily and fingering a sharp machete. Feeling uneasy, expecting to be stabbed any minute, I took the first opportunity to lift the knife from her hands and give it to the master of the house, who carried it safely away. I had begun to diagnose Fune as a walking schizophrenic with hysterical features, and I didn't feel I could safely predict her behavior.

Two nights later a disturbance occurred that I learned about only the next morning. Violence had broken out between the partisans of two rival magical healers, Fune and a man named Feo. I had known Feo slightly. He had an eleven-year-old daughter, a delightful tomboy, who was one of the better pupils in my schoolroom. Feo was one of the few adults on the island who spoke English. He had worked as a houseboy for the American Navy in World War II. I had not been aware that he conducted nightly seances and that he headed a healing cult, having a following second only to Fune's. It happened that Feo was treating Motana, a young female schoolteacher, at the same house in which Fune had threatened me with the machete. Treating two patients in the same house, Feo and Fune had clashed. On the night of April 30, a group of Feo's partisans had gone to the house and tossed Fune's things outdoors. The head schoolteacher, a Gilbertese man named Napuqau, told me that he had stayed up all night to keep the peace, going back and forth between the two healers to persuade them to keep their followers from violence. Each healer agreed to stay out of the teacher's house when the other healer was there. Nevertheless, the next morning, a group of Fune's partisans marched past Feo's house and traded insults with him.

On May 4, when I encountered Fune, she asked me to walk with her through the village. She visited a woman patient whose foot was swollen with pus from elephantiasis complicated by bacterial infection. Fune squeezed the pus out. She and Hame walked home with me, and she asked me to take over treatment of the woman's foot. I instructed her to bring the woman to me at the *tulesa*'s health station the next morning, which she did. I asked Fune why she always puffed on a cigarette while doing her treatment. She replied that her teacher, the healer on another island, had told her that her treatment would not be successful unless she smoked cigarettes during it.

On the night of May 5 Fune came to my house after supper, bringing the nurse Teaa with her as interpreter. The two young women, nurse and cult healer, of the same age, made an interesting contrast. They told of Fune's training in healing. While Teaa was a student nurse at Seabattle, Fune went to the Central Colony Hospital there for treatment of rheumatism. Partially cured, she took more treatment from a bush doctor on Tradition Island, then returned home to Expectation Island. Sick again, she went by ship to Tradition Island to see another bush doctor. She recovered her health, but it was not that healer who instructed her in the cult. Instead, a woman came and gave her a hair to eat; after eating the hair she acquired the knowledge. While telling this story, Fune came to the real purpose of her call: she proposed that the three of us, Fune, Teaa, and I, go together to Fiji on the next ship. Neither Teaa nor I took her seriously. But two days later, when the ship came, Fune departed on it and did not return during my stay on the island. She told people that I had paid for her ticket.

On May 9, I suggested to Teaa that she come with me that night to witness a session of Feo's healing practice. She refused, saying, "They can't come to our house and we can't go to theirs. For many years, Feo has made magic to kill my father." I concluded that it must be weak magic, since her father was still alive and well. Her father had been the chief (*aliqi*) of the island until the British government had abolished such titles three years before. Her father was himself a practitioner of traditional healing, she explained, but only of massage, not of magic. When their family needed magic, they went to another practitioner, Mofumu.

That night at Feo's house, some fifteen or twenty people, mostly women, were gathered, for what turned out to be a nightly session. Teaa's young sister, Mafosulu, who was married and pregnant, was among the company. Feo's wife, Faalanala, was the medium through whom the spirit Seilosi spoke. There was no dramatic process of putting her into a trance. Acting perhaps on a slight signal from her husband, she seated herself at a chosen place on the floor and at once changed character to Seilosi. Feo and his wife hesitated to conduct their usual session in my presence, and spent a few minutes conversing with me about it, perhaps to test my attitude. Feo explained that they had three healing methods: massage, medicated oils, and fire points. He said that his wife and the spirit Seilosi were clearly two different persons, because his wife did not know how to treat sick people, while Seilosi did. He asked me whether I preferred to talk with Seilosi in English or in Tuvalu. Knowing that the woman spoke no English, I tested the response by asking the spirit to speak in English. After a few minutes' debate, in Tuvalu, with "Seilosi" and others, he reported "Seilosi" as saying, "I can speak all the languages of the world, but since we are in these islands I will speak Tuvalu." I asked "Seilosi" what kind of *aitu* she was and whether she was the spirit of a dead person. She denied that she was an *aitu* at all, or a spirit of a dead person. She described herself only as a person who went around the world helping people. After these preliminaries, she got down to the business of treating people.

One patient was Nailapu, about nineteen years old, one of the most beautiful young women on the island. She had been married about five months, and complained that she had not been able to get pregnant. Feo gave her the fire treatment. He took a burning twig or rootlet of pandanus, like a lit match, and extinguished it by pushing it into the skin of her belly. He did this in a dozen places. Nailapu's husband was present, but nobody thought of treating him.

Motana, the young female schoolteacher, was the next patient. She was an unwed mother and the fattest woman on the island of her age, twenty-two. She had an itching skin rash on her chest. A kinswoman of Feo or Faalanala treated her with fire points.

At a later date, Motana explained to me, "They have helped me a great deal. I had been feeling guilty about having slept with that man who made me pregnant. He was a schoolteacher on another island, and had a wife. Now they have explained to me that the reason that I did it is that that man did magic to make me fall in love with him. Now that I know that, I feel better; I don't feel guilty anymore." This was a clear case of psychotherapy: relief of guilt feelings by strengthening the defense mechanisms of projection and rationalization. Another day she told me of a man who had fathered children out of wedlock with half-a-dozen women, and once had two women pregnant at once, including his own daughter. She explained in English, "He was doing magic also to make them love him." I asked, "Is that true?" She answered firmly, "Yes. I know that."

Another patient that night was a woman in her forties with a lump in her breast. Like most women of her age on the island, she had breasts that hung below the navel. Feo joked with me: "Are there any breasts like this in America?" His wife, Faalanala ("Seilosi") treated the lump by massage—a dangerous procedure that could spread cancer throughout the body.

I visited Feo's sessions several times more. On the evening of June 4, he had a farewell feast for the spirit Seilosi, who was to be replaced by another spirit using the same medium. On the night of June 20 I took pictures of the fire-point treatment. Feo asked me to come back the next morning and take pictures of him treating a woman for obesity, and I did so. The technique was to prick the skin of the woman's fat belly and thighs at many points to allow bleeding. He struck rapidly with a sharp implement, a stick with a shark's tooth affixed, and made about a thousand bleeding points before he stopped. His wife stood by with a cloth, wiping the blood away. The patient took it silently, scowling in pain.

The morning after my first visit to Feo's sessions, I told the nurse, Teaa, that her young married sister had been there, despite Teaa's word that the two families were deadly foes. Teaa explained that her sister had joined the enemy camp because her husband belonged to that group. When she married, she had promised her parents that she would not join Feo's cult, but she broke the promise. Now that she had joined the enemy camp, she had been disowned by her family.

On May 17, Teaa's young sister gave birth to a baby boy. The next day,

Teaa complained to me that Feo's people would not leave the young mother in peace; they kept coming around with unwanted attentions. I noted with amusement that Teaa no longer regarded her sister as one of the enemy but as a victim of the enemy. Two weeks later, I saw the young woman sitting in her parents' house, nursing her baby. The estrangement within the family was over. The birth of the grandchild had brought them together again.

On July 11, I encountered Malevole, the alleged evildoer, and asked him in Tuvalu whether it was true that he did magic to kill people. He exploded, "It's a lie!" Then he added calmly, in Tuvalu, "I only do *vai laaqau* to cure people, the same as you do." In his youth, it was said, Malevole was quarrelsome and aggressive and beat people up. As he grew older, he became taciturn and no longer fought, but when people annoyed him he would say, "Just wait and see what happens to you." It was said that such people got sick and died shortly afterward.

On July 27, I interviewed a 54-year-old man, Paoa, who had been blind for twenty-three years. He was one of the very few on the island who cherished the old stories of pre-Christian times and who felt distressed at the progressive loss of the old lore and skills. Speaking through an interpreter, he told me the following story.

"This skill [*fai aite,* 'to work with spirits'] as practiced here now is not much based on indigenous traditions; much of it has been imported from Fiji and the Micronesian Islands. Some of the techniques come from a faraway place called lipi [probably Yap]. The ghosts of that place are different. I learned my skill from Sumetu, a man from Tradition Island who had been a seaman. He had sailed to faraway places and had learned magic at lipi in the Caroline Islands. You probably know that group of islands; one of the islands is called Luko [almost certainly Truk].

"All the evil skills of our ancient people were stopped when Christianity came, ninety-five years ago. Only massage remains of our old healing practices. The evil skills that our people use to harm one another today were brought in from other places.

"The spirits I deal with have no names. Sumetu says it's a person who made the sun, the sky, the trees, and the land. So when I try to cure someone of a spell, I call on the man who made the sun, the sky, the trees, and the land to come and cure him. ["Is it the same God we worship in the Christian church?"] All I know is I've done it and it works.

"When I do it, I have a dream that I'm flying through the air, and I see all the trees that I can use to cure the sickness. When I wake I know that a sick person will soon come to me for help; and when he comes, I know that what he has is not a physical sickness but a magic; and I know already which leaves I can use to cure him.

"I already have a bottle of oil. In that bottle are leaves, well prepared. So when I try to cure a sickness I get a leaf from the wilderness. I rub oil on a *maiquiqu* [green coconut frond], I go to the sick one, I tap him on the head with it, and I touch his body with it.

"For other sicknesses, such as stomachache, I use the bottle of oil with massage. I use the *maiquiqu* only for illness that comes from *vai laaqau*. [Apparently a distinction is thus made between natural and supernatural sickness.]

["Is your method of healing like Feo's?"]

"Feo got his oil in Ocean Island from a woman named Muna from Big Island. Feo keeps having the families of his patients do things for him, prepare special foods for him. He tells them it's an order from the spirits. I think he makes it up. [The feast for Seilosi's departure may be an example.]

["What about Fune?"]

"I don't know. She has a different way. I don't know other people's methods, and they don't know mine. I don't approve of healers who go in for specially prepared foods and special clothing, as Feo and Fune do. Other practitioners on the island don't do so.

"If a patient doesn't seem to improve, I have a dream that a man comes to me and gives me food; breadfruit, for example. Then I know that's the food I am to prepare for the sick one. So I prepare food for the patient; I don't have the patient's family prepare food for me.

"Malevole learned his magic from Muna. Maalapi learned his from Taqipau, a Big Island man who lived here. Mofumu learned his from Maalapi here. Everyone has a different way.

["What are the names of the *aitu* that make people sick?"]

"All I know is that people get sick from *vai laaqau*. ["Who makes the people sick?"] From a sick person I can tell only a few things. Someone comes to me in a dream and shows me trees, seaweed, or *limu* [moss]. Then I know that the harm was done through moss or seaweed. So the cure is likewise, but not the same plant.

"A man named Faului from Tradition Island did magic to a woman here, Pomufo, making her sick. I cured her. Faului and I had a quarrel because Faului denied that he was the one that did it. This was in 1949, the year after I became blind. I told Faului, 'If you want to make sure, take it to court.' He didn't, so I knew I was right. Faului said, 'My teacher, Muna, said that she is the greatest magic-maker in the Tuvalu Islands.' I answered, 'My teacher, Sumetu, said that he has the weakest ghost, the lowest level of knowledge, but even so, let's have a contest.' Faului refused the challenge. I taunted him, 'Okay, let's see you do your magic and hurt me.' That was a Saturday. At last he said, 'Go now. Tuesday is the day you will die, at two o'clock.' I ignored him till Tuesday, and then I took my protection from the air. I went to the sea to bathe at noon, and then stood in the sunshine to let the salt crystallize on my skin to protect me. Nothing happened.

"In one case, Feo accused Malevole of making the patient sick. When Malevole heard of it, he went to Feo, who denied making the charge; he said that only the people working with him had mentioned Malevole's name.

"I can't tell whether a person is sick from *vai laaqau* till I try healing him. The other case I had was Haamea, the son of Seyana. Haamea's maternal grandfather, Sulema, was the one who had cast the spell on him. He was cross with Haamea and intended to kill him. Sulema had gone to Haamea's father, Seyana, and asked him for one of his sons, as a companion and household worker, because he had no son. Haamea was willing, and went. But Haamea's wife refused to move with him into the old man's household; to oblige his wife, Haamea moved out of the old man's household. Seyana, the father, sent Haamea's younger brother instead. That's why Sulema was cross at Haamea.

"I told Seyana that the grandfather, Sulema, was the one who cast the spell on Haamea and that he could tell Sulema if he liked. One day Sulema's daughter, Suailese, came to me and asked me whether it was true.

"Haamea was out of his mind. He couldn't sleep at night. He would wander restlessly, to the sea, to the wilderness. I treated him with the *maiquiqu*. All his wandering and talking nonsense stopped. He stayed in the house, but he was not yet restored to normal thinking. Earlier, when I was off the island, his father had taken him to the pastor, who tried to cure him by prayer. But the pastor got sick and handed him over to another minister, who told him to find another kind of treatment. If they hadn't taken him to the pastor, I could have cured him. He would have been better off either not going to the pastor at all or sticking with the pastor till he was cured. A half treatment is worse than none. Haamea died eight years later, after the *tulesa* did surgery on his testicle. So many people had tried to cure him by pressing on his back and belly that it made his scrotum swell. [Perhaps he had filariasis, which is endemic in the islands.]

"When Sulema's daughter asked me about what I had said about Sulema, I told her it was true and that Sulema could take it to court if he didn't like it. Sulema did nothing about it; he didn't come to speak to me or to the boy's father. If he had done so I would have faced him down, as I did Faului. I would have turned his own spirits against him. That's what I did to Faului, reflected his own ghosts back on him. He got sick, wasted away, and died within a month.

"Another time, the pastor and another minister, who is now the island president, had a quarrel. The third minister and the deacons tried to stop the quarrel, but they kept arguing. Someone sent for me. I went in and told them to stop speaking. The minister who is now island president wouldn't stop talking. I said, 'Wait and see what will happen to you if you don't stop.' He stopped."

Effects of Christianity on *Vai Laaqau* Practice

Let us consider the relationship of *vai laaqau* to the Christian religious beliefs, flowing from the English Puritan tradition, held by the people of Expectation Island for ninety-five years. The London Missionary Society converted Samoa, and native Samoan missionaries in turn converted Expectation Island.

In discussing Samoan beliefs in ghosts, Mead (1928) stated that such belief is inconsistent with Christian belief about life after death. But the Tuvalu people of Expectation Island, like the Samoans, are skillful at reconciling contraditions.

On June 6, the pastor preached a sermon condemning people who worked magic. "Follow righteousness. Do as Jesus did. Did Jesus do magic? No. But many people today do magic. They do wrong. It is sinful." Two weeks later, noting that the magical healers were still at their practice, I asked Napuqau about it. He answered, "I think the pastor was not condemning the use of magic to heal people, only the use of magic to harm people. He didn't make it specific. He didn't mention the use of magic in healing."

The Gospel of St. Mark is the only part of the Bible so far translated into Tuvalu. I checked it and found that it supports the local belief in evil spirits known as *aitu*. Mark 1:34 describes people possessed by devils and says that Jesus drove the evil spirits out. By using the local word, *aitu*, the translator has put the authority of the Bible behind the local Polynesian beliefs in *aitu*. The Samoan Bible, in contrast, uses the Greek word *taimona*, demons, and so avoids giving support to the local spirit beliefs. The local cult healers in Tuvalu can find their practices approved in the Tuvalu Bible; by doing magic to cast out *aitu*, and thereby cure sickness, they are following in the footsteps of Jesus.

A man whose sister had had a mental illness gave the following account, showing a rather tenuous opposition between *vai laaqau* beliefs and Christianity: "I told her, 'If you think somebody did *vai laaqau* to you, go to somebody for *vai laaqau* treatment.' She answered, 'I don't want to go to those *vai laaqau* people. They don't help. They can only hurt me. Only God will help.' But Fune tricked her. She said she'd help her against the *vai laaqau* people, the devils in her. She gave my mother some oil to put on my sister and told her not to tell her it came from Fune. . . . I believe if the *vai laaqau* people give me medicine and I drink it, it can affect me, but not from a distance. Formerly I believed they could kill me without touching me. But I read in the Bible, and I don't believe it any more."

What he seemed to be saying was that he believed in a possible pharmacological effect but not in a magical one. The same man reported that he had overcome his fear of the dark by reading the Samoan Bible, and convincing himself that belief in ghosts was inconsistent with his Christian beliefs. "God is everywhere, even at night, and I am safe." This man, unlike most people on the island, had had a high school education off the island. Some of his teachers had been Englishmen, and he had for a time joined a different Christian sect.

Commenting on the island's Christian church, which he had rejoined, but about which he still felt skeptical, he said, "The people here believe in *vai laaqau* even though they know God. I blame the pastor because he believes in *vai laaqau*. Both here and on Royalty Island the clergymen let the *vai laaqau* people into their homes and take their advice. Some say the Bible supports their views, telling of people possessed by devils. I don't know how this business can be stopped unless the pastors will preach against it. The majority of the people believe in *vai laaqau*. When my child had *ngaengae* [asthma], people advised me to seek *vai laaqau*. Fune came to me and offered to help. But I use only the *tulesa* and the massage people.

"One time the pastor, in a sermon, said that his wife had become seriously ill when she went with him to a conference on Confusion Island. He said that someone who went with him to the conference had done *vai laaqau* to her. Tonini, one of the deacons here, who had gone with the pastor to the conference and who has some skill at *vai laaqau*, felt that he was the one accused. Later that day, Tonini made an angry speech in the town hall, asking the people whether they believed the charge against him. The pastor wasn't there. Tonini said, 'If he thinks I did it, why didn't he come to me?' Other people calmed him down by saying, 'If you know you are innocent, forget it.'

"I didn't hear the pastor's recent sermon mentioning *vai laaqau*, but I've heard him preach on it before. What he says is that all powers and skills are from God, including the power to do magic [*vai laaqau*]. The skill is given us to help people. Using it to harm people is wrong."

The island people are fiercely loyal to their fundamentalist Protestant Christianity, and they would resent being told that their religion is not Christian. But their whole world view, their concept of causal relationships in the world, and particularly their view of the efficacy of spiritual and moral forces in the physical world, derive from the traditional Polynesian system of *tapu*. Christianity has only replaced one list of *tapu* acts with a new list; the Bible is read as a source or reference book for such a list.

Many Polynesian *tapu*s are, in many cases, regarded as self-enforcing. A violation often brings its own punishment, in the form of sickness and death. Thus, the woman schoolteacher seemed to believe at first that her skin trouble was a moral judgment against her sexual behavior. And the girl who was impregnated by her own father gave birth to a sickly child, apparently neurologically damaged. Western scientific practitioners would give a naturalistic explanation. The schoolteacher's *belief* that her behavior was immoral (not the *fact* that it was immoral) may have caused her skin trouble through psychophysiological mechanisms; the child born of incest may well have been homozygous for a deleterious recessive gene. But in the Polynesian belief system, the violation of the *tapu* has effects directly in the physical world, through mechanisms that no one attempts to explain. The effect may not only be biological but also meteorological. The island suffered a severe drought the year I was there, and some people believed that it was a divine punishment for the continuing high rate of out-of-wedlock pregnancies.

Conclusion

Having reviewed these incidents, we can summarize some points about the function of the indigenous healing cults on Expectation Island. One of the chief practices of the traditional healing cults, massage, is a good physical therapy for physical ills. However, massage is often used inappropriately for conditions that it cannot help, such as fractures, and for conditions that it may even worsen, possibly causing metastasis or carcinoma of the breast. Other physical agents, such as medicated oils and fire points, are probably of little or no physical value but seem to help psychologically by suggestion. The same is true, of course, of some of the treatment given by Western medical practitioners, which, intentionally or otherwise, works as a placebo.

An important function of the cult practitioners, one that Western-trained medical assistants cannot perform, is to remove the *aitu* (ghosts or evil spirits) that are believed to be causing bodily or behavioral symptoms, and are believed to have been put into a patient by someone with intent to do harm. The cult healers who can exorcise the spirits are the same persons who are believed able to cast them into a victim. A person who believes (correctly or falsely) that someone has performed such an act against him could easily fall sick by self-suggestion. In some cases (as with Lauto, who had meningoencephalitis) an organic medical illness is mistaken for a possession by spirits. Fortunately, the patients or their families usually play safe by seeking treatment from both the cult practitioner and the Western-trained medical assistant (*tulesa*) at the same time.

In some cases the cult practitioner treats psychological conditions by psychological means. An example is the teacher, whose feelings of guilt or embarrassment were relieved by the fostering of projection and rationalization. This kind of psychotherapy, working by self-deception, is the opposite of psychoanalytic or nondirective psychotherapy, which aims at self-awareness and congruence. Nevertheless, it can be highly effective.

The *vai laaqau* healing cult, based on old Polynesian beliefs, has reached a tentative compromise with beliefs of the Christian religion. Some Micronesian and Fijian methods of sorcery have been added to it.

REFERENCE

Mead, M. 1928. Coming of age in Samoa. New York, Morrow.

10.   Native Healers in Malaysia

DAVID KINZIE, Ph.D.

Department of Psychiatry
University of Hawaii
Honolulu, Hawaii

JIN-INN TEOH, M.D.

Department of Psychological Medicine
University Malaysia
Kuala Lumpur, Malaysia

ENG-SEONG TAN, M.D.

Department of Psychological Medicine
University of Malaysia
Kuala Lumpur, Malaysia

THIS PAPER deals with the theoretical framework underlying the native healing, and with the personalities of the native healers, in the three Malaysian cultures. The authors, all Western-trained psychiatrists, will describe interviews with a sample of native healers and comment on their healing methods. Rather than evaluate the therapeutic effectiveness of their methods, our goal is to convey, in a cross-cultural comparison, a sense of the diversity of their methods.

There are several reasons for studying these healers and their methods. First, the fact that they continue to help a large part of the community suggests a base of common assumptions underlying the diverse methods that operate in the several cultures. We wanted to discover what these assumptions were. Second, we wanted to determine the degree of correlation between the cultural beliefs about the causes of diseases and illnesses and the treatment offered by the native healers. Third, we wanted to find out—for obviously pragmatic reasons—how we as Westerners could work with these people in community psychiatric projects. These healers, who maintain their magical, religious orientation in an increasingly Western and materialistic environment, are widely consulted for emotional and personal problems. Is there a way they can be formally incorporated into mental health projects?

Studies on Ethnic Psychiatry

Other studies have called attention to the effects of native healing and psychotherapy. Lederer (1959) noted that primitive psychotherapies are effective in their own cultures perhaps because the native psychotherapist has a cognitive understanding of the causes of the anxiety in that culture and can therefore face the patient from a solid base of security. The therapist's own security then breaks the vicious cycle of insecurity and anxiety in the patient and his cultural group. Frank (1963) felt that the effectiveness of magical and religious healing lies in the ability to rouse hope for cure in the patient. The patient's hope is enhanced by a set of assumptions about the illness and healing that he shares with his society. The ideology and the rituals supply the patient with a conceptual framework for organizing his chaotic and vague distresses. It gives him a plan of action and helps him gain a sense of mastery. Religious healings may increase the patient's sense of self worth and focus the group's attention on him at the same time. The cure may be maintained by the changed attitude of the group, which constantly reinforces his cure. This point was reinforced by Ari Kiev (1964), who wrote that there are several universal elements in psychotherapy response and that specific cultural forces are important in the content and the techniques of psychotherapy. He felt that modern, Western psychotherapy may underestimate the emotional aspects of the process. The nonspecific effects of therapy, the group forces, and the powerful influence of the therapist have not been given the credit due them.

In her specific studies of shamans in Alaska, Jane Murphy found that the shaman has limited objectives (1964). The shaman focuses on removing the victim's symptoms and therefore his tension and anguish. The shaman does not, however, improve the victim's adaptation to circumstances or create changed attitudes that may help him in future situations. Also, there is no aim to foster independence or promote insight, which are considered goals in Western psychotherapy. Nevertheless, the shaman has a powerful combination of psychotherapeutic tools as long as the cultural group in which he practices remains intact. Kaplan and Johnson (1964) have reported that the effectiveness of Navaho curing seems to be based on two processes: (1) convincing the patient in a community that the causes of his difficulties have gone; (2) reaffirming the solidarity of the community and the Navaho deities with the patient. The ceremonies show concerned goodwill and serve to reintegrate the sick person into the social group. Torrey (1969) has also emphasized the use of native and indigenous healers in community mental health programs.

Culture and Methodology

Malaysia is a recent political union including the Malay Peninsula and the Sabah and Sarawak areas of Borneo. Our study includes the populations of the Malay Peninsula, where three major ethnic groups are located—the Malays, the Chinese, and the Indians. There is also a smaller segment of aborigines. Because of religious, ethnic, and linguistic differences, the groups have remained isolated. Despite the government's current attempt to promote a national identity and encourage ethnic mixing, isolation has persisted, and the culture of each group has remained to some extent intact. Thus, Malaysia is unique in having culturally distinct ethnic groups that are undergoing Westernization and are attempting to find both a national unity and an identity.

We are aware that our own patients at the University Hospital Psychiatric Service have a great deal of contact with native healers. A survey by Teoh and others (1971) showed that 31 percent of the patients had been seen by native healers before coming to us. Many continue to see them after leaving our service. Concurrent therapy between native healers and psychiatrists does exist.

The method we employed was an informal, semistructured interview with the healer, usually involving two psychiatrists from our department. Arrangements were made beforehand, and a time and place were agreed upon. All the healers interviewed resided within a short distance of Kuala Lumpur, the capital city. The interviews generally took between one and a half and two hours and were sometimes accompanied by the demonstration of techniques. Occasionally there was initial tension on one side or the other, but the interviews always proceeded well in an informal atmosphere, with the participants sometimes eating and drinking together. The conversations were tape-recorded, and a report of the interview made following our return to the hospital. The interview covered a wide variety of topics, but generally the following questions were asked. What kind of patients come to you? What kind of mental illness do you see? What do you think causes mental illness? What kind of treatment do you give? How would you treat a depressed patient? an agitated person? Do you give counseling or advice? What kind of counseling do you give? In addition, we covered such personal topics as the healer's training, ethics, fees, his personal life, and how he liked his work. In our report we gave an overall impression of how each healer, as an individual, came across in the interview and what personal characteristics might be influential in his counseling. In this report we will discuss only three of the cultures and only the healing activities related to psychological illnesses, whether due to physical or other problems. We will discuss aborigine healing as perhaps the most primitive and unsophisticated approach, then those found in Malay groups, and finally the healers found in the Chinese groups. These will be contrasted for simplicity of presentation.

Healers in their Cultures

Aborigines (Orang Asli).   The aboriginal peoples of the Malay Peninsula are the most primitive in terms of material culture. Their beliefs are animistic and correspond to the folk Malay religion, but without the latter's Islamic elaboration. The fifty thousand aborigines of the Peninsula tend to be scattered throughout the jungle areas, but many of them live in close proximity to urban communities. Regardless, their way of life is relatively unchanged as compared with the other groups and they have not yet received the full impact of Western culture. Many people consider the native healers of the aborigines among the most powerful and effective, probably because they are assumed to be closer to the spiritual world. The village (*kampong*) we visited is about ten miles from Kuala Lumpur and is isolated by about two miles of unimproved road. As with the Malays, the aboriginal shaman or native healer is called *bomoh*. The *bomoh* here, a man named Halim, was forty-seven years old and also the headman of the village. He met us in his loin cloth and we talked in the community meeting house. Halim treats all kinds of illnesses. The common treatment for complaints of fever and stomachache is a special kind of water. This water has received an incantation in native verse to render it more powerful. In cases of serious illness, this treatment will continue for several successive days. Halim can also give another medicine, one made up of a mixture of seven types of tree roots and barks. Again an incantation, called *jampi*, is performed over the mixture and it is given to the patient to drink. Sometimes the patient is bathed in water with a compound of seven types of flowers.

The *bomoh* said he sees some mental illness. One type, called *risau*, describes a person in a depressed state. Treatment consists of drinking a mixture of two or three varieties of roots boiled in water. Another type of illness, *terkena*, indicates a person who suddenly behaves abnormally without reason and may become paranoid, with delusions and hallucination. To treat this illness, the *bomoh* looks into a bowl of water to see how the patient became ill and to learn what type of spirit, called *gin* or *hantu*, has taken possession of him. After discovering the type of *gin* or *hantu*, he hunts for the roots and bark of trees or plants that make the particular spirit afraid. After finding them, he grinds them into a powder, which is boiled for drinking. A *jampi* is always performed before the mixture is taken, to politely ask the *gin* to leave, and sometimes it is necessary to use a *jampi* to chase out the evil spirit.

Any unexplained happening in the village is believed to be caused by *gin* or *hantu*. In the jungle there are many spirits, and a person will be attacked if he happens to offend them. In his own village Halim is usually consulted for common illnesses such as fever and headache, as well as for the mental illnesses mentioned. However, outsiders, particularly the Malays, come to ask his advice and help with love, medical, or sexual problems. He does not charge a fee for his treatment but does charge a fixed price for any charms that he uses. The *bomoh* listed various ingredients used in making charms, including elephant sperm, tiger claws, and rainwater falling on a Friday.

To us this *bomoh* appeared very vague about exactly how *gin* and *hantu* cause illnesses and the mechanism by which *jampi* or the charm cure them. His theoretical knowledge seemed quite unsophisticated and limited in connecting cause and cure of illnesses. On the other hand, he seemed to be an open, sincere, modest, simple man who was quite unpretentious in his outlook and accomplishments. Undoubtedly he was a good leader for his community.

Malays. The Malays are the biggest single group on the Malay Peninsula and generally are rural, conservative, and traditional. They are exclusively Moslem. However, their folk religion shows a mixture of animistic, as well as Hindu, and Moslem, influences. As noted by Endicott (1970), many magical elements remain in the Malay folk religion. The Malays' structural system of beliefs allows them to accept contradictory ideas such as Islam and magic quite readily.

Most illnesses are believed to be caused by supernatural forces, and healing is accomplished by magical methods that can control these forces, whether the illness is due to invasion by a spirit, loss of one's soul, or decrease in one's vitality. Resner and Hartog (1970) have classified the concepts of mental illness among the Malays. These concepts can be quite sophisticated, involving such ideas as a strain on the brain from too much studying; being charmed; and having an excessive religious preoccupation. Physiological explanations exist, too, as well as possession by spirits, *hantu* or *gin*. Susceptible people may be those who have lost their spirit (*semangat*). Healing depends on exorcising the agent that is in the person. These concepts are further elaborated by Chen (1970), who suggested that mental illness among the Malays may be the result of predisposing conditions such as the loss of *semangat*, mental stress, or incorrect behavior. These may be attributed to supernatural causes. The spirits also may act to cause physical disorders such as brain impairment or poor blood condition, which lead to mental illness.

The Malay native healer, the *bomoh*, is the culturally sanctioned person who has the power to control the supernatural world and to heal. The popular press is full of references to magical and mysterious healing powers of the *bomoh* (Danaraj, 1964). Many Western people also attest to their healing powers. Chen (1970) commented that the *bomoh* is a culturally sanctioned healer with powers that are accepted by both the patient and the social group. The *bomoh* may heal through words, acts, or rituals, in which *bomoh*, patient, and the social group all may participate. The *bomoh*'s ability to communicate with the spirit world raises the patient's hope of cure. The *bomoh*, when he goes into a trance to make a diagnosis, also makes the symptoms and problems the patient faces meaningful for him. In addition, the atmosphere surrounding exorcism is a highly charged one emotionally.

The rural Malay *bomoh* we interviewed, Inche Rahim, is fifty-five years old and owns a coffee shop about seven miles from Kuala Lumpur. In his home he showed us much of the paraphernalia he used in healing. It included a cloth, which he used as a headdress in playing various roles before a patient. He showed us a crystal in water that was alleged to contain elephant sperm, which has special healing properties. Inche Rahim said there were 199 types of mental illness, of which several were quite common. They included: *otak kening*, an illness due to a weak brain, which he was powerless to treat and would instead send the victim to a hospital; mental illness due to possession by the devil; mental illness due to a jealous person's spell; mental illness caused by contact with animals; and mental illness stemming from severe worries. The *bomoh* said that he also had a great deal of experience treating people diagnosed as having tuberculosis, which he felt was due to a poison.

The *bomoh*'s main treatment of mental illness was bathing the patient in a preparation containing lime, bones of fish or fowl aged for some time, and a number of other concoctions that included the leaves of various plants. If a person behaved abnormally or violently he was told to bathe in this water at intervals of one month. After three months he was expected to recover. Inche Rahim also used rubbing oil or oil massages and gave a talisman to the patient. Another favorite means of treatment, for a Moslem patient, was prayers. He would say a number of prayers in the patient's behalf. He treated some cases in his own home, and some in the home of the patient. Another method of treatment involved three consecutive days of bathing, prayers, oil massages, and incantations, after which the patient was sent home for three days, then brought back for three more days of treatment. By the third round, the patient was expected to be cured. Reluctantly the *bomoh* admitted to giving advice when he was faced with situations that could be remedied by changing one's attitude or looking at things in a different way.

Discussing mental illness, Inche Rahim mentioned an incident from his own experience, when he was very young. He began to act abnormally; he saw things falling on the floor, heard voices, and became very destructive, chopping down a number of trees. He remained this way for about six months and was cured by a *bomoh*, who treated him for three days.

In summary, this healer represents a blending of traditional native beliefs in spirits with some Moslem influence.

A second Malay *bomoh* we visited, Inche Lapang, lived in the urban area of Petaling Jaya. He was a retired police officer and had been a *bomoh* all his life. However, Inche Lapang did not believe in *gin* or *hantu* or evil spirits. His only belief was in God, although he admitted that many people in the rural areas still believed in spirits. He even felt that people who believed in *gin* and *hantu* were capable of being evil. Inche Lapang's long history as a powerful *bomoh* dated back to the Japanese occupation, when he cured a Japanese officer of impotence. Now he sees several patients a day in his home and also makes visits to patients' houses.

His treatment usually centers around verses quoted from the Koran. In the treatment he would mention the name of the patient, his age and sex, and the date on which the illness started; then he would murmur the verses again as he looked into a glass bowl of water. The bowl of water would be drunk by the patient, or the *bomoh* would use it to wipe the patient's face whenever pain occurred. Inche Lapang readily admits that the procedure could be done without the bowl of water, but claims that the water makes the ceremony more complete. Sometimes foil paper shaped like a ball was tied to the patient's wrist after verses from the Koran had been written on it. He doesn't see many mental patients but has had success with the few he has seen. Often his treatment of mental patients involved saying prayers from the Koran and giving the patient foil inscribed with Koran verses.

Inche Lapang acquired his experience when quite young, from various travelers in Malaysia, Borneo, and Sumatra. He said it is important for a *bomoh* to learn as much as he can from others so that he knows more ways of treating illnesses. If one method fails he could quote another verse from the Koran.

Inche Lapang is an intelligent, honest man who seemed to have a great deal of experience dealing with people. He was easy to talk with and gave helpful examples in his answers. He often emphasized the importance of the patient's faith in getting well—faith in the *bomoh* and in God. He seemed to be an effective, warm counselor with more sophisticated ideas than those we had previously seen.

It can be seen that there is a progression in sophistication from *bomohs* in jungle areas to those in an urban setting, involving a decrease in belief in the magical, spiritual world as a causation of illness and an increase in Moslem religious beliefs.

Chinese. The Chinese are the second largest group in Malaysia, making up approximately 40 percent of the population. They are located primarily in the urban areas and are widely known for their trading abilities. Although they are nominally Buddhist, their religion is actually a mixture of Buddhism, Confucianism, Taoism, and ancestor worship. As Elliott (1964) has pointed out, popular Chinese religion remains strongly oriented toward success in human affairs and tends not to see the world of man as an insignificant appendage of the spiritual world. The Chinese religion has a pantheon of many powerful, fearsome, and anthropomorphic spirits. These powerful spirits can be influenced by humans if the latter glorify them in ritual. The Chinese word *shen* indicates these spiritual beings who can possess mediums when they fall into trances. Elliott points out that many disasters in the world are believed to be caused by devils and other deities, and that only the *shen* can deal with them.

The spirit medium generally works in conjunction with a temple, which may be dedicated to a particular deity. As Comber (1958) states, when the medium goes into a trance, the spirits or the deity are believed to possess him and he is therefore in direct contact with the spiritual world. At that time, questions can be put to him concerning a wide variety of matters including sickness, misfortune, family problems, or business concerns. Most mediums are young men in their twenties, who must live blameless lives, including abstinence from alcohol and meat. Although mediums are widely patronized, their profession is not highly esteemed. They are consulted for a wide variety of illnesses, including headache, indigestion, tuberculosis, cancer, and mental illness. In the trance, the medium may suggest certain procedures for the patient to follow, or offer Chinese medicine to be taken. Occasionally the medium will advise the patient to go to the hospital for Western treatment, in which case he will give a special charm to protect the patient while in the hospital. In Elliott's 1964 survey, of 100 persons who had come to mediums for consultation, 198 topics were covered, including 53 cases of illness, 32 involving bad luck, 13 cases of possession by evil spirits, and only 3 cases involving insanity.

We visited two spirit mediums, one working alone in his own home and one associated with an elaborate temple. The former, a Mr. Lee, is an unmarried construction worker who has a small room in a crowded Chinese quarter of Petaling Jaya. He told us that he discovered that he had certain psychic powers so that he became able to contact spirits in a trance-like state. He discovered these powers accidentally and said that he uses them to help those who are suffering. He stated that his powers come from Buddha, although apparently other spirits are also involved. He generally sees three or four patients a week, all of whom were referrals from other patients he had cured or helped. Many of his cases are women with yin-yang imbalance (discussed in detail below). They complained of backache, lethargy, giddiness, bad vision, and general malaise. Other cases dealt with persons who had been put under a spell or affected by black magic. Mr. Lee would enter a trance-like state to gain contact with the spirits in the universe and to acquire psychic and spiritual powers for healing. He said that he sees two types of mental illness. One type is inherited or contracted when the patient is very young, and no cure is possible. The second type is caused either by evil spirits or excessive yearning and can be cured by the medium. Sometimes he may give the patient a prescription for Chinese medicine that can be bought from the local medical shop.

Mr. Lee went into a trance-like state for us by bringing his hands together in a praying position and by sitting in the lotus position. He then closed his eyes, concentrated intensely and bowed his head, pressing his praying hands firmly to his forehead. He made guttural noises, salivating so much that drops of saliva dripped onto the floor. His body jerked slightly, he sweated profusely, and breathed very heavily. He appeared to be in a tense state of concentration. All those in the room remained very quiet and watched calmly. During this trance he spoke in a "celestial language," which had to be interpreted by a fellow worker. Despite this, the medium a few times responded directly to questions put to him in Cantonese. He answered several personal questions put to him by our group but tended to be very vague about future problems or decisions. After a while he bowed very low to the floor, concentrated briefly, and in half a minute was out of the trance. He explained that he awoke because the spirit in his body was not free and had to go elsewhere, but he was still "in touch" with the spirit and able to answer questions. After the trance, he said that he felt much more relaxed and comfortable, but he was unable to remember what had transpired while he was in the trance.

This session was also attended by a group of local Buddhists who opposed the cult of spirit mediumship. Mr. Lee himself was tempted to join this group, but he was obviously quite reluctant to give up his mediumship. This created some conflict between him and his interpreter during the meeting. The medium liked being a medium and thought his practices worthwhile. He declared that he did not use his power for black magic or to harm others.

We concluded that Mr. Lee was a rather nondescript person having a vague idea of the theory of his work. He seemed to be a very simple, sincere man who was obviously playing a healing role within the community.

We saw more elaborate spirit-medium worship in a large temple outside Kuala Lumpur that we visited. This temple has a long history, and the building we saw was newly erected with publicly subscribed and government funds. We were met by the governing body of the temple, which had both Chinese- and English-speaking sections. We had long talks with members of this community and saw the medium in action. However, the medium was never introduced to us, and we had no opportunity to discuss his views with him directly.

The temple was intended primarily for members of the Chinese community, although others occasionally come for help. It is famous as the site of cures for physical and mental illnesses of all types. People also come for help in decision-making, family problems, and business difficulties. The system of problem solving seems to be a main preoccupation of those in the temple. About three hundred clients are seen a week. For help with an illness the charge was M$1.00, for personal problems and advice about the future, M$1.60. Common problems included where to locate one's next house and which direction a new building should face. The medium was said to be able to make contact with the spirit involved and therefore provide proper guidance for such important decisions. The client had only to say his name and the date, place, and time of his birth in the Chinese calendar. Then the medium or the spirit of the medium did some calculations and professed to know the exact reason why the client was there and made comments and recommendations. Although the temple officials said that counseling outside the mediumship was available, it seemed unlikely from our observations.

A mentally ill or psychotic individual could be brought to the medium and help would be given directly from the spirit. Or, his relatives could come on his behalf. The medium would then make some calculations and provide a diagnosis. He would then give the relatives a piece of yellow paper, with some Chinese characters written on it, and would tell them to burn it and put it in the patient's bath. He would also give them a piece of green paper with Chinese characters on it to burn and put in a drink for the patient. There were personal testimonies of mental illness cured by this procedure. Often the curing is not complete the first time and the client may return several times until he is well.

The temple clinic was open twenty-four hours a day and there was no formality about entry and registration. However, the medium worked officially from 9:00 A.M. to 6:00 P.M., with an hour off for lunch, and Fridays off as holidays. He received M$200 a month and was registered for a pension. When the crowd at the clinic becomes large enough, the medium goes into a trance and deals with the clients one at a time. His treatments lasted from five minutes to two hours. The medium usually gives the diagnosis first and then tells the patient what is wrong and what will happen to him in the future. He advised about medicines to take and prescribed certain Chinese drugs.

The medium we saw had lived far away from the temple and was allegedly chosen by the spirit who is the patron saint of the temple. He had to go through a ceremony to become a medium and had to be taught by the spirit how to play his part. Since we were not able to talk with him, he seemed merely a body in which the great spirit acted out its wishes. He did go into an elaborate ceremony for us and answered some personal questions. He seemed to be extremely perceptive in using nonverbal cues to make comments. There was no ongoing interaction between the medium and the clients, and the information seemed to go straight from the spirit through the body of the medium. The governing members of the temple seemed quite sincere in their belief in their temple. Its large following attests to its popularity. The impersonal techniques of its medium stand quite opposed to the more direct human involvement seen with the Malay *bomoh* and that is so much emphasized in Western psychotherapy.

We had a third contact with a temple medium, one who was a patient in our psychiatric ward. A young girl who was quite shy and withdrawn was encouraged by her friends to try temple mediumship in order to secure lucky numbers for the national lottery. Although quite reluctant, she somehow attained a trance state on three different occasions, but became frightened, and quite restless after each trance. On the third occasion she became extremely fearful and guilty about assuming the role of a spirit medium. She felt she was being punished by a spirit for it and became more withdrawn, developed headaches and fainting spells, and had visual hallucinations. This seemed to be a case in which a person with a vulnerable personality had an adverse reaction to being involved as a temple medium.

Chinese medicine. Classical Chinese medicine dates back 4000 years at least. It is based on the concepts of two opposing elements in cosmic forces, yin and yang, which must remain in harmony in the body to promote health (Comber, 1969). Treatment classically has been designed along the lines of applying the natural remedies based on the cosmic forces in the universe. According to Gwee (1971), in addition to the malfunction of yin-yang, disease can be caused by disruption of the flow of circulation along certain meridians in the body, in accordance with seasonal and diurnal changes. A number of diseases causing an imbalance can be put forward in the form of wind, evil or improper animus, or phlegm. Traditional Chinese medicine originally had five major groups: herbs, acupuncture and moxibustion, bone setting, surgery, magical rites, and miscellaneous practices. In Malaysia, herbal medicines and acupuncture are still popular.

In classical Chinese textbooks, according to Gwee, mental disorders are very little mentioned. There are descriptions of wind madness, ghost evil, anxiety due to wind affecting the five organs, anxiety occupation, convulsion madness, and madness of childbirth. Usually the heart is held responsible for behavior, but the heart is used symbolically rather than literally. The Chinese in Malaysia regard mental illness as a mixture of organic illness and mystical possession. When organic, it may be due to the invasion of a spirit, a bad soul, wind, phlegm, or other impurities that cause an imbalance of the organs, especially the heart and circulation. Common techniques use drugs to immunize foreign matter and to stabilize the heart. Acupuncture may be used to restore meridian circulation. There are specific types of mental illness reported. Wind madness may result from the entry of an evil wind into the yang system. The evil may come from the devil and his agents. Anxiety may be caused by the wind spirit, which affects the major organs of the body. Convulsion madness may be due to a weakness of the blood spirit. These all act upon the yin-yang harmony in the body.

An interesting study by Gwee and others (1969) cited a project in which 212 cases seen at the Chinese Physicians Association were diagnosed by Western-trained doctors. It was noted that the Chinese system of diagnosis is primarily symptomatic and that Chinese therapy is medically much different from Western. It was very difficult to compare the two systems. There was a great deal of overlap in gastric, intestinal, and dermatological matters. There was not, however, a higher percentage of neurotic illnesses than would be expected in a Western physician's practice.

The Chinese physicians who practice traditional Chinese medicine in

Malaysia are called *sinseh*. We visited two of them. The first was Mr. Ngeow, age 57, who has a large practice in the heart of Kuala Lumpur and is active in the Chinese Medical School in Malaysia. He was very open and personable. His shop was a busy one, stocked with both Western and Chinese medicines. The consultation room was large, and on his table were a stethoscope and sphygmomanometer. There were many chairs in the consultation room, and undoubtedly there was no privacy in patient consultations. He saw many cases of flu, cough, and peptic ulcer, and a few psychotic patients. There were many cases of emotional and psychosomatic problems, particularly females, who complained of palpitations, headaches, and insomnia. He believed that many of his clients have minor psychiatric disorders. He would judge by the patient's demeanor whether symptoms were due to personal problems. This Chinese physician feels that it is helpful for patients to talk about their problems, although privacy was a problem in his office. If personal problems were present, he did not investigate, because he feels it is impolite to embarrass patients. If patients were on the verge of tears, he would move to other topics because he felt that crying would further embarrass the patient. He would advise them not to worry and to be less anxious and sometimes would call them back a few days later for a second interview.

Various medications originating in China are said to help mental illness. The explanation for their efficacy is said to be that they cure yin-yang imbalance. These medicines tend to be expensive because of high import duty. Tranquilizers come in the forms of leaves, teas, barks, and roots. The latter can be given in a course of four to six doses. There is no need for maintenance therapy in any kind of Chinese treatment.

A primitive classification of Chinese medicine relates to mental illness. These are: excessive happiness (as in mania), excessive anger, excessive anxiety, and excessive preoccupation with certain thoughts, such as sorrow and sadness, or fear and fright. All these moods can lead to mental disorder. For some of these disorders Mr. Ngeow uses a "talking treatment"; for example, he tries to persuade the manic patient to be less happy. Often he would take a patient's pulse to make the diagnosis, but he said that was less accurate than using the sphygmomanometer. He also uses a thermometer, which may be more accurate than taking a temperature by hand. In many other ways he uses modern Western techniques, such as examination of the urine and blood.

Mr. Ngeow informed us that the Chinese Physicians Association in his community has about 130 members. The Association has a code of ethics but it is not backed by any government institution since Chinese doctors have no legal status. Interestingly, three of his children are Western-trained doctors, and only one was undergoing Chinese medical training. Mr. Ngeow obviously has Westernized his traditional Chinese beliefs a great deal. He was an expert on human relationships, being warm, friendly, and open. It was easy to understand how he had a large practice, though his work load gives him little time to go into the psychological problems of his patients in any depth.

Very different was the second *sinseh* we visited in a small shop in a predominantly English-speaking area. Mr. Siew is a small man who at first appeared tense and anxious in the interview. He received all his training locally, through a correspondence course and through study with a brother-in-law who is a more thoroughly trained *sinseh*. Mr. Siew's practice is small and he sees seven to eight patients a day. He described about 30 percent of his clients as suffering from psychosomatic disorders. He sees very few psychotic patients and usually refers them to a hospital immediately. The mentally disturbed patients he sees complained of insomnia, poor concentration, weak heart, fearfulness, and worries. He believed that psychiatric disorders may be due to too much heat within the body, especially in the brain and heart. He does not regard psychogenic causes as important in this type of illness. He would persuade the patient to relax, open up, and worry less. He also prescribes Chinese medicines, thirteen types in all, in various proportions and quantities. They usually must be brewed together to be effective. He encourages his withdrawn patients to laugh and to try to talk about what is bothering them. He feels that in such cases psychological release is important as well as drugs. But as he spends only a few minutes with each patient, that ventilation of feelings could not have been in depth. There is no privacy in his office; it is part of a Chinese general store.

Like other *sinseh*, he thought that five or six doses of any particular medicine would usually be effective. When pressed, he admitted that stress, as well as heat in the body, could cause illness. He found such stresses as financial loss, unfaithful spouse, ungrateful sons, unemployment, isolation, and loneliness are also common. We were struck by the fact that this *sinseh* did not charge for his consultation, only for the medicine, as he "wanted to build up his practice." He is not a member of the Chinese Physicians Association, although he reads Chinese textbooks daily to improve his knowledge.

Mr. Siew struck us as being a tense, nervous person. We speculated that he could be suffering from feelings of inferiority since he was in a locality whose residents generally patronized Western-trained general practitioners. His own personality could account for his difficulty in attracting clients.

Acupuncture. Acupuncture is a long-established Chinese method of healing, dating back at least 2000 years. In this method a needle is inserted into selected points on the skin, of which there are over six hundred. A specific point is selected for different diseases as diagnosed by the acupuncturist. The needles in current use are between two and two and one-half inches long and about the diameter of hypodermic needles. Generally, alcohol is used to sterilize the needle and the skin area to be punctured. The needles now are of metal; previously, bamboo ones were used (Chew 1963). Mann, a British-trained doctor, has written extensively about acupuncture. According to his study (1962), a Chinese concept Q, energy of life, is thought to flow in the meridians in the body in constant flux. When there are disruptions in this flow, illness can result. The meridians are paired on each side of the body, and each has a yin-yang component. Although the author used Western concepts to explain the meridians, he noted that the basic elements in the universe, yin-yang, are related to the function of acupuncture. The efficacy of this technique has not been established, but Mann quotes figures to show that, of the cases applicable, which include a wide range of illnesses, about two-thirds show cure or improvement after acupuncture therapy.

The acupuncturist we visited was actually a physician trained in a modern

Chinese medical school. Mr. Low came to Malaysia about fifteen years earlier, and since his degree was not recognized he limited his practice to Chinese medicine and acupuncture. Acupuncture actually formed a small part of his medical curriculum in China. Mr. Low has a very active practice, and regards approximately five percent of his patients as neurotic. He sees very few psychotic patients, but feels he can treat some milder forms of this illness. For some forms of anxiety neurosis he usually prescribes certain herbs in addition to acupuncture. Mr. Low feels that the steel needle activates a sensitive fiber. It stimulates the nerve, which has retrograde effects and travels to parts of the body to produce a specific tranquilizing and therapeutic effect. He also feels that acupuncture can restore yin-yang harmony in the body. The needles may be placed just under the skin, or to a depth of six to eight centimeters and be left there for a few minutes, or for about forty minutes in serious illnesses. Mr. Low readily admitted that acupuncture may be used as a placebo for people who just want to try a "new form of treatment."

Mr. Low, whose office has a great deal of privacy, felt that it was important for patients to talk about their problems. He said that many of his patients are very reluctant to talk about personal problems but concentrate on their somatic complaints. Often a patient had to come for eight to ten sessions before he was willing to reveal his personal problems. He felt that establishing friendship with the patient was important.

Mr. Low was an open and warm person. His techniques are modern, and his concepts of psychosomatic medicine are beyond those of the more traditional Chinese physicians. It was difficult to establish or understand the scientific basis for acupuncture. It seemed to be an empirical form of treatment whose efficacy is difficult to establish and whose principles are difficult to conceive in a Western frame of reference.

Analysis

This presentation has dealt with some of the activities of, and interviews with, various native healers in Malaysia. It is not meant to be exhaustive but to demonstrate some of the beliefs and practices that exist in these three ethnic groups. We purposely met with people of differing theories and various degrees of sophistication; in this manner we gained some overall impressions.

For the Western-trained psychiatrist, the experience was indeed a rewarding one. We learned of some social influences that affect our patients, and gained some understanding of the other therapies used before, during, and after our treatment. It was also rewarding to meet personally with these healers and to talk with them about their views on the healing process. The fact that we were met warmly and that the discussions were cordial implies that initial communication with this group is difficult; perhaps it is the beginning of an ongoing exchange.

Some common elements in all these groups emerge. The sincerity of all the healers cannot be doubted. They believed in their work and were dedicated to helping others, often with little financial gain. They tended to be humble about their techniques and about their own personal accomplishments. Generally they were quite approachable and easily available, which may account for their popularity in the community. Although their personal characteristics varied a great deal, most were warm, sympathetic people who undoubtedly are skilled in human relationships.

The native healers are able to communicate with their patients in idioms and nuances that are most intelligible to the patients. A Western (and in effect English-language) education gives the psychiatrist a new, and often alien, set of ethics and values that is not shared by his patients. This is not so with the native healers, who have not lost "the common touch."

In each group there are certain people who act as healers, consistent with the values of that group. However, there are great differences in their sophistication and in their understanding of their practice. We found that not all *bomoh* are the same, nor are all Chinese *sinseh*, or spirit mediums. Some undoubtedly believe in the spiritual or abstract qualities behind their work, and some recognize the placebo effect quite consciously. Although each group tends to have its own healers, there was much overlap in this multiracial region. *Bomoh* treat Chinese and *sinseh* treat Malays. (The most outstanding example, which was not reported, was that of an Indian Hindu priest, who stated that the majority of his patients were Chinese looking for spiritual support for their business ventures.)

It was obvious that these healers operate consistently on certain basic psychotherapeutic principles. Undoubtedly they all raise hopes and give the patient an understandable cause of his distress, whether it is due to a bad spirit or to yin-yang imbalance. This undoubtedly lessens the anxiety of the patients and in itself may be therapeutic. That this analysis is sometimes done in a group without privacy may indeed evoke the entire group's support and expectation that the patient would get well. As Frank (1963) has noted, if the patient does not improve, he will be letting the whole world down.

The personality of the therapist appeared more important in some systems than in others. The *bomoh* and *sinseh* would be a good example of this importance. The ones we talked to, were at best, warm, sympathetic people who seemed open and nondefensive. In line with Truax and Wargo's (1966) work on the personality of the therapist as important in psychotherapeutic change, these people may have a distinct advantage, and really promote healing on the basis of their own personality.

Many Western writers, as exemplified by what has been written above, have tended to idolize the work of the native healers. Although it may not be fair to criticize them from another frame of reference, that is, from Western psychotherapy, it does seem to us, who have worked with the same population, using our own technique, that certain problems with the approach of the native healer must be mentioned. It is rare for any of them to engage the patient in private consultation outside the group and to encourage the patient to state personally how he sees his problems. In this sense it has strengthened denial, repression, and rationalization. Our own experience with many patients in the same cultures indicates that many feel extremely relieved to be able to discuss personally and privately their own problems. In many of the native therapies, the diagnosis is entirely a work of magical, religious speculation and has nothing to do with the patient's own interpretations of the difficulty. It is extremely rare to go into the depths of the personality of the patient, and the interpersonal and intrapsychic stresses that he may be feeling.

On experience has been that these healers deal with the illnesses and problems of their patients at a symptomatic, phenomenological level and that none of them seems consciously to try to understand the psychodynamic bases for the emotional and psychiatric problems of their patients. Without doubt, they mostly respond to their patients in a psychodynamically appropriate fashion, but they never try to formulate the underlying basis of the psychosomatic or emotional problems of their patients in terms that suggested a basic understanding of psychodynamics as we know them.

Furthermore, none of these healers engages the patient in a long-term relationship. Rarely do they call the patient back for more than two visits, since the emphasis is on rapid cure. Many of our patients have needed a long-term relationship with a consistent doctor or healer whom they can rely upon for help during the illness and who will allow them freedom for increased responsibility and growth. Certainly these concepts are Western, not indigenous ones. That our patients have responded to our approach would lead us to believe that its lack is either a cultural deficiency that the native healers have not been able to remedy or that Western influences have increased the demand for it.

Generally, however, patients are not given the choice between native healers and Western-trained psychiatrists but between native healers and Western-trained general medical practitioners with extremely limited knowledge of psychiatry and perhaps of interpersonal relationships in general. The local medical practitioners are also geared to rapid consultation, with little chance for patients to discuss their own personal problems and feelings. Treatment by pills may seem vague and irrelevant. Perhaps, by comparison, the work of a native healer does seem more personal and more immediate to the needs of these patients.

A further question remains: Do the healers do any harm? Certainly, their treatment is primarily aimed toward psychosomatic and neurotic patients. We should be modest in our own ability to treat these patients; often we can offer little that is better as a means of help. This certainly is not true for psychotic patients, for whom we now have effective treatment. If the healers give false hope to or delay treatment of those psychotics in which early intervention would be decisive, then undoubtedly they are causing some harm. Some of our patients were treated by native healers before the family finally consulted a Western psychiatrist. Here again, the healers may not be particularly disadvantaged compared with some Western-trained general practitioners whose experience in psychiatry is also limited, and who themselves have difficulty referring psychiatric patients.

A final goal we had sought in our study was to determine methods by which native healers could be utilized in community mental health programs.

Undoubtedly they form a strong, active link in the management of many emotionally disturbed patients. When we asked them specifically about this question they all expressed a desire for closer cooperation with Western doctors and psychiatrists. However, they had no idea how this could be arranged, and we did not develop specific plans with any of them. The fact that the government is deprecating their position in the community also makes more formal arrangements with them difficult. The tendency for most native healers to work in isolation outside an administrative agency makes it impossible to influence them as a body. How they can be incorporated into some form of community mental health program represents a real challenge.

Summary

This report describes Malaysian psychiatrists' interviews with and impressions of local native and traditional healers in aborigine, Malay, and Chinese societies in Malaysia. The healers represent a wide range of sophistication and technical skills, but most believe in some sort of magical, religious cause of illness. They operate within the cultural assumptions of causes of illness and therefore meet the expectations of their patients, which lessens anxiety. Their sincerity and devotion to their patients seem clear, and also produce therapeutic results. However, almost universally, they aimed toward rapid cures based on appeals to authority figures or authoritative approaches. There was little concern for privacy to encourage the patient to state his problems and concerns, and to develop his own solutions. None engaged in long-term therapy or support. It would be difficult to incorporate them into mental health programs in Malaysia with their current state of development.

REFERENCES

Chen, P.C.Y. 1970. Indigenous Malay psychotherapy. Tropical and Geographical Medicine 22:409–15.

Chew, P.K. 1963. Acupuncture—an ancient Chinese art of healing. Singapore Medical Journal 4:151–57.

Comber, L. 1958. Chinese temples in Singapore. Singapore, Eastern Universities Press.

———. 1969. Chinese magic and superstitions in Malaya. 4th ed. Singapore, Eastern Universities Press.

Danaraj, A.G.S. 1964. Mysticism in Malaya. Singapore, Asia Publishing Company.

Elliott, A.J.A. 1964. Chinese spirit-medium cults in Singapore. Singapore, Donald Moore.

Endicott, K.M. 1970. An analysis of Malay magic. Oxford, Clarendon Press.

Frank, J.D. 1963. Persuasion and healing. New York, Shocken Books.

Gwee, A.L. 1971. Traditional Chinese methods of mental treatment. *In* Psychological problems and treatment in Malaysia. N.N. Wagner and E.S. Tan, eds. Kuala Lumpur, University of Malaysia Press.

Gwee, A.L., Y.K. Lee, and N.B. Tham. 1969. A study of Chinese medical practice in Singapore. Singapore Medical Journal 10:2–7.

Kaplan, B., and D. Johnson. 1964. The social meaning of Navaho psychopathology and psychotherapy. *In* Magic, faith and healing. A. Kiev, ed. New York, Free Press of Glencoe.

Kiev, A., ed. 1964. Magic, faith and healing. New York, Free Press of Glencoe.

Lederer, W. 1959. Primitive psychotherapy. Psychiatry 22:255–65.

Mann, F. 1962. Acupuncture—the ancient Chinese art of healing. London, Willam Heinemann Medical Books.

Murphy, J.M. 1964. Psychotherapeutic aspects of shamanism on St. Lawrence Island, Alaska. *In* Magic, faith and healing. A. Kiev, ed. New York, Free Press of Glencoe.

Resner, L., and J. Hartog. 1970. Concepts and terminology of mental disorders among Malays. Journal of Cross-Cultural Psychology 1:369–81.

Teoh, J.I., J.D. Kinzie, and E.S. Tan. 1971. Why patients attend psychiatric clinics: break the barrier. Proceedings of the Sixth Singapore-Malaysia Congress of Medicine. Singapore.

Torrey, E.F. 1969. The case for the indigenous therapist. Archives of General Psychiatry 20:365–73.

Truax, C.B., and D.G. Wargo. 1966. Psychotherapeutic encounters that change behavior: for better or for worse. American Journal of Psychotherapy 20:499–520.

11.   Folk Diagnosis and Treatment of Schizophrenia: Bargaining with the Spirits in the Philippines

GEORGE M. GUTHRIE, Ph.D.

Department of Psychology
Pennsylvania State University
University Park, Pennsylvania

DAVID L. SZANTON, Ph.D.

The Ford Foundation
Manila, Philippines

THE STATUS of our understanding of schizophrenia and the empirical rationale of most of our treatment programs suggest that almost all attempts to help schizophrenics should be called prescientific. Since we remain uncertain about the causes of this behavior disorder and are unable to develop satisfactory treatments because we do not know the causes, we might learn a great deal from examining an apparently successful treatment based on a conceptualization markedly different from our own.

Summary of the Case Study

In mid-1965, Juanita, a 14-year-old girl living in a lowland fishing town in the Philippines, came home from high school one day extremely agitated and then fled to a nearby town, pursued by her parents. She successfully evaded them and ultimately was apprehended by the police in a third town some ten kilometers away. She resisted the police but was forcibly subdued and held. Her family brought her back home, but during the following weeks similar episodes were repeated. Eventually she had to be restrained by ropes in her house. On the advice of a local physician, Juanita was taken to the National Mental Hospital in Manila. While there she received electroshock therapy, her symptoms subsided, and after about one year of treatment she was returned home substantially calmer than before though still obviously troubled. Shortly after her return she became violent again, physically attacking family members, ripping at her clothes, running into the street, insulting townspeople, and stealing from stores. Her family found it necessary to chain her to the floor of an old house some distance from the one in which they were living.

About this time her mother began actively seeking the help of local *babaylans*, or mediums, since there was a strong suggestion that Juanita's illness was not due to natural causes but to possession by spirits. Over the following six to eight months the mother successively called upon seventeen *babaylans* in her community and the neighboring towns and islands to attempt to cure the girl. It was only the seventeenth, a 54-year-old woman, Susang, from a town some forty kilometers away, who was able to help Juanita. The treatment was very brief. First Susang took Juanita's pulse at the radial artery and then rubbed her head whorl with ginger (a widely used medicament) and blew on it. By this means she was able to divine (*patpat*) that the illness was due to the ancestral spirits' anger at the family for failing to follow an inherited tradition. Next, she prepared a medicine bundle (*tuos*) containing a small package of rice and an egg wrapped in banana leaf, placed it on Juanita's head, and with the consent of the family promised the spirits an elaborate ceremony (*pabatak*) to be repeated annually, and on grand scale every seven years, if the spirits would release their hold on the girl. As a token or symbol of the promised ceremony, the *tuos* was left hanging in the rafters of the house. For these services Susang received ₱ 7.50 (approximately US$2.00).

In three days Juanita's symptoms disappeared. Her memories of the previous two years were vague, confused, and partial, but her behavior was fully normal. She soon returned to high school, graduating with honors two years later. She appeared quite relaxed, and in small groups and social situations she smiled easily and generally participated in a fashion typical of girls of her age. Aside from being some twenty pounds overweight, as were her mother and sisters, nothing set her apart from other girls in her age group.

The locally accepted explanation for her recovery was that Susang had been able to diagnose, i.e., divine, the root cause of the problem and then communicate with and appease the spirit(s) who had taken possession of the girl. More specifically, the logic of her illness and cure in simplified and schematic form was as follows:

1. Juanita's deceased maternal grandparents and several other ancestors were known to have been *babaylan*.

2. The skill or calling of being a *babaylan* is hereditary or traditional within a family, though no more than one member of each generation need become a *babaylan*.

3. Juanita's grandparents' spirits, and perhaps others, were angry at her mother for not having accepted the calling. The mother was indeed a *herbalario*, or folk medical practitioner, who treated natural illnesses with roots, herbs, and in her case, powdered snakeskin (the snakes, incidentally, were kept in cages under the house). But she did not—would not or could not—deal with spirits.

4. In an attempt to pressure the mother into *babaylan*ship several years

earlier, the spirits had caused the illness and eventual death of her four-year-old son, Juanita's younger brother, and several other serious family problems.

5. The ancestral spirits would be satisfied if they were promised a ceremony in which Juanita or her mother, or both, would recognize their tradition or inheritance, establish communication with the spirits via possession, and become a *babaylan*.

6. Susang's promise of what was in effect an initiation ceremony was convincing; it reached the right spirits, assuaged their anger, and prompted them to release their hold over the girl.

7. No longer possessed by the angry spirit(s), Juanita returned to her normal self.

The Philippines is, of course, a Christian country. Although small Muslim and pagan minorities exist, some 80 percent of Filipinos are Roman Catholics and another 10–12 percent profess one or another Protestant faith. Christianity did, however, arrive relatively late in the Philippines, and it overlays earlier animistic systems that are still very strong in most rural areas and among the rurally raised in the cities. It is important to stress that in this setting the Christian and animistic systems are not in conflict but are both fully functional and mutually complementary. The Christian religions (and Islam) deal with high gods and ultimate realities. Philippine animism focuses on the daily influence of ancestral spirits and an elaborate pantheon of fairies, demons, and deities, especially as they affect illness and health. As might be expected, Philippine animism is quite similar in form and content to the animistic systems underlying Islam in Indonesia and Malaysia. Thus, while the local explanation for Juanita's illness and cure clearly lay in this ancient animist world, she and her family, and all of the participants in the ceremony described below, were avowed Roman Catholics. Conflicts in this context between Christianity and animism exist only in the minds of external observers when they apply their own inappropriate categorization.

The Utility of Cross-Cultural Research

The study of disordered behavior in other cultures may sharpen or even disprove theories formulated in work with patients in Europe and North America. There are, broadly speaking, four different emphases on etiological factors: genetic, physiological, early childhood, and current social experiences, plus, of course, theories that seek to integrate two or more of these general causal domains. By and large we are powerless to manipulate gene pools, not knowing which biochemical factors to raise or lower; we do not have the authority or time to vary systematically childhood experiences; and we have only recently begun to manipulate with some effectiveness the current social pressures on a patient. Cross-cultural studies, in contrast, may provide variations in each of these four domains that would be very difficult to bring about in one society. The problem with natural experiments is, of course, that nature runs an untidy laboratory.

Mednick and Schulsenger (1968) carried out important genetic studies in Denmark, where low migration and well-kept records provide a much better setting than does our highly mobile society of recent immigrants in the United States. Rauwolfia was used for centuries in India before Europeans and Americans obtained it, and many psychotomimetic drugs have been and still are used in many different countries. If a relationship can be found across cultures between patterns of child rearing and the incidence of schizophrenia, psychodynamic formations will be supported, and the schizophrenogenic mother will be established on a broader basis than is currently available. Finally, the behavior modifier who emphasizes current reinforcement contingencies and models may find support for his position if schizophrenia varies markedly in both pattern and incidence from one culture to another.

Alien societies are not likely to provide a setting for a crucial experiment on the relative validity of these four theories of the nature of schizophrenia, but they do provide a setting in which important factors are varied or controlled to a degree that is not true in our own society. Furthermore, data from other societies may bear not only on etiology but on treatment as well. The treatment of schizophrenia is such an uncertain art that we can also learn much by observing the circumstances in which schizophrenics in different cultural settings recover.

Folk Treatments of Schizophrenia

Much of the literature on cross-cultural studies of major mental illness is concerned with symptom pictures. It seems safe to say that something like schizophrenia appears in all the societies in which it has been sought. Frequency data are more difficult to interpret, however, because criteria and case-finding methods vary. In the Philippines, the locus of our research, Sechrest (1964) has suggested that disabling mental illness is possibly only one-tenth as frequent as it is in North America. Symptom pictures vary greatly, especially the content of delusional ideas, which are intimately an expression of the community's belief systems and the current technology. We can see this if we review the history of delusional content in our own hospitals over the past century. Culture-bound psychoses (Yap, 1969) remain an unsolved riddle partly because the question of whether they are unique syndromes depends on one's conceptual system. Following a medical model, they may indeed be different pathological processes; from the perspective of a learning approach, however, they are all learned, with differences due to local variations in models and role expectations.

Much less attention has been directed to treatment, even though probably all societies try in one way or another to reduce the disruptive symptoms of a psychotic in their midst. Interestingly enough, a great contribution to the treatment of psychotics has been rauwolfia, from which the whole family of tranquilizers has been developed. This medicinal root has been used for centuries in India and elsewhere. In addition to herbs, traditional healers use a wide variety of spiritual and psychological techniques that do not involve any biochemical intervention.

Our concern in this paper is with healers' attempts to alleviate symptoms by placating spirits of various sorts or by reducing the effects of sorcery, where there is widespread acceptance of sorcery and spirit activity. These activities lend themselves to analysis by such social-psychological concepts as modeling, role playing, demand character of situations, suggestion, and the more medically oriented placebo effect. Changes once induced can be maintained by reinforcements provided by both the healer and the patient's family. The patients often recover, with no insight in the usual sense, in a therapeutic relationship that may be quite intense but in which there is little if any resolution of transference as that process is commonly conceived. After observing healing practices among Vodun groups in Haiti, Kiev (1964) suggested:

> The hope, expectation, and faith of the patient in the designated
> healer, coupled with the healer's use of meaningful symbols and
> group forces might contribute more to the therapeutic results
> than is ordinarily recognized in contemporary theories of
> psychodynamic psychiatry.

The challenge is to identify across a wide variety of treatment situations those elements that frequently accompany the reduction of symptoms. This is a difficult task within one's own culture; it is still more formidable in an alien culture. While one can conceivably record and translate the verbal exchanges involved in treatment, it is much more difficult to identify the equally important nonverbal communications and role expectations that prevail. Finally, because members of various societies have different nonverbal reinforcements that shape and maintain different behavior patterns, it becomes exceedingly difficult to identify all the ways in which a group may seek to modify the behavior of a member and to maintain the modifications after they have occurred.

One does not need to go to a preliterate society, however, to find prescientific treatments of schizophrenics. One of the authors has described powwowing among the Pennsylvania Germans, a treatment procedure that involves repeating certain incantations, prayers, the laying on of hands, and other magical steps (Guthrie and Noll, 1966). The healer, or powwow doctor as he is called, treats a wide variety of physical disorders and occasionally "tries for" the mentally ill. We first encountered the practice in a psychiatric hospital when various patients reported that they had been powwowed before they came to the hospital. Relying on a volume called the *Sixth and Seventh Books of Moses* and on incantations learned from an experienced powwower, the twentieth-century Pennsylvania healer can engage in all three orders of activity that we will outline later: intervention with higher spirits (in this case the Christian God), sorcery and countersorcery, and the treatment of natural disorders. Recovery is said to depend to a considerable extent on the patient's faith, or on the faith of his parents if he is a child. The powwower believes that he takes the illness to himself and then "puts it off." We have no idea how successful he may be with psychotic patients since we saw only cases where powwowing had failed. It is important for a psychotherapist in Pennsylvania to understand this practice because it indicates the way a certain group of Pennsylvanians understands physical and mental illness. When we learned about the process we were less puzzled that our patients and their relatives seemed not to appreciate the role of traumatic childhood experiences and of distorted mother-child relationships in the development of schizophrenia. The talking cure seemed to them a waste of time, whereas they considered pills a meaningful way of coping with whatever was causing their mental illnesses.

Research on mental illness from a cross-cultural perspective has suffered because few competent investigators have any significant depth of experience or language skill outside their own society. Psychiatrists and psychologists have no tradition of research abroad, and few anthropologists have interest and competence in psychopathology. In addition, the theoretical outlook that has dominated theory and practice with mental illness has offered explanations but posed few testable questions that could be answered by data from new settings. The result is that, from Malinowski on, observations of behavior in non-Western areas have produced no significant changes in psychoanalytic theories. We hope that with increasing sophistication, clinicians who are citizens of other cultures will carefully evaluate our Western theories against their data instead of uncritically accepting alien theories from high-status foreigners.

Prescientific Treatment of Schizophrenia

Most reports of prescientific attempts to treat mental illness come from observations in West Africa and among American Indians, fewer from the Caribbean and Malay areas. There are some remarkable similarities in explanations and treatments of illness from widely scattered points of the globe. The three categories of causes mentioned earlier—supernatural, sorcery, and natural—appear in Africa, Latin America, and Southeast Asia (Denko, 1966). Treatments follow differentially, depending on the diagnosis. Diagnosis or divination frequently depends on apparently involuntary activities of the healer such as seeing the face of the agent in some liquid, interpreting the balancing or movement of an object held in the hand, or measuring parts of the body (a sort of precursor of psychometrics?). In many instances, the healer takes the patient's pulse and intuits the causal agent in a sort of message "delivered to his mind."

A good deal of the psychopathology literature is based on a medical model, interpreting behavior disorders in the same way we interpret physical illness. Native healers, also, it would seem, embrace a medical model insofar as they tend to attribute both physical and behavioral disorders to similar orders of causes and to treat them with similar strategies.

A few examples of diagnosis and treatment may be appropriate. Levy (1967), one of the few psychiatrists who has spent long enough in the field to develop a deep understanding of an alien society, reports that the Tahitian healer differentiates natural illnesses from those due to spirits and those due to an affront to God or the natural order. Diagnosis is based on a history taken from the patient and from his family. Treatment, consonant with the prevailing Tahitian emphasis on calmness, a casual approach to life, and avoidance of interpersonal stress, causes the patient and his relatives to seek social reintegration. At the same time some of his symptoms are attributed to spirits, and these spirits are urged to leave the body of the patient. Levy notes that the healer, usually a successful, esteemed individual, serves as a model for the sufferer, while relatives and neighbors facilitate the patient's resumption of expected patterns of participation in Tahitian society.

The Zar ceremony of the Nubians of the upper Nile exemplifies a different pattern for alleviation of interpersonal stresses, and a different pantheon. Kennedy (1967) suggests that this ceremony is a sort of last resort when other treatments have failed, an acknowledgment that up to this point the spirits or *jinn* have won. The ceremony is conducted by women who have themselves been cured in earlier Zar sessions and are obligated to attend to keep the spirits satisfied. The patient is dressed in white and placed in the center of a large, dimly lighted, overheated room. There is much music and dancing addressed to various spirits, an activity in which the patient finally participates. There may be an animal sacrifice, with blood from the animal smeared on the patient. Kennedy observed that while introspection and insight are not emphasized in the Zar ceremony the patient has the constant support of the group rather than rejection, as happens in some societies.

Baasher (1967) has described the same Zar ceremony farther up the Nile in the Sudan. Again, diagnosis is a matter of differentiating between symptoms caused by sorcery, spirits, or breaking a taboo. The Zar practitioner leads a healing ceremony of drumming, singing, and dancing until a dissociative state is achieved. In addition to suggestion and demand character, the therapeutic elements include a widely shared, confident expectation of healing.

The treatment centers of West Africa constitute most interesting prescientific hospitals with inpatient and outpatient services. Those in Ghana were described by Field (1960) and those in Nigeria by Prince (1964). In the Nigerian center, the patient receives a mixture of herbal remedies and participates in a number of magical ceremonies calculated to counteract the agents causing the illness. These centers operate on a fee basis, but they provide for a good deal of participation by relatives, who maintain close contact with the patient. A second form of treatment which Prince feels is undertaken after other methods have failed is initiation into a cult dedicated to a group of spirits. This initiation involves intense participation over several days in which the initiate is subject to clear expectations which are fulfilled when the patient loses consciousness and is possessed by the spirit. Thereafter, the cult members continue treatment and support of the patient, showing their expectations of his recovery. Also in a later study (Prince et al., 1968), Prince has emphasized the effectiveness and the cultural relevance of these treatment techniques in Yoruba culture even though the insight fundamental to much Western therapy is absent.

In a society whose cultural patterns are closely related to those of the Philippines, Chen (1970) examined indigenous concepts and practices in a Malaysian community near the Thai border. Because medicine men were apparently handling the bulk of mild mental illnesses, Chen raised the question whether they might be integrated into the general mental health program. His ensuing report of their classification system and their notions about causation of mental illness shows many elements in common with African beliefs and a close resemblance to those in the Philippines. Illness may be due to evil spirits, witchcraft, or to excessive mental concentration. Chen points out that "The indigenous methods of treatment practiced by the *bomoh* [native healer] are a logical corollary of the concepts of causation." To neutralize physical causes the *bomoh* uses herbal remedies or mystical invocations, while he practices exorcism in dealing with illnesses believed to be caused by witchcraft or spirits. In doing so, Chen observes, "the *bomoh* incorporates such elements as group participation and support of the emotionally disturbed individual."

Like other countries, the Philippines show a fascinating syncretization of ancient beliefs and practices with more recent Western religion and even more recent modern medicine with its array of drugs. One finds the cross, the mass, and other Christian symbols used as amulets or as propitiating actions toward a congeries of unseen but powerful spirits. Healers provide antibiotics, incantations, and herbs t.i.d. or q.i.d., sequentially or simultaneously. Diagnostic aids may include thermometers and stethoscopes as well as the bile duct of a ceremonially sacrificed chicken.

Hart (1969) has shown that the Greek humoral theories of Hippocrates and later of Galen may well have been brought to the Philippines by the Spanish. Beyond the notion that bodily states were influenced by the balance of blood, phlegm, yellow bile, and black bile was the classification of illnesses and remedies as hot or cold. Hart makes passing reference to mental illness, indicating only that, like various physical symptoms, mental illness may be caused by a disturbed balance of body elements as well as by supernatural agencies. Treatment, of course, follows from diagnosis, with an attempt to restore the balance of hot and cold. This involves extensive knowledge of specifically what are hot and what are cold foods. Hart said that he was unable to discover the system of classifying food items as hot or cold.

Working in the same region as Hart, Lieban (1967) examined sorcery in a rural and in an urban setting. The healer (*mananambal*) had to be prepared to counteract sorcery and witches and to propitiate spirits and ancestors, as well as to deal with illness not of supernatural origin but due to such factors as fright, worry, fatigue, or exposure to wind. For diagnosis the *mananambal* relied on symptoms, the patient's pulse, his medical history or on nonsensory sources. He might suspend a winnowing basket on a string and ask a series of questions. Positive or negative answers would be indicated by movements of the suspended basket. Others "heard" directly from spiritual sources in the form of thoughts or whispers. Their treatment techniques included poultices, fumigation, anointing, prayers, incantations, and magical procedures. Most also used medicinal plants. Lieban's informants were reluctant to discuss their own countersorcery or their willingness to practice sorcery against a victim in return for a client's fee. Unfortunately for our purposes, because Lieban was not concerned with mental illness in his research, he did not give an account of the diagnosis and treatment of a behavior disorder.

In each of the instances we have cited, both diagnosis and treatment are carried out using concepts and procedures that are understood and respected by the patient, his family, and the therapist. The diagnostic procedure follows inevitably from the cosmology, and the treatment follows logically from the diagnosis. The patient and his family watch and often participate in the diagnostic and treatment activities. There are no professional case conferences, laboratory studies, or psychological testing from which the patient and relatives are excluded, both conceptually and physically. We suggest that the result is a therapeutic milieu in which social-psychological processes operate to call for behavior change and reinforce socially approved behavior as it is elicited.

Analysis of the Case Study

Background. Our background information on Juanita is limited because a case history interview was not in keeping with the junior author's relationship with her family. What we do know indicates that her childhood was similar in many ways to those of Western schizophrenic patients. Juanita's father, who was given to violent outbursts, had injured other members of the family in fits of anger. Juanita's troubles were said to have begun in a large city on another island when she was courted by a young man who later disappeared. When as an adolescent she came home disturbed, some neighbors felt that the boy had been a supernatural creature in a boy's guise sent by angry ancestral spirits to take her. Such events in her life could have laid the background of guilt and fear that is frequently found in young adult schizophrenics.

Diagnosis. As we indicated earlier, a *babaylan* goes through the familiar steps of diagnosis and treatment. We must bear in mind that without an *American Psychiatric Association Diagnostic and Statistical Manual of Mental Disorders* II, there is considerable variation from one *babaylan* to another in nomenclature, presumed etiology, and treatment strategies. The following case, however, reveals features that we believe are commonly found in the Philippines.

The initial stages of treatment by a *babaylan* usually involve three steps: diagnosis, divination, and the offering of the promise. In the first stage, the *babaylan* must determine whether the patient's illness is natural, the result of sorcery or magic, or the result of the activities of *tamawo,* usually invisible human "doubles," fairies, or various manifestations of ancestral, geographical, or divinating spirits. To determine the cause of the illness the *babaylan* takes the patient's pulse, at the radial artery immediately adjacent to the wrist, at a point some two inches farther up the arm, and finally in the patient's fingertips. The pulse may be taken simultaneously at these three points. While the one *babaylan* we intensively interviewed based his diagnosis on the patient's pulse, he was not able to tell us how the pulse differed depending on the agent of the illness. It appeared that taking the pulse and concentrating for ten minutes enabled him to develop or receive a distinct impression, somewhat like a light passing in the center of his forehead, of the etiology of the illness. Incidentally, Chinese acupuncturists also emphasize taking the patient's pulse in their diagnostic procedures.

If the illness is natural, the *babaylan* indicates that he can offer no help and refers the patient to a medical doctor or to a local healer who uses various herbal medicines as well as medications purchased from drug stores where they are sold without prescription. If the diagnostic sessions indicate that the patient is the object of sorcery, countersorcery moves are undertaken to retaliate for the misery the sorcerer has caused.

Divination. In the event the *babaylan* learns that the illness is due to a spirit, divination (*patpat*) follows. During *patpat*, the *babaylan* seeks to determine which spirit is responsible for the illness and what kind of offering the spirit will accept to make a recovery possible. He inquires in succession whether each of a number of locally known fairies or ancestors of the patient is responsible, seeking an individual answer for each name. One of many means used to obtain an answer is to attempt to stand a 10-centavo coin on its edge on a 25-centavo coin. If the smaller coin stands, the *babaylan* infers that the spirit just named is responsible for the illness, but he will complete the list of all possible spirits to make sure that none has been slighted and that all those responsible have been identified. Proceeding to the second phase of the *patpat*, he inquires whether certain offerings such as rice cakes, soft drinks, fish, chickens, or pigs are desired as a price of recovery. The answer for each of these traditional offerings may also be obtained through the balancing of a coin.

Other *babaylans* use other techniques to allow the spirits to make their wishes known. Balancing an egg on end, for instance, may serve the same purpose as balancing a coin. Another method, described in some detail by one *babaylan*, involved a piece of bamboo that extended the length of the outstretched arms of the patient, from fingertip to fingertip. After listing each name, the *babaylan* held the piece of bamboo up to the patient's outstretched arms; when the correct name had been called, it was found that the bamboo was at least six inches too long.

In both diagnosis and divination, frequent use is made of motor activities of the *babaylan* or the patient, such as balancing a coin, that are susceptible to involuntary processes. The participants experience the results as supernatural indications. We know, however, from recording muscle potentials in laboratory research, that an individual can indicate a good deal without being aware that he is doing so.

Treatment and Followup. As we indicated in the brief case summary at the beginning of this paper, Juanita recovered following the diagnosis and the promise of the ceremony to honor the wishes of the spirits. We suggest that preparations for the *pabatak* ceremony, which required many months, served to subject the patient to continuing expectations of her continued remission. The financial sacrifice of her parents in preparing for the ceremony constantly affirmed her worth to them. They knew she would continue to be well because they were meeting the conditions necessary to ward off further spirit intervention.

Juanita's family was obligated to give the promised ceremony, but they cautiously waited one month to be sure that the cure was permanent befor purchasing chickens and a pig to be fattened for the sacrifice during the ceremony planned for several months later. They then recalled the *babaylan* Susang—this was only the second time she visited Juanita—to pass incense over the animals and thus reconfirm to the spirits that the proper preparations for the ceremony were under way. It took another six months before the family had saved enough money to buy all the required offerings and pay the five *babaylans* and the small string band needed to conduct the actual ceremony.

Final preparations took several days and required the purchase of additional chickens as well as crabs, shrimp, mullet, betel, rice, bananas, bread, cooked vegetables, a variety of rice cakes, tobacco and cigarettes, *tuba* (fermented coconut palm sap), soft drinks, rice wine, and beer—the usual offerings in traditional folk ceremonies in the area. Several more chickens were contributed by kinsmen, neighbors, and friends (including the junior author). Two elaborately decorated bamboo altars (*sarimbal*) with red and white canopies were set up, one in the house where Juanita had been chained, and an identical one in the yard below. The two were connected by bamboo poles and red and white cords. Altogether, the altars, offerings, and personnel fees came to over ₱400 or more than US$100.

Because it was stressed that all of Juanita's relatives should be present, her mother, sisters and brothers, their spouses and children (some of whom lived a considerable distance away), as well as numerous more distant kinsmen attended the ceremony. Only her father was absent. As he openly indicated, he did not believe in such things and had been against holding the ceremony and the large expenditure it entailed from the beginning. Many local children and neighbors watched from a respectful distance.

Quite unexpectedly, several months before the ceremony, the wife of the junior author was asked to serve as godmother, *comadre*, to one of Juanita's nieces. We were thus considered kinsmen at the time of the ceremony and were allowed to photograph and tape-record the entire proceedings. Susang also invited an elderly male *babaylan*, Pablo, to act as a kind of master of ceremonies. He claimed to be 121 years old. In turn, Pablo called in another female *babaylan*, Pepita, and two younger male *babaylan*, Carlos and Abing, to assist. All were said to be his students or disciples, but Abing was the only one of the group actually from the immediate area. He arranged for the string band and was generally regarded as second in authority and skill.

The ceremony began at about 6 o'clock in the evening and lasted eighteen hours, with several breaks, until noon the following day. The entire proceeding was conducted in the local language, though many unrecognizable terms were regularly inserted. Some were undoubtedly Latinate in origin, probably picked up from Catholic services, but most seem to have been derived from older, now archaic, forms of the dialect.

We will give only a brief summary of the long and complex ceremony. The food offerings were first arrayed on banana leaves on the split bamboo floor of the house. Passing over the food a coconut filled with smouldering incense, the *babaylans* invited all of the local and regional supernaturals and the spirits of the family's ancestors to the ceremony. They could remember the names of only eight ancestors. Then they transferred the food offerings from the floor to the two altars in a traditionally specified arrangement. Next, the *babaylans* put on red and white hats and red and white cloth sashes around their waists and over their shoulders, crossing them over the chest and back. Juanita was dressed in the same outfit.

The *babaylans* and Juanita then seated themselves in front of the altar, and Pablo began the first of numerous formal invocations to the spirits with an Our Father and a Hail Mary. This invocation, like most of those that followed, had three goals: first, to invite the distant, local, and family spirits to come and partake of the goods offered, and in so doing to show their goodwill toward the hosts; second, to convince the spirits that by the very fact of offering the ceremony the family accepted its tradition or inheritance and would indeed follow the spirits' desires; third, to ask that the spirits recognize and enter their new initiate, Juanita. Towards the end of the invocation all the participants began beating on plates, glasses, and brass gongs to summon the spirits. When the invocation was finished, the band started playing, and the five *babaylans*, with Juanita in tow, began to dance around the altar. The *babaylans* stepped lively to the music, but Juanita simply shuffled around, willing but clearly uninspired. After a while the music stopped and there was a brief rest period.

Then Susang went to the altar and the entire process of invocation, music, and dance was repeated. However, after ten or fifteen minutes of dancing, Susang's manner suddenly changed. She became more intense and excited, and everyone said she had gone into trance, i.e., was possessed by a spirit. After dancing in this manner a few minutes she was seated in front of the altar and the other *babaylans* gathered round to encourage the spirit in her to speak to them. The spirit identified itself as Juanita's maternal grandfather, and he was invited to eat some of the offerings. He agreed but continually urged Juanita to follow his wishes and become a *babaylan*. The others, though not in a trance, encouraged her in this and had her feed snacks to the spirit and tell him that she would obey. After a few minutes this spirit left Susang and another briefly entered and left. Then a third, the girl's paternal grandmother, entered Susang. She broke out in a sweat and grimaced and complained of the bitter stomach pains with which that grandmother had died. Everyone present encouraged Juanita to massage and thus "cure" her. She reluctantly followed the instructions but seemed to do little for Susang or the spirit, and eventually that spirit left Susang.

After another rest period, Pablo started a new invocation, followed by one from Abing. The dancing resumed and Abing went into trance, and began speaking as an unidentified grandmother of the girl. Juanita was prompted to feed the "grandmother," dance around the altar with her, and agree to obey her. Simultaneously the other *babaylans* repeatedly requested the spirit to release its control over Juanita because she was obeying, i.e., accepting her inheritance. The spirit responded, "She's the inheritor, she will inherit my ability," but this still had no apparent effect on Juanita. There followed a brief rest period, and then the invocations, dancing, clanging of gongs, music, and occasional shouts continued.

Close to midnight Pablo began a new invocation directed to the *taglugar*, spirits of the place, asking that they not disturb the ceremony or invite other evil spirits who might do so. Soon the dancers were carrying about food items, a pot filled with pottery chips rattling with a sound like coins, and a bead necklace as offerings to the *taglugar*. After dancing seven times round the upstairs and down-stairs altars, the dancers buried these items in a shallow hole in the ground at a nearby well. The music and dancing resumed back at the house.

Shortly before 2:00 A.M., each of the *babaylans* started new invocations, and the dancing grew faster and wilder with increasing yells and shouts. Bamboo swords were distributed to the dancers, and to Juanita. They went downstairs, where they were soon dancing with their swords over the agitated but well tied sacrificial pig and through the scattered embers of a small fire. All the *babaylans* stepped on live coals in their bare feet without any noticeable discomfort. Juanita followed but picked her way through the coals with care. Next they returned up-stairs, where the dancing continued, while the pig was slaughtered by helpers below. Soon after, about 2:15 A.M., the dancing, shouting, and music rose to a peak and then stopped.

Juanita had stood beside the *babaylans* during their invocations, had gamely danced with them, fed and massaged them when in trance, and listened to their exhortations that she follow her "tradition." But clearly nothing very special had happened to her. Although pressured into playing the role of *babaylan*, the role had obviously not taken. She remained an ordinary 16-year-old girl following the instructions of her elders.

From about 2:30 to 4:00 A.M., parts of the neck, breast, and intestines of the sacrificial pig were cooked in four different ways. During this extended break most of the participants rested or slept, including Juanita's mother. When the mother awoke she announced that a spirit had entered her in her sleep and that she would now join the performers as a new initiate to *babaylan*ship. After a new set of invitations to the spirits and the *taglugar* by each of the *babaylans* both upstairs and downstairs, the mother was dressed in a red and white cap and sashes, and joined the *babaylans* in front of the altar. The cooked portions of the pig were distributed on both altars, but the great bulk of the animal was set on the altars in the house.

Pablo then began a new invocation, calling on the various spirits to par-take of the pig and treat well their "followers," i.e., the people providing the feast. As Abing took up the next invocation, the music and ringing of bells rose and the mother began to dance rapidly around the altar with the other *babaylans*, crying and occasionally screaming aloud while waving a bamboo sword. She had been entered by a spirit, and soon many other women and children in the house were screaming and crying. Two *babaylans* were now carrying two cloth-covered stick dolls said to be invested with the spirits of the mother's parents. After some thirty minutes of continuous wild dancing, Juanita's mother fell back on a seat, moaning, crying, and babbling inarticulate sounds. All the other *babaylans* gathered around her, attempting to make sense of what she was saying and who the spirit was that had entered her. She calmed down after a while, but they never did determine clearly who the spirit was, though they expressed no surprise at this since it was said to be a frequent occurrence when a person functioned as a medium for the first time.

After a break for breakfast, and now in the light of day, the ceremony began again with invocations, music, and dancing around both the upstairs and downstairs altars. Once more a fire was lit, the coals scattered, and the *babaylans*, in a trance, walked through them without any apparent sign of pain. Juanita's mother was entered again by a spirit, but her attempts to speak remained incomprehensible and the others could only guess who the spirit might be. Juanita continued to follow the others, but by now it was obvious that only her mother was to be affected. The dancing continued with brief breaks until close to 11:00 A.M., when the food offerings were removed and set aside and the altars dismantled. Pablo then gathered all the participants around him in the house and delivered in effect a sermon on the significance of the ceremony. Next the *babaylans* removed their caps and sashes and everyone present joined him in a brief meal composed of the offerings to the spirits.

Everyone was pleased because after some serious worries that the entire costly ceremony might have to be repeated if a spirit did not enter Juanita, her mother was finally entered. Thus, in effect, she accepted the calling she had long resisted. The spirits would have no further cause to complain. After some formal picturetaking at noon, the group dispersed. Later that day a hind leg of the sacrificial pig was delivered to the junior author's home.

Now, three years later, Juanita remains a normal young woman and her mother an active, practicing *babaylan*.

Implications

Before we discuss implications, we must deal with the question "Was Juanita realy schizophrenic?" The answer, of course, depends on what one means by the term. Juanita showed bizarre behavior of relatively sudden onset that persisted at home, in the hospital, and at home again for several years. Her behavior seemed like that that one sees in others who are called schizophrenic. There is, of course, no final answer to the question because no unequivocal diagnostic sign of schizophrenia was found—no bacillus, no lesion, no characteristic blood or urinary indication. It is not acceptable to say that she could not have been schizophrenic because she recovered. To do so would mean that one could never use the term schizophrenic in light of the possibility that the patient might recover.

Her sudden recovery from her behavior disorder might be called a spontaneous remission, a term that is an even greater confession of ignorance than is the term schizophrenic. There is no way in a single case to say why she recovered except to reverse the expectations of her mother and other relatives and to arrange for a *babaylan* to offer ceremonies designed to cause rather than cure the disorder. If she became disordered again, we would have increased confidence that the expectations or demand characteristics played a significant role. Such a procedure being out of the question, all we can do is observe that recovery occurred in conjunction with the treatment rituals.

Throughout this presentation, we have not employed psychodynamic concepts but have followed a social-behavioral approach. Space does not permit an extended defense of this approach except to assert that in day-to-day clinical settings it allows the testing of cause-and-effect relationships between environmental events and the patient's behavior. The inferred inner states of psychoanalytic thinking are both untestable and unnecessary.

These were dramatic events, fascinating in part because, like schizophrenia, they differ so much from our everyday experience. We can, however, learn something about possible methods of treating schizophrenia from these observations. Certainly one of the most mystifying and devastating of disorders, schizophrenia remains perplexing because we are uncertain about the factors that produce and sustain the behavior. Earlier we mentioned four emphases that appear among theories of the origin of the disorder: genetic factors, physiological characteristics, early childhood fixations, and current social pressures. As we see it, our data bear on factors in the last of these domains only.

Whatever else may be involved, schizophrenia is experienced as a catastrophic loss of self-esteem. It is made worse in many cases by the rejecting and punitive actions of the important people in the patient's life. We have now begun to realize that in our society, hospitals produce and sustain many of the symptoms that have classically been regarded as the inevitable manifestations of chronic, deteriorating disease. Other societies do not produce our backward syndromes because they expect different behavior and behave toward patients in ways to fulfill that expectation.

As Kennedy (1967) has pointed out, in some societies the family gathers around the patient, mobilizing their resources in his behalf. Treatment goes on within the family structure; the patient is not put away or even sent to the hospital where specially trained people can help him. The family keeps him in their midst partly because they feel threatened by the forces that are causing his illness and partly because they believe it within their power to help him. They do not hold him personally responsible for his aberrant behavior; they may, as Juanita's family did, place responsibility on other members.

Diagnosis and treatment are in terms of concepts understood by the family, and they are carried out in the presence of the patient and family with their active participation. With each step there is a sense of hope and efficacy. Behavioral scientists have ignored sudden conversion and possession experiences, largely because they reject the participants' preternatural explanations. Juanita's mother's possession was a convincing event to Juanita, her mother, and the other participants, an event that dramatically changed the social dynamics of Juanita's family. Juanita's recovery was thus affirmed by the spirits. Now, in the world we understand, Juanita and her mother have a new relationship in which both are confident of Juanita's recovery.

Of the four components of psychotherapy that Torrey (1972) found in the psychotherapy of both modern and traditional therapists, three are clearly operative in this case. The patient, her family, and the *babaylans* shared common views and terminology with respect to the patient's disordered behavior. The *babaylans* and Juanita's mother showed strong expectations of the girl's recovery.

Their expectations and their careful enactment of the rituals created a situation conducive to suggestion. We noted, however, little about Susang's personality that would set her apart from others in genuineness, empathy, or warmth.

It has been assumed that schizophrenics are not likely to lose their symptoms as a result of suggestion. Therefore, therapeutic efforts have followed other strategies. Certain situations can, however, elicit symptom-free behavior from patients considered to be quite regressed. When lights and movie cameras were moved in to record the deteriorated behavior at mealtime of a ward of chronic schizophrenics, the patients changed completely and ate as they thought people should while they were being photographed. Or, as a psychiatrist acquaintance once remarked, "I can always get a patient ready for a funeral." Susang and Juanita's mother created a set of powerful expectations based on widely shared beliefs about Juanita's disordered behavior, and Juanita responded by carrying out the suggestions. The preparations and the ceremony itself maintained the suggestion. Juanita's complete recovery was enhanced by two factors:(1) those around her believed that the spirits who caused the illness had withdrawn completely; and (2) because her symptoms were attributed to external agencies, no one looked for residuals. On the contrary, they welcomed her back into full membership in the family and the neighborhood.

These observations suggest some of the benefits to be gained from cross-cultural studies of the treatment of mental disorders. In this instance, treatment proceeded within the family and in terms and practices Juanita and her family understood. Powerful expectations were created that the patient would recover. Following recovery, the family's preparations for the thanksgiving ceremony reinforced Juanita's new behavior patterns. Her mother's new role as a *babaylan* led mother and daughter to expect that Juanita's symptom-free experience would continue.

Where schizophrenic symptoms are seen as externally imposed, and not a sign of failure or wrongdoing on the part of the patient, the symptoms can be reduced by creating a situation with powerful demand characteristics, to use Orne's term (1962). Behavior can be dramatically modified under these circumstances in a sort of conversion experience. Furthermore, in Juanita's case, and in many others, the recovery continues; the patient does not lapse. The likelihood of recurrence of symptoms is reduced because the recovered person, his family, and his neighbors believe that he is free of his difficulties and strongly reinforce his normal behavior patterns. Prescientific though many of their theories are, they lead to a social climate of optimistic expectations. It is the effect of these society-wide variables not readily manipulated in laboratory research that can be evaluated in cross-cultural research.

In the United States we are witnessing the movement of treatment from large hospitals to smaller community centers. We would like to suggest that therapists adopt the *babaylan's* practice of bringing the family actively into diagnosis and treatment.

REFERENCES

Baasher, T. A. 1967. Traditional psychotherapeutic practices in the Sudan. Transcultural Psychiatric Research 4:158–60.

Chen, P. C. Y. 1970. Classification and concepts of causation of mental illness in a rural Malay community. International Journal of Social Psychiatry 16:205–15

Committee on Nomenclature & Statistics. 1968. Diagnostic and Statistical Manual of Mental Disorders. Washington, D. C., American Psychiatric Association.

Denko, J. D. 1966. How preliterate peoples explain disturbed behavior. Archives of General Psychiatry 15:398–409.

Field, M. J. 1960. Search for security. Evanston, Northwestern University Press.

Guthrie, G. M., and G. Noll. 1966. Powwow in Pennsylvania. Pennsylvania Medicine 69:37–40.

Hart, D. V. 1969. Bisayan Filipino and Malayan humoral pathologies. Ithaca, New York, Cornell University Southeast Asia Program.

Kennedy, J. G. 1967. Nubian Zar ceremonies as psychotherapy. Human Organization 26:185–94.

Kiev, A., ed. 1964. Magic, faith and healing. New York, Free Press of Glencoe.

Levy, R. I. 1967. Tahitian folk psychotherapy. International Mental Health Newsletter 9(4):12–15.

Lieban, R. W. 1967. Cebuano sorcery. Berkeley, University of California Press.

Mednick, S. A., & F. Schulsenger. 1968. Some premorbid characteristics related to breakdown in children with schizophrenic mothers. *In* The transmission of schizophrenia. D. Rosenthal and S. S. Kety, eds. Oxford, Pergammon Press.

Orne, M. T. 1962. On the social psychology of the psychological experiment, with particular reference to the demand characteristics and their implications. American Psychologist 17:776–83.

Prince. R. 1964. Indigenous Yoruba psychiatry. *In* Magic, faith and healing. A. Kiev, ed. New York, Free Press of Glencoe.

Prince, R., A. Leighton, and R. May. 1968. The therapeutic process in cross-cultural perspective. American Journal of Psychiatry 124:1171–76.

Sechrest, L. 1964. Mental disorder in the Philippines. The University of the Philippines Research Digest 3:2, 5–9.

Torrey, E. F. 1972. The mind game: witchdoctors and psychiatrists. New York, Emerson Hall.

Yap, P. M. 1969. The culture-bound reactive syndromes. *In* Mental health research in Asia and the Pacific. W. Caudill and T. Y. Lin, eds. Honolulu, East-West Center Press.

12.   Folk Psychotherapy in Taiwan

WEN-SHING TSENG, M.D.

Department of Neuro-Psychiatry
School of Medicine
National Taiwan University Hospital
Taipei, Taiwan

FOR MANY CENTURIES, in times of great psychological stress, Chinese have visited shamans, consulted fortunetellers, and gone to temples for divination by *chien* drawing. In Taiwan these customs have survived even the recent rapid development of modern psychiatry and the increasing tendency of the mentally disturbed to seek help at the modern mental hospital in Taipei. Due to staff shortages, modern psychiatric clinics everywhere in the world are usually able to serve only a limited number of patients who visit. In Taiwan, many people still seek help at the hands of shamans, fortunetellers, and physiognomists, all of whom are readily available in each town or village. In light of the fact that the mental health of most people seeking therapeutic support still depends largely upon the practice of such folk psychotherapists, it becomes obvious that the study of shamanism, fortunetelling, or divination by *chien* drawing is useful to the modern psychiatrist.

Modern psychotherapy has emerged gradually through time as man has learned to help his fellows with their emotional problems in more sophisticated ways. The method of helping others with emotional problems has changed radically in techniques and theories; however, the human mind itself has essentially remained the same. That traditional methods of treating mental problems have functioned so long and so well in the past indicates that they must work to some extent (Frank, 1961). Scrutiny of traditional ways of mental treatment may reveal some important psychotherapeutic methods that heretofore have been disregarded or neglected in modern techniques. From them we may learn how to improve our modern method of treatment. As the Chinese say, "We can obtain new knowledge by studying the old."

Although psychiatrists have developed increasing interest in the study of culture and psychiatry in the last few decades, that interest has focused mainly on the cultural differences in symptomatic manifestations. It is very important to study further how people handle their problems in ways which are provided for and channeled by their culture. From this point of view, the study of folk psycho-therapy will certainly help us learn more about how the problems of life have been traditionally perceived and interpreted by the local people and what coping strategies have been specified by the culture. Thus, we can learn how to modify modern psychotherapy in culture-relevant ways, so that treatment will be more effective.

This paper describes and analyzes the practices of shamanism, divination by *chien* drawing, fortunetelling, and physiognomy as ways of folk psychotherapy in contemporary Taiwan. An effort is made to compare them with each other and with modern psychotherapy in the hope of increasing our knowledge and understanding of the basic process of psychological treatment in general.

Shamanism

Practice in Taiwan.   A shaman is a person who is supposed to have special powers to communicate with gods. At will he can induce himself into a trance state, speaking and behaving like the god possessing him. In this state, he is supposed to be able to help people solve the problems of life. Traditionally, as far back as recorded history goes, a shaman was called *wu* in China. Nowadays, a shaman is called *dang-ki* "man of divination," by indigenous Taiwanese. Though Taiwan is a civilized society, shamanism is still prevalent, and many shamans practice both in rural and suburban areas.

Usually a shaman is a man, sometimes a woman. He may be young or old. He usually holds a regular job during the day and practices shamanism at night. A *dang-ki* is consulted at his home in the early evening. When he is about to perform the ritual ceremony, he sits quietly in front of the home altar, praying for about five minutes. His body gradually starts to shake rhythmically all over, and he begins to speak after making some peculiar movements indicating that he has been possessed by the god. He states which god he is and asks why he is being called.

The client is supposed to tell the *dang-ki* what problem he needs help with, such as sickness, misfortune, and so forth. Then the shaman interprets the cause of the trouble. For example, if the client is suffering from diarrhea, the shaman might say that it means his fate is going to change, according to the calendar in heaven, and the god wants him to clean his stomach. If the client has nightmares and cannot sleep well, then his ancestor's spirit is disturbing him. Following this, the shaman gives the client a piece of paper on which he has written some characters and symbols. He orders the client to affix this charmed paper to the top of his door to prevent the devil's entrance, to carry it on his body as a charm, or to burn it and put the ashes into water to drink as medicine.

The *dang-ki* performs a ceremony while he is praying for the client. He gestures as if he is expelling evil spirits from the client's body. He may order the client to observe some taboo, such as to avoid food considered hot according to the herbal medicine concept, or to follow a ritual, such as putting a dozen pieces of stone into the bathtub while bathing. Occasionally the *dang-ki* may suggest that the client adopt a child, or suggest a "ghost marriage" between the client and a deceased young girl's spirit, but these practices are unusual. If the client is suffering from physical illness, the *dang-ki* usually prescribes herb drugs for him. In these ways the *dang-ki* helps the client cope with his problems.

Ordinarily, ten to twenty clients visit a *dang-ki* in one evening. They wait in line for their turn. The *dang-ki* sees each one individually over a period of two or three hours. During this time he remains in the trance state. When the *dang-ki* is finished for the evening he leaves the trance state and returns to his normal state. The *dang-ki* never charges for his services. However, when the client consults the *dang-ki*, he will offer money to the gods. People who visit shamans are usually superstitious and have little education. They are predominantly women, of various ages. They may consult a physician for physical illnesses that require medicine or injections, but they prefer to visit a shaman for any problems which they view as relating to the mind, to god, and to supernatural powers.

Psychotherapeutic implications. The outstanding characteristic of shamanism is the basic belief in supernatural powers and the existence of an omnipotent god. That belief is reinforced and enhanced by the dramatic, theatrical performance of the shaman's possession by the god. The shaman usually perceives and interprets the causes of problems as having to do with supernatural power, such as a disturbance made by the devil or an ancestor's spirit, or the client's loss of soul. Violation of taboos or bad luck is an alternate explanation. With the interpretation that a god, a devil, a soul is the potential source of disruption, the shaman provides clients with a specific, concrete enemy to cope with.

The interpretation is given not in the logical terms of the secondary-process thinking that the modern psychotherapist uses but in the symbolic terms of primary-process thinking. For example, the explanation, "the soul has been away from the body and has not returned yet," to a client who has recently had to face several successive misfortunes due to his own error, gives him a comprehensive and adequate cause for what happened to him and persuades him to accept the advice to behave cautiously until he gets his mind back, or until "the return of his guardian god." This symbolic interpretation is no doubt equal to the explanation that modern therapists might give: "your emotions are not stable and you have been making several irrational decisions that have caused the occurrence of the recent unhappy events." The message in symbolic terms is sometimes so much more concrete and compact than the language in logical and sophisticated terms that it might be more easily understood and accepted by people who are used to it. "Your tongue has gotten lost and has been replaced by a male tiger's tongue." This statement might give clear and precise insight to a woman, implying that she has been so nagging, sarcastic, and castrating to her own husband that she must try to get her natural female tongue back.

Furthermore, there is psychological significance in the interpretation that supernatural power is the cause of the client's problems (Kennedy, 1969). A devil, a ghost, or a god can serve as a symbol of a significant person in one's real life. The client may not be able to tolerate the awareness that there is something wrong with himself that he cannot control, such as his relationship with his spouse, his parents, or his neighbors. It is easier to perceive a deceased relative's spirit, a ghost, or any spiritual person as the possible source of one's problems (Wittkower and Weidman, 1968). For instance, a young man who had been reared as an only child by his foster mother had a heterosexual adjustment problem that was manifested in frequent psychosomatic disorders after his marriage (Tseng, 1972). The shaman he consulted interpreted his trouble as the result of a disturbance by the spirit of his deceased "mother," his foster father's first wife, and he was advised to propitiate the "mother" by offering sacrificial food. Actually the problem involved conflict and tension between him, his wife, and his foster mother. But instead of pointing out the actual fact that the foster mother was jealous of the young couple's happy life and resented being neglected, the shaman chose the more easily accepted symbolic substitute, not in the immediate family, as the explanation. This is particularly appropriate in a society where the relationship of family members is close and overt conflict between generations is prohibited. A successful shaman who has been trained to use his sensitive perception to discern the clients' problems (Kraus, 1970) also knows how to give explanations and advice in terms that are relevant to his clients' cultural background and are readily accepted by them.

The ways suggested by a shaman for coping with problems are usually magical in nature such as prayer, the use of charms, performance of a ritual ceremony, observing a taboo, or following some order. Although some shamans frequently prescribe herb drugs, whether they function as medicine or magic is not clear. Occasionally a shaman may give advice in psychological terms, but the advice is always represented as originating from the god. Although the advice given by a shaman may be full of magic and symbols, its value should not be denied, as the remedies suggested by a shaman are not illogical. For instance, when a shaman suggests to a young male client "not to pass by women's underwear that is drying in the sun," it may sound as if the shaman is asking the client to observe a superstitious taboo. Actually, he is suggesting that the young man practice sexual abstinence to deal with his neurasthenic symptoms, considered the result of excessive masturbation.

Divination by *Chien* Drawing

Practice in Taiwan.   Many people in Taiwan still visit a temple not only to worship and pray to gods but also to draw bamboo sticks called *chien* for divination, particularly when they encounter problems they cannot cope with. Drawing bamboo sticks as a way of divination has existed for many centuries in China. It is said that after the Sung Dynasty it became so popular among people as to become a part of their daily life.

In each Chinese temple a bamboo pipe is placed near the altar. It contains a set of bamboo sticks, usually one hundred in number. On each stick a number is marked. A *chien* client, after worshipping the god at the altar and presenting his problem to this god, goes to the bamboo pipe and takes one stick from it at random. He receives a *chien* paper of the corresponding number from an old man sitting on the desk in the temple. On each *chien* paper an answer to a problem is written in the form of a special poem. However, as the poem is difficult to understand, people usually ask the old man at the desk for an interpretation. He is experienced in such work and does it on a voluntary basis. The poems on the *chien* papers are usually ordinary Chinese poems that describe in a vague and symbolic way something such as nature, events, or ideas. Associated with each poem is a set of specific answers regarding problems in business, marriage, health, and the like. The interpreter can interpret them as he sees fit with a great deal of flexibility.

The client usually presents his problem briefly in the form of a question, and the interpreter replies simply yes or no. For example, if the client asks whether it is all right to give up his present job and start a new business, he may simply get the answer that it would not be good to change his job. However, another interpreter might inquire in detail why he wants to change his job, whether it is because he does not get along with his boss or because he is not making enough money, and so on. According to the information he obtains, he provides appropriate advice as if it came from the *chien* poem.

As there is no charge for this service, and temples are so numerous, people visit the temple quite often for *chien* divination. This is particularly true of people with little education who live in rural or suburban areas. Women engage most in the practice. People of all ages go. Many young people visit the temple to obtain guidance about their future. Young girls always want to know whom they should marry. In one of the biggest temples in Taipei City, there are regularly about ten interpreters sitting behind desks serving clients every day. Several hundred people visit for worship and divination almost every day.

Psychotherapeutic implications.   People who visit the temple for divination by *chien* drawing are those who believe in gods and depend on supernatural powers for solving their problems. However, for them a god is an unseen being rather than a concrete one. Therefore, they do not need to reinforce their beliefs with the dramatic performance of the shaman. Their need is to pray earnestly to a god for divine guidance. An interesting point is that the whole system of *chien* poems and their interpretations was designed for this purpose many centuries ago and has been used continuously up to now. Thus, by studying the content of *chien* instruction we can better understand the traditional way of viewing problems and the suggested customary ways of coping with them.

Analysis of the content of the *chien* interpretations discloses that explanations for disastrous events in life are given exclusively in fatalistic terms. Good examples are: "things are arranged by heaven," "the time has not come," "fortune has not arrived," "bad luck comes after the good luck is gone," and "things change as easily as the weather changes." The explanations given by shamans—that ghosts or the devil have interfered, or the soul is lost, or that one has been cursed by another—are not found in *chien*. It is believed that certain natural processes and guiding rules for human life are influenced by supernatural powers. Therefore, any problem or misfortune is understood as the result of an offense against them. However, one can find out what his specific offense was only through divination.

Consequently, the ways of coping with problems suggested by the *chien* poems and their interpretations have a unique quality: namely, the answers tend to be conservative. The client is always told to "be conservative," "maintain the status quo," "it is not good to try to change," "you may meet disaster if you try to move." The client is frequently told to be patient, to endure through everything, and to wait for an auspicious time. "Things will become better if you wait long enough," "the spring will come after the long winter," and so on. People are always advised to make peace and not to fight with others. Litigation is discouraged. The client is frequently encouraged to do good things to cultivate virtue whenever he has a misfortune.

Contrary to what one tends to think, the nature of fatalism and conservatism is not to view the world pessimistically with a passive attitude (Lieban, 1966). Though people accept failure with greater ease by believing that fate caused it, fatalism does not necessarily stifle efforts to find a solution. Rather, it provides a hope that in the future, when the right time comes, things may change. This is a great help to those who are experiencing misfortune. As for conservatism, it always provides people with stability in life, as it does not force them to face, the threats implied in drastic changes.

A statistical analysis of the proportion of unfavorable versus favorable answers in *chien* poems revealed that nearly two-thirds of the *chien* drawn indicate favorable results and less than one-fifth show an unfavorable outcome (Hsu, 1972). Instead of relying on chance or probability, the results have been "fixed" in such a way that more answers favor a good outcome. Apparently the purpose is to encourage people to view the future optimistically. This is the essence of supportive psychotherapy: no matter how difficult the situation may be, always provide the client with hope to help him deal with his problem.

Fortunetelling

Practice in Taiwan. Fortunetelling is called *suang ming* in Chinese, which literally means "calculation of fortune." The basis of fortunetelling rests upon the idea that certain universal principles rule nature. According to the ancient Chinese text *I Ching*, or *Oracle of Change*, everything in the universe is in a state of flux. Nothing is final; changes follow one another in a recurrent cycle, and every end is also a beginning. The process of change can be seen everywhere: in the flow of the tides, the phases of the moon, the cycle of the seasons, and the fortunes of mankind (Douglas, 1971).

According to the *I Ching*, change arises from the interaction of the two primal forces of yang and yin, the positive and negative elements of existence. The complex interplay of energy between the two poles results in the perpetual creation and transmutation of all things. The traditional Chinese calendar divides the year into two halves, the first six months being ruled by yang and the second six months by yin. During the six months of yang, spring and summer, the masculine pursuits of farming, hunting, building, and marriage are considered important, while in the six months of yin, autumn and winter, more feminine activities come to the fore: weaving, recreation and childbirth. Timing is of great concern to farmers. Therefore it is the custom for the people to want to begin projects at the most auspicious time. The *I Ching* was designed to reflect all phases of the process of transmutation in the universe, from creation through growth, maturity, decline, dissolution, and re-creation. It is a complete reflection of the natural order in miniature. From it one can tell his fortune and whether the changes in his life will be favorable or not.

Associated with the concept of yin and yang is the concept of the five elements. It is believed that the universe is composed of five elements: metal, wood, water, fire, and earth. Each element represents numerous things in the world at different levels, ranging from the material to the conceptual. For example, the metal element represents the actual metal, but also money, wealth, and so on, and the fire element represents fire, warmth, temper, and danger. It is thought that certain relationships and order exist between the five elements: Metal creates Water, Water creates Wood, Wood creates Fire, Fire creates Earth, and Earth creates Metal (terms capitalized to denote this special meaning). There is antagonism between Water and Fire, Fire and Metal, Metal and Wood, and so forth. The relationships between aspects of life represented by the elements are revealed by the relationships between the elements themselves. For example, it is good for a woman of the Water element to marry a man of the Wood element, as water helps the woods to grow; but a woman with the Water element is not suitable for a man of the Fire element since water will put out fire. With this knowledge, the skilled fortuneteller has unlimited scope for calculating judgments.

The fortuneteller usually sets up his stall or office near the market, inside a temple, beside the road, in the park, or another place where people can visit him easily. There is no need of ceremony to worship the god as seen in the divination by lot drawing in the temple or in shamanism. The client simply tells the fortuneteller the time, day, month, and year of his birth. Based on these four numbers, the fortuneteller will calculate his fortune. It is believed that a person is born with his destiny predetermined at the moment of birth. Everyone has eight characters associated with his birth: two are related to the year, two to the month, two to the day, and two to the hour of birth. These characters are in turn related to the five elements, which in turn are related to other systems in life, such as the seasons, interpersonal relationships, and so on. With these numbers as a basis, the fortuneteller can interpret issues of the client's past, business, marriage, health, wealth, and future. The purpose of fortunetelling is to calculate the changes that are constantly operating throughout all levels of the universe. When a person is given insight into the forces that guide his fate, he can then pattern his life so that the future can be faced and experienced in the best possible manner.

In practice, the fortuneteller will observe carefully the responses the client makes during the sessions and also will ask for further information from the client in addition to his birthdate before he starts with his interpretation. The important point is that regardless of the assigned meanings of the set of numbers, elements, or figures that emerge, he can interpret them as he sees fit to help the client solve his problems. The numbers or elements are usually just a steppingstone from which he can produce a story for the client, as if he knew all the principles in the world.

The client is supposed to pay a certain fee to the fortuneteller for the service. The fee varies according to the status of the fortuneteller and the intensity of the fortune he is asked to calculate. Generally, the fee is low enough so that anybody can afford to consult a fortuneteller if he wants.

Psychotherapeutic implications. The main characteristic of fortune-telling is that, in contrast to divination by *chien* drawing, it does not depend on belief in gods. The basic assumption in fortunetelling is that certain universal rules and principles of nature determine one's destiny. It does not entail the worship of gods or discerning their will. The basic idea is to study and learn the complicated system that governs nature and thus learn how to live in the universe. Although the frequent use of numbers and elements may seem arbitrary, they actually represent time, space, events, people, et cetera, and are thus a systematic method for describing the basic cycles of life.

Fortunetelling implies that things are wrong either because something relating to yang and yin or the five elements is amiss in a person's predisposition, or that the timing of events has gone against the basic laws of nature. This kind of interpretation combines abstract concepts and actual reality. The best example is that frequent occurrence of illness in a family may be attributed to the unfavorable location of a part or all of the family's house, such as the height of the door, the number of windows, or the direction of the house, whereas the wind, sunshine, humidity, or ventilation of the house may be the real reason for the physical as well as emotional condition of the family members. The lack of the Fire element in someone's body may be singled out as the cause of failure in his business, whereas his lack of enthusiasm in business transactions is the actual cause.

As events are viewed as being predetermined by a person's innate disposition and the temporal cycle of changes in life, the fortuneteller always advises the client to be aware of his own predisposition, to learn what the chances are for the attainment of his goals, and to obtain a more harmonious combination of factors to improve life. As a result, there is a great concern for time, order, relationship, and harmony. For example, if someone is getting married, the households of both families should be well balanced, the ages of the engaged couple should be matched, the time of the marriage ceremony should be auspicious, and so forth.

Many people who believe in fortunetelling are often impressed by the accuracy of the fortuneteller's predictions. Observation of psychological factors can explain to some extent why the fortuneteller gives people such an impression. The prediction made by the fortuneteller is always vague in nature and has many possible out comes. But it is the client himself who gives focus to the answer, giving concrete information to support or confirm the prediction. For example, if the fortuneteller predicts that there is a superior man of middle age who always helps the client attain success, the client is very likely to think of his boss, his uncle, or any person who fits such a description. Since a "superior man" exists in almost everyone's life, the client will be impressed by the accurate prediction. A taxi driver consults a fortuneteller for his dizziness. The fortuneteller interprets that he almost killed a living creature by running over it several months ago, and he has been distressed by the event. This interpretation will cause the taxi driver to recall some event in the past in which he may have almost run over a cat, a dog, or other living creature, an event which so often happens to taxi drivers. He will be surprised to find that the fortuneteller was so "accurate" in discovering what had happened to him.

Another phenomenon is that the client tends to remember the accurate interpretation or prediction and disregard the inaccurate one. Consequently, what is left in the client's mind is the successful prediction. The fortuneteller always has a way of proving to those who believe that the prediction is right. If he predicts that a great disaster is going to happen at a certain time, and some kind of misfortune does occur, no matter how serious, he can claim to have made an accurate prediction; if no disaster happens, he can say that the client has followed his advice, which prevented it. The fortuneteller always wins the game. The important point is that if the client is told that an opportunity is a favorable one, he is thereby encouraged to act on his interests and thus make good use of his potential ability. He may eventually be successful. But if he is told that things are not favorable to him at the time, he will be conservative, patient, cautious, and wait for good fortune to come. Either way, the client is affected by the fortune-teller's suggestions.

Physiognomy

Practice in Taiwan. Physiognomy is called *kahang shiang* in Chinese, "reading the face" or "examining the features." Physiognomy is based on the theory that there is such a close correlation between the mind and body that one's character, life, and fortune can be read by examining his features. It is not as concerned with the rules and principles of the universe as is fortunetelling. It focuses mainly on the individual, with the idea that things are determined by the person's predisposition and how he makes use of it. Therefore, the major concern is the human being himself. It is related to phrenology or palmistry to some extent. In fact, some people may practice fortunetelling, physiognomy, phrenology, and palmistry in combination, while others specialize in only one field.

The principle of physiognomy—that a person's character, life history, and fortune can be read from his face or other parts of his body—is based partly on projection and partly on physiological fact. The assumption that a person's life span can be read from the top of the face downward to the bottom of the faces, that the forehead represents youth, the area between the eyebrow and the nose adulthood, and the area below the nose old age, is a good example of how a person's life is divided and projected on certain parts of his face in corresponding order. However, part of the interpretation apparently is based on physiological characteristics plus the physiognomist's experience in observing the correlation between physiological character and mental character. For instance, a wide forehead is said to represent wisdom, and a narrow one indicates lack of intelligence.

Like fortunetellers, physiognomists are readily accessible to people in Taiwan, for they set up their stalls in the streets or near the market. When a client consults the physiognomist, his features are examined first. Based on the location, shape, size, and relationship of the client's forehead, eyebrows, eyes, nose, mouth, ears, and so on, the physiognomist will describe and interpret the client's life in the past, personality, behavior patterns, and fortune in the future. Generally the physiognomist will explain to the client what possible problems the client may encounter in matters such as business, family, marriage, love affairs, friendships, and so on, and will advise the client of the best way for him to cope with such problems; thus the process of therapy takes place.

Psychotherapeutic implications.   What is unique about physiognomy is that it is based on the assumption that a person is born with a certain predisposition, which is shown in his physical appearance; this predetermined personal character will lead the person to manifest certain behavior patterns, which in turn will determine his success in all aspects of his life. In contrast to fortunetelling, physiognomy attempts to reveal the nature of the man himself, not the nature of the universe.

Misfortune is interpreted as the consequence of having a bad predisposition. For instance, a criminal person is criminal because he possesses a certain kind of physical character that predisposes him to behave as a criminal; a person suffers from sexual impotence if he has a "flat temporal region"; a woman who always quarrels with others does so because she has a long tongue. Thus, the person himself is responsible for his behavior, although it is predetermined to be so; things are interpreted in physiological terms.

A physiognomist tries to help a client understand himself, learn about his characteristics so that he can make good use of what talents he has, and try to make up for his shortcomings. The physiognomist may tell a client with a wide forehead that since he is intelligent he can study very well; thus he encourages the client to attain high academic achievement. If the client has thick lips, which indicate that he is an honest man and is not good in social interaction, the physiognomist will tell him it is better to avoid involvement in businesses that require diplomatic talent.

The physiognomist may occasionally suggest that a client do something which is magical in nature, such as wear a ring or keep the fingernails long, if he interprets something on the client's finger as the cause of misfortune. Or, he might suggest that the client wear plain glasses to compensate for the shortage of "spirit" in his eyes. However, the conversation between physiognomist and client is usually psychotherapeutically oriented.

A businessman was brought by his wife to a physiognomist. He inquired why he was always a failure in business. Looking at the man's face, the physiognomist immediately said, "You do not smile! A man should always smile at people if he wants to be successful in business." The client needed encouragement but also honest advice. The successful physiognomist is skilled in making use of his alert and sensitive perception of the client. From the appearance, expression, and behavior of the client, the physiognomist tries to grasp the characteristics of the client's personality. Physiognomists are not only sensitive but also will not hesitate to tell a client anything he should know. Therefore, a good physiognomist is described by people as a man with an iron mouth.

Comparative Analysis

Common psychotherapeutic elements. Although, at first glance, the practice of shamanism, divination by *chien* drawing, fortunetelling, physiognomy, and modern psychotherapy may seem different and unrelated, they may all be considered psychotherapeutic activities if one defines psychotherapy in broad terms (Reider, 1955). In each practice there is (1) a healer, who presents himself as an authoritative figure with superior ability that enables him to help others deal with their problems (Lederer, 1955; Murphy, 1964), (2) a sufferer, the client, who consults the healer to seek relief from his problems with the firm faith that he can be helped (Opler, 1936; Pattison et al., 1970) and (3) a process of psychological interaction between the healer and the sufferer.

During the process of interaction, the healer always interprets for the client the cause of the problems presented. The interpretations vary a great deal according to different practices; they include: (1) interference by supernatural powers, (2) incompatibility with the principles of nature, (3) the client's predetermined physical predisposition, and (4) conflicts at the intrapsychic level. These interpretations may be related in symbolic terms, conceptual terms, or rational terms. However, no matter what kind of interpretation is given to the client, it can greatly alleviate the client's anxiety, for when a person is facing a serious problem, he always wants to know why it has happened to him. Merely supplying an answer to the question, whether it is accurate or not, surely helps the client reduce his anxiety.

Besides the interpretation, the healer always advises the client to do something to cope with his problems. No matter what the way is—whether to perform a magic ceremony, to take action to change the environment, to reorient his relations with others, or to change his value system about himself and about the world—it has a definite psychological effect (Leighton and Leighton, 1941). When a person is facing a problem he always feels the need to do something to cope with his anxiety, whether it has a practical effect or not. However, he is always uncertain about what he should do. If the healer is skillful or capable enough to provide the client with a convincing answer to his problem, he helps the client make decisions at a difficult time and thus do something about his problem.

It is not easy to evaluate what the therapeutic factors in such treatment are. In early psychoanalysis, the encouragement of insight by the interpretation of repressed ideas was regarded as the crux of therapy. Later, the abreaction of affect, the resolution of transference distortion, and then the corrective emotional experience were emphasized. Recent behaviorist theories stress the importance of the learning process in the psychotherapeutic transaction. No matter what style of treatment is carried out with what kind of theory, the successful healer always seems to be someone who knows how to provide the client with hope, which motivates the client to make good use of his potential ability to cope with his problem (Frank, 1968). The efforts to heighten the client's positive expectations about the future will certainly help him gain the strength to readjust to himself, to others, and to his environment.

Differences. In spite of the similarities which exist among various kinds of folk psychotherapy, comparative study of them reveals that they are different in many respects. The greatest difference lies in the basic idea behind each practice (Kiev, 1964).

Shamanism tends to view a devil or a soul as the interfering power, so that magic is suggested for coping with the interloper. All problems are externalized, and the clients are taught "how to cope with such supernatural power" (Boyer, 1964).

Divination by *chien* drawing views things as being predetermined by supernatural rules. Therefore, the client must find out what they are so he can "live compatibly with nature according to the rules."

Fortunetelling is based on the belief that an underlying principle of the universe rules nature. The client is taught how to "adjust to nature by following the principle of nature."

Physiognomy views problems as originating inside the individual. Although nature rather than the self determines a person's predisposition, the client is encouraged to "know about yourself so that you can live with what you are."

The modern psychotherapist also tends to interpret things as being wrong with the self; he is concerned with the client's behavior, his intrapsychic life, and his relation with the environment. He thinks that one is responsible for his life and that he can change his life. Therefore, the focus is on how to "train the self or change the self for better life" (Kiev, 1964).

It is obvious that there is a shift of focus in these methods of treatment from the supernatural world to the natural world and then to the individual person. This does not necessarily mean that the theory and modes of mental treatment have developed in a historical path from shamanism, divination, fortunetelling, and physiognomy to modern psychotherapy. But the shift does illustrate that different psychotherapies can vary greatly in their basic ideas. It is amazing that such different styles of treatment can exist and function together at the same time in a contemporary society.

Evaluation. Although it is worthwhile to study folk treatments from the theoretical point of view, one should not forget to evaluate and criticize their practicality. From the clinical point of view, folk psychotherapies may be a great help to those who have minor psychiatric problems in the category of neurotic and psychosomatic disorders, and those who have normal coping problems in ordinary daily life. However, their validity is questionable for the severe psychiatric cases labeled psychotic. If the unexperienced shaman, fortuneteller, or physiognomist were so ambitious as to pretend that he is omnipotent and able to solve all the problems presented by his clients, then there is the possibility he might do harm to a client by delaying the effective psychiatric treatment that that client needs.

By definition, the shaman, the fortuneteller, and the physiognomist are supposed to be superior in that they know everything about the client. In practice, they can only use their sensitive perception to speculate about the client rather than to inquire directly. This certainly limits them in obtaining enough information to make appropriate suggestions.

Communicating with the client in symbolic terms and suggesting that the client cope with problems by magic methods may easily gratify the client's needs, since a person who is under stress tends to function and think at the primary level. However, there is always the risk that such treatment will lead the client to remain at this level, making him reluctant to mature and learn to think at the secondary level and to function more rationally—as is desirable according to modern therapy.

Suggestions for Modern Psychotherapy

The study of various kinds of folk therapy provides us with the insight that psychotherapy should be always carried out in a way that is culturally relevant. This implies understanding the client within his cultural context, interpreting problems and suggesting ways of coping with them that are appropriate to the client's sociocultural background, and maintaining the therapist-client relationship in a culturally relevant way.

Based on respect for a person's potential independence and basic freedom, the therapist in the West is supposed to play the benevolent authoritarian (Doi, 1964). He is trained to conduct treatment in such a way that the client seems to be the one who discovers the answers and solves the problems (Pande, 1968). But people who are used to following and being dependent on autocratic authority are easily frustrated when the therapist does not take an active guiding role. Toward such clients, the therapist should not hesitate to present himself as a very confident, powerful, authoritative person. Otherwise, the client may feel insecure when he learns that he is in the hands of someone who is not authoritative enough.

The modern therapist should be sensitive to the client's social and cultural background to facilitate more appropriate and comprehensive communication and interaction with his client throughout their time together. No matter what kind of language is used, an interpretation will be more meaningful if presented in the proper cultural context (Deane, 1961). For instance, if an un-educated Chinese patient complains that he has "fire in my liver" or that he is suffering from "kidney insufficiency," it is better not to regard those as "unscientific" descriptions, to look down upon them or disregard them. The patient is actually stating that he has been feeling very tense (which results in "fire in my liver"), or that he is suffering from a psychosexual difficulty (and thus he feels "weakness in his kidney"). The patient is actually presenting his psychological problems in somatic terms (Tseng, 1972).

When he is about to suggest how the client can cope with his problem, the therapist should always consider the traditional ways for dealing with such a problem (Devereux, 1958). For example, if a person is used to doing things actively and aggressively within his environment, telling him to solve problems in a passive way will be unacceptable; on the contrary, if a person has been trained to be conservative and fatalistic, to suggest that he deal with things aggressively and radically will cause him even greater stress. The problem is better solved by the way that is most congruent with the client's cultural background.

While modern therapists are busy trying to discover and develop specific ways of treating specific kinds of problem and are concerned with which particular therapeutic effects bring about improvement, a good psychotherapist must (1) convey qualities of self-confidence, enthusiasm, and controlled emotional warmth, (2) supply an adequate interpretation for the cause of problems, (3) suggest certain answers for coping with problems, and (4) provide support and cultivate hope to motivate the client to utilize his potential to improve. No matter what the mode of treatment is, the successful therapist should not forget these factors, which are fundamental to successful treatment.

REFERENCES

Boyer, L.B. 1964. Folk psychiatry of the Apaches of the Mescalero Indian reservation. *In* Magic, faith and healing. A. Kiev, ed. New York, Free Press of Glencoe.

Deane, W.N. 1961. The culture of the patient: an underestimated dimension in psycho-therapy. International Journal of Social Psychiatry 7:181–86.

Devereux, G. 1958. Cultural thought models in primitive and modern psychiatric theories. Psychiatry 21:359–74.

Doi, L.T. 1964. Psychoanalytic therapy and "Western man": a Japanese view. International Journal of Social Psychiatry, special edition 1:13–18.

Douglas, A. 1971. How to consult the *I Ching*, the oracle of change. New York, G.P. Putnam & Sons.

Frank, J.D. 1961. Persuasion and healing: a comparative study of psychotherapy. Baltimore, Johns Hopkins Press.

———. 1968. The role of hope in psychotherapy. International Journal of Psychiatry 5:383–95.

Hsu, J. 1972. Counselling in the Chinese temple. Paper presented at the Fourth Conference on Culture and Mental Health in Asia and the Pacific, Honolulu, March 20–24. See chapter 16 in this volume.

Kennedy, J.G. 1969. Psychosocial dynamics of witchcraft systems. International Journal of Social Psychiatry 15:165–78.

Kiev, A. 1964. The study of folk psychiatry. *In* Magic, faith and healing. A. Kiev, ed. New York, Free Press of Glencoe.

Kraus, R.F. 1970. A psychoanalytic interpretation of shamanism. Transcultural Psychiatric Research Review 7:5–9.

Lederer, W. 1955. Primitive psychotherapy. Psychiatry 22:255–65.

Leighton, A.H., and D.C. Leighton. 1941. Elements of psychotherapy in Navajo religion. Psychiatry 4:515–23.

Lieban, R.W. 1966. Fatalism and medicine in Cebuano areas of the Philippines. Anthropological Quarterly 39:171–79.

Murphy, J.M. 1964. Psychotherapeutic aspects of shamanism on St. Lawrence Island, Alaska. *In* Magic, faith and healing. A. Kiev, ed. New York, Free Press of Glencoe.

Opler, M.E. 1936. Some points of comparison and contrast between the treatment of functional disorders by Apache shamans and modern psychiatric practice. American Journal of Psychiatry 92:1371–87.

Pande, S.K. 1968. The mystique of "Western" psychotherapy: an Eastern interpretation. The Journal of Nervous and Mental Disease 146:425–32.

Pattison, E.M., N.A. Lapins, and H.A. Doerr. 1970. Faith healing: a study of personality and function. Transcultural Psychiatric Research Review 7:73–77.

Reider, N. 1955. The demonology of modern psychiatry. American Journal of Psychiatry 111:851–56.

Tseng, W.S. 1972. Psychiatric study of shamanism in Taiwan. Archives of General Psychiatry 26:561–65.

Tseng, W.S., and J. Hsu. 1969–70. Chinese culture, personality formation and mental illness. International Journal of Social Psychiatry 16:5–14.

Wittkower, E.D., and H.H. Weidman. 1968. Magical thought and the integration of psychoanalytic and anthropological theory. Transcultural Psychiatric Research Review 5:125–30.

13. Shamanism in Taiwan: An Anthropological Inquiry

YIH-YUAN LI, Ph.D.

Institute of Ethnology
Academia Sinica
Taipei, Taiwan

Chinese Shamanism

Shamanism has a long history in China. Its practice can be traced at least to the Shang Dynasty, and various forms of spirit mediumship are still prevalent in all parts of China (De Groot, 1892–1910; T.S. Hsu, 1940). However, it is in the two most southern provinces, Fukien and Kwangtung, that Chinese shamanism developed into its most elaborate form. It followed the immigrants from these two provinces into Southeast Asia and Taiwan and has been common in the religious life of the Chinese in these areas (Elliott, 1955; Kokubu, 1941). Among the Fukienese, the shaman is popularly known as *dang-ki. Dang-ki* means "divining youth" or "youth into whom a spirit descends." It is believed that a *dang-ki* is one whose horoscope indicates that he is bound to die young, so serving as the medium of a spirit or god is a way to save his otherwise ill-fated life. Therefore, in the classic case, a *dang-ki* is young and had some physical or mental defect before being selected by a god. Nevertheless, there are many instances in which older persons take up mediumship, and they may not show any prior symptoms.

The main work of the *dang-ki* is to be possessed by a god and convey the god's instructions to worshippers and clients. In performing the ritual, a *dang-ki* puts himself into a trance and behaves like the god who is possessing him. A *dang-ki* is possessed by only one god, usually a particular god familiar to him or even a tutelary spirit. But some *dang-ki*s can be possessed by different gods on different occasions. Before a *dang-ki* becomes possessed, his body becomes cold. The first overt sign that he is being affected is that he stretches and yawns several times; later there is a gentle quivering of the limbs. When the quivering becomes stronger, the *dang-ki*'s whole body starts to sway and his head begins to swing around in circles. He suddenly jumps up and for a few minutes leaps about, portraying the characteristics that are expected of him.

It is usually at this stage that self-mutilation takes place. It usually takes the forms of cutting the tongue or the back with swords, piercing the cheeks with iron rods, and flailing the back with a nail-studded ball. Self-mortification seems intended to dramatize the shaman's performance and gain the confidence of the worshippers, and is more frequently practiced at a communal feast than in private curing rites. However, the blood from the wound is believed to be useful in curing the sick.

For the clients, the most important event in the ceremony is the verbal pronouncement by the *dang-ki*. The *dang-ki* will usually speak a kind of language that is unintelligible to all but the interpreter, who acts as his assistant. Often he mutters petulantly, in a shrill and artificial voice. In many cases, each phrase contains three parts: a meaningless prefix and suffix with a meaningful iteration in the middle. The meaning of the instruction becomes intelligible when the middle segments of successive phrases are added together. An interpreter, therefore, is not required by a regular worshipper, but for the occasional client the interpreter s help is essential not only in translation but also in obtaining charms and prescriptions.

Since this paper focuses on the effectiveness of the *dang-ki* rather than his practices, we will not go further into the performance of the *dang-ki*. The studies of De Groot (1892–1910) and Elliott (1955) cover this aspect of Chinese spirit mediumship.

The *Dang-ki* in Taiwan

In the rural areas of Taiwan today and also in certain districts in the cities, the *dang-ki* plays quite an important role in the daily life of the people (Tseng, 1972). Since the seventeenth century, when the Fukienese first established pioneer communities in Taiwan, the *dang-ki* has been closely connected with the gods of the pestilences, epidemics, and plagues that were so prevalent among the pioneers, and has earned the trust of the people. In almost every Taoist or folk temple in Taiwanese villages there is a *dang-ki* for the worshippers to consult. Usually the *dang-ki* practices his mediumship only part-time. He may be a farmer or a shopkeeper during the day, shifting to his role of *dang-ki* in the late afternoon or at night. Even so, the *dang-ki* performs rituals only at the request of clients or at feasts to honor the gods of his temple. The ritual performed in a sick person's behalf may be conducted at the temple or even in the client's home. In the latter case, a statue of the temple god has to be brought with him. After the assistant has conducted preliminary ritual procedures such as burning incense sticks and joss papers, the *dang-ki* falls into a trance. He examines the case and gives a diagnosis and prescriptions, which may include Chinese herb drugs and charms. Each session may include up to a dozen clients.

Within the last decade, the *dang-ki* has become even more popular in Taiwan, and several different kinds of practice have developed. One of these is the professional *dang-ki*, who practices full-time, opens a "clinic" at his home or in a temple, and is available for consultation during specified hours. Another recent development is the collective performance, or cult sect. In an ordinary *dang-ki* ritual, only the *dang-ki* goes into a trance. At a large feast, several *dang-ki*s may be possessed at the same time, and a couple of "insanes" may suddenly fall into a drowsy state, but the worshippers never all follow the *dang-ki* into a trance. However, in the developing cult sect, the master *dang-ki* performs a curing rite for the patient, who, after being healed, becomes the *dang-ki*'s follower and learns to go into a trance. The followers come to the altar very often, some of them every night, to join their master in possession.

Let us look more closely at the first of the new types of practice by examining a case study of a professional *dang-ki*.

A Case Study

Mr. Chuang, the *dang-ki* we studied, lives in a typical rice-cultivating village in the north of Chu-Shan township, Nan-tou County, in the central part of Taiwan. He is 39 years old. He is assisted by his elder brother, who acts as his interpreter (*dou-t'au*). Mr. Chuang and his brother started their career in 1956, when the former was 23 and the latter 30 years old. A year or so before, Mr. Chuang had suffered from a minor mental illness. A neighbor had suggested that he consult a god called Kai Chang Sheng Wang, a famous local god of the Fukienese, and he was healed. In gratitude, the family brought an image of this god to their own house altar to worship, and gradually a cult developed on the instructions of the god. In the beginning, they practiced the ritual part-time, only at night, for their fellow villagers. In the last few years, because many clients came from other villages and neighboring townships, they began performing the ritual in the afternoon too, and Mr. Chuang became, in fact, a professional *dang-ki*.

We observed Mr. Chuang's practice between November 1 and 30, 1971, during which time the *dang-ki* was consulted by 220 clients. Five of the clients lived in other townships, and invited him to their houses; each trip took him an afternoon or a whole day. Therefore, excluding those five days, he had an average of more than nine clients per day. For each of the 220 cases we obtained background information and analyzed the consultations.

When performing his ritual, Mr. Chuang goes into a fairly deep trance. He behaves feverishly and impatiently, beating the table frequently with his left hand when he is not talking. In giving instructions from the god he speaks the ordinary Fukienese dialect, but in a rather peculiar and low tone, so it is necessary for his brother to interpret for him. The interpreter is in charge of all the business in the ritual, including preparing charms and amulets, writing down the herb drugs prescribed, giving supplemental instructions and advice, recording case information, and so forth.

Every case of consultation includes three essential procedures: (1) identifying or diagnosing the case, (2) explaining the causes of the trouble, and (3) treatment.

Identifying the case, or the diagnosis. When he comes to consult the *dang-ki*, the client first informs him what his problem is. When it is a case concerning disease, the client usually states the symptoms and also what he thinks the illness is in traditional Chinese terms. The *dang-ki* usually takes the accuracy of the report for granted and sometimes makes a few additional comments. The *dang-ki* does not take these "diagnoses" too seriously, but he does give a label to each case. The problems of the 220 cases are grouped by category in Table 1. From the table we see that the problems are primarily concerned with various kinds of physical suffering and secondarily with unfavorable or inauspicious conditions. Actually, these two categories, which include almost 90 percent of the cases, can be combined into a general category, anxiety about personal and family well-being. Indeed, it is characteristic of Chinese templegoers to merge physical illness into the general category of calamities and disasters, since they attribute all calamities to a supernatural, or more accurately, metaphysical, cause.

Explaining the causes of the trouble. Except in those cases where it does not apply (problems listed under "Others" in Table 1), the *dang-ki* gives one

Table 1: Clients' Problems

Problem	Number of Cases (percent)	
Psychophysical Problems:		
Physiological illness	126	
Insanity	12	
Accident	4	
	142	(65)
Unfavorable or Inauspicious Conditions:		
Concerning the whole family	30	
Concerning the individual	8	
Man's indulgence in gambling and women	15	
	53	(24)
Others:		
The choice of auspicious dates	11	
Need for business advice	7	
Desire for news of a distant relative	4	
Miscellaneous	3	
	25	(11)
Total	220	(100)

or several reasons to explain why the patient, but not others, has suffered from disease or disaster. I think this is the most important point in understanding the *dang-ki*'s practice. Elliott (1955), in his study of Chinese *dang-ki*s in Singapore, gives a detailed description of many aspects of this spirit mediumship. However, in his conclusion he lists only the data concerning the topics of consultation, as we have in Table 1, giving no explanation of the causes of trouble. More accurately, he combines these two things into one category. It seems to me that is the reason Elliott does not arrive at a convincing conclusion.

Among the 195 cases of consultation for which explanations were relevant, Mr. Chuang gave explanations for 148 (67.28 percent) and no explanations for 47 (21.36 percent). Among the 148 explained cases, 110 were given single causes; 25, double causes; 11, triple causes; 1 case, four causes; and 1, five causes. Altogether there were 202 causal items given. I have classified them into several categories, as is shown in Table 2.

Table 2:   Explanations for Clients' Problems

Explanation	Number of Cases (percent)	
A. Disasters caused by spirits of deceased relatives:		
Deceased spouse	8	
Male agnates	23	
Female agnates	17	
Affinal kin	6	
	54	(27)
B. Disasters caused by spirits of nonrelatives or evil specters	29	
	29	(14)
C. Black magic conducted by relatives or nonrelatives	6	
	6	(3)
D. Ancestor's grave or *feng-shui*	25	
	25	(12)
E. Other *feng-shui* issues	48	
	48	(24)
F. Temporal elements:		
Year span	14	
Short period span	14	
Accident	9	
	37	(18)
G. Miscellaneous	3	
	3	(2)
Total	202	(100)

Some comments on the correlation between explanations and problems should be added before we go to the third subject, treatment by the *dang-ki*. The 47 cases for which no explanation was given were all simple physiological illnesses. Not a single case had to do with mental illness, accident, or general inauspicious conditions. However, we failed to find correlations between problems and specific categories of explanation. The only exception may be that the multiple explanations were mostly given for unfavorable or inauspicious conditions concerning the whole family. Twenty-one out of the 30 cases shown in Table 1 have multiple explanations.

Treatment.   After identifying the case and explaining the cause of the trouble, the *dang-ki* gave instructions, advice on remedies, and prescriptions. For most cases, paper charms and spells were prescribed. For some cases, especially those of obvious physical illness, Chinese herb drugs, usually of a common variety, were prescribed. For disasters caused by the spirits of deceased relatives, by *feng-shui* (geomantic) problems, and those concerning temporal factors, special advice and arrangements were necessary. A few affinal kin troubles arose from disputes over the inheritance of property; several such cases were attributed to a quarrel between paternal and maternal ancestors because their tablets were placed in the same temple hall. For the latter situation, the *dang-ki* suggested that the tablets bearing a different surname from that of the household be moved from the main hall. In the case of a deceased spouse or ascendant relative, the spirit had to be properly worshipped or pacified with offerings. The *dang-ki* instructed the patients not to neglect the worship rituals. In the case of a male relative who died young, the *dang-ki* suggested that the patient assign a descendant to him, so that he would have a proper position in the family altar with other ancestors. In the case of a deceased girl, there were two alternatives: an honorary tablet could be installed in a temple, or a "ghost marriage" could be arranged. Mr. Chuang preferred the first method. In other parts of Taiwan, ghost marriages are often arranged (Li, 1968; Jordan, 1971).

Problems concerning *feng-shui* are also complicated. If the ancestor does not feel comfortable in his grave, a new site has to be arranged. This is true both for primary and secondary burials. Sometimes a grave site is not suitable for group burial, and those interred must be separated. In the case of "bad" *feng-shui* (geomantically an unsuitable habitation site) of a house, its situation must be changed. For the cases of offense to other people's *feng-shui* and retaliation by death, the *dang-ki* suggested the performance of a propitiatory ritual.

The category that I call temporal elements is close to the concept of fate. It includes troubles attributed to the incompatibility of the patient's horoscope characters and a specific time span. For cases of incompatibility within a short time span, a ritual may be suggested and the client is asked to behave carefully within the period. Should the crisis span a year, the *dang-ki* suggests a rite called *kai-yun*, to "cover" and "freeze" the time span. The ritual involves sealing the soul of the patient in a small pot and covering the pot with a charm. Only when the period of crisis is over will the soul be released.

Analysis

In our observations of the curing procedures of the Chinese *dang-ki* in Taiwan, one thing stood out. Neither the *dang-ki* nor the client paid much attention to pathological issues, either in the Western medical sense or even in the traditional Chinese medical sense. They both seemed interested only in the reason why disaster befell a certain individual or group. Thus, the explanation of the causes of disaster is the key to understanding the *dang-ki*'s practice and needs further discussion.

It seems to me that all the explanations the *dang-ki* gives can be grouped into three main categories: (1) man-to-man relations, which are purely social, not involving the intervention of nature in the genesis of the problem; (2) nature-to-man relations, having to do with the influence of time and space on man; and (3) a category that mediates between man and nature.

The category of man-to-man relations includes explanation groups (A), (B), and (C) in Table 2, including disasters caused by the spirits of relatives or nonrelatives and disasters caused by black magic conducted by living relatives or nonrelatives. Together these three groups explain 44.06 percent of the cases, and group (A) is the most important one, with 26.73 percent. These items really concern, both for the *dang-ki* and for his clients, the proper conduct of interpersonal transactions, especially among relatives or kinship members, both living and dead. On this aspect of Chinese society, F. L. K. Hsu declares most clearly (1967:259):

> The really miserable individual is he or she who has no
> place in the kinship structure or who does not live among the
> members necessary for the successful functioning of the
> structure, whether because of his or her own fault or because of
> circumstances beyond his or her control. Such a person will be
> very much at the mercy of the individuals with whom his lot
> is cast.

In a more recent article Hsu states (1971:30):

> Along with this, the Chinese individual is most likely
> to be strongly concerned with knowledge, artifacts and rules of
> conduct centralized in the kinship sphere. Hence filial piety is the
> cornerstone of all morality, ancestral land is the basic
> attachment. . . .

Therefore, the remedies the *dang-ki* prescribes for this category of disaster are focused on observing the duties and obligations of kinship rituals and taking the proper place in the family or kinship line. In other words, the emphasis is on maintaining the harmony and order of man-to-man relations, a focal point of being a man in Chinese society.

The second category of explanation, nature-to-man relations, refers to explanation group (F) in Table 2, temporal elements, which accounted for

18.32 percent of the cases. This category differs from the one discussed above in that the explanations are the result of the pure influence of time and space, with man playing no part in the genesis of the problems. About this system of Chinese thought, which is popularly known as the concept of fate, Yang states (1961:35):

> Each time unit stood for a certain combination of heavenly and earthly forces at work. The meeting of these forces at a certain hour in combination with a certain day in a certain month in a certain year might be harmonious and lead to good luck, whereas another combination might mean an antagonistic meeting of force and lead to misfortune.

The *dang-ki*'s remedies for such causes are intended mainly to avoid the antagonistic meeting of natural forces and to find a compatible or lucky date based on the patient's horoscope.

The third category of explanation, problems concerning *feng-shui*, includes explanation groups (D) and (E) in Table 2, or 38.15 percent of the cases. *Feng-shui* mediates between the first and second categories in the sense that it brings all the elements to bear on the problems of man adjusting to the universe. The following quotes will further illuminate this point. In his classic work, De Groot (1892–1910) says:

> *Fung* means the wind, and *shui* water. *Fung-shui* consequently denotes the atmospherical influences, which bear absolute sway over the fate of man. In a hyperbolical sense, however, *Fung-shui* means a quasi-scientific system, supposed to teach men where and how to build graves, temples and dwellings, in order that the dead, the gods and the living may be located therein exculsively, or as far as possible, under the auspicious influences of nature.

Freedman (1969) calls *feng-shui* a system of mystical ecology and says:

> It is very important to grasp the idea that in the Chinese view a building is not simply something that sits upon the ground to serve as a convenient site for human activity. It is an intervention in the universe; and that universe is composed of the physical environment and men and the relationship among men.

And in another essay (1967):

> The geomancy of graves is part of a large system of ideas and practices in which topography and man are made to interact. The Chinese have elaborated for all sorts of constructions (houses, government offices, villages, cities, and so on, as well as graves) a theory and set of practices which rest on the idea that men are, so to say, members of the universe.

They do not walk the world as intruders. Changes made in the
landscape are not simply modifications of nature; they are
changes of man-in-the-world. As an important part of Chinese
culture, *feng-shui* has gone where that culture has gone.

Thus, it is obvious why the *dang-ki* emphasizes *feng-shui* as an explanation for
human disasters and why the remedies he orders actually follow the doctrine
of this system of Chinese thought.

Summary

The three kinds of explanation that the *dang-ki* gives for his clients'
problems are derived from Chinese thought regarding the constitution and
working of the cosmos, ideas that bring all the elements to bear on the problems
of man adjusting to the universe. In this we can discern the Chinese sense of the
wholeness of the universe, of which man is a part, an inseparable part. The
concept that man and nature are interrelated parts of one system is shown in
many ways in traditional Chinese culture: in the philosophical writings, in
popular religious beliefs, and in the ethical codes. The Chinese *dang-ki* not only
provides a specific answer for the client, he also draws upon the whole cultural
system to give a meaningful explanation to the client.

The *dang-ki* realizes that under this integrated and balanced system of
the universe problems can arise in two main ways: (1) from man's inability or
unwillingness to play his proper role in the functioning of the system, or (2) from
contradictions inherent in the system. Hence, the remedies he prescribes are
designed to maintain harmony among the various components and to ward off
the antagonistic forces that may jeopardize the functioning of the system. Viewed
in this way, the *dang-ki* appears almost as a systems analyst or even a practicing
social scientist of the functionalist school. Therefore, the *dang-ki* may act as a
practitioner for the client, in some sense, but more accurately he serves as an
adviser or a consultant. He explains and brings insight into the causality of the
client's problem, but he leaves rehabilitation up to the client himself.

ACKNOWLEDGMENTS
The author is grateful to Mr. and Mrs. James P. McGough for their help in
polishing the English and their constructive comments on this paper. Fieldwork
assistance was given by Mr. Chuang Ying-chang, Assistant Research Fellow of
the Institute of Ethnology, Academia Sinica.

REFERENCES

De Groot, J.J.M. 1892–1910. The religious system of China. 6 vols. Leiden.

Elliott, A.J.A. 1955. Chinese spirit-medium cults in Singapore. London School of Economics Monographs on Social Anthropology 14.

Freedman, M. 1967. Ancestor worship: two facets of the Chinese case. *In* Social organization —essays presented to Raymond Firth. M. Freedman, ed. Chicago, Aldine.

——. 1969. Geomancy. Presidential address 1968. London, Proceedings of the Royal Anthropological Institute.

Hsu, F.L.K. 1967. Under the ancestor's shadow. Garden City, New York, Anchor Books.

——. 1971. Psychosocial homeostasis and *jen*: conceptual tools for advancing psychological anthropology. American Anthropologist 73:23–44.

Hsu, T.S. 1940. A study on the superstition of *fu-ki*. Shanghai, The Commercial Press. [In Chinese]

Jordan, D. 1971. Two forms of spirit marriage in rural Taiwan. Bijdragen, Deel 127. Leiden.

Kokubu, N. 1941. A study of *dang-ki*. Taiwan Folklore 1:1–3. [In Japanese]

Li, Y.Y. 1968. Ghost marriage, shamanism and kinship behavior in rural Taiwan. *In* Folk religion and the worldview of the Southwestern Pacific. N. Matsumoto and T. Mabuchi. Tokyo, Keio Institute of Linguistic Studies.

Tseng, W.S. 1972. Psychiatric study of shamanism in Taiwan. Archives of General Psychiatry 26:561–65.

Yang, C.K. 1961. Religion in Chinese society. Berkeley and Los Angeles, University of California Press.

14.   The Korean *Mudang* as a Household Therapist

YOUNGSOOK KIM HARVEY, M.A.

Department of Anthropology
University of Hawaii
Honolulu, Hawaii

KOREA is frequently described as a country without religion, a gross misrepresentation. In Seoul, residents often go to bed with the rhythmic beating of the shaman's drums in their ears and are roused at dawn by the pealing of Christian church bells.

The predominant religion is shamanism, despite its lack of organization, coherent doctrine, the outcaste status of its practitioners, and a long history of official suppression extending back at least to the fourteenth century. I have no current statistics on the ratio of practicing female shamans, or *mudang*s, to the general population. One source (Clark, 1932) estimated one *mudang* per 300 residents in 1930 in P'yŏngyang, then the second largest urban center, and this at a time when Japanese suppression of shamanism was most thorough. Judging from the apparent proliferation and thriving of *mudang* today, I would guess that the ratio is not much lower.

The traditional attitude of Korean elite, whether the old gentry class or modern intelligentsia, has been to scoff at shamanism and dismiss it as the foolishness of women or other ignorant citizens. The fact remains, however, that shamanism is supported in practice by the majority, and its role in the lives of the people therefore cannot be ignored.

So far as I can determine, there is no *mudang* Korean counterpart to the American soothsayer, Jeane Dixon, who forecasts national events in syndicated newspaper columns, or to "Dear Abby," who gives personal counseling through her columns. Notwithstanding, the *mudang* serves both as fortune-teller and as therapist to her clients in personal sessions. It is this therapeutic role to her clients and their households that the *mudang* comes to assume in the course of exercising her spiritual mediumship that I shall focus upon in this paper.

The *Mudang* as a Household Therapist

Since the *mudang* is consulted almost exclusively by women, and by housewives in particular, and seldom sees other members of her clients' households, the claim that she functions as a household therapist requires some explanation. Since every client who is a mother and wife is the embodiment of her household, the *mudang* who has access to and influence over such a client has, *ipso facto*, access to and influence over the household's internal affairs—which inevitably have external consequences as well.

The division of labor between husband and wife in the management of household is dichotomized, with minimal overlap of mutual participation and decision making. Korean male dominance and superiority in the public sphere has garnered much gratuitous sympathy from foreign observers for the Korean woman's lot. Less well known, but no less poignant, is the predicament of the Korean man, who is an outsider in the heartland of his own household. His formal authority is hardly ever challenged, but his actual authority within the household is much curtailed, for, like the king who knows only what his ministers choose to tell him, he is often ignorant about his domestic affairs.

In some households, the husband is completely in the dark about his wife's visits to the *mudang* and her resultant plans for the household, which involve the entire household, including him. If the husband's objections are strenuous, or are anticipated to be, the wife most probably will choose to keep her dealings with the *mudang* secret from him (and sometimes even from older male children). She thus avoids confrontation, yet preserves her reliance on the *mudang*. It is possible, of course, that there is collusion between husband and wife in sustaining such a situation. The important point is that, facilitated by this family situation, shamanism remains a strong religious force in the lives of Koreans, emphatic denials by the male elite to the contrary.

The *Chŏm* Session

No single Korean term applies uniformly to the consultation session with the *mudang* in her home. I have chosen one term, *chŏm*, meaning divination and fortune-telling, to refer to it. Both the internal structure and the external setting of the *chŏm* session contribute to the therapeutic function of the *mudang*, the former by facilitating information elicitation and the latter by providing a setting for group therapy.

A *chŏm* may terminate in a single transaction or lead to other action, such as a *kut* (an exorcism rite). The *mudang* usually works at home, with neither formal office hours nor appointments; nor does she publicize her work. She receives clients in a special room where her altar is kept. Clients come from all levels of society, and usually alone, though friends and relatives sometimes accompany to give support. Occasionally, clients come in pairs, one presenting the other as the source of the problem. Clients do not like to patronize *mudangs* in their own neighborhood; they suspect that such *mudangs* may use personal knowledge of clients in divination. For their part, most *mudangs* explicitly refuse to see neighbors or relatives, fearing that it might impair their personal relationship with them.

Waiting clients behave as though at an informal social gathering, participating in the *chŏm* in progress with comments and cluckings of the tongue. The *mudang* sometimes uses this audience to muster a consensus support of her advice vis-à-vis the client of the moment.

The *chŏm* structure is relatively uniform among *mudang* during the initial phase. The *mudang* asks for the information necessary to cast divination and proceeds, repeating the process for every member of the client's household. Then, as special problems or requests are presented, each *chŏm* varies from this point on, depending upon the problem, the client, and the *mudang*. Generally, however, it goes through the stages of interpretive reformulation of the problem, analysis, and giving advice. In the process, the *mudang* makes gestures and utterances that seem incomprehensible. Interspersed with these activities, she manipulates the client by clever interview techniques to elicit crucial information. Another effective technique is impromptu chanting, in which she gives an empathic recitation of the client's problem and the sufferings involved, pleads to the spirits for help, and reports on the progress of divination. During this, the client usually volunteers additional information to ensure the accuracy of all the essential features of her problem before the spirits, sometimes revealing her own suggestions for solution.

Speaking personally, the first few times I observed *chŏm* sessions, I was haunted by a sense of *déjà vu*. As a child in Korea, I was wooed by Presbyterian and Maryknoll missionaries from America. They used to oblige me to kneel with them in prayer—they doing all the talking with God and I being permitted to interject "amen" where appropriate. They would narrate the plight of my unsaved soul, declare me a true seeker after the truth, and fervently beseech their Lord to show me the way, through the agency of the Holy Ghost.

The Clients and Their Problems

From my observations of the work of seven *mudangs*, I have chosen six *chŏm* sessions to analyze.[1] They include only those dealing with interpersonal problems; requests for general fortunes, selection of auspicious dates, and so forth were excluded. The following cases come from four of the seven *mudang*. I shall give a fuller account of the first to convey the flavor of a *chŏm* session.

Case 1. A 28-year-old woman, whose appearance bespoke a harsh life, wanted to know if her husband's behavior would change in future. She was torn between leaving her husband, as he daily told her to do, and staying for the sake of their two sons. She was undoubtedly a regular client, for the *mudang* greeted her familiarly: "What! You again! Haven't seen you around for awhile—have things settled down a little?" Looking askance at the unanswering client, she continued: "You've been making the rounds of *mudang*s again, haven't you? Can they tell you any differently, when your fate (*p'altcha*) is such?"[2]

This client had been supporting her family since her husband's business failed. The husband, with whom she had made a love marriage,[3] had been chronically unemployed, spending his days lounging at home and his evenings out drinking up her meager earnings. He often beat her, accusing her of hiding money from him. If she complained, he would tell her to get lost. She asked the *mudang* to determine if his future behavior would change.

Barely going through the initial motions of divination, the *mudang* poured forth like an exasperated mother: "If you come 12 times or 12 × 12 times, it's the same story. . . . Your fate is harsh, . . . makes no difference whether you stay or leave. As for your children, they were born with lousy parental luck (*pumo-bok*) . . . their lot will get easier as they get older. . . . You've been coming here for two years with the same lousy story. . . . You support the lot, must you take the abuse? What do the kids get from that father? . . . What have you to lose? A house? Bah, you live in a rented room! . . . You just take your day's earnings and make the rounds of every *mudang* you ever heard of. . . . What do you make in a day? What are the kids going to eat today? Here, take this [grabbing the client's money from the offering table] and buy something for their stomachs —the gods will have indigestion on that kind of money. The truth is, you are just stuck on that no-good husband of yours! . . . Don't just sit on the threshold . . . jump one way or another and keep to it."

When the client refused to take back her money, the *mudang* asked her maid to wrap up some rice cakes for the children. As the client waited for the cakes, another client confided that, widowed with two infant sons, she had been able to raise them both to manhood, adding, "You are luckier . . . I didn't know the first thing about earning a living."

Case 2. Two sisters-in-law, both 20 years old, one married to the other's elder brother, had been sent by the mother-in-law, who was too ill to come herself. Their problem was a puzzling illness that alternated between the mother-in-law and one daughter-in-law, resisting medical treatment. Now in its third cycle, the illness had begun with the daughter-in-law soon after marriage. Upon her recovery, the mother-in-law fell ill. When the mother-in-law's recovery was followed by the daughter-in-law's second illness, the latter was sent to her natal home, where she quickly recovered and stayed three months. During this time the mother-in-law was also in good health.

The second cycle resumed with the mother-in-law falling ill upon the daughter-in-law's return, followed again by the daughter-in-law's illness. The daughter-in-law was once again sent home, where she recovered. The mother-in-law's present illness began shortly after the daughter-in-law's return from her family.

Although an ardent Christian convert who had forsaken ancestor worship, the mother-in-law was now despondent. Not only was she ill again but her only son was becoming withdrawn, depressed, and without appetite. She wanted to know if her daughter-in-law, as a newcomer, was disagreeable to the spirits of the household and thus the locus of their problem.

The *mudang*'s analysis was that the illness was caused by an angry and unappeased female ancestral ghost, supported by other ancestral ghosts, who resented their neglect. She advised the mother-in-law either to give up Christianity, resume the duties to the ancestors, and have an exorbitant *kut* to purify the house,[4] or let the son and his wife start a separate household and assume the duties of ancestral rites, which are his responsibility.

Case 3. This 44-year-old client was visibly agitated. Her husband, a prosperous merchant, was in the grip of a passionate extramarital affair with a young girl. She requested sorcery to make her husband lose interest in the girl, whom she had just that morning tried unsuccessfully to bribe off.

Rejecting the request, the *mudang* cast divination for the client's household, thus establishing the configuration of her family life. Her eldest son, just out of the army, was unemployed but unwilling to work for his father. The second son divided his time between brooding at home and roaming the streets, having failed the entrance exam at the college of his choice two years in a row, and military draft was imminent. A narcissistic, 15-year-old daughter, showed a precocious interest in boys.[5] The youngest was a boy of ten with no particular problems.

Attributing the husband's behavior to the incompatibility of their signs, the *mudang* gave the following advice: "Don't take to bed with your own burning. . . . Get your first son a wife. . . . Take him into your confidence and get control of the family business. . . . Bribing the girl won't work; . . . you'll lose double that way. . . . She's a leech . . . will bleed your husband for at least ten years. . . . Get your second son into a vocational school; I see he's good with his hands. . . . If he goes into the army in his mood, he will harm someone and bring sorrow on your head. The girl . . . better pin her tail down and teach her to look after the brothers, or others will be after it soon. . . . Your youngest boy should avoid water at age 16. . . ."

For the client, the *mudang* foresaw a comfortable and peaceful old age: " . . . if you do right, your children will respect you. . . . Your husband will come crawling back. He won't be able to talk big . . . you can keep him in his place." She also warned that any more direct intervention by the client in the husband's affair would be like fanning a burning fire and suggested that she offer periodic devotions at the *mudang*'s altar instead.

Case 4. This 41-year-old upper-class woman was so striking in appearance that as she entered the room every gaze turned to her. She had come to ask if her family should move to a different house. Ever since they had moved to Seoul for the children's education, and particularly since moving into their present house, nothing had gone well for them. The client's husband was involved in a complex fraud involving the sale of their country estate, and the fraud was now being exposed. If her husband's role was discovered, imprisonment was likely. Their numerous investments had not paid off.

The *mudang*'s analysis confirmed the client's suspicion of the house but went further, revealing the *mudang*'s own hostility toward the client: "You have no shame ... you go to the Christian church and sing in their choir ... why come to me? ... why not pray to your god for guidance? ... You want me to tell you what's ahead.... Your husband is likely to go to jail in July ... if not, then better move by September.... Consolidate your investments into one or two and put your heart into it ... or bank it and live on the interest.... Better for people like you, too scared to trust anyone.... All your worries are 'bought' worries.... your future looks best if you go back to your home province, make good the damages, regain trust.... You have enough to eat ... why not quit Seoul and this struggle with city shysters?" If they stayed in Seoul, the *mudang* insisted that they must relocate and have a *kut* in the new house.

Case 5. This young matron, 26 years old, obviously well off and a college graduate, wanted to know if her husband should quit a good salaried position to go into his own business. Using information gained in part from the client, the *mudang* gave the following analysis and advice. "An only daughter in a son-less family, you married this man for love against your parents' wishes. They took him in [the couple was living with her parents] and found him a good job.... He has a good business personality but he is restless.... He wants to start his own business but your parents object; ... you are in the middle....He grew up an orphan ... doesn't know how to be warm with people but he is a good man ... a lonely man, too, in his wife's house, ... an outsider. There is nobody to understand him if not his wife.... Your parents won't abandon you, so if you stick by him they will have to also.... The signs are auspicious for his success ... but he should give up his stepfather's name and take back his own father's name before going into business...."

Case 6. This 26-year-old barmaid, who was also a prostitute, requested sorcery to break up her lover's marriage. Having borne her lover a son, which his wife had failed to do, she had been taken into the family by his mother and had given them another child. When the mother died, she was forced out by the wife, who promised to raise the children for her if she would not see the husband again. Even having no place to go, she had agreed, but now she longed to go back. Her lover also missed her; he telephoned her at work every evening, urging her to see him.

The *mudang* rejected this request for sorcery. But after casting the client's divination, she assured her that her life would be a bed of roses when she reached her late thirties or early forties. She would meet a man who would take care of her well into old age, but if she were to go back to her lover there would be tragedies, especially for the sons. Her advice was to forget "this spineless man" of hers, be sober and thrifty, avoid deep involvement with men, and concentrate on getting some real estate. Signs were auspicious for investing in houses and land. She reiterated that after forty the client's life would be trouble-free and that she could renew ties with her children when they were older.

Conclusion

The foregoing material makes clear that *mudang* make no systematic attempt to help their clients develop insight into their own problems, as modern psychotherapists attempt to do. Rather, they dispense supernatural explanations and common-sense advice to their clients in an authoritative manner totally in keeping with Korean culture. Nevertheless, they perform a real therapeutic role.

A number of factors combine to cast *mudang* in a psychotherapeutic role for clients and their families. First, they are readily available. Second, they provide a relatively safe and hospitable social setting for clients to unload their problems. Third, they satisfy clients' needs to make sense of their problems and gain some control over future events by knowing what lies ahead. Lastly, they give advice for action that is pragmatic and often effective because of its common sense and heavy reliance upon tradition.

In themselves these are significant services in a society where open and direct communication, particularly across sex and generation barriers, is severely inhibited and strained, as in Korea. For Korean women, the majority of whom lack access to other forms of counseling or social counterparts to male drinking fellowships, these services assume magnified importance. Visits to the *mudang* become social occasions with their own significance. Minimally, they provide a break in the monotony of housework.

More important, in consulting the *mudang*, women have a chance to define and express their problems, the first active step in any problem solving, and not without cathartic effects. If, in the course of analysis, clients have been induced to feel guilt or regret, they are not left with it. Instead, the *mudang* uses it for leverage in motivating the clients to certain activities designed to resolve it and simultaneously solve the problem. In this and other ways, clients have an active part in carrying out their own treatment but bear no responsibility for prescribing it. Hope is born of anticipated activities, but no anxiety arises from personal responsibility for their efficacy. In addition, clients have a way out of their immediate impasse, and confidence born of foresight to cope with events to come.

The *mudang*'s analysis and advice often have the effect of distracting clients from preoccupation with their own problems and redirecting their concern to other persons or matters. Prognosticating future events far more grave than current problems and suggesting appropriate, anticipatory measures for coping with them, or projecting realistically the durability of certain problems presented for analysis are only two such instances. The public nature of the *chŏm* also contributes to this effect. Clients are sometimes enabled to obtain a more realistic perspective on their own problems through vicarious participation in the problems of other clients.

In her analysis of problems and the counseling that follows, the *mudang* relies heavily on traditional values to provide herself and her clients with a mutual frame of reference and congruence. The strong emphasis on linear kinship ties found in every case and the not inconsiderable hostility shown toward Christianity in some cases indicate support of the traditional values among the *mudang* I observed.[6] Though the *mudang*'s advice, typically based on the traditional wisdom of coping strategies, fails to deal with factors unique to certain situations and people, it is effective for adjustive behaviors and, to a lesser degree, for adaptive behaviors in most situations for most clients.

Clients of the *mudang* have the additional advantage of being her social superior and sexual equal. *Mudang*s as women, have much in common with their female clients. They are in the unique position of being able to see their clients' problems from a similar viewpoint without threatening them with moral judgment or social injury. Their outcaste status gives their clients immunity to their personal opinions of them as individuals.[7]

How consciously do *mudang* perform the therapeutic role attributed to them? Most are, I believe, aware of it at least on the intuitional level. Lacking a body of systematically developed professional knowledge to draw upon in ministering to people, they usually advance their best educated guesses, embedded in supernatural symbolism for greater credibility. *Mudang* are, on the whole, keenly intuitive and perceptive persons who make good use of their knowledge of people and human problems in helping their clients make the best of their situations. They give conservative advice, provide clients with outlets for potentially disruptive emotions, and get substantial help from the passage of time in solving clients' problems.

In so doing, they use individual techniques that elicit clients' life histories and psychological attitudes. Open-ended sentences are a favored method.[8] They carefully segregate their professional relations from their personal ones, and take full cognizance of long-term effects of their ongoing treatment, though their concern is focused on the consequences to themselves rather than to the clients.

For an inside view on this point, I would like to quote a *mudang* I interviewed. After our third interview, she asked me: "Do you think you are really getting to the inside of me with all your questions? . . . Well, that's not so different from what we do. Some newly initiated *mudang* are stupid and short-sighted . . . they say whatever they feel like to clients. . . . They are usually finished in a year, at best two. . . . I've been in this *mudang* business for sixteen years; the best of us can't be right all the time so you have to be careful. You want your clients to come back, . . . to send others to you. . . . So, your advice has to bring good results. . . . Just like a doctor's job, this one is a popularity enterprise. . . . There are doctors in three-story clinics with hardly any patients and others, in tiny places, with patients lined up outside to see them. . . . Why? Because they know how to treat a person right . . . to make him feel right. . . . With regular clients I hardly bother with divination . . . I know their family histories inside out, . . . sometimes I can guess their problems before they tell me, and I know what will work with them."

Another *mudang* put it this way: "We give them hope. . . . They see it's not so bad. . . . There are certain things they can do. . . ."

Given this picture of the *mudang* as a household therapist, what are the chances for her continued role in Korea?

Today there are fewer than one hundred psychiatrists in South Korea, with a population of thirty million. If the present high level of social instability and stress in Korea continue, the prospects of modern mental-health care for the people are grim beyond imagination. Under the circumstances, it seems reasonable to consider the possibility of cooperation between mental-health professionals and *mudang*, at least until there is a sufficient increase in the number of mental-health professionals. Although a few Korean psychiatrists have recently shown an active interest in Korean shamanism, cooperation between the two groups seems unlikely because of the general contempt in which *mudang* are held and the suspicion with which *mudang* regard mental-health specialists. But I expect that, for the foreseeable future, the *mudang* will continue to function as household therapist.

NOTES

1. I attended the *chŏm* sessions, took notes, and made tape recordings.
2. *P'altcha* refers to "the cyclical characters forming binomial designations for the year, month, day, and hour of the birth of a person; these are supposed to have influence upon his fortune." It is usually used to denote destiny, fate, one's lot, one's star, fortune, and luck (Martin et al., 1968).
3. "Love marriage" refers generically to marriages that are entered into by nontraditional modes of negotiation. Their chief common attribute is that the partners choose each other and that the marriage is agreed upon before a go-between is engaged to complete the negotiation.
4. A *kut* of the proportion that this *mudang* was prescribing would have cost approximately what an average man in Seoul earns in a year.
5. Generally speaking, it is not expected or tolerated for girls to show overt heterosexual interest until after high school.
6. Korean ethnographers and folklorists seem agreed that the *mudang* is the most reliable repository of traditional knowledge in such disparate matters as healing, burial rites, ancestral rites, cooking, clothing, and even etiquette. I observed that *mudang*, without exception, present themselves in the image of the traditionally ideal Korean housewife and mother. Their hairstyle is traditional to the point of seeming anachronistic on some of the younger ones, and they always wear the Korean costume (*ch'ima-jogori*) when acting in the capacity of a *mudang*.
7. Although legally emancipated from their outcaste status in 1894, *mudang* are still subject to considerable social discrimination. One indication is that *mudang* have difficulty finding spouses for their children from non-*mudang* or non-outcaste families.
8. The Korean cultural pattern of using double entendres and open-ended sentences in normal conversation facilitates the use and effectiveness of this technique.

REFERENCES

Clark, C.A. 1932. Religions of old Korea. New York, Fleming H. Revell Co.
Grajdanzev, A.J. 1944. Modern Korea. New York, John Day Co.
Han, W. K. 1970. The history of Korea. Lee Kyung-Shik, trans., and Grafton K. Mintz, ed. Seoul, Eul-Yoo Co.
Hulbert, H.B. 1903. The Korean *mudang* and *pansu*. Korea Review 3:145–49; 203–08; 257–60; 301–05; 342–46; and 385–89.

Lebra, W.P. 1964. The Okinawan shaman. *In* Ryukyuan culture and society. A.H. Smith, ed. Honolulu, University of Hawaii Press.

———. 1966. Okinawan religion: belief, ritual, and social structure. Honolulu, University of Hawaii Press.

Martin, S.E., Y.H. Lee, and S.U. Chang. 1967. A Korean-English Dictionary. New Haven, Yale University Press.

Osgood, C. 1951. The Koreans and their culture. New York, Ronald Press.

Palmer, S.J., ed. 1967. The new religions of Korea. Transactions of the Korea Branch Royal Asiatic Society 43.

Rutt, R. 1964. Korean works and days: notes from the diary of a country priest. Tokyo, Charles E. Tuttle.

Song, U.S. 1969. Marriage and the family in Korea, *In* Marriage and family in the modern world: a book of readings. Ruth Shonle Cavan, ed. New York, Thomas Y. Crowell Co.

ETHNOPSYCHIATRY AND ALTERNATE THERAPIES

15. Cultural Time Out: Generalized Therapeutic Sociocultural Mechanisms among the Maori

JAMES E. RITCHIE, Ph.D.

Professor of Psychology
University of Waikato
Hamilton, New Zealand

THERE IS virtually no recent literature concerned with the ethnopsychiatry of the Maori.[1] Those working in the clinical field are aware that specific cultural practices such as *makutu* (witchcraft) or *tapu* (sacred prohibition) get caught up in both the etiology and the symptom production of contemporary Maori psychotics. Thus a psychiatrist has reported to me that some Maori parents have shown a preoccupation with urine as a ritual purifier, for it is thought to remove contamination by contact with *tapu* objects, persons, or events. It was so used in traditional society, and the belief persists. I have myself, at the case level, found specific personal interpretations of and obsessions with myth, with possible witchcraft, and with particular tribal culture heroes, taken by psychotics as identity models, spiritual guides, and mentors. These utilizations of specific cultural content are, like artifacts to an archaeologist, meaningless until placed in the matrix of cultural influence and social process. They are sometimes puzzling, possibly trivial, but equally possibly significant keys to understanding cultural processes that lead to both reduced functioning because of stress and to its alleviation.

In this paper I propose to speculate—a little shamelessly I confess, for the data we need to do more do not yet exist. I am therefore engaging in that well-known academic sport of generating hypotheses. But I do not do so in a careless way. The nature of Maori culture, as it was, as it is now, and will be for some time ahead, reveals balances that heal, and it is to an examination of the nature of these that I wish to direct the thrust of such empirical and historical observations as I may make.

Elsdon Best reports that in the classic Maori culture, insane persons, called *keka* (deranged) or *kikiki* (idiot) were supposed to be possessed by a *kikokiko*, the ghost of a dead person (or malevolent demon), or to have been reduced to that condition by *makutu*, the practice of malignant magic or the casting of spells. Such magic often involved body products and nail parings; hair clippings and excretions were therefore a matter of personal concern. Delirium was recognized and referred to by a variety of names including *kuawa* (wild or deranged talk), *kutukutu ahi* (delirious raving, wandering) and *ngutungutu ahi* (incoherent babbling, excessive grumbling, or abusive talk). The only recorded specific therapy was the rite of *kai ure*, the recitation of a ritual formula (*karakia*) while clasping the phallus in the hand. The use of fresh, flowing water as a ritual cleansing agent was also recorded.

Two other terms in current use are *porangi* (beside oneself, out of one's normal mental state, confused) and *haurangi* (mad or deluded, drunken, irrationally enraged, or showing excessive exasperation). Neither term was recorded by Best, but both are quite common in present-day Maori comment on such matters or incidents.

No clear classification emerges from these terms, though one probably existed and its nature might well be revealed by detailed linguistic analysis and the techniques of ethnoscience. Though unclear as to categories, the ethnographic record is rich in information relating to a person's mental health status. This was considered historically determined. Though no clear mind-body distinction was made, certain body organs were especially thought to be the seat of certain faculties. The head and brain were not considered organs of thought. Rather, they were the major repository of *mauri*, the essence of life, a nonmaterial spirit stuff generally distributed through the body and forming an aura around it, but especially concentrated in the head, hands, and, in the male, penis. *Mauri* was like an electric charge, present at birth by status in kinship, increased by prestigious action, *mana*, and giving to the person his own *tapu* or sacred status. It was largely discharged at burial, but its counterpart, *tapu*, remained on the body, at the burial place, on possessions, and in personal locations, and it could actively continue to have influence for a very long period of time.

Contact with another's *mauri* was dangerous. A priest could invest it in a tree or stone where another person might inadvertently encounter it. Any breech of *tapu* (sacred regulations) could result in loss of *mauri*, and therefore sickness, death, malaise, or insanity. In warfare the destruction of *mauri* was the chief aim, next to which killing was incidental. *Mauri* was invalidated by killing, but a greater indignity still was to consume the head, flesh of the palm, or eyeballs of an enemy, or to force him, if not killed, to crawl through the legs of a woman. In battle the hand, an agent of *mauri*, directly afflicted the head, the repository of *mauri*, of the enemy. For this reason, possibly, hand-to-hand fighting was preferred and missiles were not used.

There were, it seems, no specific culture-bound psychiatric syndromes. But generalized contact with a specific malignant influence, spell casting and counteracting spells, offense against a variety of natural and supernatural spirits, fairies, and monsters, as well as the ghosts, *mauri*, or memory of dead ancestors or other people, and spirit possession by a person or an influence—all offered a rich store of cultural explanations of odd or peculiar behavior.

The frequency of such behavior cannot be estimated, but since Maori culture provided considerable individual license, had apparently a rather loose normative system, and had a well-established system for redressing grievance and offense in warfare, the recognition, or labeling, of stress reactions was not conceptually precise.

Nonetheless, the mad were mad and had to be handled socially somehow. When this was necessary the services of a healer, one of a variety of skilled men called *tohunga*, were employed. Or, perhaps, a practitioner of counteractive magic and divination might be called. While the disordered were feared, they were not, so far as one can tell, ostracized or maligned. Indeed, the practices of the *tohunga* were an active and available means of reintegrating the person in a social sense and probably in a psychological sense as well.

There were, however, strong elements of seclusion, positively sanctioned withdrawal, and special attention and support in the traditional Maori way of handling psychological stress. They constitute the traditional form of what I shall term "time out." A person receiving *tohunga* rites as therapy would be isolated since the *tapu* of the proceedings was grave and his *mauri* vulnerable. He might be secluded with the *tohunga* in a remote place till the cure was effected, or at least the rites completed. He might withdraw and live in a solitary state till his return, when, no doubt, he would receive attention and social reinforcement for well behavior. For all of these there is evidence in accounts of tribal histories as well as tradition.

Some states were positively valued. Seers or diviners, termed *matekite*, were recognized by their capacity to foretell death or other events. Such visionary power might run in the family or be more expected in some families than in others. Or, it could result from a sickness or other psychic crisis in which the power was given or received, or from epilepsy. Telling natural omens, recognizing and using familiars, such as owls as messengers or bearers of omens, might be part of the repertoire of a *matekite*, but mostly they were visionaries having special insight through dreams, awareness, and revelations of future events.

In the wide range of ritual cleansing, protecting, and healing rites, the practice of *ngau paepae*, biting the sitting bar of a latrine, which Best interprets as going right to the dividing line between life process and death process, has interesting conceptual connotations. A parallel was the *ngau tawhito* rite, biting the perineum of a dying man in order to inherit his *mana*, knowledge and power, symbolically a place exactly between the source of generation and the origin of dead waste, excretion. That the perineum is also unusually sexually sensitive and significant is not without note.

Indeed, the number of rites is legion—spells to alleviate the pangs of thwarted love, to secure the love of another, to be protected from another's hate, to ensure fertility, to give protection and potency in battle—on and on the list goes. One is tempted to think that rites were not set in form but invented by the specialists, tailor-made to suit the case, its occasion and circumstances.

Overall what this adds up to is an extraordinary catalogue of psychiatric competence: for every ill a rite, for every apprehension a panacea, for every crisis a specialist. And so comprehensive an ethnopsychiatry was surely needed, for conflicts over land, tribal jealousies, women and status-striving were quite extreme. Clearly this was a culture with a high stress level and a high level of servicing stress with reassurance, placebo, and time-out therapies. It is no wonder, therefore, that specific culture-bound syndromes simply do not appear. In such a system, therapy was applied before diagnosis was even required, perhaps even as stress was experienced, and an enormous variety of successive therapies could be employed if necessary.

But such a system is potentially unstable. Either an increase in stressors or a decrease in social therapeutic agents, services, or mechanisms could result in psychiatric explosions.

Such a series of explosions did occur after European contact in the early decades of the nineteenth century. They appeared in several forms, notably mystical religious cults, loss of morale, widespread alcohol use, and depressive reactions. Attempts to suppress the *tohunga* and their practices exacerbated the situation, but were rather unsuccessful. Stress levels rose, and at the same time cultural coping mechanisms lost form and structure.

Not understanding Maori religion and spiritual awareness, European observers, administrators, and missionaries saw Maori rites as "black" magic. The word *tohunga* is technically a noun meaning "expert," and it requires an adjective to be meaningful. But it was readily equated by Europeans with negative associations, with the idea of witchdoctor, sorcerer, or charlatan. Western medicine, physical in its orientation, philosophically myopic, and metaphysically barren, struggled to eliminate "mumbo jumbo" such as *makutu, tapu,* the protective rites, and rituals such as the *tohi* rite of baptism of children to protect them at birth. The baby literally went out with the bathwater, and the destruction of native healing, its crafts and wisdom, proceeded with apparent rapidity.

But the story does not end there. Had Western psychiatry the potency and power of Western medicine, then pragmatism, that sternest of arbiters of change, would have won the day. But, in the continuing context of Maori belief, the native practices, at least in their most generalized sociocultural mechanisms, were seen to be, and were, more powerful, more potent. So belief persisted and persists, and from it new cultural practices were generated and continue.

Let us now turn to the present. What survives? How is it expressed in behavior and what social mechanisms service the stress levels of Maoris in New Zealand now?

I discount entirely official records of the incidence of psychiatric disorder among Maoris now for three very good reasons. First, the classification of who is and is not Maori is racist, that is, defined in terms of amount of Maori blood, not in terms of cultural saturation or even stated identity and allegiance. Secondly, in the last twenty years the Maori population has moved massively toward towns and cities, so that the apparent eruption of psychiatric disorder among Maoris may be no more than an artifact of more efficient recording, the readier availability of services, and more total detection of cases. Finally, this change has disrupted Maori community care, so that more cases are dumped on mental health facilities or come for medical attention. No epidemiological studies have been conducted, so no firm statement concerning incidence or the rise or fall of Maori mental health rates can be made.

There are surviving cultural beliefs, though these too are of unknown incidence. Belief in *tapu* is still strong for many contemporary Maoris. A hat is not placed on a table, for food is *noa*, or "common," and destroys the *tapu* of the hat. If the hat is returned to the head while *noa*, then evil effect could result. The whole *mauri* concept and its links with *tapu* and *mana* are implicit in this. For the same reason, cooked food is never passed over the head of a person. Many Maoris retain apprehensions about nail parings and hair clippings. Many feel uneasy in places known to have traditional strength of *tapu*; even driving past a rock on the roadside I have known a Maori in his twenties to express apprehension and resist my wish to stop and have a look.

Tapu is significantly present at times of death, and funeral ceremonies reflect this. Many protections are still applied. The clothes of the deceased are burned or buried with him, often, too, the bedding on which death occurred. After one leaves a funeral, water or bread is passed over the head and hands to remove contamination from *tapu*. Burial grounds are not visited without similar ceremony. Even photographs of deceased persons have an aura.

Makutu is still believed in by older Maoris, and there are still some practicing *tohunga*, combining both white and black magic in their ritual repertoire. One whom I once accompanied on his daily round treated in turn, (1) a case of sterility (for which he prescribed more uninhibited sexual intercourse) with appropriate chants and the clasping of a tree he asserted had special *mauri* specific to such a condition, and (2) a limb hysterically paralyzed, with chants, lengthy manipulation, and deep massage, showing some chiropractic sophistication. He also gave (3) reassurance therapy, and (4) a blessing to two girls en route to a boarding school in territory traditionally hostile to their tribe, by anointing them with seawater, freshwater, and olive oil, and by chanting. The same practitioner was often called to the cottage hospital near his locality to increase the efficacy of Western medicine, overcome terror, to prepare patients for surgery and rehabilitate them afterwards, and to deal, first of all, with psychiatric crises. He had priestly status in the Maori religion of Ringatu and performed lawful offices as well as conducted services.

There are, therefore, specific cultural survivals both in belief and in therapy, but, in general, psychiatric practice takes little account of them. Even less acknowledged are cultural practices that have developed through acculturation that prevent major breakdown, sociotherapies of some considerable effectiveness but which are of low social visibility or apparent note.

There is a common belief that sicknesses are of two kinds, one that can be cured by Western medical therapeutics, and the other, *mate maori* ("Maori illnesses"), that cannot. For the latter, a prescription of herbal remedies (mainly purgatives) and a regimen of correct behavior may be set. Or, the individual may consult a *tohunga*, though these days they are not at all commonly available. Or, an older person or relative may perform an appropriate ritual, usually praying over the patient and anointing him with fresh or salt water. In one locality a throat-scraping ritual was performed until a few years ago, when the old woman who did this died. Or, the illness may be recognized and not treated except with rest and care. But in many cases no particular treatment is given. *Mate maori*, when recognized as such, entitles the sick person to "time out" and to this we should now turn.

This practice was a conscious method of treating psychological disturbances in a community we will call Rakau, which we studied over a period of six years. I have since had reports that "time out" is far more widespread but perhaps less consciously a sociocultural therapy than it was with the tradition-oriented Tuhoe people of Rakau.

When a person in Rakau felt disturbed or stressed he might simply declare himself sick, go to bed, expect and receive convalescent treatment, and be visited by relatives as a sick person should. Later, again at self-election, the person would be well again, would be welcomed back into the normal pattern of life, received back in a restorative way as though from a bout of physical illness, and would proceed in ordinary life as before.

There were in this community of 350 people two clear psychotics and two other borderline cases. They had no specific "time out." They were all recognized as *porangi*, though in varying degrees, and were regarded as casualties to be tolerated, suffered but not encouraged greatly, regarded as incurable but better kept in community care. No person from Rakau had ever gone to a mental hospital at the time of our study, and it was felt shameful to suggest that anyone should. The community wanted to care for its own.

"Time out" was a generalized way of dealing with situational stress and potentially neurotic behavior. It did not prevent obsessional ideas, depressions, outbursts of hostility or irrational rage, fear, anxiety, or apprehension. Nor did it cure them. But it put the person with any such symptoms into a cultural-social safety lock when things got too much for him, thus preventing either personal breakdown or an excessive and intolerable degree of interpersonal disorder.

If a non-Maori New Zealander did this, the consequences would be different. The behavior would possibly be negated ("get up, you're not really sick"), the illness denied, and the need for time out denied. Or, it would be taken to indicate a psychological state likely to become progressive. No one wants to care for a continuously bedridden dependent ("so pull yourself together and get out of there"). Persistent resort to bed would indicate moral laxity ("laziness"), deception ("swinging the lead" or avoiding responsibility), or mental illness (the so-called nervous breakdown). Not only would others find such a course of action unacceptable, irresponsible, and personally disturbing, but the actor involved would too, and would get worse, not better.

In all probability, most Westerners when stressed would not take "time out" but would rather regard symptoms as signs that they should try harder to keep going, to cope, till breakdown intervenes.

In the Maori case there are several features that make "time out" positive and the response therapeutic:

- It is self-initiated.
- The physical-mental distinction is held in abeyance or not even applied at all. Nor is the person judged. Incompetence is accepted as temporary.
- The behavior is excluded from European health concepts altogether; it becomes a case of *mate maori*.
- The individual is isolated from further stress.
- No worrying attempt is made to solve the precipitating problems the person has had, so no impairment of future autonomy or responsibility occurs.
- In many cases the stressor disappears as a matter of course or is placed in reduced perspective.
- The social ecology is not disturbed by the disturbed person and so can move on, permitting his reintegration when he is ready to emerge.
- Social events from which the person is excluded while "sick" are reported to him. He is thus kept aware of what is going on, and the opportunity and inducement to return to normal operation are offered continuously.
- Dependency needs are satisfied during the "time out."
- The continuous stream of solicitous visitors avoids frustrating, over-stimulating, or otherwise disturbing the person.
- The "therapy" is applied quickly and as soon as it is needed.
- The person chooses when to terminate his "illness."
- There is massive reinforcement of well behavior when the person leaves his bed and returns to normal life.
- Often issues that stressed the person have been simply dropped in the meantime and may not be revived at all.
- After "time out," work to reintegrate the person keeps him busy, but he is not required to catch up on things not done.

There are negative aspects to this form of sociotherapy. It won't work with a nagging wife (or suspicious husband). It is not compatible with Western demands by employers or school authorities for medical certificates. It is defined as illegitimate behavior in the dominant culture and recorded as absenteeism or truancy or worse.

Western psychiatry has become specialized. In doing so it has narrowed its vision and scope. Characteristically it individualizes the person as the locus of illness and places the illness either in a physical context or in a quite unphenomenal context that divides physical and mental functioning. It has developed specialized treatment settings that disrupt social mechanisms of healing. For these reasons, some aspects of its recent development need to be examined and some trends reversed.

Like other specializations in the development of urban-technocratic culture, modern psychiatry has taken from people some of their competence—in this case the competence of the ill person to act autonomously and for those around him in normal life to act in a healing way toward the sick. The continuance of "time out" in the social management of stress in the Maori community indicates that there are functions that need to be returned to the people, among them the right to heal.

There is also a prevalent idea, particularly among the more cynical critics of psychiatry, that some benefit will accrue from any sort of therapeutic intervention. The so-called Hawthorn effect, that any change will lead to some improvement, is involved. This is a mindless bit of nonsense. The power of belief to cure cannot be denied, but not any old belief will do. The really therapeutic act is that which reduces belief dissonance, so therapy must rest on a knowledge of the nature of the patients' beliefs and the expectations that flow from them. We may, indeed, in psychiatry, as in psychoanalysis, spend much of our time building up a belief system in which the patient is then invited, induced, or seduced to believe. But he had beliefs before we began this process, and he must return to a world where his beliefs must be seen, by him, to be valid and viable.

In a sense, every patient "knows" (at some level of knowing) what kind of therapy will cure. If he has in fact lost this knowledge he is beyond reality contact altogether, and possibly beyond cure until some belief system can be built by him, or accepted by him, or forced down his throat. But if one "knows" or explores the matrix of social forces around the person into which his belief system is locked, one is then in a position to utilize his own therapeutic system in his own behalf.

Why should we reject exorcism, placebo therapies, or "time out" if these do, in fact, restore a person to functioning. Their use can be no more questionable, no more ethically dubious, no more blindly pragmatic than drug therapy or electroshock therapy. On the contrary, a therapy based on the patient's own belief system (not the therapist's), supported by the mechanisms of his own social and cultural ecology (not that of the mental hospital), and initiated and terminated by him (not by an impersonal bureaucratic decision) has probably served mankind in some form in every culture through all of human history, or at least till very recently.

Perhaps, indeed, what is really therapeutic in modern orthodox therapies is our own cultural form of "time out" (asylum), made less efficient because we do not live in communities. Perhaps what has made the "therapeutic communities" innovation therapeutic is parallel to, but less efficient than, "time out" in Rakau. On the other hand, the removal of the patient from the reinforcement supports for sick behavior may let well behavior emerge and be reinforced more strongly. In Rakau the sick role is played in order to get well, whereas in most of Western psychiatry such behavior would be a desperate attempt to convince others that the person was really as sick as he thought himself to be. In Rakau the shift to dependence is a step toward restored independence, and autonomy is never really lost. In the West the collapse into dependency may be total, progressive, and regressive and consequently require a long journey back.

Many have observed that to catch stress reactions before the person's coping system collapses, before breakdown occurs, is the real objective of the mental hygiene movement. Well and good, but where can people take their troubles? In Rakau the answer is, to bed. By this the individual signals to others his need. They, understanding this, respond with healing behavior. A good deal of humanity, given the chance, will do the same. The psychiatrist of the future, like the Maori practitioner of old, may have to invent a new therapy for every patient and rely more on the supports that existed before, and will exist after, he gives his services. And if it worked then, why not now?

NOTE

For early Maori beliefs see Elsdon Best, *The Maori* (1924), *Spiritual and Mental Concepts of the Maori* (1922), and *Maori Religion and Mythology* (1924), all published by the Government Printer, Wellington, New Zealand. Recent hospital data on the incidence of mental disorders among the Maori are available in the reports of the Statistics Centre, Health Department, Wellington. For further information on the contemporary Maori see J.A. Metge's *A New Maori Migration* (Athlone and Melbourne University Presses, 1967) and J.E. Ritchie's *The Making of a Maori* (Wellington, Reed, 1963), which contains other references to Rakau. A useful overall survey of Maori life is *The Maori People in the Nineteen Sixties*, edited by Eric Schwimmer (Auckland, Paul, 1968), but it contains no direct information on mental health or illness. The spirit and quality of Maori life are strongly evoked in a photographic survey by Ans Westra and J.E. Ritchie called *Maori* (Wellington, Reed, 1967).

16. Counseling in the Chinese Temple: A Psychological Study of Divination by *Chien* Drawing

JIN HSU, M.D.

Tien Medical Center
Taipei, Taiwan

MANY PEOPLE in Taiwan still go to the temple in times of life crisis to seek advice through *chou-chien* (divination by drawing bamboo sticks). Popular Chinese religion is strongly oriented toward success in human affairs and shows little tendency to regard the world of man as only an insignificant passage to a spiritual world (Dawson, 1948). As such, its main purpose is not to teach people to find a place in heaven but to help them be happy and content in the "human world." Therefore, the practice of *chou-chien* is more a type of psychological counseling than a religious ritual (Watts, 1961).

The persistence of the practice of divination by *chien* drawing through the ages reflects its efficacy in helping the Chinese cope with psychological problems. It is certainly a challenge for the modern psychiatrist, whose goals are similar, to study such a practice to understand culturally sanctioned ways of psychotherapy and of dealing with life crises. This paper will describe the practice of *chou-chien,* analyze the content of *chien* responses and their interpretations, and discuss the psychotherapeutic elements of *chien* drawing, with the aim of understanding the meaning of that traditional way of counseling within the Chinese cultural context.

The Practice of Divination by *Chien* Drawing

Chou-chien literally means "drawing a divine stick." The practice of divination has existed in China since prehistoric times. In the past, a simple method of foretelling the future involved burning a cow's shoulderblade or a tortoise shell while a question was being asked. The heat produced cracks in the bone or the shell, and a skilled interpreter deduced the answer to the question by the position and shape of the cracks. Divination is based on the belief that there are continuous, regulated changes operating throughout all levels of the universe; and that we must learn to know the cycles and tides of fortune if we are to achieve success. This idea is well reflected in the ancient Chinese book the *I Ching*, or *Oracle of Change,* one of the oldest books in the world (Douglas, 1971).

The method of divination has been refined over the centuries. It is said that the contemporary method by drawing divine bamboo sticks, evolved during the Sung Dynasty, A. D. 960–1120 (Zuon, 1928). It is now one of the most popular methods of divination and is carried out in almost any Chinese temple, whether in Taiwan, or in Japan, Korea, Singapore (Elliott, 1964), or the United States.

The *chien* client goes to the temple and, in the classic way, she makes an offering, worships the god, kneels facing the god's image, and silently tells the god her problems. Then she picks up a bamboo vase and shakes it. The vase contains a set of *chien* sticks, usually one hundred in number. The shaking of the vase causes a few of the sticks to begin to rise up. She removes one of them and then casts a pair of "divine blocks" to see whether she has chosen the "right" *chien*. The divine blocks are bean-shaped, usually made from bamboo roots, with one side flat and the other side rounded. When she casts these and both blocks land with the same side up, it indicates that she has not drawn the right *chien*, so she draws again. If the blocks land with one rounded side up and one flat side up, the god is indicating his approval. Then the client can go to the desk in the temple and ask for the *chien* paper corresponding to the number indicated on the bamboo stick that she chose from the vase. To keep pace with modernization and industrialization, *chien* drawing has become much simpler in procedure and thus more convenient for modern people: anybody can go into a temple, pick up a bamboo stick without an offering or any ritual and, in several famous Japanese temples, there are even vending machines selling, not cigarettes or soft drinks, but *chien* papers.

For each bamboo stick there is a corresponding *chien* paper printed with a classic Chinese poem. The poems, composed of four sentences with four, five, or seven characters in each sentence, usually describe some historical event. Associated with each poem is a set of specific interpretations, each appropriate for a particular problem. The range of problems represented cover topics that clients would most likely ask about–marriage, business, lawsuits, and so forth. If not printed on the paper, the answer can be found in a divination book available to the interpreter.

Although the client may *read* the poem and the interpretations for his problem, classic poems describe things in old-style Chinese in abstract and vague terms that are difficult for the ordinary person to understand. Sometimes there is no interpretation on the *chien* paper, and sometimes the client wants further elaboration. For all these reasons, an interpreter in the temple is usually consulted.

The *chien* interpreter is generally an old man who does this job on a voluntary basis. He is a person who reads the Chinese classics and history and is familiar with the poems and the historical events described. He is also old enough to have had a rich life experience and be wise and skillful in giving advice.

The client, who is usually a woman, presents her problem in the form of a question to the interpreter, who answers yes or no according to the *chien* poem and the associated interpretations on the *chien* paper. If the question concerns an important decision, the interpreter will ask for more information, both about the client's background and the nature of her problem so that he can provide suitable instructions. The *chien* poem is written in an abstract and symbolic way, thus allowing the interpreter to explain it in the way he thinks is the most helpful for the supplicant. Even though the advice is given as if it is provided by the god, and thus to have maximum effect upon the client, there is no doubt that psychological counseling by the interpreter takes place. This is illustrated by the following observed cases.

A young man asked whether it was "blessed" for him to change his job. The interpreter read to him the *chien* poem on the paper he had drawn and then asked several questions before he made any interpretation, including how long had he been on the present job, why was he thinking of changing his job, and whether he had any opportunities for a new job. The young man replied that he had been on his present job for only a month or so, having just graduated from school. He did not like the job because of its long hours and low pay. He had made no plans for a new job and had no idea how to go about it. Upon hearing this, the interpreter said that it was not "blessed" for the young man to change his job at that time, that young people should make more effort than demands, and that if he worked hard and long enough he would eventually be paid more.

A woman of forty asked the interpreter whether it was good for her to leave home and to take up residence in a temple with the intention of becoming a nun. When questioned by the interpreter, she told him that she had only an adopted son, who did not care for her very much. She was so disappointed that she decided to donate all her money to the temple and stay there for the rest of her life. The interpreter advised her not to go to the temple because she would be taken care of only so long as she had money to donate. "But," the woman said, "I have lots of money." The interpreter said: "There is an old Chinese saying that even a mountain will break down if you keep digging at it. How long do you think your money will last if you continue to donate it?" When the woman failed to reply, he again advised her to stay home with her son. He said: "A son is a son. He is still young and does not appreciate the invaluable relationship between mother and son. Give him a little time. When he grows older he will learn to treat his mother better."

It should be repeated that, during both interpretations, no emphasis was made in terms of belief in or worship of a god, or belief in a future world. Instead, recommendations were given to improve personal and social adjustment.

Observation of many instances of *chien* drawing revealed that: (1) four times more women than men visit the temple for divination, (2) about 40 percent of the clients have had a grade-school education, and 50 percent are illiterate, (3) there is no significant age grouping. In spite of past speculation that only old people visit the temple, many young people go also. As to the problems the clients present, the most frequent questions are about future fortune (30 percent), social achievement (30 percent), sickness (17 percent), marriage (9 percent), moving (5 percent), wealth (1.6 percent), birth of a child (1 percent), and others (Shai, 1968). The number of clients visiting for divination varies a great deal according to the popularity of the god worshipped in the temple. But it is safe to estimate that, at the most popular temples, between fifty and one hundred clients visit a temple per day. This is supported by the fact that in one popular temple there are about ten interpreters simultaneously available to meet the demand, although at most temples only one interpreter is needed.

The Content of *Chien*

Because the Chinese worship many different gods, and because there are special *chien* books for the different gods worshipped, one does not necessarily find the same sets of *chien* books in all temples. For example, the number of sticks and papers required for a set of *chien* varies from 100 to 64 to 60 to 36 to 24 and so on (Zuon, 1928). The *chien* poems are different also. In this study the sets of *chien* books considered the most popular in contemporary Taiwan were chosen for intensive analysis.

Each *chien* by itself is classified and labeled in terms of the amount of luck it indicates, such as "*chien* of great luck," "*chien* of average luck," and "*chien* of bad luck." An analysis of *chien* according to its classification of luck reveals that about 50 percent of the total *chien* poems are classified as indicating good luck, about 25 percent indicate average luck, and 25 percent indicate bad luck (see Table 1). In other words, the *chien* sets have been designed so that most people will draw a *chien* that indicates good fortune, with a lower chance of drawing a bad-luck *chien*. In contrast, studies of divination by cards in Peru

Table 1: Distribution of *Chien* in Terms of Good or Bad Luck

Chien Set	Good Luck			Bad Luck	Total
	Very Lucky	Lucky	Average Luck		
A	10	46 / 56	24	20	100
B	17	36 / 53	17	30	100
C	13	13 / 26	12	14	52
D	3	8 / 11	7	6	24

showed a high-frequency occurrence of misfortune cards. This enabled the healer to tap the patients' particular personal conflicts and stresses, which might be contributing to physical or emotional complaints (Dobkin, 1969). Both findings suggest that divination systems are carefully designed to fulfill special therapeutic purposes.

The response of a *chien* usually deals with several specific problem areas, such as social achievement, wealth, lawsuits, traveling, sickness, mate-matching, childbirth, moving, and farming. For the convenience of the present study, we classified the responses given concerning these problem areas into the following categories:

Favorable response: definitely a favorable outcome.

Delayed favorable response: a favorable outcome subject to certain conditions or delay.

Uncertain response: an uncertain outcome, with the implication that it may be unfavorable.

Unfavorable response: definitely an unfavorable outcome.

Commentary response: comments, either prohibitive or encouraging, instead of a prediction of outcome.

Based on the above criteria, the responses of each problem area were examined for two sets of *chien* books. The results are illustrated in Table 2. Examination of the figures reveals that no matter which problem area is of con-

Table 2: Distribution of *Chien* Responses by Character of Response and Problem Area

Chien Set	Favorable Response	Delayed Favorable Response	Uncertain Response	Unfavorable Response	Comment
Set A (N = 100):					
Social achievement	21	33	6	12	12*
Wealth	20	26	5	12	21*
Lawsuit	16	26	2	12	36*
Traveler	43	6	21	12	
Sickness	25	18	10	10	25+
Mate-matching	32	9	11	6	12+
Childbirth (safety)	21	1	2	4	2+
Set B (N = 60):					
Social achievement	12	11	2	26	
Wealth	16	32	1	9	2*
Lawsuit	15	11	21	7	3*
Traveling (going away)	11	15	2	8	21*
Changing residence	14	8	2	9	29*
Mate-matching	35	5	6	14	
Childbirth (sex of baby)	32 (boy)			17 (girl)	10+

* Prohibitive comment.
+ Encouraging comment.

cern, there are always more favorable responses than unfavorable ones. This supports the previous statement that *chien* drawing has been designed to encourage the client with the prospect of a favorable outcome, in the present or in the future.

Social achievement.   Social achievement is a broad term that includes reputation and success in politics, the military, and academic life. It usually refers to extraordinary achievement. In set B, it is the only area in which responses indicate more unfavorable outcomes than favorable ones. In set A, there are 12 commentary responses that discourage too much ambition. They include: "one should not be too eager to be socially recognized" and "it is dangerous for a person to seek success in extraordinary ways." These findings may reflect the fact that in traditional Chinese society it was socially valued for a person to seek certain degrees of sociopolitical achievement, but too much ambition was not encouraged, as one might become too threatening to the authorities.

Wealth.   Wealth refers to material achievement for an individual, his family, or his business. Although most responses are favorable, there are 21 commentary responses in set A that warn people not to be greedy and urge them to be satisfied with what they have: "Wealth depends on your allotment by fate, and with wealth Heaven sends down misfortunes." This is in line with the traditional Confucian idea and Buddha's teaching not to overvalue material benefit.

Lawsuits.   In set B. there are 21 uncertain responses, the highest of all, indicating that a lawsuit will last long and have an uncertain outcome. This may simply reflect the actual situation in the society. In set A, there is a comparatively large number of commentary responses (36) which recommend that people not start a lawsuit and suggest negotiations with others when there is conflict. Open expression of aggression is discouraged in traditional Chinese culture, even through the channels of law. The importance of harmony is greatly emphasized in the culture and is obviously reflected in the *chien* papers. Actually it is very useful advice, since it may prevent people from doing something that is costly and often unfruitful.

Traveler.   The term traveler refers to any person who travels away from home, such as a soldier, fisherman, or businessman. Usually someone in the family, worrying about the son or husband far away, comes to the temple for divination to learn whether the traveler is safe and, more important, when he will return. The responses are largely favorable, indicating that the individual is safe and is on his way home. Such answers aid greatly in relieving the anxiety the family is experiencing.

Traveling.   The auspices for traveling are sought when a person plans to go away from home for business, study, or better opportunities. Nearly one-third of the responses are prohibitive comments, indicating that it is not good to travel. This is understandable in an agricultural society, in which it is better for people to stay in the same place than to move around. This attitude is also reflected in the area of "moving," in which almost 50 percent of the responses suggest not to move out or change residence. Agriculture tends to locate the family in certain places and to preserve spatial coherence.

Sickness.   In set A, most responses indicate favorable outcomes. There are many commentary responses; nearly half of them state that sickness is caused by spirit invasion and suggest praying to the god for improvement, while the other half suggest some kind of change in medical treatment, either in the physician or the medicine, or discontinuing the medicine. Only one response says that the physician now treating the patient is a good one. It should be mentioned that there are sets of *chien* available for choosing medical prescriptions that were not included in this study.

This is the only problem area in which the supernatural terms *devil* or *ghost* appear and praying is suggested. The strong emphasis on supernatural beings in the interpretations of sickness may be due to the fact that, among all the problems presented, sickness is the most threatening, and is relatively beyond human control. Therefore one has to rely on a supernatural power for explanation and help. Maple (1971) suggested that the notion of death is the common denominator underlying all our apprehensions, and that superstition is one of the ways by which mankind seeks to protect itself from what is considered the enemy of survival: "Take away death, and there is no fear, nor any devil nor the need for gods to counter-balance them."

Mate-matching or marriage compatibility.   In traditional Chinese society, marriage is arranged by the parents and a matchmaker. The individuals have little opportunity to get to know each other and few facts by which to estimate the compatibility of the marriage except some information on social background. Under these circumstances, it is very natural to consult *chien* to foretell the outcome. The *chien* responses in this area, both in set A and set B, suggest favorable matches and encourage marriage, although some responses in set A comment that one should "think twice" before making the final decision.

Childbirth.   People who inquire about childbirth usually have two questions in mind. The first concern is whether or not the process of childbirth will be smooth. In the past, especially in rural areas, when no adequate medical care was available, "to have a child is only paper thin away from death." The second is whether the baby will be a boy or a girl. In patriarchial societies like the Chinese, it is extremely important to have a son to carry on the family name. In *chien* set A, about 75 percent of the total responses indicate that the process of childbirth will be safe. Among these, 10 indicate the birth of a boy, and 2, a girl. In set B, there are twice as many responses predicting the birth of a boy than of a girl. When a girl is predicted it frequently comes with the comment that the girl baby will be a "noble" person and will bring good luck to the family. A certain number of responses comment that both a boy and a girl are good luck for the family. This is apparently an effort to minimize the parents' disappointment at the prospect of having a girl baby.

Special remarks.   In addition to the responses to each problem area, the *chien* paper usually bears some general comments or remarks. In set A, we found 71 such comments out of 100 *chien*. They can be grouped in the following way: 19 suggest that the client be satisfied with what he is, to be conservative, to be traditional, and the like; 10 warn the client not to be too aggressive, ambitious, or to do things that are inappropriate to his role and status; 11 encourage the client to be patient, to look toward the future, to wait for improvement in his situation; 16 urge the client to cultivate himself, to practice virtuous behavior, to learn to be a "good" person; 7 indicate that a "noble" person (i.e., someone who is influential in society) will foster his success; 4 advise the client to be more insightful, not to be preoccupied with material gain, and to learn to know the true meaning of life; and 4 encourage the client to be diligent and cautious.

Thus, the person is encouraged to be conservative, patient, and non-aggressive, and to pay attention to personal cultivation and accept his situation rather than rebel against it. This is apparently the culturally sanctioned way of coping with problems.

Psychotherapeutic Implications of Divination by *Chien* Drawing

Divination by *chien* drawing might be dismissed as only superstition by the modern psychiatrist. However, close examination of the practice reveals that, except for the basic belief that a supernatural power superior to man that directs the course of nature and of human life exists and can be appealed to for guidance, the emphasis of *chien* interpretation is on not the supernatural and the esoteric but on behavior and social adjustment. This is particularly striking when *chien* divination is compared with divination practiced in other places (Beattie, 1966, 1967). The whole process of divination by *chien* drawing can be better understood from the psychological than from the religious point of view. If psychological counseling or psychotherapy is defined in broad terms (Frank, 1961), the practice of divination by drawing *chien* can be viewed as a folk-style counseling.

The psychotherapeutic elements apparent in the practice of divination and the process of interpretation are the giving of hope, the elimination of anxiety, the strengthening of self-esteem, and the reinforcement of adaptive social behavior.

Giving hope. As *chien* responses are predominantly favorable, it is evident that the system is clearly designed to provide the supplicant with an optimistic view of his problem and of the future. It has long been pointed out that mobilization of hope is an important factor in producing favorable changes in mental illness (Frank, 1961). Studies on the effectiveness of placebos offer evidence that man's mental states are strongly influenced by his view of the future, and efforts to heighten the patient's positive expectations may be as genuinely therapeutic as any other form of therapy. Thus, part of the therapeutic effect of *chien* lies in its ability to mobilize hope, inspire a feeling of well-being, and thus spur actions that lead to the fulfillment of the hope. The wide acceptance of *chien* and faith in its reputed high rate of accurate prediction is probably due to its self-fulfilling nature.

The elimination of anxiety. Among the many causes of anxiety, one of the most common is not knowing what will happen in the future. This is particularly true when a person is facing drastic situations, when the outcome of a change or decision in one's life is uncertain or beyond human control. The uncertainty of success or failure in one's career, the difficulty of extricating oneself from a bad situation, the uncertainty of winning or losing—such things produce anxiety. This is especially true when a family member might be lost by sickness, accident, childbirth, or the like.

When people are suffering from such anxiety they will visit the temple for divination because *chien* responses almost always provide some concrete answers as to what will happen in the future. No matter what the result is, "knowing" something about it beforehand, learning the correct course of action to choose from several possible alternatives (Shelton, 1965), or just the act of "doing something" about a misfortune (Leighton and Leighton, 1941) help to reduce the intensity of anxiety.

In other words, people become anxious in the face of the overwhelming and unpredictable power of nature, particularly sickness and death and similar phenomena that are beyond human control. To ward off the threat of anxiety and the intolerable feeling of helplessness, the individual looks for some way to manipulate or control the situation. The belief in the existence of a universal order that can be made known to men through divination, enables the individual to turn the unknown fate to his advantage, (Douglas, 1971), thus giving him some control over previously uncontrollable situations. As Freud put it, spirits and demons are nothing but the projections of man's emotional impulses; it was the "omnipotence of thought" that was projected onto the gods. Man can thus control the gods by influencing them in some way or other in his own interests (1946).

The strengthening of self-esteem. The comments of *chien*, by expressing a fatalistic view of the world, provide rationales that soothe the pains of frustration and make one's self-image more acceptable. For example, a poor person who inquires about wealth and is told that "one should not be greedy after wealth" is thus encouraged to see himself as a blessed person who operates in accordance with the Law of Heaven rather than as a failure. Unlike many other methods of divination, *chien* does not simply foretell future events and recommend passive acceptance; on the contrary, it offers sound advice on how to act so that the future can be faced and experienced in the best possible way. It encourages a person to do as much as he can to improve his life; however, it puts the final responsibility on Heaven. So if the person fails and becomes depressed (the time when he would most likely go to the temple), divination puts the responsibility for failure on Heaven, and thus the person can better accept the frustration with less damage to his self-esteem. However, the person who depends too much on divination is similar to the neurotic who overuses ego defense mechanisms (A. Freud, 1966): he creates a fantasy castle in the air that affords him not the slightest protection against the very real dangers in the world in which he lives (Maple, 1971).

The reinforcement of adaptive social behavior. The *chien* books, like other culture products such as folklore (DeVos and Hippler, 1969), reflect the traditionally sanctioned way of assessing problems and the sociocultural pattern of coping with them. The supplicant is urged to follow traditional ways of behavior so that he can function well within his social and cultural environment (Devereux, 1958). The adherence to a complicated system of prohibitions and restrictions in guidance by divination evolved not only because in primitive society the element of social control is provided by religion and magic rather than by political and legal organization, but also because the emphasis of Chinese religions is not on the supernatural but on behavior and the fulfillment of special duties (Dawson, 1948).

Comment

The practice of divination by *chien* drawing in contemporary Taiwan has been studied as a folk method of psychological counseling. It is additional evidence that the study of such traditional ways of mental healing provide new insights for the theory and practice of modern psychotherapy in Taiwan.

First, the Chinese are used to submitting to authority instead of dealing with people on an equal basis. As the therapist is seen as an authoritative figure, he is expected to be more active and, in contrast with the Western therapist, to give approval or disapproval, and suggestions or prohibitions without hesitation. If he fails to do so, the Chinese client will not only be disappointed and frustrated but will also discontinue psychotherapy. This is a common complaint made by the Western therapist about the Chinese patients. Interpersonal relationships of the Chinese have been oriented toward mutual dependency (Tseng and Hsu, 1972). This differs greatly from the value of individuality and independence in the West, and allows the therapist treating the Chinese patient more opportunity to gratify the patient's need for dependency without evoking undue shame. *Chien* papers and their interpreters, almost without exception, give instructions. This can explain the persistence of *chien* drawing through the ages and the fact that it is still widely accepted in contemporary Taiwan.

Second, the Chinese consider it rude to express emotions directly and openly and value subtle and symbolic ways of expression. They cannot comfortably discuss personal feelings directly in psychological terms (Tseng and Hsu, 1969). For example, it is very rare for a Chinese to say "I love you" except in English, as to say so is considered in bad taste. But to say "the moon is beautiful" sometimes communicates the same meanings, and "I like you" is the strongest expression a person can give in the spoken language. A common frustration for the Western therapist who treats Oriental patients is the patient's strong resistance to talking about emotions and to accepting psychological interpretation. He would be less frustrated if he could learn to put his interpretation in broad and philosophical terms, like the *chien* commentary responses. What Y.Y. Li said about the Chinese shaman is also true of *chien* divination. *Chien* responses, like Chinese shamans, use the whole cultural system as background in giving a meaningful interpretation to the patient (1972). The work of the Western-trained therapist would be more rewarding to himself and more helpful to his patient if he could fit his theory and practice of psychotherapy into the Chinese cultural system instead of simply transplanting the Western one. After all, even for organ transplantation, homogeneity between the recipient and the donor is essential for success.

Third, different types of psychotherapy have different goals. For example, the goal of psychoanalysis or analytically oriented psychotherapy is primarily self-realization—to broaden one's abilities for choice by broadening the conscious dimensions of awareness. Only secondarily is it to achieve more effective adaptive behavior. It is not the role of the therapist to direct the patient's behavioral choice but to equip him to do it himself. In the United States, where psychotherapy is most popular, there are already demands for more direct and manipulatory means of resolving immediate crises. As Aaron Stern expressed it: "One can afford the luxury of long-range individual maturation only when the house is not on fire" (1967). This is particularly true in Chinese society. The popularity of divination by *chien* drawing, which can be regarded as an ultra-short-term therapy, indicates the great demand for such a therapy, not only because the need for psychological help is greater than modern psychotherapy can meet, but also because it better suits Chinese culture.

REFERENCES

Beattie, J.H.M. 1966. Consulting a diviner in Bunyoro: a text. Ethnology 5:202–17.
———. 1967. Consulting a Nyoro diviner: the ethnologist as client. Ethnology 6:57–65.
Dawson, C. 1948. Religion and culture. New York, Sheed & Ward.
DeVos, G.A., and A.A. Hippler. 1969. Culture psychology: comparative studies of human behavior. *In* Handbook of social psychology. Vol. 4. G. Lindzey, ed. Boston, Addison-Wesley.
Devereux, G. 1958. Cultural thought models in primitive and modern psychiatric theories. Psychiatry 21:359–74.
Dobkin, M. 1969. Fortune's malice: divination, psychotherapy, and folk medicine in Peru. Journal of American Folklore 82:132–41.
Douglas, A. 1971. How to consult the *I Ching*, the oracle of change. New York, G.P. Putnam & Sons.
Elliott, A.J.A. 1964. Chinese spirit-medium cults in Singapore. Singapore, Donald Moore.
Frank, J.D. 1961. Persuasion and healing: a comparative study of psychotherapy. Baltimore, Johns Hopkins Press.
Freud, A. 1966. The ego and the mechanism of defense. The writings of Anna Freud. Vol. 2. New York, International Universities Press.
Freud, S. 1946. Totem and taboo. New York, Random House.
Kiev, A. 1964. The study of folk psychiatry. *In* Magic, faith and healing. A. Kiev, ed. New York, Free Press of Glencoe.
Leighton, A.H., and D.C. Leighton. 1941. Elements of psychotherapy in Navaho religion. Psychiatry 4:515–23.
Li, Y.Y. 1972. Shamanism in Taiwan: an anthropological inquiry. Paper presented at the Fourth Conference on Culture and Mental Health in Asia and the Pacific, Honolulu, March 20–24.
Maple, E. 1971. Superstition and the superstitious. London and New York, W.H. Allen.
Shai, W.H. 1968. The study of divination in a Chinese temple in Taiwan. Thought and Word 6, 2:85–88. [In Chinese]

Shelton, A.J. 1965. The meaning and method of Afa divination among the Northern Nsukka Ibo. American Anthropologist 67:1441–45.

Stern, A. 1967. Social goals in psychotherapy. *In* The contribution of the social sciences to psychotherapy. L. Bernstein and B.C. Burris, eds. Springfield, Illinois, Charles C. Thomas.

Tseng, W.S., and J. Hsu. 1969–70. Chinese culture, personality formation and mental illness. International Journal of Social Psychiatry 16:5–14.

———. 1972. The Chinese attitude toward parental authority as expressed in Chinese children's stories. Archives of General Psychiatry 26:28–34.

Watts, P.W. 1961. Psychotherapy East and West. New York, Pantheon Books.

Zuon, T.T. 1928. The origin of divination. Bulletin of Institute of History and Philosophy 1 (1):47–87. Canton, National Institute of China. [In Chinese]

17. Social Change and Psychiatric Illness in Ceylon: Traditional and Modern Conceptions of Disease and Treatment

NANCY E. WAXLER, Ph.D.

Department of Psychiatry
Harvard Medical School
Cambridge, Massachusetts

MANY WESTERN PSYCHIATRISTS have been intrigued with the question of how "their" treatments and "their" theories might fare in a culture in which people traditionally see madness as supernaturally caused and supernaturally cured. Being intrigued may come partly from the suspicion that there is basically little difference between the shaman's treatment and the psychoanalyst's methods. However, that is the suspicion of a small minority of practitioners. The majority would most likely expect that Western treatments, when introduced into a peasant society, would swiftly prove themselves, and the indigenous treatments would wither away; this rather one-sided battle might vary in duration, but eventually science would win.

The relation between Western and indigenous medical systems, of course, is more complex than either of the above explanations. One might think of the real issue as Gould states it (1965): Folk and scientific medicine are intertwined, each serving a function for the social system, each altering its methods, theories and practices in response to the other, and therefore each leading to changes in use by members of the society. The nature of these interrelationships is the interesting empirical question.

The island of Ceylon provides a suitable laboratory for examining this question. As we will see, the Sinhalese of Ceylon have several elaborate supernatural theories of mental illness and, over the centuries, have developed a system of magico-religious treatments for such problems. Side by side with these methods stands Ayurvedic medicine, another non-Western but physically based treatment mode used for a number of illnesses that we would call psychiatric. Yet, within this century Ceylon has opened three government mental hospitals as well as a number of public outpatient clinics and psychiatric wards in general hospitals, all Western-oriented in patient management and treatment. Who goes to these hospitals? Have they tried other treatments before resorting to Western medicine? How do they explain the illness to themselves? In other words, in a peasant society like Ceylon's, how are indigenous treatment systems and Western psychiatry interrelated in the minds and actions of families forced to do something for their ill members?

Psychiatric and anthropological studies in other cultures suggest that the answers to these questions are not simple. Gould (1957, 1965) has shown, in one village in India, that both the quality of the illness and the nature of the personal relationship between family and practitioner are variables that may send a family to a specific treatment agent. Western medicine is usually chosen for an acute or life-threatening illness, while indigenous agents treat a more circumscribed range of illnesses consisting of chronic and poorly defined complaints, probably including mental illness. Field (1960) reports a sequential pattern in Ghana in which mentally ill villagers first go to a native shrine, where the social or supernatural cause of the illness is established, before going (or not going) to the Western hospital for treatment. Hartog's impressions (1972) also support this sort of functional difference between the *bomoh* (native healer in Malaysia) and the physician, with the *bomoh* serving as the front-line referral agent for psychiatric illnesses. Ames (1963) writes that the Sinhalese villager in Ceylon thinks of Western medicine as simply another form of magic; to him it is neither the "best" nor the "last resort"; his observations suggest that one treatment system seems to be a simple substitute for the other.

In these and other studies it is apparent that the use of indigenous and Western medical systems is closely linked to the ideology and values of the culture as well as to the economic and social structure. For example, Gould says one reason Western medicine is used in India for acute disabling illnesses is that the medicine is quickly effective and can return a worker to the fields, where he is sorely needed, very soon. It would follow, then, that when cultural values change and the structure of the social system is altered, we might expect a change in the use of medical systems and in the explanations or understanding of illness.

We know from historical data that Ceylon is in the process of rather rapid social change, centered on increasing urbanization and industrialization, which is resulting in a larger middle class (Ryan, 1952; Wriggins, 1960). Structural changes in the society and in dominant values have been reported (Ryan, 1952; Pieris, 1952), especially an increase in concern with competition, individualism, and acquisitiveness. Recent changes in Buddhist beliefs and practices from passive acceptance of one's karma to active search for merit (through home meditation centers, social action groups, and the like) reflect a shift in these dominant values toward individual responsibility for one's own life situation (Ames, 1963; Obeyesekere, 1970a).

We would expect, then, that such changes in Ceylonese social structure and values would lead to new definitions of deviance, particularly mental illnesses, bringing with them new ideas about etiology and new modes of preferred treatment. For example, with increasing stress on individual responsibility we might predict that the occurrence of a mental illness would increasingly be attributed to the patient's own life-style and past social experiences rather than to an external agent such as a ghost or a neighbor who has done witchcraft. If this line of argument is true, we might predict that Ceylonese who hold modern values and are of middle-class status are most likely to use Western medicine and to hold ideas of causation that mesh with the ideology of Western psychiatry.

Thus, the question we will investigate is this: Does social change, as represented by modern values and mobility, lead to changes in beliefs about the etiology of mental illness and to changes in the choice of treatment? We will examine this question by looking at the actions and ideas of family members as they try to make sense out of the strange behavior of their own psychiatric patient and as they search for a treatment that will cure.

Psychiatric Treatment Systems in Ceylon

For the treatment of psychiatric illnesses, Sinhalese villagers currently recognize at least seven different agents upon whom they might call for help with a psychiatric illness in their families. (Some of these are described in detail in Wirz, 1954, and Yalman, 1964.) The Ayurvedic physician, or *vederala*, follows the ancient Indian theory that illness is generally due to an imbalance of the three body humors, wind, bile, and phlegm; imbalance may be explained by such things as poor diet, extreme climate, and inappropriate styles of life. Mental illness is commonly understood by Ayurvedic physicians to be caused by an excess of bile that results in an increase of heat in the head. Treatment for this may consist of herbal decoctions, oil rubbed on the head, an irritant put into the nostrils, and a regimen of baths. Some Ayurvedic physicians have been formally trained; the large proportion, however, have learned their skills through apprenticeship and may practice medicine as an adjunct to other jobs in the villages (Obeyesekere, 1970b, 1971).

The Western doctor, practicing either privately or in a government hospital, also treats psychiatric illnesses, usually with drugs or electric shock, and seldom with psychotherapy. His conception of psychiatric illness is oriented toward British psychiatric theory and thus has a relatively large organic component.

Besides these two treatment agents specializing in physical illness, the villager may look to others. The astrologer may be consulted, since a psychiatric illness may have descended upon a person because he is under the bad influence of the planets. An astrologer is useful especially because he can estimate prognosis; he reads the patient's horoscope and determines how long the bad influence may last. Secondarily, he diagnoses illness and may make treatment suggestions. The soothsayer (*sastara-karaya*), too, gives diagnoses and prognoses by looking into a flame, globe, or bottle of oil. Very often these diagnoses have to do with supernatural phenomena, particularly witchcraft done by a jealous acquaintance.

The exorcist (*kattadiya*) may be called to diagnose and treat possession by demons or ghosts that are believed to have entered the patient's body when he was in a weakened condition or in an unsafe place. He carries out sometimes simple rituals and sometimes elaborate ceremonies to rid the patient of these devils and thus to relieve the symptoms. The *kattadiya* is, as we will see, commonly consulted in the villages, perhaps because he is a fellow villager who practices his profession along with another job.

The *kapurala*, who is the priest of the *devale*,[1] also helps rid psychiatric patients of possession by the lower gods and devils. Treatment may consist of ritual threats to the gods and symbolic beating of the patient by the priest. When the problem is perceived to be less serious, the family may promise to present a gift to the temple if the temple deity intervenes through entreaty by the *kapurala*'s prayers and if the patient is thus cured.

Since a psychiatric patient's suffering may be explained by his having accumulated demerits in a past life, or by sinful behavior in his present life, a Buddhist priest may be asked to carry out ritual readings of holy verses and to receive alms in order to increase the security of the patient or his family and to ward off demons. These *pirith* ceremonies and alms-givings may be extensive affairs involving many priests, or, if the problem is less serious, religious verses may be chanted by a family member or neighbor.

The range of theories of causation—some supernatural, some physical, and some social—is apparent in the range of treatment agents. Treatments are designed to deal, for example, with demon possession, too much bile in the system, and bad living. However, it would be a mistake to think that each treatment agent deals with only one type of causation; in practice there is considerable overlap. For example, the Ayurvedic physician whose patients we studied prescribes both herbal decoctions and charmed coconuts, and attributes illness to both humoral imbalance and witchcraft. The fact that treatment agents do not adhere strictly to one etiological theory, when attempting to cure, hints that families of patients, as well, may not necessarily link, in a logical way, their beliefs about the cause of the illness with the treatments they select. Nevertheless, the culture does provide a wide variety of beliefs about the cause of mental illness as well as a wide range of possible treatments.

Methods

To investigate how families explain psychiatric illness when it occurs in their own family, and to understand why they select certain treatment agents from all of those available, we interviewed a sample of such families. The sample was limited to Sinhalese Buddhists, the majority racial-religious group in Ceylon, from the Kandyan up-country area, the more traditional part of the country that was, historically, less affected by colonialism. Eighty-nine families were selected from the two sources. (1) A Western hospital psychiatric ward; all first admissions over a four-month period in 1970 were interviewed, yielding 55 families. (2) An Ayurvedic treatment center run by a Buddhist monk who specializes in Ayurvedic treatment of psychiatric patients. We interviewed families of all inpatients and outpatients whom he had diagnosed as mentally ill, yielding 34 familes.[2] A comparison group of families of tuberculosis patients was also interviewed; data from this sample will not be presented here.

Families were contacted by a letter that explained the purpose of the study and emphasized the research goal. With a few exceptions all interviews were done in the family home, with several family members, sometimes the patient, participating. There were no refusals, although a small proportion of families could not be found.

The interview, consisting of a set of standard, open-ended questions, was conducted by the investigator through an experienced interpreter. It was tape-recorded and later retranslated and transcribed. Since we were concerned with ways in which social background and values may explain theories of illness and treatments selected, we included questions on all of the following topics: (1) the social background of the family and the patient; (2) traditional and modern values; (3) the patient's social performance and symptoms at the sampling point (the hospital or the priest's clinic); (4) the patient's social performance and symptoms at the onset of the illness; (5) the family's and patient's ideas of the cause of the illness; (6) a detailed treatment history, including information on why each treatment agent was selected, what he did, whether the treatment helped, and so forth; (7) what treatment agents were available to the family in the village.

The data presented here are, therefore, from 89 families, each of whom had a member judged to be mentally ill and who was eventually treated either at a Western hospital psychiatric ward or at an Ayurvedic treatment center.

Social Change and Beliefs about Illness

Traditionally, the Sinhalese had two general ways of explaining the symptoms and behavior that we would label mental illness. The illness could have been caused by supernatural phenomena, for example, being possessed by a *yakka* (demon), or it could have resulted from physical phenomena such as having worked in a hot climate. Within the supernatural category, of course, are a number of subtypes, since a mentally ill person may be possessed by lower gods, demons, or ghosts, or suffering from witchcraft, from the bad influence of the planets, or from bad karma. Implied in this list of causes is also the idea that some causal agents are more noxious than others; the bad influence of the planets may predispose a person to attack by a *yakka*, for example, but the planetary influence by itself may not be enough to cause the illness. The "physical" explanations generally involve ideas of humoral imbalance, which may or may not be touched off by such things as a hot climate or eating "hot" foods.

With the introduction of Western medicine came the new idea that psychiatric disorders could be explained by current and past interpersonal experiences or by some physical damage to the brain or nervous system. As we have noted, the interpersonal explanation, in particular, does not fit with the traditional conceptions of illness. However, with value changes and social mobility deriving from urbanization and industrialization, we would predict that the Sinhalese who are on the forefront of social change—who hold modern values and belong to the middle class—will change their explanations of psychiatric illness to fit with new ways.

We measured "modern values" by a series of sixteen questions that determined, for each respondent, how much interest and information he has about the world outside his village (e.g., does he read newspapers regularly), how much he believes in and practices the traditional village rituals (e.g., worshipping one's parents), and to what extent he has taken on new ideas imported from the West (e.g., family planning). These value questions were asked of the most active and knowledgeable interviewee, a summary score was obtained, and this score was used to classify the family as having either traditional or modern values.[3]

The family's belief about the cause of illness came in response to questioning about their particular patient: "At the time you first noticed his illness, what did you think had caused it?" Their answers were classified into three categories: supernatural beliefs, physical beliefs and social beliefs. The physical category includes both Western-oriented causes ("She had a brain tumor") and traditional physical causes ("Heat went to her head from too much bile"). In the social category are included any mention of an interpersonal experience of the patient (the death of a relative, losing a job, failing an examination) to which the illness was attributed. Some families gave multiple reasons; these families have been multiply classified in the data tables.

In Table 1 is evidence that, in contrast to our expectation, there is no significant relationship between values and the family's belief about the cause of the illness. Even more interesting is the fact that modern families are somewhat less likely to explain an illness in social terms than are traditional villagers, and they are equally likely to use supernatural explanations. This is not to say that they did not give social explanations. Indeed, modern people did say such things as, "We thought it was from the sorrow of his sister's death; he fell by the dead child and hit himself." But modern families also said, "Someone has charmed him; we thought he was poisoned." It is clear from the data that social values and

Table 1: Values and Beliefs about the Cause of Mental Illness

	Beliefs about Cause		
Values	Supernatural	Physical	Social
Traditional	36% (16)	39% (17)	25% (11)
Modern	33% (15)	48% (22)	19% (9)

NOTES: Frequencies in the table add to more than 89 because some families gave multiple explanations for cause. The 90 responses represent the opinions of 71 codable families.

$X^2 = .83$; df = 2; n.s.

beliefs about the cause of a mental illness are unrelated, and more significantly, that Sinhalese villagers who have taken on modern values and are in touch with the world beyond their village have not dropped the belief that supernatural phenomena can cause mental disorder.

Another aspect of modernization in Ceylon may be related to one's beliefs about causation, however. There has been increasing social mobility and the development of a middle class composed not only of government white-collar workers, a phenomenon of British colonialism, but also of educated, relatively well-to-do village families. One might predict that the increasing education, opportunities, and awareness that accompany middle-class status may lead to an alteration in traditional beliefs about mental illness.

Our sample of middle-class families is mainly "village middle class" and thus is a special subgroup of the larger system. Their children are usually well educated, some with university degrees. They are interested in the world beyond the village, have access to it through radios and travel, and yet the occupation of the household head is usually the traditional one of cultivator, and they live in rural areas. The sample we have labeled "lower class" is composed of families who own little or no land, live in small wattle-and-daub houses and, typically, work as day laborers in the village. Our indicator for social class comes from questions about ownership of six highly valued items: a radio, wall clock, dining table, sewing machine, bed, and car. Village middle-class families own three or more of these items.[4]

In Table 2 are data showing that social class is not significantly related to the family's beliefs about the cause of the mental illness. While we might expect that village middle-class families would have taken on social explanations of illness, they are most likely to attribute the illness to the supernatural—demon possession, witchcraft, and the bad influence of the planets. The lower-class families most often think of physical explanations.

This rather consistent trend in the data, that modern and middle-class families prefer supernatural and physical explanations of illness over social ones, led to further investigation. The value and social-class measures are uncorrelated in this sample of families ($X^2 = .01$; 1 df =; n.s.), and thus it is possible for a

Table 2:   Social Class and Beliefs about the Cause of Mental Illness

Class	Beliefs about Cause		
	Supernatural	Physical	Social
Lower	27% (13)	48% (23)	25% (12)
Middle	39% (21)	35% (19)	26% (14)

NOTES: Frequencies in the table add up to more than 89 because some families gave multiple explanations for cause. The 102 beliefs represent the responses of 81 codable families.

$X^2 = 2.07$; df = 2; n.s.

family holding modern values to be lower class, or for a middle-class family to hold traditional values. When we sort the families by values and class, we find that knowing both things about a family helps us understand their beliefs about mental illness.

First, in Table 3, it is clear that the village middle-class families, regardless of their values, explain a psychiatric illness supernaturally. Secondly, physical explanations seem to be typical of lower-class villagers. However, middle-class families who have modern values also are very likely to give physical explanations. It is instructive to examine the content of these beliefs about causation, which we have, for the sake of convenience, lumped together into one "physical" category. Examination of the lower-class families' explanations shows that they are predominantly in terms of traditional Ayurvedic theory, with mention of such things as "too much bile" as the causal agent. In contrast, nine of the ten village middle-class families who also hold modern values use physical explanations that recall Western medicine. For example, "He had high blood pressure," or "We thought her brain had gotten muddled in school, from studying too hard." While these differences are not statistically significant, there is a hint from the different types of physical explanations given that, if beliefs about illness do change with changing social structures and values, such change may require not only middle-class status but also the adherence to modern values.

It is clear from the findings at this stage, however, that neither the taking on of modern values nor the increasing education, experience, and interest in the external world that comes with social mobility leads the family to shed traditional explanations of a mental patient's predicament. To some extent, especially for middle-class families, these traditional beliefs may, in fact, be reinforced. Certainly there is no evidence that along with new values about such things as marriage based on love, and new ideas about family planning, modernization has inculcated beliefs in social or interpersonal explanations of mental illness.

The persistence of supernatural beliefs in a modernizing peasant society should not be a surprise, however, if we keep in mind the fact that beliefs about illness are functionally tied to aspects of society beyond the family and its internal problems with a patient member. Several anthropologists have noted, following Foster (1965), that the belief in supernatural phenomena, and particularly in

Table 3: Values, Social Class, and Beliefs about the Cause of Illness

		Beliefs about Cause		
Values	Class	Supernatural	Physical	Social
Traditional	Lower	28% (6)	48% (10)	24% (5)
	Middle	41% (9)	32% (7)	27% (6)
Modern	Lower	24% (5)	52% (11)	24% (5)
	Middle	42% (10)	42% (10)	16% (4)

NOTE: $X^2 = 3.3$; df = 6; n.s.

witchcraft, by middle-class families serves an important purpose for everyone. Hostility and guilt arise in a peasant society, especially one like Ceylon's in which high value is placed on village cooperation, when one family obtains more of a good thing than another family. Thus, village families who control more land and valuables may perceive sanctions and retribution against them from poorer neighbors as witchcraft, and use this perception as a convenient explanation for the psychiatric illness that befalls their families. Belief in supernatural causation, in this case, then is functional, since the "battle" the family must fight is not with its neighbors but with demons and ghosts. The village equilibrium is maintained. It is interesting to note that in one village in Mexico (Nash, 1967) a curing ritual is directed toward the witch who, it is believed, has caused the illness out of envy for the greater goods of the attacked family. Then, in order to carry out the treatment ceremonies properly, the family or the patient may be forced to sell the excess cattle or crops that originally gave them economic advantages over others. Thus "the resources expended in the process of curing eliminate the initial advantages of the envy." Obviously, an alteration in the belief patterns in this case would require significant alterations in other segments of the social system.

Traditional beliefs about mental illness may persist because they are linked with the functioning of institutions in the larger society. Our finding that middle-class families use traditional explanations for the illness of a family member may also owe to their greater knowledge of traditional myths, religious stories, and Ayurvedic theories that are available in the culture to explain the peculiar behavior of the patient. Our impression from interviewing these families was that many village middle-class families were in close touch with the indigenous beliefs and practices, and were more able than lower-class families to link these beliefs to their family's experience and to verbalize them. This impression is consistent with the fact that only 3 percent of the middle-class families were unable to give any reason for the cause of the patient's illness, while 9 percent of the lower-class families could give no explanation at all and usually said, "We don't have any idea why he got sick." Thus, it may be true that village middle class, instead of dropping old beliefs and taking on new ones, serves as the active carrier for the traditional culture.

Gould (1965) does not present data specific to the above hypothesis, but his conclusions regarding Indian villagers confirm our finding that belief systems regarding the causes of illness do not change with the introduction of Western medicine. He writes, " . . . the acceptance of modern medical help for critical incapacitating dysfunctions involved no concomitant conversion to scientific thoughtways concerning the causation and etiology of diseases." Much more important to these villagers was the effectiveness of treatments offered and the personal relationship with the treatment person. Sinhalese villagers may be much like their Indian neighbors, pragmatists who, as Gould describes the process, filter new medical experiences through their cognitive system in such a way that ideas about the new medicine become consistent with old ways of thinking. "One therefore wonders whether it is correct to say that the villagers accepted modern technology or that they converted modern medical technology into folk medicine." Evidence in our interviews of the incorporation of Western medicine into the traditional system comes from our observation that many families explain the effect of Western pills and syrups in the terms of traditional Ayurvedic theory.

Social Change and the Selection of Treatment Agents

Even though traditional beliefs do not change, perhaps the family's choice of treatment agents does alter as a result of mobility or new values. When someone becomes ill we know that his family has available to at least seven different treatment systems, many with practitioners living in the family's village. Also we know that the predominant orientation toward illness in Ceylon is toward cure. Sick people and their families will travel from one treatment person to another, stopping only briefly to try out his medicine; if the first bottle of medicine (or first chant, or first prayer) does not cure, they move on. Thus, there is stress on an active search for help, concomitant with the availability of a wide network of treatment agents for every family.

If Western scientific medicine has had an impact upon families with modern values or middle-class status, we might expect that these families would limit their search for a cure to Western medicine, or at least would avoid the use of treatment agents whose modes of treatment were most alien to Western medicine. On the other hand, villagers holding traditional values and lower-class status might be more likely to take advantage of all the indigenous treatment systems.

Here we can examine several aspects of the actions that Sinhalese families take when confronted with a mentally ill family member. The most general is this: Do modern or middle-class families limit the number of treatment agents whom they consult? We have created this global measure by simply counting how many different treatment agents the family had consulted before they arrived at the sampling point (the general hospital or the monk's clinic). This number ranged from none for a few families to 100 for one family.

In Table 4 are data showing the statistically significant relations between the number of treatment agents consulted and the social class and value status of the family. In contrast to our expectations that middle-class families' networks would be small, it is clear that they consult more treatment people, an average of 6–20, than do lower-class families, who generally consult fewer than 5. However, this class difference is much clearer for families having traditional values; when a family holds modern values and middle-class status, the number of people consulted before the family appears at the hospital (or temple) is somewhat less than the number consulted by families with more traditional values. Again, as with beliefs, it may require a combination of middle-class status and adherence to modern values before families limit the network of people they consult.

However, the most important thing to be learned from Table 4 is that, while modernization and social mobility do not imply a change in one's explanations of a psychiatric illness, they do lead generally to new actions, to a more active or extensive search for a cure. In particular, middle-class families spread a wider net when confronted with a deviant family member.

Another aspect of the family's selection of treatment agents, important to our prediction regarding class and values, is the range of treatment types that

Table 4:   Values, Social Class, and Number of Treatment Agents Consulted

Values*	Class†	Number of Treatment Agents		
		0-5	6-20	20-100
Traditional	Lower	62% (10)	12% (2)	25% (4)
	Middle	33% (6)	22% (4)	44% (8)
Modern	Lower	53% (10)	37% (7)	10% (2)
	Middle	26% (5)	53% (10)	21% (4)

NOTE: $X^2 = 12.9$; df = 6; $p < .05$.
*Traditional x Modern: $X^2 = 7.1$; df = 2; $p < .05$.
†Lower x Middle: $X^2 = 5.6$; df = 2; $p < .10$.

the family chooses. As we have pointed out, it is possible for each family to select seven different types of treatment for a psychiatric patient; yet we might expect that the more modern and middle-class families would not choose some of these types, perhaps because the explanation of illness and the methods used are inconsistent with their understanding of illness, or because the personal style of the treatment agent does not fit with their own.

We measured range of treatment types by counting how many of the seven possible types the family actually used in searching for help. In Table 5, in which we examine the effect of social class upon the selection of treatment agents, we see that the data fail to confirm our prediction, in that middle-class families do not limit the range of treatment agents used, but instead select a wider range than do the lower-class families. The significance of the family's social class overshadows the effect of values on treatment selection, although this latter relationship is also interesting. If a family has lower-class status, the holding of modern values has a minor limiting effect on the network of treatment agents the family consults. The same effect exists in the middle-class families; 50 percent of those with traditional values try almost all types of treatments, while somewhat fewer of the middle-class/modern-value families use as many as 4 to 7 types of treatments. There is a tendency, therefore, for families who have adopted modern values to use somewhat fewer of the types of treatment available to all Sinhalese villagers. However, social class makes a bigger difference. Apparently, access to information, travel, knowledge about the world, and financial resources allow the middle-class families to spread their treatment networks much wider than the lower-class families can.

Then which specific treatments are selected? Within their more limited network of treatment agents, do lower-class villagers avoid the use of Western medicine and continue to do what has traditionally been done, call in the Ayurvedic physician and conduct an exorcism ceremony, just in case there has been a "scare"? In Table 6 we have tabulated the proportion of each family type that has selected each of the seven treatment agents.

Table 5: Values, Social Class, and Number of Treatment Types Used

Values*	Class†	Number of Treatment Types		
		0-5	6-20	20-100
Traditional	Lower	35% (6)	35% (6)	30% (5)
	Middle	39% (7)	11% (2)	50% (9)
Modern	Lower	22% (4)	61% (11)	17% (3)
	Middle	26% (5)	32% (6)	42% (8)

NOTE: $X^2 = 10.9$; df = 6; p < .10.
*Traditional x Modern: $X^2 = 4.3$; df = 2; p < .20.
†Lower x Middle: $X^2 = 6.6$; df = 2; p < .05.

Table 6: Values, Social Class, and Treatment Agents Selected

Treatment Agent	Traditional Values		Modern Values		X^2
	Lower Class	Middle Class	Lower Class	Middle Class	
Ayurvedic physician	61% (11)	67% (12)	50% (10)	63% (12)	ns
Western doctor	50% (9)	72% (13)	70% (14)	68% (13)	ns
Exorcist	44% (8)	61% (11)	50% (10)	42% (8)	ns
Kapurala	44% (8)	44% (8)	20% (4)	42% (8)	ns
Astrologer	22% (4)	33% (6)	25% (5)	32% (6)	ns
Buddhist priest	17% (3)	44% (8)	20% (4)	32% (6)	ns
Soothsayer	28% (5)	11% (2)	0% (0)	16% (3)	ns

NOTE: X^2 across each row; df = 1.

Despite family differences in social class and adherence to traditional values, there are no significant differences in these families' selection of any specific type of treatment, except that the soothsayer is more often used by lower-class families having traditional values.[5] Thus, class and values do not determine whether any specific type of treatment is used or avoided. Middle-class families go to Western doctors no more often than do lower; families holding traditional values use the exorcist and Ayurvedic physician no more often than do modern families. The fact that a family is middle class or modern, therefore, does not mean that it avoids the use of supernaturally based treatment agents such as the exorcist, nor does it consult the Western physician more often.

If we examine the relative use of specific treatment people by families of different types, we see, comparing percentages across each row, that the traditional, middle-class families are most frequent users of every type of treatment for their psychiatric patient, with the exception of the soothsayer. This finding is, of course, related to our earlier one showing that middle-class status predisposes a family to spread a wide network in their search for help; Tables 4 and 5 revealed that traditional, middle-class families consulted more practitioners, and more types of practitioners. Here, we see that their search is indeed a broad one since it spreads across all possible treatment sources. This combination of traditional values, which may predispose the family toward all indigenous treatments, and financial and informational assets, which allow them to carry out these choices, may push traditional, middle-class families to try everything, including the Western doctor.

The most popular treatment choice for all except the lower-class, traditional families is, in fact, the Western doctor. The latter families most frequently consult the Ayurvedic physician, but even with them, the Western physician is a close second, chosen by 50 percent of these families. The reverse pattern holds true for all others; they still alternate between the Western doctor, their first choice, and the Ayurvedic physician. Further, for all families, particularly modern and middle-class ones, it is important to note that supernatural treatments are not avoided; approximately half of all families—no matter who they are—call in the exorcist to rid the patient of demons or other bad influences.

In his report on indigenous and modern medical practices in an Indian village, Gould (1965) suggested that even very poor Indian villagers had the inclination to use Western medical treatment (at least for acute illnesses) but very often did not follow this inclination because they lacked funds. If they had no money they fell back on native treatments. It appeared that the economic factor was most important in explanining differential use. In Ceylon, in contrast, lower-class, traditional families do consult Western doctors; this is their second most frequent choice, in fact. Here the economic explanation may work the other way since the services of Western doctors (at least in government hospitals and clinics) are entirely free, while a fee (or a gift in kind) is expected by all the native practitioners. This economic difference may partially account for the relatively high frequency with which Western doctors are consulted by all Sinhalese villagers.

The use of supernatural treatment agents by modern and middle-class families has not disappeared. However, Table 6 hints at some internal shifting in the relative popularity of these agents. Soothsayers are significantly more often consulted by lower-class, traditional families; the other three modern or middle-class families more frequently consult an astrologer. Both serve similar functions, giving prognoses and, secondarily, diagnoses. However, the work of astrologers is considered, at least by middle-class Sinhalese, much more "scientific." Some describe it, in fact, as if the astrologer were a computer into which one feeds certain data and out of which comes an objective and valid prediction, subject only to computational error. Astrologers seem to be more acceptable to the more educated and knowledgeable family looking for the security of a prognosis. Firth suggests (1967) that even though people believe in the truth and validity of a ritual performance (as many still "believe" in the soothsayer), if the propriety of its use is questioned, then in the long run it will tend to be abandoned.

Thus, while middle-class status and modern values do not imply changes in a Sinhalese family's beliefs about the mental illness of their own family member, they do imply changes in a family's practice in one specific way. A middle-class family is more willing and able to spread a wide treatment network to find a "cure" for the patient's illness. Rather than limiting the numbers and types of treatment people, their knowledge and experience with the world and their financial resources give them greater access to all treatment people. In their search for help they include all the indigenous treatments as well as Western medicine. Thus, with greater knowledge and access to possible treatments, middle-class families will try everything.

The values a family holds have only minor implications for treatment selection. While there is a tendency for a family holding modern values—new ideas about achievement, marriage based on love, the priest-layman relationship, for example—to limit slightly the extensiveness of their search for a cure, these values have very little effect on which treatment person is consulted. Certainly, modern families have not eliminated supernaturally oriented treatment agents from their field of choice favor of Western practitioners.

Thus, despite some expectations that social change might lead to new patterns in the use of treatment agents, it is clear here that structural change has a much more limited effect upon medical decisions made by Sinhalese villagers. Middle-class access to knowledge and funds leads to what could be described as a more complete use of the treatment system available in the indigenous Sinhalese culture. One's basic values or beliefs about what is important in the world seem to have little import for the family's actions. Instead, selection of treatment people may be, as Gould suggests (1957), a much more pragmatic process. If a family knows about the treatment, hears that it is good, and can afford to try it, it will.

Comment

What we see here is that Sinhalese villagers do not change their traditional beliefs about the cause of mental illness. Beliefs in demon possession, ghosts, planetary influence, and witchcraft are all used by families with modern values and middle-class status to explain the strange behavior of their mentally ill family member. Western medicine is also used by everyone, in somewhat different proportions perhaps, but always as a first or second choice. It has not replaced indigenous treatment methods, however, since these, too, are frequently selected by families of varying values and social class.

Only in one way do middle-class families behave differently from lower-class families when a psychiatric illness in their family forces them to take action. They spread their treatment network wider. Middle-class families leave no stone unturned. As the wife of a psychotic patient said, "I thought I should try everything to get my husband cured." Gould suggested (1957) that in India the villager's evaluation of a medical system is based upon its effects, not upon its theory of causation. The Sinhalese villager, similarly, searches for a cure without regard for what his beliefs about cause are, or whether his belief about the illness is logically consistent with the treatments selected.[6] Middle-class status simply brings with it the greater awareness of all possible cures, whether they be traditional or modern, and the easier access to these cures that comes with knowledge and financial resources.

This leads back to our original question. What is the process through which Western medicine and indigenous treatment systems come to be reconciled in the minds and practices of the Sinhalese? Crozier (1970), in discussing the modernization of medicine in China and India, has suggested that: "One might expect some resistance to modern medicine at the popular level when traditional habits and beliefs inhibit rapid acceptance of new practices; ... medical acculturation [is] one of the less easily introduced technological changes in a traditional society." Underlying his conception of medical acculturation is the idea that once the traditional habits are broken down the new medicine will find acceptance. But our data do not support that conception. We have found that the old beliefs are retained and yet Western medicine is now one of the two most popular treatments for mental illness for all classes.

Perhaps it is more reasonable to think of the impact of Western medicine upon traditional cultural beliefs and practices not in terms of a battle between old and new in which one will eventually win but in terms of incorporation or syncretism. Singer (1971) proposes a series of steps through which any alien object, method, or system may move when introduced into a traditional society. In its first stages, the method may be handled by enclavement; for example, when first introduced into Ceylon, Western medical treatment may have been defined as something "for foreigners only" and thus isolated from Sinhalese society. Later, there may have been a ritual neutralization of the enclave such that marginal members of Sinhalese society may take part, and the norms of the society do not apply. This is evident in Ceylon now in that caste proscriptions do not apply in Western-trained doctors' contacts with patients. Compartmentalization and then incorporation may occur, allowing villagers to use the imported method to the point that it simply becomes "another option," a legitimate choice for the family to consider.

The incorporation of Western treatments into the traditional system attests to the strength of that system and to the intimate ties between it and medical beliefs and treatment. We have alluded to this in our interpretation of the function of witchcraft beliefs for middle-class village families. As Firth (1959) has argued, the traditional beliefs and practices in the medical system are closely linked to political, religious, and economic structures. Indigenous treatments not only function to help the distressed individual but also serve as sanctions for the community, making clear to all what kind of behavior is deviant and bringing deviating members back in line with the norms.

We saw this phenomenon in operation in the village where one of our sampled patients lived. An all-night *bali* ceremony was held and was explained by the family as serving to remove the bad influence of the planets from the patient. This dancing and chanting ceremony brought together more than fifty of the family's neighbors, including many children. The gathering functioned also to integrate the patient back into the community, to publicly define him as now "well" and, finally, to reconfirm the values and norms for proper behavior of the whole village.

The extent to which medical systems are tied to the larger social system is quite apparent in New Guinea (Schofield and Parkinson, 1963), where the traditional use of the village sorcerer for medical problems has become less frequent, not because beliefs about sorcery have changed or because new and better Western medicine has been introduced, but because the power structure has altered. Whereas in the past village men gained influence and wealth through sorcery, now another pathway to power is available, membership in an elected village council. The powerful network established by the sorcerer is weakened and villagers no longer feel the necessity of consulting him. Thus, Firth (1959) may be correct in his judgment that only radical changes in nonmedical institutions will lead to basic changes in the beliefs about illness and the use of medical systems. If this is true, then it is apparent that in Ceylon social change has not been so extensive or radical as to have overturned these basic belief systems.

If the traditional structure is still largely intact and thus the pressure to retain indigenous medical practices still apparent, how has Western medicine been incorporated? Our experience and our data suggest that this process is largely one of redefinition of the new in terms of the old. The function of Western medicines are often explained by the family in terms of Ayurvedic theory; in fact, some Western doctors have accommodated to this by explaining their own medication in this way and by adding to their medical prescriptions recommendations about diet consistent with Ayurvedic theory (Obeyesekere, 1971). Probably more important, however, is our observation that Western-trained Ceylonese physicians tend not to challenge the supernatural belief systems of their patients. Patients in the Western hospital's psychiatric ward were sometimes discharged in time for an important exorcism ceremony at home. Hospitalized patients continued to wear talismans: the ward staff was not disturbed if an exorcist (*kattadiya*) appeared with family visitors to recite some verses and to tie a charmed thread on the patient's wrist. In Gould's experience (1957) with Indian villagers this attitude seemed to be crucial in determining whether a village family would continue with Western treatment. Here, as well, if the Western doctor is as pragmatic with regard to treatment as the Ceylonese villager, then his treatment is accepted, redefined, and added to the list of possible options. The result, as Firth predicts (1959), is that the social system incorporates the new treatment method, thus enlarging the scope of therapy available, rather than radically overthrowing the framework of the health ideology.

If we return to Ames' observation (1963) of Sinhalese villagers' medical practices, we would have to agree that they think of, and use, Western medicine neither as the "best" treatment nor as the "last resort." However, Western treatments are not "just another perhaps somewhat more efficacious and wondrous system of magical remedies" (Ames, 1963), but instead are more often seen as another form of Ayurvedic medicine. Beliefs in Ayurvedic medicine and in supernatural causes and treatments are well entrenched because they serve a function not only for the family and patient but for the entire village social system. Change in this system—in terms of increasing education, mobility, and the introduction of new values—has simply meant that all families have added Western medicine as another option to be used alongside indigenous treatment methods when the family is confronted with the disturbing and strange behavior of a mentally ill member.

ACKNOWLEDGMENTS

I would like to thank Elliot G. Mishler, Virginia Abernethy, Stephen Leff, and Jean Hendry for their comments on an earlier draft of this paper. Thanks go, too, to several friends in Ceylon who made important contributions to my work: Sena Bulankulame, H.K.J.R. Bandara, Angelo Rodrigo, and Sunimal Talwatte. This work was partially supported by Research Scientist Award K2-MH-38,842 from the National Institute of Mental Health.

NOTES

1.   The *devale* is a small temple dedicated to the Sinhalese version of a Hindu god. It is usually built adjacent to the Buddhist *vihare,* or temple. Many Buddhists, when visiting the *vihare,* regularly stop at the *devale* to entreat the god for help with current problems. The nature of religious syncretism in Ceylon has been discussed by a number of authors (Yalman, 1967; Ames, 1963).

2.   Thus, this analysis mixes the Western with the traditional Sinhalese orientation toward psychiatric illness in the sense that classification of a sampled person as mentally ill was done from two different perspectives, the perspective of a Western-trained (but Ceylonese) psychiatrist in a general hospital and the perspective of a traditionally trained Ayurvedic physician. It was apparent from discussing diagnostic and treatment issues with both physicians that their criteria for mental illness overlap to some extent, as one would expect since both are in close touch with the cultural definitions of deviance, but that there are also major differences. For example, the Ayurvedic physician in practice included in the mentally ill category such diseases as viral encephalitis, while the Western physician treated as "depressed" some women whom the Ayurvedic physician called "lazy." In later analyses we will investigate the relationship of this dimension—the disease orientation of the diagnostician—to beliefs and actions of patients' families. (See Fabrega's discussion [1972] stressing the need to make clear the frameworks used to conceptualize disease in order to understand health and illness cross-culturally.)

3.   The sixteen-item value measure was developed by extensive pretesting of visitors to the outpatient clinics at a general hospital. The validity of the items was established by comparing value questions with background information (e.g., education, occupation, use of English), of the respondents. Some items were suggested by Ryan's original value measure (Ryan, 1952).

4.   This ownership measure is significantly correlated with other indicators of social class in our sample: occupation of the head of household, family income, size

of the family's house, the type of house, and whether any family members speak English.

5.   See significance levels for the Chi-square comparisons across each row of Table 6.

6.   The relationship between beliefs about the cause of the illness and the treatments selected will be explored in later studies. We can be fairly certain, however, from examining data in Tables 1, 2, and 6, that this correlation will not be strongly positive. It is apparent that most families still believe in demon possession, and at the same time accept the pills offered by the Western physician. Some investigators have implicitly assumed that belief and treatment must be consistent, or that the selection of a treatment agent is determined by one's belief about causation. For example, Weinberg (1963–1964:259) suggests that the urbanized Ghanian "contemplates the intervention of supernatural forces which contributed to his particular misfortune. With this frame of mind he would seek help from the native doctor who shares his frame of reference and idiomatic aspects of his personal expressions." In Ceylon other social variables are probably much stronger determinants of treatment selection than the individual's belief about the cause of his illness.

REFERENCES

Ames, M. 1963. Ideological and social change in Ceylon. Human Organization 22:45–53.

Crozier, R. 1970. Medicine, modernization and cultural crises in China and India. Comparative Studies in Society and History 12:275–91.

Fabrega, H. 1972. The study of disease in relation to culture. Behavioral Science 17: 183–203.

Field, M.J. 1960. Search for security: an ethno-psychiatric study of rural Ghana. Evanston, Northwestern University Press.

Firth, R. 1967. Ritual and drama in Malay spirit mediumship. Comparative Studies in Society and History 9:190–207.

———. 1959. Acculturation in relation to concepts of health and disease. *In* Medicine and anthropology. I. Galdston, ed. New York, International Universities Press.

Foster, G.M. 1965. Peasant society and the image of limited good. American Anthropologist. 67:293–315.

Gould, H. 1965. Modern medicine and folk cognition in rural India. Human Organization 24:201–08.

———. 1957. The implications of technological change for folk and scientific medicine. American Anthropologist 59:507–16.

Hartog, J. 1972. The intervention system for mental and social deviants in Malaysia. Social Science and Medicine 6:211–20.

Nash, J. 1967. The logic of behavior: curing in a Maya Indian town. Human Organization 26:132–40.

Obeyesekere, G. 1971. The impact of Ayurvedic medicine on culture and the individual in Ceylon. Unpublished paper presented at the Burg-Wartenstein Symposium on The Comparative Study of Asian Medical Systems.

———. 1970a. Religious symbolism and political change in Ceylon. Modern Ceylon Studies 1:43–63.

———. 1970b. Ayurveda and mental illness. Comparative Studies in Society and History 12:292–96.

Pieris, R. 1952. Character formation and the acquisitive society. Psychiatry 15:9–28.

Ryan, B. 1952. The Ceylonese village and the new value system. Rural Sociology 17:9–28.

Schofield, F., and A. Parkinson. 1963. Social medicine in New Guinea: beliefs and practices affecting health among the Abelam and Wam peoples of the Sepik District. Medical Journal of Australia 1:1–33.

Singer, M. 1971. Beyond tradition and modernity in Madras. Comparative Studies in Society and History 13:160–95.

Weinberg, S. 1963–1964. "Mental healing" and social change in West Africa. Social Problems 11:257–69.

Wirz, P. 1954. Exorcism and the art of healing in Ceylon. Leiden, E.J. Brill.

Wriggins, H. 1960. Ceylon: dilemmas of a new nation. Princeton, Princeton University Press.

Yalman, N. 1967. Under the Bo tree. Berkeley, University of California Press.

———. 1964. The structure of Sinhalese healing ritual. *In* Religion in South Asia. E. Harper, ed. Seattle, University of Washington Press.

18. Nonmedical Healing in Contemporary Japan: A Psychiatric Study

YUJI SASAKI, M.D.

Saitama Mental Health Center
Saitama, Japan

IT IS WELL KNOWN that Japan, though extensively modernized and Western-ized, still retains many practices bequeathed from the past. For instance, modern medicine, which was introduced in the late nineteenth century and which has since grown enormously under official sanction, does not seem to prevent a large number of people from flocking to various nonmedical healers. Moreover, it appears that though nonmedical practices are increasing with modernization rather than diminishing, it is very difficult to obtain proof of this, especially in the field of mental health. The question occurs as to why such methods of healing would flourish with modernization.

On December 9, 1970, a murder case was reported in the Japanese newspapers. The caption was "Mother's faith in shaman killed her son. Super-stition never dies out."

A carpenter's wife, 47 years old, in Aomori Prefecture had worried about her 18-year-old son's headache, which had not improved despite various medical treatments. One day she asked an *itako*, a kind of shaman [Sasaki, 1969], to cure his headache. The shaman diagnosed it as possession by an evil spirit. In order to exorcise the evil spirit the family forced him to fast for three consecutive days, and then beat him on the head and face again and again. The son failed to respond to their efforts and died.

I read a newspaper account of such a death, induced by a shaman, at least once or twice a year even now, but unreported incidents may be even more common. In addition, the various sectarian newspapers regularly report many miraculous cures: "Thanks to faith, I am cured of diabetes mellitus . . . schizophrenia . . . gastric cancer" et cetera.

This might suggest that nonmedical healing has reached full bloom in Japan. As a matter of fact, if we add up the number of believers claimed by each sect, the number of sectarian adherents amounts to one and a half times the total population. However, according to a recent sociological field survey (Nishihira, 1970), the actual number of present-day participants is perhaps no more than 20 percent of the population, with another 10 percent marginal. Nonetheless, in times of trouble people frequently become religious, and there is an illustrative proverb, "Once on the shore, we pray no more," which probably holds true for about 60 percent of the population, according to Nishihira (1970). Whatever the actual state of affairs may be, there can be no doubt that those who have a psychological problem often turn to religion. My report on this phenomenon derives from a field survey of religious healing on an island community and from a study of healing practices in two new religious sects.

Religious Healing on Hachijo Island

In 1961, my colleagues and I (Akimoto et al., 1964) made an epidemiological and social-psychiatric field survey of Hachijo Island. Hachijo is an island located 300 kilometers south of Tokyo in the Pacific Ocean, with an area of 70 square kilometers and a population of 12,000. The island can be divided into two districts: area A, more urbanized, lies in the open area of the central part of the island; area B is a rural, highland community. In brief, A is the town, and B the village.

One hundred seventy-five psychiatric patients were found on the island. Curiously enough, the percentage of medically treated cases in district A was lower than in district B (32.5 percent vs. 44.9 percent). Analysis of various factors such as psychiatric diagnosis, age, occupation, economic status, and level of education could not explain this difference. The attitude toward religion appeared to be the significant factor to be taken into account.

We undertook to determine the percentage of families with religious adherents in districts A and B in terms of presence or absence of medical patients, somatic patients, psychiatric patients, and schizophrenic patients. Our random sample included approximately one-fifth of the families (households) on Hachijo. Respondents were asked if they, or any member of their family, had ever been treated by folk healers such as shamans or other religious practitioners or by participation in religious cult healings. We were concerned that the answers to such a query might not be too reliable, for Japanese, unlike Americans, are usually resistant to attitude sampling and evasive in their responses. So we also asked, "Apart from healing, have you or your family ever visited a shaman?" and "Do you or your family have faith in some religion?" If they answered Yes they were counted as believers.

An average of 27.2 percent of the random sample of families indicated a religious commitment. When we compare the other four family groups—families without patients, with somatic patients, with psychiatric patients, and with schizophrenic patients—we can see that religious involvement rises with sickness, and especially so with psychiatric problems. Moreover, 66 percent of the believers in our random sample gave sickness as the motivation for becoming active religious adherents.

We also found a marked difference in religious commitment between districts A and B. Although that difference among the randomly sampled families was merely 4.4 percent and did not seem very significant, it increased to 20 percent among families with schizophrenic patients. This might indicate that patients in district B have access to more medical attention, but it is more likely, we feel, that the number of people who prefer to take recourse to, and/or who have access to, magico-religious practices is relatively greater in the urbanized segment than in the rural segment of the population.

I have good reason to believe that the foregoing findings for Hachijo Island can be taken as representative of contemporary Japan as a whole. In fact, this was corroborated at the Tokyo Metropolitan Mental Health Center, where I worked from 1966 to 1971. The facts that 44 percent of the cases at the center professed some faith in religion and that 83 percent of them belonged to one of the new religions indicate the importance of religion among urban mental patients. Therefore, religious healing has vital significance for mental-health professionals. For this reason we have given our attention to research on the new religions and their healing activities.

Healing in Two Contemporary Religious Sects

Although Japan has a variety of traditional folk therapies, those employed by the new religions can be regarded as the most important of the nonmedical therapies. Previously, my colleagues and I (Fujisawa et al., 1966) reported on several sects and their healing practices. Here I shall present two contrasting sects, S and K, as illustrative (see Table 1).

Sect S. Sect S is one of the largest new religions in contemporary Japan, claiming a membership of 1.5 million. It has a systematic doctrine, whereas Sect K is a small regional cult. At the 10-day summer training camp of Sect S, we administered 359 questionnaires. From among the 127 respondents who stated that they came to the camp to be cured of their illness, we interviewed and diagnosed 70 at the beginning of the camp and followed up on 59 of them at the end of the camp. Among the latter group the case of a 48-year-old female, a beauty specialist, with an anxiety neurosis, may serve as illustrative.

On the second day of the training camp, she stated, "I have always been dissatisfied with my husband because of his stubborn personality. A few years ago my son joined the student movement (*zengakuren*), since then I began to have palpitations and the fear of death every night. In spite of various medical and psychiatric treatments, my anxiety didn't get any better, and I was almost forced by a friend to join Sect S." At the second interview on the ninth day,

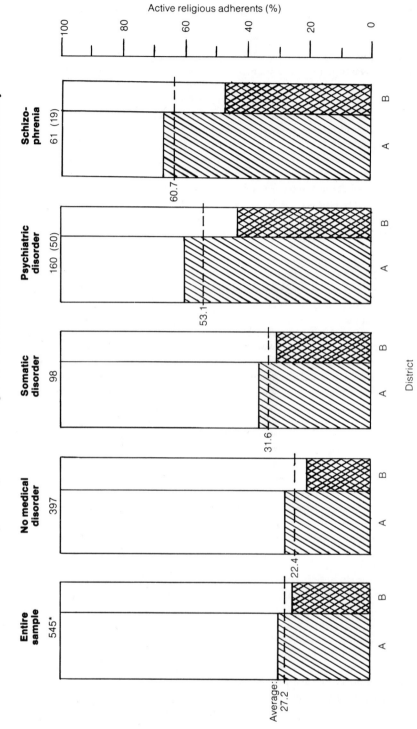

Districts A & B Compared by Active Religious Adherence and Medical Disorder in Family

Active religious adherents (%)

Schizo-phrenia
61 (19)

Psychiatric disorder
160 (50)

Somatic disorder
98

No medical disorder
397

Entire sample
545*

District

Average: 27.2

60.7

53.1

31.6

22.4

*Figures denote number of families examined. Figures in parentheses indicate number occurring in sample.

Table 1:   Characteristics of Sects S and K

Characteristic	Sect S	Sect K
Doctrine	Systematic	Nonsystematic
Organization	National	Local
Number of adherents	1,500,000	About 500
Notion of cause of sickness	A shadow on the mind	Imbalance of mind and body
Notion of healing	Be thankful for everything	Accelerate metabolism; drive out toxin; absorb spirit of cosmos
Methods of healing	Lecture and discussion of personal experience; ritual activities	Kahli massage; spiritual-wave therapy

her anxiety and sad expression were gone. She spoke with confidence and animation, "I have felt myself getting better these past several days. At last I could find the cause of my sickness. It is me! I am guilty! I have been lacking in gratitude to my husband. I will do my best for him after the camp. As for my heart, it can't be sick because it was created by God. I am no longer anxious, although I have some palpitations still." Six months after the camp, when we inquired how she was, she answered, "Quite well."

What actually happened at this training camp? It might be termed a severe brainwashing exercise in two parts. One part consists of lectures and confessions of personal experiences. Here the doctrine is strongly emphasized that the real man is harmonious and perfect, without sickness. The other part consists of religious rites that are, in effect, a combination of group therapy and work therapy.

Early every morning a loudspeaker awakens all the participants with religious songs. They salute one another, saying *Arigatō gozaimasu* ("Thank you very much"), with their hands pressed together in prayer. A variety of ritual activities, cleverly arranged, follow one after another. The rhythmic prayer *kanzen enman jissō* ("perfection, harmony, and real life") is repeated frequently. In the "laughter training" sessions the leader forces the participants to laugh. In other sessions they stand facing each other and pray that one another's unhappiness will diminish. As the sessions progress, the atmosphere of the camp becomes charged with excitement. In particular, the participants are enormously moved by their confessions of personal experiences, thus becoming highly suggestible and susceptible to cure.

Sect K. Sect K is a small local group with several hundred followers grouped around a healer in the suburbs of Tokyo. We have studied this sect from 1964 until the present, and we have followed up with periodic interviews 41 selected cases who visited the healer during the summer of 1965.

As shown in Table 1, the healing methods of Sect K are principally two, Kahli massage and spiritual-wave therapy. Kahli massage, which is derived from Yoga, consists of violent massage using a coinlike piece of metal after the entire body has first been covered with vegetable oil. This obtains from the sect doctrine that sickness is cured by driving the toxin out of the body by accelerating blood circulation and metabolism. In spiritual-wave therapy, the healer stands apart from the worshipers and holds up her hands, which are thought to transmit the spirit of the cosmos to the adherents through her fingertips. The whole or a part of the patient's body begins to vibrate spontaneously, which is called spiritual movement. During violent spiritual movement the patient is considered to be in a state of trance. Prior to treatment the suggestion is given to the patient that the sick part will move most violently. Here one case may suffice as illustrative.

A 52-year-old female, the wife of a farmer, had cancer phobia. Ten years before, her grandfather and her father had died of cancer in succession. Since then, suffering from nausea and hyperexia, she has visited many physicians one after another in her fear of gastric cancer. She received many diagnoses such as gastritis, gastric ulcer, gastroptosis, and even a clean bill of health. The differences in diagnosis made her more and more anxious, and she lost considerable weight. She was finally induced to enter the sect at her neighbor's suggestion.

The healer confidently diagnosed her condition. "Don't take any medicine, because it is toxic. You can eat everything. Your stomach is not sick." The confident diagnosis by the healer and the warm welcome by her "therapeutic brothers and sisters" quickly reduced her anxiety. She received both Kahli massage and spiritual-wave therapy, and as she entered into the spirit of the movement, her trust in the healer became very strong. She developed a good appetite and became quite happy.

Table 2 compares the characteristics of the cases we studied in Sects S and K. In terms of medical diagnosis, as shown in Table 3, more psychiatric disorders are found in Sect S, whereas in Sect K more somatic cases are found. This may be because a kind of physical therapy, Kahli massage, is employed by Sect K. As is shown in Table 4, which gives the effects of the sects' healing practices, remarkably favorable changes in neurotic clients are produced in both sects. Only epilepsy became worse as a result of the treatment. During the training period the two epileptics, who had discontinued taking their drugs, suffered grand mal attacks. Curiously enough, they felt happy despite their attacks and insisted that even epilepsy could be cured when their faith became more earnest. This poses a real problem for psychiatrists to think about. As to types of neuroses, hypochondria strikingly is dominant in Sect K, whereas no single type is so clearly predominant in Sect S, as is shown in Table 5.

Table 2:   Characteristics of Cases Interviewed

Characteristic	Sect S	Sect K
Number of cases	70 (23 male, 47 female)	41 (11 male, 30 female)
Distribution	national	local
Average age	34.0	46.5
Educational attainment (within compulsory education)	29.0%	53.8%
Occupation	various (6.6% farmer)	50.0% farmer

Table 3: Psychiatric Diagnosis of Cases Studied

Diagnosis	S	K
Schizophrenia	11	0
Schizophrenia?	0	1
Epilepsy	2	0
Neurosis	25	12
Alcoholism	2	0
Psychopathy	3	0
Organic psychosis	0	5
Somatic disease	19	23
Other*	8	0
Total	70	41

*These persons were in good health themselves but were participating on behalf of sick members of their families.

Table 4: Effect of Healing

Disorder	Change for the worse	No change	Some change for the better	Hard to judge	Total
Sect S:					
Schizophrenia	0	6	4	0	10
Epilepsy	2	0	0	0	2
Neurosis	0	6	17	0	23
Alcoholics	0	0	0	2	2
Psychopathy	0	0	0	3	3
Somatic disease	0	15	3	1	19
Subtotal	2	27	24	6	59
Sect K:					
Schizophrenia?	0	0	1	0	1
Neurosis	0	1	11	0	12
Organic psychosis	0	3	2	0	5
Somatic disease	0	9	14	0	23
Subtotal	0	13	28	0	41
Total	2	40	52	6	100

Table 5:   Disorders of Neurosis and Effect of Healing

Disorder	Number	No change	Some change for the better
Sect S:			
Nervosity	6	1	5
Hypochondria	8	1	7
Anxiety Neurosis	5	4	1
Hysteria	4	0	4
Subtotal	23	6	17 (74%)
Sect K:			
Hypochondria	11	1	10
Anxiety Neurosis	1	0	1
Subtotal	12	1	11 (91%)
Total	35	7	28 (80%)

For some adherents high expectations of being healed through cult participation are crucial factors, and they enter the faith willingly after many disappointments with long-term medical treatments. But these cases account for only a few, and the majority of our cases followed a course of taking both medical treatment and participating in cult healing. Such a practical course of action may be true of most of those who are ill among the followers of new religions in Japan. Unfortunately, there are some individuals who endanger their lives by consulting the healer without receiving any medical treatment, but their numbers are not great.

As to the question of how the patient's expectation is related to the effect of healing, we believed that there must be a close relationship but the results proved us wrong. The process of brainwashing was so skillfully designed that the results seemed almost inevitable, as if the adherents were traveling on a conveyer belt. In terms of the dynamics of psychotherapy the healing process has four stages. Stage one involves entrance into the faith and the process of acceptance. By having one's suffering accepted by others, one gains a new feeling of belonging. In stage two, intense relationships with the healer and the congregation develop. Some obtain a kind of oceanic feeling of unification with the cosmos, as in the second case described; some develop a great sense of gratitude toward others, as did the first case we described. Obligations and responsibilities toward the ancestors are utilized to the utmost. In stage three, conversion may take place, induced by suggestion and doctrine. The convert gains a new kind of insight and acquires a new sense of moral responsibility. Complete healing, the fourth stage, can only be achieved, it is believed, when one leads a religious life.

Summary

In Japan, despite modernization and Westernization, a large number of people are flocking to various nonmedical healers, especially among the new religions. Field studies and clinical experience have indicated that those who have a psychiatric problem seem especially inclined to take recourse to magico-religious cures. Moreover, it appears that the numbers of psychiatric cases pursuing such practices are relatively greater in the urban areas than in the rural. The question immediately occurs as to why such methods of healing would flourish with the availability of modern medicine. My field research and follow-up studies of selected cases reveal that remarkably favorable changes among neurotics can be achieved by magico-religious practices, and particularly by participation in some of the new religious cults that offer healing. Religious conversion apparently produces a beneficial change for neurotics by facilitating greater self-insight, social awareness, and moral responsibility. Comparing the insight induced through analytically oriented psychotherapy with that induced through religious conversion is a worthy subject for further research.

REFERENCES

Akimoto, H., et al. 1964. An epidemiological, genetic, and social-psychiatric study of mental disorders on the isolated island of Hachijo. Psychiatria et Neurologia Japonica 66:951–86. [In Japanese]

Fujisawa, T., et al. 1966. A social-psychiatric study of religious movements in Japan. Seishinigaku 8:928–32. [In Japanese]

Nishihira, S., et al. 1970. A study of Japanese national character. Vol. 2. Tokyo, Shiseido. [In Japanese]

Sasaki, Y. 1969. Psychiatric study of the shaman in Japan. *In* Mental health research in Asia and the Pacific. W. Caudill and T.Y. Lin, eds. Honolulu, East-West Center Press.

19.   The Origin of Morita Therapy

KYOICHI KONDO, M.D.

Department of Psychiatry
Jikei University
Tokyo, Japan

MORITA THERAPY is a unique psychotherapeutic approach that was established in the early 1920s. The name of the therapy comes from its founder, Shoma Morita, who was then professor of psychiatry at Jikei University in Tokyo.

Psychotherapy is without doubt the branch of psychiatry that is most closely related to the cultural milieu of society. Hence, though the theory and the treatment method are the direct result of Morita's original and unique thinking about the etiology of neurosis, it is very important to understand the historical-cultural context and interpersonal milieu in which the psychotherapeutic approach identified with the Morita school arose. As far as I know, we have had, up to now, few papers written in English that described the historical development of Morita therapy. Frequently, Morita's method is deemed an approach based on the concept of Zen Buddhism. Though Morita himself has denied it, it is only natural that Zen or other traditional Japanese concepts might be reflected in the philosophy behind his treatment method. However, we should also remember that Morita, who was educated and trained in the thought and scientific methodology of Western medicine, rediscovered the therapeutic value of traditional and indigenous ideas after twenty years of trial and error using a variety of therapeutic methods imported mainly from Europe.

I would like to give you a fairly detailed exposition of those therapeutic methods, which became in a sense the heuristic idea for Morita. Then, on the assumption that most of you here are not familiar with Morita therapy, I shall outline it briefly.

Morita was born eighteen years after Freud was born and died one year earlier. At about ten years of age, Morita was said to have been horrified upon looking at a picture of hell in a Buddhist temple. After that fearful personal experience he became concerned with problems of life and death and a variety of parapsychological phenomena.

At about 16 or 17 years of age Morita began suffering almost incessantly from so-called chronic neurasthenic symptoms, such as severe headaches, languor, palpitations, frequent mental and physical fatigue, poor concentration, and so forth, especially after attacks of paralytic beriberi and severe typhoid fever. Anxiety attacks struck him two or three times a month and were accompanied by a fear of death. Furthermore, in his early days in medical school, his parents could not meet his monthly expenses. His mental and economic plight drove him to such despair that he completely gave up the medicines and therapeutic regimens to which he had clung and became absorbed in his studies. Quite unexpectedly, his neurasthenic symptoms abated. His schoolwork improved markedly. Hence, in his youth, Morita had the personal experience of finding a way out, after long and desperate efforts to rid himself of the inveterate malaise. I hold that his earlier experience was a great impetus to the development of Morita therapy eighteen years later. Morita's unbiased, practical mind, his keen interest and piercing intuition into the human psyche, his intellectual tendency, and his strong will also contributed to the shaping of his unique treatment method for neurosis.

Even though the therapy was the fruit of Morita's own wisdom and continual effort, it cannot be evaluated without taking into account its relationship with the state of psychiatry in his day.

The inception of Morita therapy is usually reckoned at 1920, thirty years after Western psychiatry was first introduced in Japan by Yasuasaburo Sakaki, then professor of psychiatry at the Imperial University in Tokyo. At that time, in Europe, the psychiatric system of Emil Kraepelin had been established, and the theories and treatment methods for mental disorders had taken great strides. The chief concern in academic circles at the time had been gradually shifting from psychoses due to organic causation to psychogenic psychoses and neuroses. Freud made public his unique theory and therapeutic method of psychoanalysis, which by then had taken shape. Needless to say, such trends in psychiatry in those days undoubtedly exerted a direct or indirect influence upon Morita and offered a provocative impact on his critical mind for the development and elaboration of his therapy.

Morita therapy was not worked out at a stroke. Around 1909 Morita began to employ his therapy as a specific treatment for *shinkeishitsu* (the term Morita used to denote one form of neurosis originating from the strongly introverted, hypochondriacal disposition; the Japanese term means nervosity, or nervous temperament). He reported this in 1919 in a treatise entitled *The Nature of Shinkeishitsu and its Treatment,* which was published in 1922 (see Morita, 1960). In 1929 he reported his clinical experiences with *shinkeishitsu* patients whom he had treated by his method from 1919 to 1926, the period during which we may consider Morita psychotherapy completed. Therefore, Morita seems to have worked by trial and error for nearly twenty years before he established his therapy. As the nature of neurotic disturbance was poorly understood and its innumerable symptoms had not been classified, no effective treatment for it existed in Japan, nor in the West.

It is thus natural that Morita found it difficult to arrive at a definitive interpretation of neurosis. His keen interest in the study of psychotherapies is evidenced from the following episode: in 1902, when he was specializing in psychiatry he told his guidance teacher, Professor Shuzo Kure, that he hoped to study psychotherapy, and he tried to engage schizophrenic patients in indoor or outdoor work. This experience seems to have provided him with a clue to the effectiveness of a psychotherapeutic approach.

Professor Kure had an important academic influence on Morita. Kure opened the door to modern psychiatry in Japan. He had studied psychiatry in France, Austria, and in Germany under Kraepelin. He succeeded to the professorship of psychiatry at Tokyo Imperial University after Sakaki's sudden death. Morita, as a student of Kure, may be regarded as a fully pedigreed psychiatrist. It is said that Morita sometimes professed to be an unacquainted disciple of Kraepelin. Kure introduced and popularized the descriptive, nosologically oriented psychiatric system of Kraepelin. He also pushed forward in Japan the Pinelian movement of humanitarian emancipation of psychotic patients; and he was one of the few persons who had an interest in, and recognized the therapeutic value of, the scientific psychotherapy that prevailed in Europe at that time. He presented the theme of psychotherapy to Morita, already motivated to study it, as previously stated, so Morita learned through Kure the clinician's attitude, the importance of objective observation and description, and a humanistic approach to the suffering person.

When Morita started his career as a psychiatrist, the clinical term neurasthenia, whose main syndrome consists of irritable weakness including headaches, various manifestations of hypersensitivity, undue fatigue, mental distraction, reduced productivity, and so forth, was thought to be related to exhaustion or enfeeblement of the central nervous system. According to this general concept of the cause of neurasthenia prevalent then, Morita tried at first to cure the patient mainly with biologically oriented means, but he found those almost ineffective. In the meantime, he had such a spirit of inquiry that he became interested in and tried out several treatment methods that were being introduced in Japan. He modified and critically employed these new procedures, and then systematized his own method on the basis of insight obtained from the results of this therapeutic experience.

Next I would like to enumerate these procedures, which happened to serve as the forerunners of Morita therapy, and explain their relative significance to this therapy.

Forerunners of Morita Therapy

Rest therapy.   Morita found that compulsory rest was highly efficacious for manic-depressives and other psychotic patients. He adopted especially the idea and method that Weir Mitchell employed as a routine: enforced bed rest and a high-calorie diet for neurasthenic patients. Through the follow-up of this method, he found that physical rest seemed to have a favorable influence upon the patient's mental state. At that time rest therapy appeared as an antithesis of the physical treatments that were current but have since been proven ineffective for neurotic patients (Kawai, 1962).

Occupational therapy.   In the history of Japanese psychiatry Morita stands as a pioneer in the use of occupational therapy. As previously stated, he began to engage in work therapy with chronic schizophrenic patients in 1904 under the open-door system. He obtained gratifying results. It later became evident that physical activity as a treatment method could be adopted for *shinkeishitsu* patients. He also discovered that the *shinkeishitsu* patient has a strong "desire to live"—a key concept in Morita therapy both practically and theoretically—when he recognized the difference in craving for activity among *shinkeishitsu* and other psychotic or psychopathic patients. Though its effectiveness had already been ascertained, Morita found the therapeutic value of occupational therapy to be even greater than supposed.

Life normalization method.   The original method of life normalization by Otto Binswanger (n. d.) consists of a five-week treatment course in which intellectual and manual activity is imposed on the patient under a strictly regulated timetable. It seems that Morita might have received a suggestion from this method as to the limitation and length of time for his own therapy (the original Morita therapy lasts on the average 40–60 days). However, at the same time, he felt it crucial that the patient is made to submit to the regulations so mechanically and rigidly that his inherent spontaneous, creative desire for activity is hampered. After finding that strict regulations were unsuccessful, he decided not to prescribe detailed rules and to let the patient engage in work quite freely and spontaneously at his own will as much as possible; he dropped the diversional elements from the original method, which tended to distract the patient's mind. This idea arose from the successful therapeutic experience which Morita had in trying to cure some patients in his own home.

Dubois' method of persuasion.   From the end of the nineteenth to the beginning of the twentieth century in Japan, works on psychotherapy were written mostly by men of letters along philosophical, ethical, and religious lines of orientation. Lay sermons were very popular. Such cultural circumstances might have paved the way for persuasion to be easily accepted and popularized. It is likely that that is why P. Dubois' method won popularity. Becoming familiar with the work of Dubois (Morita, 1922), Morita tried to adopt Dubois' method of treatment by rational persuasion, but he eventually came to the conclusion that treatment merely by intellectual communication was useless and perhaps even harmful at times.

At first Morita tried to persuade obsessive-compulsive patients by the Dubois method, but without success. In fact, Dubois' persuasion technique brought about a reverse effect in which the patient became worse, as it intensified his anxiety. Intensified obsession caused anxiety, and anxiety in turn strengthened obsession, producing a vicious circle. Morita realized through this experience that the most important thing in psychotherapy is to begin by removing the patient's anxiety and letting his mind follow its natural course. As a result, Morita adopted a method that runs counter to Dubois' method, which G. Usa, Morita's disciple, termed "rational nonverbalism." In the *modus operandi* of original Morita therapy, it is of secondary importance to give a verbal and logical description or explanation of the client's psychological mechanism and experience. Over and above conceptions, ideas, and verbal communication, the transformation of experience itself is the therapeutic aim.

However, it may be worth remembering that Dubois also recommended a combination of bed rest and a treatment regimen for severe cases. Nor is Morita always against words. He uses a method of persuasion that is markedly different from the ordinary persuasive method because it is founded on the patient's insight through his own personal experience. Morita's method of persuasion involves guidance of patients through diaries they write, group meetings, and outpatient treatment.

Hypnosis. For about ten years (1911–1921), Morita was as keen on hypnotic treatment as Freud was until he adopted the method of free association. After 1921, however, Morita began to feel doubts about the therapeutic value of hypnosis, which Takeyama regards as the very beginning of Morita's technique of psychotherapy. It is of great interest that Morita, like Freud, tried out hypnosis before originating his own unique method.

What effect did his encounter with the works of Freud have on Morita? Several years before the official introduction of Freudian psychoanalysis in 1912, Morita became familiar with some of Freud's earlier works. *On Psychoanalysis* and *Psychopathology of Everyday Life* are actually quoted in Morita's main work, *The Nature of Shinkeishitsu and its Treatment* (1922). Since Morita studied and was trained according to Kraepelinian German orthodox psychiatry, he was naturally critical of the Freudian theory of the day. Another reason for his lack of sympathy with Freud might owe to his basic conceptions of human nature and his Weltanschauung, which are deeply rooted in the cultural matrix where he was born and bred.

Morita frequently expressed his interpretation in a comparison with Freud's theory, and his phenomenological viewpoints were confirmed in this way. Thus it might be said that Morita, in a sense, was subject to the influence of psychoanalysis, and that in the laying of the foundation of his psychotherapeutic system, his critique against the earlier Freudian concepts was an unconscious formative and contributory factor.

Mature Morita Therapy

As mentioned earlier, Morita therapy was originally devised for treating certain types of neurosis, which he termed *shinkeishitsu*, literally "nervous temperament." However, since the English term is only approximate, and misleading as well, I will use the original Japanese term in this paper. From the beginning Morita had a limited range of illnesses in mind when he used the term *shinkeishitsu*, and he emphatically stated that his therapy would be most effectual when applied to this specific type of neurosis. It includes chronic or constitutional neurasthenia, obsessive-ruminative states, and anxiety neurosis, all of which, Morita contends, arise from the "hypochondriacal temperament." This is, in brief, a personality tendency that makes a person overly introspective, hypersensitive, always worried about his bodily and mental conditions, perfectionistic and idealistic, and ruminative about his worries. Such people are quite prone to believe that their normal physiological functionings are due to some serious disease or weakness.

Here I would like to emphasize Morita held that such a hypochondriacal tendency is quite a common and normal phenomenon which occurs in ordinary human nature. It seems to me that here enters the traditional Oriental attitude toward human psychology. Morita therapy is always concerned with the transformation of states that are common in human beings, and in this sense it might be called a psychotherapy for "normal" people. Neurotic conflicts are not understood in terms of deviation from normalcy. Its main therapeutic concern is not just with the particular neurotic frustrations, but also with the general frustration that ails almost every member of society. According to his idea, this tendency is only a negative side of the universal "desire to live" that exists to a greater or lesser degree in every human being; hence, the "desire to live" and the "hypochondriacal tendency" are nothing but parts of the whole. Such a view of human nature is the most central idea in Morita therapy in the sense that it is the dynamic concept that ties together Morita's theory and his method for treating *shinkeishitsu*. When the hypochondriacal tendency is extreme, there occurs a neurotic turn of mind, and complicated neurotic symptoms appear.

Morita also used the term *shinkeishitsu* to denote a morbid condition. However, this term is ambiguous because it can be easily mistaken for the general term that indicates a personality or a temperament, not the pathological state. Therefore, Kora (1964) proposed a new term, *shinkeishitsu-sho*, to denote the morbid state, by adding the suffix *sho*, which means "disease." He also intended to give the term "hypochondriacal tendency" a broader interpretation by regarding it as an anxiety state in which a person feels that his present condition of mind or body is adversely affecting his very existence. In other words, the anxiety ·makes the person believe that he cannot adapt to his environment in his present physical or mental condition. Kora gave the name "inadaptability anxiety" to this premorbid state. Kondo (1966), analyzing in full this basic mood from another point of view, found the main characteristics of it in the subjective-idealistic, egocentric, and perfectionistic attitudes, and contended that this state of feeling is essentially the same as inadaptability anxiety.

Morita proposed another factor as contributing to the development of *shinkeishitsu* symptoms. He called it the "psychic interaction of attention and sensation." It is a process by which sensation intensifies when attention is directed to it by chance, and attention is directed to it all the more when sensation thus intensifies, thereby creating a vicious circle. He used this theory to explain the development of *shinkeishitsu* in such cases as so-called cardiac neurosis, head-heaviness or headache, and erythrophobia (morbid fear of blushing). Nomura (1962) cited the hypothetical example of a person who wakes up one morning and feels his head to be heavier than usual. It may be due to a hangover, to over-sleeping, or to a host of other causes. The point is that the person has taken note of his condition, and it is his hypochondriacal tendency that makes him do so. Once a particular condition of the body is taken note of, the vicious circle of psychic interaction of attention and sensation goes into play to fix the symptoms. By this theory Morita also described the pathogenesis of obsession, and success-fully applied his treatment to cure obsessive neurosis.

Taking erythrophobia as an example, Morita's method of psychotherapy would explain the development of the obsession as follows. A person first notices his blushing by chance but that is because of his hypochondriacal tendency. His blushing intensifies through the vicious circle of psychic interaction of attention and sensation. Fearing the blushing, the person constantly worries about it and devises ways to avoid it. As it is impossible to do so, he will be trapped in a psychic conflict, which is nothing but an obsession.

As these examples show, the conditions from which *shinkeishitsu* patients suffer are states that are seen in normal people. The only difference is that the patient intuitively interprets the condition as abnormal and harmful to his exis-tence, and he tries to get rid of it in vain. Therefore, treatment should be aimed at making the patient realize, at the deepest level, through personal experience, that his mentality is not wrong, that his symptoms are normal phenomena which only he is interpreting to be abnormal and pathologic, and that he should and can live with them.

The goal can be achieved if the patient's hypochondriacal tendency is destroyed so that the desire to live, which is the underlying vital force creating this personality tendency, can be properly utilized in a more constructive way. It can also be achieved if the patient learns to free himself from the vicious circle of psychic interaction of attention and sensation by accepting the symptoms as they are and stopping his futile attempts to get rid of them. Accepting the symp-toms does not mean resignation. It is rather an indispensable and basic step of "integrating" the patient's self-contradiction, which is caused by a division of experience into subject and object, thinker and thought, feeler and feeling. In Morita therapy the goal is not an increase of conscious control over the uncon-scious by the ego. It is, rather, an integration of the unconscious and conscious preparatory to the type of living, thinking, and acting that in Zen is called *mushin*, a state where acts and decisions are handed over to the same unconscious process that organized the ingenious structure of the body.

To achieve this goal, Morita devised his unique therapy, which he called "personal-experience therapy." He chose this phrase because it is only through personal experience that the patient can overcome his symptoms, gain insight into his disease, and realize his true self. It was his followers who renamed his method "Morita therapy." The basic aims of Morita therapy are to help the patient understand human nature, admit and realize the psychic reality of human life, respect the value of constructive efforts, and to improve and elevate his daily life.

Shinkeishitsu patients are treated either as outpatients or as inpatients. In the original Morita method of treatment, patients were hospitalized; however, that is not always done today. Throughout the therapeutic process, the patient is encouraged to understand the actual situation he is in and to become aware and experience, just as they are, the diverse emotions that have arisen and will arise. Furthermore, he is taught to understand his own personality traits and is encouraged to enhance his personality and advance in the concrete aspects of life.

Hospitalized patients are seldom given direct advice or suggestions concerning their struggle with conflict. The original hospital method consists of four phases, each of which runs about one to two weeks. Today, in our practice, no strict demarcation exists among the last three phases. The first phase is distinct from the rest in that the patient is bedridden during the entire period, whereas he is engaged in physical activity during the other stages. During the bed-rest phase, the patient is secluded from all the unessential paraphernalia of his former life and kept continuously in bed. In this stage the patient will mentally reexperience his process of conflict, arriving at a state where he is hungry for stimulus and action. The object of treatment at this stage is to block the flow of the innate "desire to live" to the worries and have it accumulate sufficiently to be channeled later into constructive living through the subsequent three phases of physical activity. At the beginning of the second stage the patient will engage in light work, then gradually in more complicated work, and finally in learning to be more constructive in actual life. What is unique during the phases of physical activity is that the patient is not told specifically what to do but merely pointed in the general direction and told to look for work himself. After getting up from his bed, the patient is asked to keep a diary, which he is to show to the doctor every morning. Through the diary the doctor can get a general idea of the present status of the patient and follow his course. When interviews are regarded as necessary and the patient wants to meet the doctor, the patient is called in any time. However, advice on the patient s attitude toward his symptoms, his problems, and his life is usually given more informally during work therapy or at meetings held regularly to discuss the conditions of the patients. By being made to work, in spite of his symptoms, the patient learns that he can accept the symptoms and live with them. This enables him to rid himself of the vicious circle that is enslaving him.

Morita therapy, in its broadest sense, encompasses a wide range of methods and forms. It is impossible for me to describe them fully here. Although a great variety of studies on *shinkeishitsu* treatment methods have been done by many authors, I believe there still remain many points which need further elaboration. In my opinion to comprehend Morita therapy from the cultural-historical viewpoint is of great importance, and I shall be glad if my paper could make some contribution toward that point, especially for the foreign reader.

ACKNOWLEDGMENTS

This paper was prepared while the author was a Fellow in the program of research on Culture and Mental Health in Asia and the Pacific, which was funded jointly by the Social Science Research Institute (under NIMH Grant #MH09243) and the East-West Center, University of Hawaii, Honolulu. He gratefully acknowledges this assistance.

REFERENCES

Binswanger, O. n.d. Grundzüge für die Behandlung der Geisteskrankheiten. Vorträge für prak. Therapie, Heft 3.

Kawai, H. 1962. A medico-historical study of Morita therapy. Shinkeishitsu 3(1):33–41. [In Japanese]

Kondo, A. 1966. Morita therapy. Seishin Igaku 8(5):2–10. [In Japanese]

Kora, T. 1964. Morita therapy. Festschrift for Professor Kora. Tokyo, Jikei University Press. [In English]

Morita, M. 1960. The nature of *Shinkeishitsu* and its treatment. Revised edition with commentary by H. Kawai. Tokyo, Hakuyosha. [In Japanese]

Nomura, A. 1962. Psychotherapy in Japan—Morita's psychotherapy. Shinkeishitsu 3(1): 25–29. [In English]

20.   Naikan Therapy

TAKAO MURASE, M.A.

Psychological Research Division
National Institute of Mental Health
Ichikawa, Japan

NAIKAN THERAPY (*nai*, meaning "inside" or "within," and *kan*, "looking"[1])
is a form of guided introspection directed toward attitude and personality change.
It has been practiced in Japan for the past thirty years. Developed by a lay practitioner, Inobu Yoshimoto, Naikan therapy was originally employed in correctional
institutions but is now widely used in medical and educational settings as well.

Although the method was derived from the Jōdo-shin sect of Buddhism,
the most popular Buddhist sect in Japan, it is unrelated to any professional psychotherapeutic form, Eastern or Western. Naikan therapy is based upon the
philosophy that the human being is fundamentally selfish and guilty, yet at the
same time favored with unmeasured benevolence from others. In order to acknowledge these existential conditions deeply, one must become open-minded toward
oneself, empathic and sympathetic toward others, and must courageously confront his own authentic guilt. Only then will he achieve new identity.

This Naikan philosophy is intimately related to Japanese culture and,
at the same time, is firmly based upon the universal nature of the human mind.
Both the culture-bound and the more universal aspects are found in the specific
Naikan procedures and clients' behavior in Naikan setting. Let me start by
describing the specific Naikan procedures.

The Method

In short, Naikan therapy is a process of continuous meditation based upon highly structured instruction in self-observation and self-reflection. Accordingly, the content of instructions and themes for meditation or reflection, as well as the way of giving instructions, are of central significance.

The volunteer Naikan patient is asked to examine himself in relationship to others from the following three perspectives: (1) "Recollect and examine your memories of the care and benevolence that you have received from a particular person during a particular time in your life." (Beginning as a rule with an examination of his relationship to his mother, the client proceeds to examine, reexperience, and reflect on relationships with other family members and with other persons whom he has been close to, from childhood to the present.) (2) "Recollect and examine your memories of what you have returned to that person." (3) "Recollect and examine the troubles and worries you have given that person." These three perspectives can be named, for the sake of convenience, "benevolence given," "benevolence returned," and "trouble given" to others.

The examination is conducted in a boldly moralistic manner, placing the burden on the patient rather than on the "other." No excuses, rationalizations, or aggressions toward others are permitted except in the earliest meetings, when the counselor is more passive and tends merely to listen to what the patient describes to him. Following the introductory session, however, the counselor places more demands on the patient and is prepared to lead him if the patient faithfully follows the instructions. Mr. Yoshimoto used to give his clients such instructions as, "Examine yourself severely, like a prosecutor indicting the accused."

The patient begins his Naikan recollections and reflections at 5:30 in the morning and continues them until 9:00 in the evening. He sits in a quiet place surrounded on two sides by a Japanese screen and walls on the other two so that he is cut off from distractions and is free to concentrate exclusively on his inner world. Since he is not allowed to leave this very narrow space except to visit the bathroom or go to bed, the place inside the screen constitutes his whole environment. Such small confines facilitate concentrated self-reflection. For seven successive days he follows the same schedule so that at the end he has sat more than 100 hours almost continuously except while sleeping. This continuation of the same mental activity is essential for Naikan insight.

The counselor interviews the patient briefly (five minutes average) approximately every 90 minutes to ask what he has been examining. Total interview time amounts to 40–50 minutes a day. The role of the Naikan counselor is very different from the ordinary role of the professional counselor or therapist. The primary function of the Naikan counselor is to directly supervise the patient in a highly specific routine of private meditation. He is mainly concerned with making sure that his patient is following instructions and reflecting successfully on the topics assigned for his self-examination. In this respect, the Naikan therapist is more concerned with procedure than with content or with the counselor-patient relationship. In other words, it is not necessary for the counselor to achieve a full, empathic understanding of the patient's intricate inner world. The counselor accepts and respects the patient as a person, as one who has the potential to realize himself; at the same time, the counselor is negative and critical about any non-Naikan or anti-Naikan attitude that the patient might have toward himself. In this sense, the basic counselor-patient relationship in Naikan is authoritarian. Although direct contact with the patient is sporadic, it is nevertheless intensive and highly directive. Accordingly, transference is kept as uncomplicated as possible.

The Process

Patients following the instructions often find them rather difficult. At first they may be unable to concentrate on specific themes in the way they are instructed. For some, the psychological and physical isolation or confinement is too much to stand. The counselor uses several techniques to help them overcome the first barriers. Usually it takes two to three days for the patients to adjust to the new situation.

Occasionally and unexpectedly, forgotten memories come up and sporadic or diffuse guilt feelings and gratitude are experienced. At the same time, various kinds of resistance against the practice may come out, usually not the deeply rooted idiosyncratic resistance observed in psychoanalysis, but rather a more conscious reaction to such an unusual, harsh situation as Naikan. Patients are free to discontinue the method if it proves too difficult for them. Simple emotional catharsis is observed in some cases.

As the process goes on, the patient becomes more and more meaningfully involved with his past. For some the process is gradual, whereas for others abrupt insights into the guilty aspects of their present and past emerge. Insights into other people's love for them and their dependence upon them for this love also occur. Toward the end of therapy they accept the newly recognized guilt along with feelings of self-criticism and repentance. They also feel truly grateful for love from others and become empathic with the pain and suffering that they experienced.

The Outcome

The most common result of successful Naikan therapy is an improvement in the patient's interpersonal relationships. The improvement is brought about by the increase in, or the fresh appearance of, real feelings of gratitude for others; an inclination toward self-examination rather than an extrapunitive or impulsive attitude; empathic and sympathetic ability; regard for others; and the realization of one's responsibility for his social role(s). From another angle, the establishment of identity; strengthening of ego-ideal; and achievement of security, confidence, and self-disclosure may be the most obvious factors in the improvement.

This method has proven effective with many types of patients, except psychotics, without any modifications of technique. Notable success has been achieved with delinquents, criminals, and drug addicts. Even though few scientifically rigorous follow-up studies have been done, in many correctional institutions the Naikan method has proven more effective than other methods of treatment.

Contraindications and Ill Effects

As a rule, Naikan is ineffective for patients diagnosed as having an endogenous psychosis. Severely self-punitive types of compulsive neurotics difficult to treat by any method may gain nothing from Naikan. It must be emphasized, however, that the depressive state that is accompanied by strong feelings of guilt is not necessarily a contraindication for Naikan, because the guilt and the self-criticism stemming from the systematic examination of objective experiences in Naikan differ essentially from feelings observed among depressed patients. This will be illustrated in the first case study, below.

Case Studies

Case 1: a woman suffering from depressive reaction.   Mrs. NGK was a middle-class housewife, 32 years old, when she began Naikan treatment. Previously she had worked as a primary schoolteacher. When she came in for treatment, she had been in a depressive state for ten months, manifested by an increasing loss of interest in activities and a certain amount of obsession about her inability to accomplish things as she had before. She suffered from serious insomnia and had at times contemplated suicide. Her depressive reaction seemed to be precipitated by two incidents: maladjustment to her work following a change of teaching assignment two years previously, and an unexpected pregnancy several months before admission. The pregnancy increased her despair because losing her job as a result would have had harsh economic consequences for her family. Prior to these difficulties, she had reported no previous serious depressions. There were no reported familial or hereditary factors that might have effected her psychological disturbance. Medication given prior to Naikan treatment had been totally ineffective.

When she arrived for treatment, her motivation for Naikan was quite low. She cooperated with the treatment but in a very passive and almost reluctant manner. For three days she was not deeply involved in meditation but devoted most of her time to making accusations about her own incapacity and worthlessness. She seemed unable to adapt to the situation and was on the point of asking her father to take her back home. Her father, however, strongly encouraged her to continue trying. Mrs. Yoshimoto also strenuously encouraged the client to continue. Following this, after the third day, the patient suddenly began to be able to carry out the practice of Naikan. She accepted the method with seriousness. She was then able to examine what her mother-in-law had done for her and through this was able to feel how deeply her mother-in-law cared for her. Following this emotional insight her whole attitude toward life underwent a drastic change. She found everything shiny and bright. Let me cite an interview from that time. Mr. Yoshimoto asked, "What have you been examining?" Mrs. NGK replied, holding back the tears:

> Last year we bought a piano for our daughter. I realize now that this was only made possible by using the money that my mother-in-law had saved. I had forgotten this and thought that I had bought it with my own money, completely forgetting her contribution. I was so egocentric. When she was hospitalized, I only visited her once, bringing her a small gift, although my father-in-law visited her more frequently. (This was accompanied by a lot of self-deprecatory crying.) When I was hospitalized after the delivery of my last child, she visited me almost daily, bringing expensive fruits and walking up to the fifth floor to see me in spite of her heart condition. At this time she very, very kindly took care of me and really acted like a loving mother. I think about that now and I am aware at last how egocentric and unaware I had been as a *yome* ("daughter-in-law"). I really don't know how I can express my gratitude to her now. I am full of the feeling that I wish to beg her pardon on my knees right now.

She spent the hours following this revelation reflecting on her relationship with her father-in-law, thinking about how he had expressed love and shown care for his daughter-in-law. She again realized how relatively ungrateful she had been, not only to her father-in-law but also to her real father.

Thinking about the troubles that she had given her father-in-law in the past, she realized that she had not been *sunao*,[2] "obedient." She described herself as feeling like a "poisonous snake." She also said that she had become increasingly aware of a tremendous amount of guilt toward people in her home and worried that she could not beg her father-in-law to forgive her for her faults and imperfections.

On the fifth day of Naikan exercise, Mr. Yoshimoto felt that she had become in some ways too dramatic and excited to continue the practice of Naikan properly. He therefore asked her father to come and discuss taking her back.

The father, on seeing his daughter's drastic change, was quite overwhelmed. They reunited, embracing each other in joyous tears. The day following her return home her excitement subsided but her improved state of mind continued.

When about two weeks had passed, she became unstable and a little depressed. But this time the amount of depression was significantly less than she had experienced prior to Naikan. She overcame the crisis by employing Naikan exercises at home by herself. Through this she regained courage and hope. Her former rigid attitudes toward life changed, and she became more flexible and accepting. She could relate herself to everything with gratitude, warmth, and naturalness.

Although at the time of my second follow-up study (one year and four

months following her Naikan treatment) there was still a possibility of her becoming depressed in the future, her attitude toward life had fundamentally
changed as a result of Naikan treatment. The likelihood of subsequent psychological disturbance seemed lessened following her treatment.

To summarize, this woman recovered from a severe depressive reaction
by undergoing Naikan therapy for only a few days. Naikan brought her the
insight that she had been very selfish and without any real regard for beneficence
and love from others, especially her family members. This insight was accompanied by the deep feeling of authentic guilt and gratitude. Her strong defensiveness, which may have been mainly due to her distrust of others, was remarkably
decreased, and her aggression toward herself seemed to disappear. She came to
have a much better understanding of the feelings of others and gained vital hope
for the future.

Case 2: a male student with ego-identity problems.   Mr. M. was a male
undergraduate student studying to be a primary schoolteacher. Although superficially his social and academic adjustments were normal, he seemed to be worried
by emotional problems and wanted to "change himself." In the initial interview
he told me that he had a feeling his personality was composed of a lot of small
sins, which he was extremely afraid of facing. He had asked himself whether he
could be a "real" adult since he realized he was dirty and "diffused."

After two days of the introductory stage he gradually became involved
in examining himself. He kept thinking of his "dark" self and asking, "Who am
I," and wondering how he could go on living. He recollected the warm treatment
he received from his primary schoolteachers and realized that he had done nothing
for them. He felt especially lonesome, miserable, and remorseful when he recollected an episode in which he accidentally broke a window in the school and his
teacher did not reprimand him at all. With tears in his eyes, he kept on thinking
about this incident. Then suddenly he felt alive, full of determination and insight.
Sobbing, he told Mr. Yoshimoto, "Right now, at this very moment, I clearly
realize what I should do right after graduation from the university; I must bring
up children the way my primary schoolteachers did me. I believe this is my mission.
That's all." Following this incident, when he was recollecting and examining his
memory of the relationship with his mother, he had another experience of extremely strong emotion and feeling. When he was eight years old he still wet
his bed, and whenever it happened his mother would change the wet sheet and
let him come into her own bed. The recollection of the warmth of his mother's
bed was combined with the recollection of another kind of warmth he experienced
more directly in his babyhood, when he was carried by his mother in her arms or
on her back. When he realized that he had completely forgotten this warmth up to
the present, he felt so sad and sorry that he could not help but burst into tears.
Sobbing, he went to Mr. Yoshimoto and asked for permission to go back to his
parents immediately in order to do anything he could for them and also to tell
them how his feelings and thoughts had changed. Mr. Yoshimoto advised him
not to be so overwhelmed by sheer emotion but to try harder to examine himself.
He simmered down and reached a tranquil state of mind.

Both of these experiences are primarily based on the acknowledgment of warmth from others. He said, "My mother and my first-grade teacher, these two persons are now closer to me, I feel."

In recollecting and reflecting upon his relationship with his father, he remembered one incident about which he felt deeply ashamed. Once when his father suddenly lost consciousness, his first worry was taking over his father's debts. Mainly for this reason he wished for his father's recovery. He also had to admit to himself that he had been jealous of his brother and had hated and distrusted him in spite of his brother's kindness to him. He found himself always being exploitative, not only of his brother but of others as well.

On the final day of his Naikan treatment he said, "Before Naikan, I wished I could completely forget such bad memories as having been slapped by my teacher or being a truant in junior high school days; but right now, I keenly feel that I exist here, now, only after I have done those things. That's why I really think I must not forget my sinful past." He felt strong enough to face the guilt squarely and found it most meaningful.

According to the follow-up interview and psychological testing carried out three months after he finished concentrated Naikan therapy, his interpersonal relationships in general showed marked improvement. His previous exploitative and antagonistic attitude toward others changed to a cooperative, accepting, and open-minded one. He began to listen to others and to see himself from another person's point of view. He also began to be more responsible, stable, and confident of himself, with greater hope for the future. The fundamental change in his attitude toward life made it possible for him to speak very easily in front of nearly 200 people in church. That he could do such a thing was beyond his imagination before Naikan therapy.

We must note, however, that in spite of the marked improvement in his attitude toward life, according to the TAT his essentially negative relationship with his father seemingly remained almost unimproved.

Tentative Analysis of the Therapeutic Function of Naikan

The major task that the Naikan patient is asked to accomplish is to see himself in another's position and reflect on both the beneficence given to him and the harm he has done to others.

In vividly recollecting memories of "having been loved and cared for,"[3] especially by maternal figures, the Naikan patient reexperiences the deep security and satisfaction that he once had in his relationship with the person being recalled.[4] The Naikan setting reinforces the positive aspect of the client's image of others, especially his mother. His deep gratitude for his parents is transferred to others in general and he becomes more accepting of himself and others. He discloses himself, moves toward others, and becomes more empathic with them.

It may be also reasonable to assume that to recollect the experience of "having been loved and cared for" in earlier days gives the patient a feeling of inherent continuity and consistency between his present self and his basic trust of the world. This experience brings about a more solid and more integrated ego identity.

From the cultural standpoint, the character of the Japanese mother,[5] who is essentially very nurturant and interdependent with her child, may contribute in creating the above-mentioned therapeutic condition.

One additional significant therapeutic aspect of the acknowledgment of "having been loved and cared for" is that it prepares the ground for confronting and accepting one's guilt. One can never have authentic guilt feelings toward a person whom he feels he does not love or who he feels does not love him. This is probably the most decisive aspect of recollecting benevolence, because acknowledging guilt is, after all, the central experience of Naikan therapy.

Now let me discuss the therapeutic meaning of the acknowledgment of guilt. In contrast to the prevalent idea of guilt as being more or less negative and very often pathological, Naikan emphasizes the existentially positive meaning of guilt-consciousness[6] if one is able to confront it. Experiences related to guilt-consciousness tend to be forgotten and alienated from the ego unless one dares to face them. Once the person examines his past guilty conduct, relates himself directly with it, and accepts it as belonging to himself, he naturally changes his self-image and reorients it toward responsibility, courage to be, and a humble attitude toward life. (He then achieves a broader and more integrated identity.) His selfish attitude and lack of empathy or sympathy lessen, often radically, when he realizes he is not qualified to demand and criticize others without respecting and understanding their feelings.

It is necessary to note that for a Japanese to do harm to those close to him, such as parents, is a severe violation of social morals. Thus, the acknowledgment of such misconduct produces especially strong guilt feelings in the Japanese. As R. Bellah (1957) and G. DeVos (1960) proposed, *on* obligation is very closely related with guilt among the Japanese. Naikan seems to facilitate guilt-consciousness skillfully by reinforcing the sense of *on* obligation, particularly the *on* obligation regarding one's mother. It is interesting to note that among Westerners, superego anxiety is said to have its origin in the father-son relationship, which is basically determined by fear of authority perceived in conjunction with sexual rivalry as well as by the more or less "universalistic" nature rather than by the "particularistic"[7] one. Japanese guilt, on the other hand, seems to be very closely related with the mother-son relationship, in which the fundamentally empathic and sympathetic attitude of the son toward his mother brings about guilt in him when he realizes he has done harm to his beloved mother, who may have raised her child in a rather "morally masochistic" (devoted), self-punitive way. He also tends to feel guilty when he realizes that he has had an unconscious intent to hurt his mother, due to the natural ambivalence that arises from living under very close parental control. The whole traditional social system of *on* obligation may reinforce this profound personal attitude toward guilt.

Thus, Naikan therapy utilizes very effectively such basic characteristics of the Japanese personality as strong potential guilt feelings, *on*-consciousness, the predominant significance of mother, and specific moral values in the context of highly "particularistic" interpersonal relationships. The more universal basis of Naikan may be found in its emphasis on insight into, and a positive relating with, one's guilt,[8] in contrast to the mere feeling of guilt.

ACKNOWLEDGMENTS

I wish to acknowledge the sincere cooperation of Mr. Inobu Yoshimoto, the founder of Naikan, and the patients who agreed to record their Naikan interviews, to have research interviews, and to take psychological tests. I also gratefully acknowledge the assistance of the Social Science Research Institute (NIMH Grant # MH09243) in the preparation of this paper. Lastly, I wish to thank Frank Johnson, M.D., who discussed the basic concept of Naikan with me and whose comments from the standpoint of a Westerner and a psychoanalytically oriented psychiatrist helped my thinking.

NOTES

1. *Kan* literally means "observation" but carries a specific meaning in the context of Japanese Buddhism. It implies observing or visually imagining an object during meditation with intensively integrated states of mind.

2. The Japanese word *sunao* is almost impossible to translate into English. It contains such implications as naturalness, naïveté, straightforwardness, simplicity, frankness, open-mindedness, mildness or gentleness, and compliance. Japanese culture attaches high moral value to this trait, and the word is often used in negative form by Naikan patients when they criticize themselves.

3. Discussing the dynamics underlying the Naikan method may pose some difficulty for Westerners, since the recollection of affection for a parent (along with guilt about one's transgressions against the parent) is usually said to be discovered only after the analysis of unconscious anger toward the parent. Furthermore, for Westerners, hostility toward the parent often is deliberately intensified through the process of recollection and free association. This is much less prominent in Japanese patients than in Western patients. The cultural differences responsible for this may have to do with the different ways of gratifying dependency in Japanese culture when contrasted with a culture originating in Continental Europe (see Doi, 1961, 1962). The relative absence of aggression in Japanese family life cannot be accounted for simply on the basis of repression but is due to significantly different cultural practices in child rearing and family life. I think that recognition of guilt and the realization of love in a way exacerbates and intensifies the conflict within the patient over his responsibilities for other people in his life.

4. In connection with the recollection of early experiences of being loved, it may be necessary to discuss the possibility of regression in Naikan therapy. We notice that many Naikan patients experience something similar to regression, though very mildly and temporarily. Since Naikan is an exclusively conscious and judgmental procedure, even though regression tends to occur, it is in conflict with the conscious, self-observational, and reality-directed way of thinking in

Naikan and thus is readily and quickly suppressed. Although the therapeutic meaning of this oscillating process of repeatedly arising mild conflict and its resolution is not clear to the author yet, he assumes that the regression-like experience in Naikan must be therapeutic to a certain degree in making the patient relatively free from his perceived-reality-bound and rigidly patterned way of experiencing.

5. Those interested in the character of the Japanese mother can refer to Tomomatsu (1939), Yamamura (1971), and Caudill (1961). Yamamura, a Japanese sociologist, analyzed the image of mother among Japanese delinquents treated by Naikan therapy. In his findings almost all of the delinquent boys who underwent Naikan therapy realized either that they had returned evil for their mother's kindness or that they had been given love and care by their mothers in spite of the harsh treatment they gave their mothers.

6. Tillich (1952), Pattison (1969), and others call this recognition "existential (ego) guilt," which follows the violation of essential relationships between men. One might also call it "authentic guilt" after Buber (1958). This feeling should be contrasted with guilt based largely on repressed hostility since existential guilt involves realization and confrontation on a conscious level of actual violations of essential moral values in regard to a particular person. It is interesting to note that there is a striking similarity between what Buber (1958) proposed as the way of confronting and overcoming one's existential guilt and what Mr. Yoshimoto has actually practiced under the name of Naikan therapy.

7. "Particularism" is the term advocated by Parsons (1951) to refer to a specific value orientation based largely upon a particular person or a particular group; "universalism" refers to a value orientation that is based much more upon universal principles than upon a particular person or group.

8. Yasunaga (1967), a Japanese psychiatrist, contends that the significant therapeutic meaning of pure guilt-consciousness, which is defined as the feeling accompanied by the realization that one sees himself responsible for his conduct, is that he also has done harm to a particular person. In this sense this "pure feeling of guilt" differs from the ordinary feeling of guilt. Yasunaga noticed that this kind of guilt feeling is brought about by a truly empathic understanding of another's pain and suffering. This experience of pure guilt has the positive effect of (1) melting away even the very strongest defense, (2) resolving one's *amae*, or dependent attachment on others, (3) successfully overcoming one's bitter consciousness of being hurt by others, and (4) increasing the possibility of confronting oneself honestly.

REFERENCES

Bellah, R.N. 1957. Tokugawa religion. Glencoe, Illinois, Free Press.
Buber, M. 1958. Schuld und Schuldgefühle. *In* Martin Buber Werke, Erster Band. München, Kösel.
———. 1965. *In* The knowledge of man, selected essays of Martin Buber. M. Friedman, ed. New York, Harper & Row.
Caudill, W. 1961. Around the clock patient care in Japanese psychiatric hospitals: the role of the *tsukisoi*. American Sociological Review 26:204–14.
DeVos, G. 1960. The relation of guilt toward parents to achievement and arranged marriage among the Japanese. Psychiatry 23:287–301.

Doi, L.T. 1961. *Sumanai to ikenai*—psychodynamics of guilt in the light of Japanese concepts. Seishin Bunseki Kenkyu 8:4–7. [In Japanese]

———. 1962. *Amae*: a key concept for understanding Japanese personality structure. *In* Japanese culture: its development and characteristics. R.J. Smith and K.K. Beardsley, eds. Chicago, Aldine Publishing Co.

Parsons, T. 1951. The social system. New York, Free Press of Glencoe.

Pattison, E. 1969. Morality, guilt and forgiveness in psychotherapy. *In* Clinical psychiatry and religion. E. Pattison, ed. Boston, Little, Brown.

Tillich, P. 1952. Systematic theology. Chicago, University of Chicago Press.

Tomomatsu, E. 1939. Boshin (Mind of mother). Tokyo, Kaseisha. [In Japanese]

Yamamura, Y. 1971. Nihonjin to haha (Japanese and their mothers). Tokyo, Tōyokan Shuppansha. [In Japanese]

Yasunaga, H. 1967. Chiyu-kiten to zaiakukan (Healing and guilt feelings). Tokyo, Seishin Igaku 9:281–85. [In Japanese]

PROBLEMS OF
TRANSCULTURAL PSYCHIATRY

21. Psychotherapy as "Hide and Seek"

L. TAKEO DOI, M.D.

Department of Mental Health
University of Tokyo
Tokyo, Japan

IN THIS PAPER I attempt to provide a theoretical model that fits all kinds of psychotherapy, ancient and modern, East and West. It is deceptively simple. I propose that the essence of psychotherapy is "hide and seek."

Hide and seek is probably the most primitive and hence the most international children's game. Because it is so elementary, books on children's games do not describe it. Interestingly enough, Eric Berne, author of the famous book *Games People Play* (1964), did not mention it either. It must have eluded his discerning eyes (to put it ironically, because it was the very game he was playing professionally).

There is, however, an even earlier game of disappearing-reappearing called *inai-inai-bah* in Japanese. This is not purely a children's game, for adults have to engage infants to play it. For instance, a mother will cover her face with her hands, saying, "*Inai-inai*," which means "Now gone," and then will remove her hands, saying "*Bah!*," a special exclamation that means "Here now." The repetition of these two acts invariably elicits a smile from the infant, which indicates, in psychoanalytic terms, that the infant has beginning object relations. The infant comes to learn the trick and enjoys immensely trying it himself on the adult. Japanese play this game quite often from a very early age, even at five months; perhaps other nationalities also have a similar game. Peek-a-boo is one example, although the emphasis there is not upon the repetition of disappearing-reappearing but upon the sudden appearance of a familiar face. Hence its onset must be later than *inai-inai-bah*. A game called "fort-da" by a little boy of one-and-a-half observed by Freud (1920) definitely has the theme of disappearing-reappearing. The boy held a reel by the string and threw it over the edge of his curtained cot, so that it disappeared into it, at the same time uttering an expressive "o-o-o-o." He then pulled the reel out of the cot again by the string and hailed its reappearance with a joyful "da." According to Freud's interpretation, he apparently made into play his experiences of letting his mother go and seeing her back again later. This was a solitary game invented by one particular boy. What interests me is the fact that the disappearing-reappearing play, or something like it, seems to be a precursor of hide and seek, and that there is a developmental continuum from the disappearing-reappearing play to hide and seek.

Hide and seek is played between several people who hide and one who tries to find them. In abstract terms, one could say that the game involves two activities: secret formation and its discovery. So it presupposes a certain level of psychological development, which in my observations includes a capacity for a kind of lying. This should not be equated with delinquent lying, however; rather, it is innocent lying for the sake of preserving one's separate self. For instance, a child who doesn't want to be asked by his mother every morning if he has washed his face might say one morning that he had washed it when he had not. To put all this in psychoanalytic terms once again, only those who have reached the oedipal stage can and will play hide and seek. Hence, a child who is made to play the game before he is old enough will often announce himself from his hiding place, and if forced to seek others in hiding, he is likely to cry or give up playing unless the others make it easy for him to find them. He is still fixed at the stage of the disappearing-reappearing play. Incidentally, Japanese call the seeker role *oni*. This word is usually translated "demon," but it may refer to a person who for one reason or another isolates himself from society, that is, "the alienated one." So it is very appropriate that the one who is first discovered in hide and seek—that is, the one who loses the game—becomes *oni*. In English, the seeker is referred to simply as "it." I wonder if this appellative carries the same feeling as *oni*. Perhaps it does.

When I say that the essence of psychotherapy is hide and seek, it is because the patient is induced to look for the secret of his illness by the therapist. The patient can be thought of as a frustrated and lost *oni* whom the therapist comes to help. But since the secret of his illness, which they work together to find out, lies hidden in the patient himself, the psychotherapeutic hide and seek is really played within the patient himself. That is why it is so difficult and the therapist's help is needed. Sometimes it might appear that the therapist is the real *oni* and the patient the one who tries to escape his attention. Or, the patient might act like *oni* toward the therapist and wish to pursue the therapist's secrets. Still, if the patient is within the neurotic range, he can rather easily be made interested in discovering the secret of his illness. But if he is psychotic, it is hard to engage him in the psychotherapeutic hide and seek. He is either in no mood to play the game or is feeling terrified because he is convinced that his "secrets" are out; that is, he feels exposed and defenseless. In such a case one may say that he is literally *oni*, the alienated one not interested in playing the game. Then the therapist first has to bolster the patient's ego and again persuade him that his secrets are within himself.

The formulation of psychotherapy as hide and seek seems to apply best to psychoanalytic therapy. It was, after all, Freud himself who tried to discover the secret of neurosis and became convinced that he succeeded in this. He bequeathed his personal experiences to posterity in the form of psychoanalytic therapy. But I wonder if the hide-and-seek formulation cannot be applied to other kinds of psychotherapy, too, or any kind for that matter. What is thought of as the secret of neurosis will differ according to various schools. One should add, however, that the sense of secret and its discovery may not be so pronounced in other schools as in Freudian psychoanalysis.

Here I would consider the Oriental psychotherapies that are discussed at this conference. For shamanistic therapies, the secret is of course what a shaman divines. For Morita therapy, the secret is the patient's *toraware*, the state of being bound up with one's physical and mental conditions, which is attributed ultimately to the self-preservation instinct. In actual therapy the patient is supposed to develop insight into and at the same time transcend his *toraware* by engaging in various kinds of work within a setting of communal living. For Naikan therapy, the secret is one's unconfessed sins or unacknowledged indebtedness, and here again the therapeutic process takes place in a setting of communal living.

I believe the therapeutic use of communal living is characteristic of Japanese psychotherapies. Also it should be noted that the emphasis in Japanese psychotherapies is not so much upon seeking a hidden secret as upon rescuing the person entrapped in his hiding place and bringing him back to communal living. Thus, in these therapies the psychotherapeutic hide and seek is heavily slanted toward the disappearing-reappearing play. Along with this difference in emphasis, there is also a subtle difference in the meaning of "secret," for what strikes the patient as well as the therapist as secret is not really one's inner secrets, but rather what makes man transcend them; in other words, the therapy itself becomes shrouded with the sense of secret, or perhaps mystery. A sense of mystery is of course more pronounced in not only Japanese but in all religiously inspired therapies or healing cults.

In this connection it may be relevant to point out that for the awakening infant the object is always something wondrous or even mysterious. That is why he can be delighted by *inai-inai-bah* or peek-a-boo. This is not to claim, however, that the sense of wonder or mystery is just infantile, since both philosophy and religion may owe their origin to it. One may recall that Plato declared wonder the instigator of philosophical endeavor, and also recall the frequent references to the face of Yahweh in the Old Testament. Of etymological interest is the fact that the Japanese word *himitsu*, which was originally coined as a Buddhist term, can signify both "secret" and "mystery," like the German word *Geheimnis*, though nowadays it more often denotes secret, and the Buddhist meaning has almost been lost.

Psychoanalytic therapy has never caught the fancy of Japanese people. Without meaning to disparage them, one may compare them to small children who are reluctant to play hide and seek. It is not that they are not troubled by inner secrets. On the contrary, they are often greatly troubled by them, since inner secrets keep them from satisfactory communal living. But they are not interested in finding out about the secrets. So they wish them away or pretend that they have none. Do they not behave like small children who, still being fixed at the stage of the disappearing-reappearing play, come out from hiding in order to be found or become grieved if nobody comes around to find them?

This argument is essentially the same as the one I expounded in another paper, "Psychoanalytic Therapy and 'Western Man'—a Japanese View" (Doi, 1964). There I stated, using the concept of *amae* (dependency), that Japanese who tend to value dependence and shy away from the dichotomy of subject and object will not warm to psychoanalytic therapy as it is practiced in the West. However, there is an element of the disappearing-reappearing play in psychoanalytic therapy itself. It is understood by the name of transference, though, according to the rules, it also has to be analyzed eventually, that is, be identified for its real nature. In other words, it is assumed in psychoanalytic therapy that disappearing-reappearing play has to be resolved into hide and seek.

Now Japanese as children do play hide and seek, and there is no reason why they cannot play psychotherapeutic hide and seek if they are skillfully encouraged to do so. It is interesting to note that the activities of secret formation and its discovery constitute the antipode to *amae*, whereas *amae* represents the desire to merge with others, to cultivate or pursue secrets, to establish one's separate self and master the world. So it is not that Japanese lack the native inclination for the latter activities; it just seems that they have not given free rein to it for some historical or sociological reason. In the West, on the contrary, there has been a tremendous upsurge in the rationalistic pursuit of finding out whatever one can in the world. At the same time, Western man has come to appreciate the worth and individuality of a human soul. The peculiarly Western blend of individualism that has evolved in recent centuries can be described figuratively as contentment at being in hiding, along with the freedom to go out at will. And I wonder if these achievements and developments were not prompted by a keener sense of secret in the West, which in turn may have been created by a deeper sense of mystery to begin with.

Finally, a few words about the climate of the present age and its implications for psychotherapy. We know that people everywhere in the world are now having the curious sensation of being driven out of their hiding places. This is undoubtedly related to the fact that the natural habitat of man is being destroyed rapidly by the enormously accelerated advance of technology. The outward changes are matched by changes in man's inner world, too. It seems now that every secret of not only nature but man and society as well is being laid bare. I think the unmasking trend in literature, which began in nineteenth-century

Europe and spread over the whole world, has greatly contributed to this outcome, along with the advances made in every field of science.

Significantly, sex no longer spells secrecy in our contemporary society. In such an atmosphere it would be extremely difficult to play hide and seek, because, like psychotics, man feels exposed and denuded. Man then hankers for mystery anew or tries to create artificial secrets, as can be seen in the recent rise of popular interest in occultism or mysticism and in mystery stories and political secrets. I think the fact that psychoanalytic therapy is no longer in vogue—even in the West—is also related to this change in the mental climate of the age, although it is an irony that such change may be at least partly due to psychoanalysis itself, i.e., the dissemination of psychoanalytic knowledge among the public. Contemporary man would rather engage in disappearing-reappearing play than in psychotherapeutic hide and seek. This helps create, I think, two apparently unrelated opposite effects. One is the search for effective therapy to rescue man from the modern predicament, hence the renewed interest in all kinds of brief therapy such as crisis intervention, encounter therapy, sensitivity training, and traditional folk therapy. The other is that psychoanalytic therapy, if it is undertaken nowadays, tends to be a long, drawn-out business stretching over many years, inasmuch as man gets easily stuck in disappearing-reappearing play, which is its legitimate ingredient. Accordingly, I may be not too far from the truth if I assume that the present conference also has come about in the last analysis by the requirement of the present age as I have described it here.

REFERENCES

Berne, E. 1964. Games people play. New York, Grove Press.
Doi, L.T. 1964. Psychoanalytic therapy and "Western man"—a Japanese view. International Journal of Social Psychiatry, Special Edition 1:13–18.
Freud, S. 1920. Beyond the pleasure principle. *In* The standard edition of the complete psychological works of S. Freud. J. Strachey, ed. London, Hogarth Press, 1955.

22. The Interrelationship of Social and Psychological Structures in Transcultural Psychiatry

GEORGE A. DEVOS, Ph.D.

Department of Anthropology
University of California, Berkeley
Berkeley, California

Adaptation Versus Adjustment

Can there be a comparative science in psychiatry? Psychiatry, insofar as it is a social as well as a biological discipline, has discovered in itself the difficulties suffered generally in the social sciences in their attempts to become an integrated true science of man. Not only are there difficulties in overcoming taboos on objectivity or prejudgment related to value judgments, but the very perceptions and concepts around which the still-separated social sciences are organized tend to be heavily influenced by the enthnocentrically perceived social realities of the culture in which they are developed. When carefully examined, psychiatric theory as an amalgam of psychology and sociology as well as anthropology continues to manifest internal evidence of ethnocentrism in what are initially presumed to be culturally transcendent, scientifically based hypotheses or conclusions. As a consequence, psychiatry today is undergoing a crisis of confidence concerning its capacity to diagnose seemingly aberrant behavior, let alone to understand causality in mental illness.

Indeed, psychiatry is being criticized from outside by some members of the sociological profession (Scheff, 1966) for mistaking culturally conditioned role behavior for symptoms. Some anthropologists (Honigmann, 1969) criticize psychiatry from the standpoint of a cultural relativism that permits no judgments about maladjustment. According to some extreme adherents of this position, all behavior must be viewed as cultural. Mental illness is an ethnocentrism that does not really exist.

Psychiatry is also being criticized from within by some, such as R.D. Laing (1967; with D.G. Cooper, 1971), who are moving toward a Marxist-oriented view that the presently accepted psychiatric tradition—and the "disease" it is treating—is itself an aspect of capitalist exploitation. Franz Fanon (1968), for example, documents the possibilities of using psychiatry as a support for colonial domination by citing extreme cases he witnessed during the Algerian war. No one can deny the possibilities of abusing scientific knowledge for political purposes. There is no doubt that psychiatrists may be called on to help "adapt" individuals to a status quo that is itself brutalizing for those whose social role makes them an integral part of a pathological social system. One cannot therefore state that psychiatry itself is to blame, as some do. From another perspective, Thomas Szasz (1961), attacking psychiatry more from the right than from the left, would have us believe that the concept of mental illness itself may be a spurious metaphor, or that many forms of what we see as mentally ill behavior are actually elaborate forms of malingering (Sarbin, 1964, 1969).

From my viewpoint as an anthropologist who has had experience with the manifest universals of mental illness in more than one culture, what is most disturbing is not that such injudicious or tendentious writings appear periodically but that they receive the relative popularity that they do among social scientists. One may ask whether, indeed, there is not occurring at the present time a political as well as social failure of nerve in psychiatry, as well as in the related social sciences generally, concerning the validity of what has been previously trusted as methods of gaining truth? The total ramifications of this crisis cannot concern us here. Suffice it to say that the question of cultural, or more specifically, social-class bias in science generally, not only psychiatry, is being raised both injudiciously as well as judiciously with the contemporaneous realignment of forces in world politics. There is an unfortunate tendency to mix political and scientific judgments as well as to assume one-sided arguments from the standpoint of a single specialized discipline.

Some social scientists, however, are continuing to avoid political or disciplinary dogmatism. Efforts continue to try to combine in empirical research the methods and perspectives of both anthropology and psychology as well as other disciplines. Some, like myself, have found that some form of dualism in social theory is necessary to resolve at least some of the issues raised. Ultimately, from the perspective of man's common human biological heritage and his culturally transcendant growth potential toward psychosociological maturation, it is necessary to reject on the one hand any totally relativistic anthropological position that qualifies all judgments about human behavior as value-laden or culture-bound. From a scientific standpoint it is also necessary to reject as insufficient any sociologistic intentions that seek to do without some conceptualization of underlying psychological functioning. I believe the evidence so far points toward the universality of human psychology, from which it therefore follows that potentials of hereditary or traumatically induced malfunctioning of various sorts will appear cross-culturally in a limited, scientifically definable number of ways regardless of cultural differences or social attitudes or beliefs. Some of these emotional and physical states of functional disorder or "disease" cause human misery, regardless of the culture in which they occur. A transcultural ameliorative science of psychiatry is possible, and we must continue to work toward it. I do agree, however, with the anthropological critics that would question whether there should not be a serious reexamination of present psychodiagnostic categories and treatment on a transcultural basis.

The distinction between adjustment and adaptation. For the most part, in the literature of psychology as well as anthropology and sociology, the concepts of "adjustment" and "adaptation" are loosely used in a roughly equivalent manner. They indiscriminately refer both to the internal structures which we subsume under the concept of personality, or, in many instances, to mutually adaptive processes of human communication and interaction that occur in social-role relationships. More generally, they are used indiscriminately as concepts referring to man's response to his environment. The converse concepts, maladjustment and maladaptation, can refer to some deficiency or structural lack in a capacity for response in an individual or simply to some form of response itself that is inadequate to the purposes or survival of the individual.

Some distinction is necessary. The term adjustment as I use it here is not culturally and situationally relative; it assumes an ideal progression of maturation that is potential for all human beings, but the realization of which may be culturally fostered or deformed. It is often said today that to be "well-adjusted" in a "bad environment" itself can be pathological. This is not the proper use of the term adjustment in the psychodynamic sense intended here. Indeed, a person can be deformed maturationally by his culture in such a way that he adapts well to situations of human brutality. One cannot at the same time assume that he is internally well-adjusted in the psychodynamic sense. While it is possible for an internally well-adjusted person to survive in a bad environment, one presumes, however, he will attempt to effect alloplastic changes outside of himself in the environment, whereas a person who is maladjusted will not be as well equipped to bring about desired ameliorative change. To put it the other way is to define adjustment in terms of adaptation rather than maturational potential. It is most helpful theoretically to maintain a clear distinction between the internal structuring of personality related to the concept of adjustment and social-behavioral responses, which can be seen as adaptive or maladaptive for the individual within his social nexus.

This distinction has been elaborately elucidated by Clyde Kluckhohn in his publication on Navaho witchcraft (1944). Kluckhohn, in a detailed study of the social and psychological functions of witchcraft beliefs and practices, kept this essential distinction: adaptation, for him, was defined as the relationships of individuals within society. For example, witchcraft was functionally adaptive in deflecting aggressive feelings out of the group onto more distant outsiders. Internally, for the individual, Kluckhohn considered witchcraft beliefs or practices to be adjustive in that they acted as an outlet for emotional states that otherwise would be disruptive to psychological functioning. The same witchcraft could be seen in some other contexts as relatively maladaptive to the social group, or as evidence of relative maladjustment in one person compared with another who had less need to have recourse to witchcraft but could handle his relationships more directly. In this latter sense, adjustive functions are to be viewed solely in the context of personality organization or personality structure. Adaptive functions pertain to judgments, not of personality, but of social functioning. Witchcraft seen in a dual functionalist framework is the institutionalized form of an external relational adaptive function. The individual practicing it may be more or less socially adaptive. He also may or may not be discharging potentially disruptive states of internal tension—an internal adjustive function. These ideas and relations are depicted in Table 1.

To complicate a dualist functional theory a bit further, one must point out that a structural-functional analysis of anthropology or social psychiatry is incomplete when limited to one level of analysis. What is involved in psychocultural research is a necessity to examine and to explain human behavior on a series of interrelated levels. In the analysis of human behavior one must relate one level of functioning to the next level of structure. For example, a sociologist or anthropologist can study "possession" behavior simply as a function of social structure. But a psychological anthropologist or social psychiatrist attempting to understand the interrelationships of social structure, possession behavior, and personality must use a dual level of analysis with a structural-functional distinction to delimit and interrelate the concept of adjustment to psychological structure on the one hand, and adaptation to social functioning on the other. In one sense, each level has its structures and these structures are at least bifunctional with respect to other levels.

The concept of psychological structure itself can be subdivided and examined on yet another level of analysis for the relationship between adjustive psychological functioning of possession states and organically determined physiological structure. The human brain or the human psyche, or whatever concept is congenial to the reader, has a limited number of variable modes of functioning or malfunctioning. There can be malfunctioning due to environmental stress without any physiological deficits, or there can be malfunctioning due to particular lesions or physiological trauma or toxic effects on the body.

If we relate these distinctions in relation to the field of psychiatry, we see that the traditional problems in psychiatry have been to distinguish between structure and function in respect to organic problems versus functional adjustment problems. In social psychiatry, or transcultural psychiatry, however, a new dichotomy appears. The distinction must now be made as to whether or not relatively debilitating or painful adjustments or maladjustments are socially adaptive or maladaptive within a given cultural context.

Psychiatrists and psychologists, when viewing "mental health," are usually concerned specifically with psychological adjustive mechanisms with which they have become familiar in Western culture, and to this extent they tend to slip

Table 1:   Psychocultural Adjustment and Adaptation: A Schema

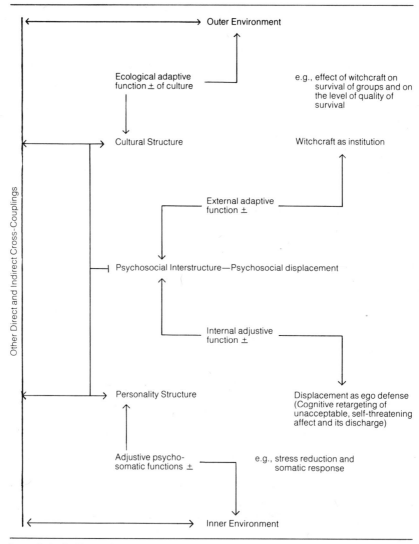

Source: Devised by Theodore Schwartz.

Note: The schema depicts the adaptive and adjustive functional relations among the various structural levels mediating between man's inner and outer environments as well as the other cross-couplings of structural levels and environments that are nonadjacent in this schema. A given, ongoing state of such a psychocultural system is a first derivative set of adaptive and adjustive functions. Change may occur in any part or parts of this system, initiating chains of second derivative adaptive and adjustive responses.

into ethnocentric value judgments that govern the diagnosis and treatment of what they perceive to be psychiatric illness. Anthropologists in turn, are focused on patterns of social adaptation, that is, whether the individual remains, or how he remains, or how he was brought into, or excluded from, social participation. Caudill (1959) suggested that comprehension of the working relationship between anthropology and psychology requires today, for the psychiatrist as well as others, some understanding of the concept of culture as a key concept, just as it is necessary for anthropologists to understand personality structure or personality functioning as keys to motivated human behavior. He suggests that we must avoid tendencies to reductionism in either group in studying the interrelationship of these systems. It is from this standpoint that I, too, find it necessary to remain a bilevel psychocultural dualist in social theory, using both social structure and social function as orienting concepts helping to explain the meaning of human behavior on the one hand, and personality structure and psychological functioning on the other, as concepts referring to interpenetrating sets of determinants influencing social behavior.

For modern psychiatry, operating both within and outside Western culture, there is the disturbing consideration that, to the degree that a malfunctioning is not based on an organic problem, knowledge of the causes of malfunctioning by itself may not help in the treatment of problem behavior—unless there is a sharing of beliefs and symbol systems between therapist and patient concerning the efficacy of treatment. To that degree, treatment is irreducibly symbolic, in the literal sense of the word. What is already apparent to some social or transcultural psychiatrists in extending or reinterpreting the causes of mental health or illness is the necessity to clarify or differentiate between those concepts or definitions of behavior pervading a given culture and those concepts that are being imposed externally upon the meaning of behavior from a Western psychiatric framework. If no attention is paid to indigenous perceptions of "mental illness" or to the meaning of its particular forms within the culture, there can be no therapeutic process. Western-trained psychologists or psychiatrists studying what are recognizably disturbed patients in radically different cultures tend to rely too heavily on their own background in their diagnoses, perhaps using traditional descriptive psychiatry or psychoanalytic formulations, which, in a sense, alienate them from symbolic communication with members of the culture in which they are functioning (Prince, 1964).

The anthropologist very often notes what might be considered clinically bizarre behavior but he also notes how it is highly integrated and socially adaptive within its cultural setting. Cultural usage or the cultural definitions given to the behavior seem to alter the "meaning" of the symptom for the individual so that he in fact remains socially integrated within his group. In our own culture, what we now define readily as neuroticism was in a previous age defined as sainthood or scrupulosity in adherence to religious directives. Certain forms of internal maladjustment in other cultural contexts may be seen as requiring not treatment but a special vocation such as that of the shaman. A deviant way of life may be proposed for the sufferer, who can thus employ a specialized, socially adaptive pattern that may relieve the internal pressures resulting from the experience of the inner stress. The particular symptoms of his illness are thus channeled in such a manner that the behavior becomes more controllable, hence, socially useful. The personality structure may not change, but a socially positive climate fosters adaptation rather than alienation. We have not as yet explored, for example, how some shamans learn to use ecstasy rather than remaining passive subjects in seizures (or, we do not as yet know by systematic study if those actually suffering become the shamans for the group. It may well be that their symptoms are mimicked by others who "borrow" such symptoms as signs of possession for religious purposes).

The Distinction between Culturally Normative Functioning and Clinical Symptoms

The relationship between adaptation and adjustment is indeed complex, whether examining the behavior of one individual from two points of view or examining similar behavior of different individuals in different contexts. To help clarify it, Theodore Schwartz (n.d.) has introduced the innovative concept "pathomimetic behavior." Such behavior is socially adaptive behavior which, for purposes of strengthening religious belief, an individual mimics, unconsciously or consciously, forms of behavior that usually are indicative of maladjustment or organic pathology. For example, a shaman may indicate behaviorally that he is possessed by a deity by exhibiting seizure phenomena of a type observed to occur in epileptics. In native medicine, epileptic seizure, a frightening form of behavior to behold, is usually explained as the intrusion of an alien force, often a deity, into the body. The possessed person, therefore, manifests a seizure. In the case of the epileptic, the behavior is maladjustive in the personality-structure sense. In the shaman, whatever his state of consciousness or self-hypnosis, the behavior becomes socially adaptive as a socially usable symbol of religious ecstasy. In pathomimetic phenomena, the possessed individual has somehow learned to manifest convulsions as a sign that a spirit has entered his body so that communication becomes possible with the supernatural.

Is there any way to make some scientifically objective judgment of adjustive behavior by ascertaining something about personality structure cross-culturally? I contend that there is since I am an adherent of the use of psychological testing procedures cross-culturally. Unfortunately, some previous attempts have not been free of ethnocentric judgments; but past failures in any field of scientific endeavor should not deter future efforts. Some tests have been improperly used; again, this does not mean that better attempts should not be made. Despite criticism to the contrary, I contend that one can make some objective judgments of psychological structures and the relative prevalence of given psychological adjustment patterns in different cultures. Both individual and group differences in adjustive functioning are obtainable cross-culturally. I must concede, however, that, generally speaking, adequate training in the use of testing procedures, not only in other countries but in the United States, which has been the center for most training in clinical psychology, has not been forthcoming to the degree necessary to provide more than sporadic examples of what might be accomplished given more money, effort, and talent devoted to cross-cultural work in personality psychology.

In the course of my own work applying psychological tests such as the Rorschach and the Thematic Apperception Test (TAT) cross-culturally, it has become apparent to me that there are some further distinctions necessary between the relative presence of psychiatrically recognizable states of social or personal maladjustment and the relative presence, within any given culture, of given "coping" or "defense" mechanisms and patterns of cognitive funtioning operative as aspects of personality. The problem is a very complex one. I can only attempt in this context to briefly touch upon some of the main dimensions of my thoughts in seeking answers.

I shall briefly illustrate three necessary distinctions.

1. There is cross-cultural universality in the appearance of organically based mental illness. In every culture, therefore, physiologically based impairments of cognition or emotional expression must be distingushed from nonorganic "defensive" personality patterns. Peculiarities in aberrant thought content, interesting as they may be, may tell us nothing about the organic cause of psychiatric pathology.

2. There are universally recognizable capacities in human beings that go through a process of maturation. Whereas all human beings have the potential to think rationally or "causally" in problem solving, there are cultural differences in how such a potential maturation is facilitated or impeded. There are cultural differences also in the areas of culture (technological, political, social) in which the use of rational problem solving is permitted or emphasized. A propensity to "regress" to precausal cognitive patterns under emotional duress or stress is also a universal in human beings regardless of culture. Given cultures will differ in the degree of readiness with which their members will manifest regression of this nature. Cultures also differ in the degree to which they "educate" their members toward rational causal thinking, or the degree to which they induce in many of their members severe traumatic experiences that result in defensive personality rigidifications impeding both cognitive and emotional maturation. That is to say, in comparing cultures, one must distinguish, by testing levels of maturation, between cultural limitations consisting of growth and actual traumatic impairments that result in defensive ego maneuvers maladjustive in nature.

3. A psychological universal in human beings is what might be broadly termed the capacity for altered states of consciousness, which may or may not betoken the presence of psychopathology.

There is a necessary distinction to be made between the capacity to utilize some form of dissociation, for example, a possession state or a trance, and the uncontrolled appearance of a dissociated state as part of a hysterical neurosis of a temporary or chronic nature. For example, certain features of personality structure in a Balinese individual going into trance as part of a religious drama, as reported by Bateson and Mead (1942), may or may not resemble those in someone developing a "dual personality" in the United States at the turn of the century, or those in the recent outbreak of hysterical possession in a girls' school in Malaysia reported earlier in this volume. Regardless, in each instance the mechanism of repression is brought into play; but the social and personal contexts are highly different. In Bali the condition is induced in a religious ritual. In the second instance it is part of a socially debilitating individual neurosis. In the third instance it is part of a collectively reinforced outbreak of hysterical acting out on the part of immature adolescent girls.

To illustrate briefly rather than completely each of these three topics, I shall draw informally on my experiences with the analysis of psychological tests and observation in psychiatric settings in Japan and elsewhere in both clinical and normative research.

Distinctions between culturally induced aberrant patterns and organically based psychopathology. Psychiatry may never be able to distinguish completely between the psychological and the social determinants of what is perceived as aberrant behavior. We still have much to learn about what is caused organically and what is induced socially or experientially in psychopathology. It is very obvious, however, to those who have some cross-cultural experience that "queer," socially disturbing, or defective behavior in every culture can result from organic causes. When the organic cause—be it the operation of an outside chemical agent or an internal chemical or hormonal imbalance—is corrected chemically, behavior changes, regardless of the previous peculiarities of cultural content through which the organic disturbance received external expression.

The peculiarities of the cultural or symbolic content in cases of organically induced psychopathology may nevertheless be of interest in suggesting cultural differences in personality. Some attempts should be made to examine cultural differences in thought content in situations where the same types of organically induced psychopathology can be compared. The appearance of mechanisms or of peculiar thought content, with the use of drugs for example, may or may not be related to the nature of the chemical agent rather than to the culture. One cannot easily decide. During the 1950s there was an almost epidemic use by urban Japanese youth of an amphetaminelike stimulant called *hiropon*. Individuals with symptoms of overdose appeared in psychiatric hospitals with paranoid delusions, usually of a grandiose nature. One could say that the general weakening of ego controls by use of the drug permitted the appearance of underlying paranoid propensities already present in some of the users. Or, one could say that the paranoid symptomatology was a characteristic effect of the drug. Similar paranoid-like symptoms have been noted in more recent reports on the use of "speed" in the United States. Detailed study would be necessary to decide whether it is indeed the characteristic of amphetamines, regardless of culture, to produce in some of their users paranoid symptomatology. It may be that there is some selectivity in different cultures as to who will begin to use such a drug. It may also be that the paranoid-like content in both cases may have some interesting differences. It is obvious that further transcultural research would help enlighten us.

Comparative research and culture in mental health—A comparison of problems in the actualization of human potential. The degree, extent, and social context in which members of a culture realize their human potentials for rational, causal, objective thought, or for a mature control of emotional responses, depends heavily on how cultural traditions are passed on as each new generation is socialized. Depending on how individuals are socialized, one finds relative degrees of readiness in particular culture groups or individuals to regress to precausal cognitive patterns under emotional duress or stress. There are also cultures in which individuals are encouraged by collectively held beliefs to maintain "magical" or "mythological" forms of thought on matters about which other cultures encourage a more objective scientific approach.

Malinowski (1948) well cautioned us, however, from falling into the error of Levy-Bruhl (1926), who tended to dichotomize too absolutely between so-called modern rational man and so-called primitive man. The biological and social fact is that man's maturational capacities, regardless of culture, are the same. As Malinowski points out, a Trobriand islander learns to use "scientific" methods, when they are culturally available to him, in planting his crops. But when rational problem-solving behavior is insufficient, he resorts, as does modern man, to magical practices or religious supplication, especially when he is uncertain and anxious about the outcome of his endeavors. A "modern" man who finds himself in a social, technological, or personal crisis may offer prayers to a personal god, who is anthropomorphically endowed with a sense of pity which may cause him to intervene in the usual working of impersonal laws of nature on behalf of his supplicant. A modern man praying is usually not thereby classified either as primitive or as mentally ill. The people in a Texas town who call in Indian rainmakers to stage a dance of magic during a drought display the same level of helplessness and consequent anxiety about capricious nature as did the Indians who lived before them on the same land with the same problems.

Granted the universality of man's capacity to think illogically or "superstitiously," as well as logically and objectively, one can nevertheless find differences in cultures in the degree to which the individual is "educated" or socialized toward the use of objectivity and logic in solving problems, is discouraged from giving way to the press of emotionalized thought associations. One must distinguish, for example, between cultural explanations from a precausal nature which result simply from a lack of available knowledge and those resulting from an immaturity in personality structure. One must also distinguish between a culturally permitted emotional display of temper in interpersonal crises and forms of structured incapacity to control the emotions that may indeed be fairly common in a culture due to its method of socialization. There are obvious difficulties in social or psychological theory related to a conceptual incapacity to express adequately the complex and continuous interrelationship existing between intellectual maturation and the maturation of the emotional structure of the individual. Problems resulting from the ego weakness to manage previous unresolved emotional experiences strongly influence the course of maturation of intellectual processes in all stages of cognitive development.

Questions of "psychopathology," therefore, do not relate as much to the cultural content of beliefs as to the type of personality structure that is to be found in individuals sharing in given beliefs. Individuals with more mature personality capacities, regardless of the paucity of scientific knowledge available within given cultures, will be flexibly capable of picking up new experiences and using them adaptively in problem-solving behavior when new instrumental needs become available. Conversely, an individual with a structural rigidification in personality is less capable of adapting in situations of change.

Let me illustrate these rather abstract statements by referring to my work with Horace Miner (1959) on materials obtained from Algeria. Miner not only obtained samples of belief from various informants in Algeria, he also carefully noted to what degree certain beliefs in culturally widespread magical practices or given attitudes about the chaperonage of women were found in specific individuals. He also obtained Rorschach protocols from a number of these individuals. In our work together later, we were able to find that there was indeed systematic correspondence between personality rigidity and the strength of particular magical beliefs and projective attitudes on the part of given individuals.

To make scientific progress in culture and personality research one cannot simply formulate in general terms the belief system common to a given group. Especially in times of change one must go further and attempt to demonstrate how the members of the group do not equally share in the common belief system. Nor do all the members of any group share completely or even partially in the psychological or structural characteristic of personality that is common for the group. For example, we found that paranoid-like thinking was a characteristic of a number of individuals in Miner's sample of Algerians, to a degree that group norms would readily distinguish these individuals from samples of American Indians or Japanese. There was, for example, a propensity in Algerian Arabs to employ arbitrary forms of thought, putting together precepts that have no logical juxtaposition. Also evident in a number of the records were types of suspicion and defensiveness, expressed in symbolic content, that give ample evidence of the use of projection as a mechanism of defense. There was other symbolic evidence of concern over homosexuality and passivity, which is also characteristic of individuals with paranoid personality structures who periodically appear in American psychiatric settings. How is one to judge these data?

The first question usually asked is whether or not the material obtained is valid; whether we can indeed give the Rorschach test to people of another culture and hope to obtain material from which one can make valid comparative inferences about thought processes, and the like. One reads in present-day literature on culture and personality a number of opinions that such comparative work is impossible. Many of these opinions are voiced by self-styled authorities on the subject who may not have had any firsthand experience with the particular tests they are judging, let alone any experience of giving the tests they are criticizing in several cultures to check out results with other behavioral evidence.

Contrary to such opinions, I have found test materials with which I have become familiar to be generally valid and capable of being analyzed as is such material obtained from Americans. I do not generalize and say that in all instances and settings it may be possible to obtain valid, analyzable material, but my qualified judgment would be that Rorschach material can indeed be used comparatively in an effective way if the same type of qualitative analysis is applied. I must note that I do not believe in a type of analysis that depends simply on a quantitive comparison of percentages of whole responses and the like. One must use certain flexibilities in interpretation. The danger to validity in using the Rorschach test cross-culturally is not that one obtains invalid material but that individuals trained only in clinical practice may make overly rigid interpretations based solely on their clinical experience. Anthropologists without test experience, on the other hand, have no qualifications for making valid interpretations of data.

In the particular case of the Algerian material, one must conclude that there is a paranoid-like structure suggesting maladjustment in a percentage of the population that exceeds that found in other cultures, for example, the American Indian. In the Rorschach records obtained by June Helm from two groups of American Indians, the Slave and Dogrib Athabascan Indians of the Northwest Territories in Canada, one gains an overall impression of "normal" but very constricted personalities. We found signs of maladjustment, such as mental subnormality, in some of the Dogrib families, but no other characteristic that would exceed that expected in a normative population. The Indian records were characterized by intellectual constriction rather than signs of defensive personality rigidification suggestive of paranoid propensity, as in the Algerian Arabs.

So far, please note, I have made no attempt to assess comparatively the overall social adaptation of the cultural groups concerned. Such assessment would involve a value judgment. But judgments of relative adaptation within groups are possible, however. In the case of the Arabs, to illustrate, there was seeming correspondence between what Miner noted as the person's social behavior and the severity of disturbance noticed on the Rorschach. In the case of the Slave there was no general correspondence, although in individual cases, such as that of a family in which parents and children evidenced some obsessive-compulsive features, we also found observational evidence to support the test findings (Helm et al., 1960).

In general, I would consider it possible, given a sufficiently large population of records and observational data from a particular group, to judge individual differences in social adaptation within the group, but the Rorschach test would have only a very limited ability to predict breakdown or social incapacitation, except in cases of very deviant records that show a severity of maladjustment far below the expected norms for the particular group. Working blindly on the Algerian material, that is without behavioral materials, I found it easier to predict positive adaptation from some of the protocols, which I judged to be superior to the norms of the group, than to differentiate and indicate relative social incapacity among those with relatively disturbed records.

In working with Japanese protocols, on the other hand, it was not too difficult for me using ordinary clinical criteria to make assessments of the different types of neurotic behavior to be expected of given individuals who came to the attention of psychiatrists at Nagoya University. In general, in Japan we found relatively few signs of florid symptomatology in the normative population of over 800 Rorschachs obtained in two cities and three villages. For example, in our normative population we had only one record with direct sexual content. One can see that in such a normative population the appearance of sexual content would mark the giver as deviant from his group. Therefore, when sexual responses appear, they are of peculiar significance within the context of Japanese culture. The absence of sexual responses in the Japanese records is indicative of the type of conscious control over symbolic expression that is characteristically Japanese.

Recently, working as a consultant with an Israeli psychologist doing research on the acculturation of Moroccan Jews in Paris, I noted the appearance in several of the protocols of obsessional concern with sexual material of such proportions that the individual was unable to respond adequately to the testing with other associations. Such protocols were found among individuals who were not acculturating to social life in France but had been living an encapsulated existence for a number of years. To summarize, in my experience I have found that the Rorschach results not only can differentiate between normative populations of different cultures but also can, to some degree at least, make intracultural differentiations relating possible maladjustment problems to some possible forms of social adaptation among individuals living within a given culture.

The significance of primitive intellectual and emotional coping mechanisms. From the foregoing cited experience it has become my conviction that a normative population of any given culture can be approached with testing procedures permitting some forms of personality assessment to determine the relative utilization of particular mental mechanisms related to progressive maturational levels. The relative use of coping mechanisms, such as repression or projection, by certain members of a cultural group can be elicited by a flexible use of some already existing tests such as the Rorschach when they are adapted to special problems of rapport and communication. What is then the relationship between evidence of the ready use of projection or repression and psychopathology in the predictive sense?

It stands to reason that tests cannot be rigidly applied by seeking quantitative comparisons in cross-cultural work. In some instances they must be adapted to elicit qualitative indications of the presence or absence of particular psychological processes.

Certain test results obtained from individuals accompanied by disturbed behavior in an American or European psychiatric clinic are usually indicative of social malfunctioning; in another culture setting similar protocols may not be accompanied by any manifest signs of social maladaptation. The question again arises therefore whether or not the test results are valid or whether they are suitable for personality assessment outside their culture or origin. The tests are testing, in one way or another, universals of maturation in psychological (not biological) functioning. Manifest immaturities in thought processes or primitiveness in emotional control, however, do not bear a one-to-one relationship to either socially or psychiatrically recognizable symptoms. I have witnessed results obtained with the Rorschach on Americans outside psychiatric clinics that indicate the wider presence in the American normative population of very "primitive" modalities of thought. For example the presence of prelogical "magical" thinking, emotional rigidifications, and the like are found in a good number of individuals who have never manifested obvious psychiatric symptomatology. Test signs indicating a propensity to use immature coping mechanisms are not limited to individuals whose obvious symptoms of disturbance have brought them to the attention of a psychological or psychiatric facility. The tests used clinically do indicate, in the clinical states at least, that signs of primitive emotional functioning of primary-process thinking will be significantly over-represented in a psychiatric population. They work well, especially to distinguish between neurotic and psychotic structural problems in the personality organization of individuals whose disturbed behavior has caused them to refer themselves, or be referred by others, to a psychiatric facility. The point is, however, that tests of personality do not usually in any way control or measure the pressures or problems of the individual's social environment—or its supportive functions. Yet it is the effect of the pressures or stresses of the social environment that partially determines whether or not the pressure of certain personality rigidifications or immaturities within individuals will result in the acute or chronic appearance of an obvious clinically recognizable symptom in the usual psychiatric sense.

One can, for instance, conclude as a result of a psychological assessment that an individual has what is termed a "schizoid" personality. This judgment may be based on an assessed proneness to cope by withdrawal from social communication coupled with evidence of the presence of some form or other of primary-process thinking. Whether or not this person would at some time or other become manifestly "psychotic" and be diagnosed psychiatrically as a schizophrenic is not within the power of the testing procedure to determine, since environmental factors are not predictable. He may continue to function tolerably in simple, nondemanding social situations that do not require his use of complex reasoning processes relatively free of emotional interference or subjective preoccupations.

Individuals may reveal on tests a proneness to employ an arbitrary, projective type of thinking termed "paranoid," as did some of the Algerian Arabs whose records I examined with Horace Miner. The degree to which such propensities would become manifest or recognizable would depend on the sensitivity of the individual's social group as well as the necessity for the individual concerned to make reasoned decisions under stress. What Miner and I concluded in the case of the Algerians in our sample was that a propensity for paranoid-like thought processes was indeed present in some Algerians, but that such thinking was not necessarily recognizable directly as socially disruptive. What is socially acceptable or explainable differs with the culture. What would be taken in Europe or in the United States as a sign of psychosis, such as sitting mute and unwashed in the street for days, would be more apt to result in the individual being classified as a "holy man" in Algeria. Should he immodestly remove his clothes, however, he would be immediately recognized as "crazy." So, too, with thought processes. For an Algerian to share in socially common beliefs about the plots of Jews and

French, for example, to see Jews involved in a plot to undermine one's health or potency, would not be considered "queer" by fellow Algerians. For thinking to be recognized as "queer" it must go counter to that allowable by the society. Paranoid Americans who join a special Christian religious group or the John Birch Society to defend America against a "Communist conspiracy" are usually not judged to be "paranoid" with the same rapidity as are those whose paranoid thinking leads them to think they are famous persons or that they are being persecuted by radio waves from Mars.

There are in all cultures some particular situations of crisis for the individual in which a massive regression to more primitive levels of function can occur. Psychological tests such as the Rorschach can find such potential for regression in the individual. Samuel J. Beck, at Michael Reese Hospital, Chicago, tested individuals during acutely manifest schizophrenic episodes. He then retested the same individuals five years later. When retested, most of the individuals had made more or less satisfactory forms of social adaptation. In one instance, the individual learned not to reveal his continuing hallucinatory experiences to others because such revelations "disturbed them." The Rorschach test-retest results were notably stable, showing little change in personality pattern despite the fact that these individuals for the most part had made at least marginal social adaptations. In the judgment of its users at Michael Reese, the Rorschach test was valid in revealing persistent schizophrenic personality structures in this sample of subjects. It was incapable, however, of commenting on whether or not the social environment would be supportive enough to allow for some level of adaptation given the limitations of schizophrenic weakness in the ego.

Potential maladjustment due to personality immaturity becomes evident when the individual reveals he is incapable of alternative forms of coping should they become personally or socially necessary to him. The potentially maladjustive individual is rigidified in such a way that he cannot alter his behavior relative to its appropriateness for resolving reality situations. He has matured to a point of being able to exercise alternative capacities except under optimal conditions. Under stress, his coping capacities readily revert to less adequate, more psychologically primitive levels of functioning. It is more taxing, hence very costly in mental and emotional energy, to maintain functioning at a higher level—he is less "structured" to do so. The individual has not developed sufficient capacities at a higher level to sustain himself well through any excessive stress so that he more or less readily "regresses" under duress to the use of less adequate and more primitive modalities of coping. It is this proneness to regression as well as the rigidification of earlier forms of maturational capacity that characterize the maladjusted individual.

On a social level one must also look at what is culturally available as patterns either of knowledge or of behavior to aid the individual in coping with particular situations. Given social roles, expectations can support or impede. Social role expectations may pull the person toward the expression of one form or other of behavior, acceptable or nonacceptable. If, for example, a woman in a given society is forbidden direct expression of overt aggressive behavior, she may feel constrained, and therefore may more readily adapt some masochistic mechanisms to handle the amount of affect engendered in a highly emotional situation. Masochism can therefore become a socially reinforced method of coping for some women in certain social circumstances. On the personality level the woman may be capable of alternative forms of action, but because of her social definition of herself and of her conscious self, she is incapable of exercising them, given her society.

Values—a therapeutic concern. So far in this discussion I have been arguing against some of the notions of cultural relativism, especially against the contention that no comparative judgments about social adaptation or personal adjustment are possible. While I am firmly of the opinion that cross-cultural evaluations can be made in terms of maturation, I agree to some extent with the point made by some of the cultural relativists who criticize the too-ready use of the concepts of psychopathology to label various forms of incomplete maturation that appear in every culture. Optimal maturation is relatively rare among individuals. It is an ideal state seldom recognized in any society. It is not the scientific task of comparative psychological anthropology to judge "pathology" per se. Nor to suggest that if one finds witchcraft, for example, in a particular society that the society should be compelled to initiate some kind of social amelioration program of personal therapy. The task, rather, is to objectively describe personality functioning as well as possible and to recognize how social adaptation occurs. In most instances, what one perceives in comparing patterns operative in one society with another are alternative forms of less than optimal realization of social harmony or the development of personal capacity. Value judgment comes in readily when one attempts to assess the relative virtue of one imperfect pattern compared with another. It is indeed difficult to judge what must be considered relatively satisfying or unsatisfying as a form of human social life.

Though I believe it possible to do scientific comparisons between cultures to a great extent without succumbing to value judgments, I believe value judgments are unavoidable in the practice of psychotherapy within a given culture. Values are always involved in the sense of malaise as it is subjectively experienced by an individual suffering some disorder. Values are invariably involved in considering the goal of alleviation. Since values differ within cultures, it is natural to find that the psychotherapists working within a culture have culturally bound concepts of how to aid a person who is maladjusted, how to help him realize a more adequate form of social adaptation. The objectives of therapy cannot avoid being determined, at least partially, by the shared values of a culture.

In looking at the goals of psychotherapy cross-culturally, including the practices of native healers, it seems clear that most do not work with the concept of effecting an actual change in personality structure. That is a Western goal in psychotherapy. I would argue, indeed, that when positive results are obtained through the practice of psychotherapy, it is very rarely due to any actual change in personality structure. Much more often it is due to a reordering of social perceptions, which permits the individual to adapt himself better without feelings of animosity or resentment toward something in his actual life pattern. Whether it is acknowledged or not, Western psychotherapy, regardless of the particular theoretical school involved or the goals stated, does not often result in change in the actual personality of the individual but, rather, in his ability to function more adequately with the kind of personality structure he has.

Let me illustrate the interrelationships of these two points—first, the fact that some form of value judgment seems unavoidable, and second, that psychotherapy consists of helping an individual to function more adequately within the limits of his personality—by comparing some practices of therapy in Japan with those observed in the United States.

In the United States, individuals tend to be socialized toward the best possible development of "individualistic" life patterns, stressing hard work and long-range goals leading to success. American culture demands as much of its members in the way of competition. They are subject to a great deal of tension and strain as a result. In such a culture, it is of some social advantage in many occupations to have obsessive-compulsive personality propensities. An individual with such propensities may be able to function quite successfully in a number of occupational roles where obsessive-compulsive traits are socially adaptive. At the same time, he may find that his personal social relationships are difficult and unrewarding. Such an individual may come to psychotherapy to help resolve a sense of internal malaise. The psychotherapist may find in working with such a person that some of the issues involved that exacerbate problems in individual relationships are due to unresolved feelings held toward parents or siblings. The aims of psychotherapy would be directed toward easing the type of strain the individual places upon himself and easing the behavioral rigidifications with which he is plagued. At the same time, the positive value of achieving an individualistic resolution will be emphasized. The individual may be helped to break unsatisfactory relationships with family or others that are difficult and stressful for him to maintain. In such a type of psychotherapy the individual may be helped to adapt better to his environment without actually undergoing any radical change of personality. He may still have personality traits that appear to cause him difficulty, but with the help of the therapist he learns to avoid falling into situations where his obsessive-compulsive personality gets him into unnecessary stress that may be unmanageable.

In Japanese culture, similar goals of hard work, striving, and covert competition are stressed, but the value of family harmony and social harmony is generally more important than personal independence and individualism. Japanese society also produces its share of individuals who can be considered from a psychiatric standpoint obsessive-compulsive in their personality or configuration. It is unknown whether the number of individuals with this type of difficulty is proportionately larger in Japan or the United States. There is no easy way of answering that question statistically. Work in any psychiatric clinic in Japan reveals the presence of individuals with the same structural personality problems of this nature as would appear in a clinic in the United States. An individual with such a personality has a good chance of arriving at an impasse that will cause him to seek psychotherapy. Chances are that in Japan, however, regardless of the school of psychotherapy followed, he will encounter a therapeutic regime that will be attuned more toward reestablishing his intrafamily harmony than toward freeing him from the burdens of difficult primary family relationships. In Japanese therapeutic regimes, such as Naikan therapy discussed elsewhere in this volume, and Morita therapy, there is an implicit cultural value in the therapeutic aim of restoring the individual's interpersonal family harmony. The individual is helped to subdue his idiosyncratic propensities and feelings in the name of family adaptation.

Whatever the relative level of maturation of a Japanese or an American, he will seek to achieve within himself a way of living which subscribes to the central values of his culture. Idealistically conceived goals of perfect independence or of complete social harmony may never be achieved. Indeed, seeking to actualize such a goal may produce in the individual continual stress, which for his "mental health" should not exceed manageable proportions. The values of a culture, whatever they may be, are achieved at a price. But at the same time, they provide forms of satisfaction for those living within the pattern. Again, I would suggest that what is achieved therapeutically most often is not actual modification of personality structure but the resolution of some inner tension by a realignment in the way the individual thinks about what has occurred to him and his past experiences. In both cited examples, there may be a deep, abiding, unresolved sense of resentment directed toward specific others. In either culture, entering a therapeutic regime or becoming involved with a particular religious group may help change an internal balance of a perceived life situation in such a way as to dissipate resentment and to permit the individual to obtain a better level of interpersonal functioning. In the one instance, he may be assisted toward "independent" behavior; in the other, resignation to an expected family role. What has been resolved therapeutically is a feeling state. In tests before and after therapy in the United States only rarely does a personality structure show dramatic change.

Altered states of consciousness—pathology or adaptive social function? A central issue in examining human behavior cross-culturally from a standpoint of personality structure as related to psychopathology is how to interpret altered states of consciousness that appear as religious phenomena or as signs of possession. Are individuals who manifest an altered state of consciousness mentally ill? Again, I find it meaningful to consider this issue in a maturational framework in which the coping mechanisms of an individual are progressively socialized to be socially adaptive.

In personality diagnosis one must distinguish between a type of loss of reality wherein the ego boundaries are ruptured, causing confusion in the recognition of internal and external stimuli, and various forms of repression as a method of maintaining self-consistency. By and large, the altered states of consciousness that are reported in the anthropological literature are of the second variety. Psychotic syndromes are generally less manifest in religious phenomena than are the dissociated states variously described as trance or possession. In these latter instances, the mechanisms of repression seem to be utilized as part of the social ritual. In Western culture, during the modern period, dissociation phenomena have been diagnosed most frequently as a form of hysterical psychoneurosis.

Repressed material does not remain disorganized and fragmented. What cannot be taken in and accepted as part of one's concept of self may assume some consistencies of its own. An alternate personality may wait to "appear" during a dissociated state. A person in a trance state seems often to assume "personality" traits opposite to those exhibited while normally conscious. To the observer, he is "possessed" by an alien being.

Since repression has come to be recognized in psychiatry as the major mechanism involved in hysterical neurosis, various sorts of dissociation phenomena are usually considered to appear as a characteristic of individuals with so-called hysterical personalities. Looking at the phenomenon of dissociation cross-culturally, however, it does not appear suitable to call all individuals capable of trance "neurotic." We do not even know whether trance is selectively characteristic of those who employ repression inflexibly as a major operative mechanism. It would be more appropriate to limit the term "neurotic" for use in situations where an individual has developed a subjectively realized, rigidified incapacity that limits his adaptive responses in such a way that he has an acute inner malaise, or to those who become manifestly socially incapacitated in a form recognized as deviant by his social group.

I am of the opinion that those who are prone to use repression (so-called hysteroid personality types) can be induced more readily to utilize possession or trance. It has not been demonstrated, however, that given the proper social circumstances other individuals, who must be considered within the normal range of maturation, cannot also be induced to enter an altered state of consciousness in which dissociation plays a major role.

In 1954 at Nagoya University, I participated in the analysis of a case of fox possession. A young bride was brought to the clinic exhibiting unseemingly aggressive behavior uncharacteristic of her usual demeanor. Her family considered her to be "possessed." She had previously been taken to a Shinto exorcist, but for some reason the fox remained stubbornly resistive and would not leave. She was given a number of psychological tests as well as extensive interviews by the staff and was admitted to a ward for observation. In studying her Rorschach material, I found her to exhibit a pattern that closely resembles those obtained from individuals in the United States with hysterical symptomatology. It must be noted that any person in Japan who is possessed by a fox is considered disturbed. It is not a consciously sought-after state, nor is it part of an institutionalized religious ritual. It does, nevertheless, depend upon the sustaining belief of others that fox possession is a real occurrence. Today, this has become very rare.

I do not think that one can readily transfer what we find in such a situation to what occurs in a culture where possession is utilized socially in a positive sense rather than a negative sense. Seen functionally, fox possession in Japan could be utilized unconsciously by young brides to overcome difficulties of harassment from a stringent mother-in-law. Indeed, in the Nagoya case we found a type of family situation often reported wherein the young bride found herself unsatisfactory in the eyes of her new family. The fox took over and possessed her at a point where she could no longer maintain her usual psychological equilibrium under the pressure of her demanding mother-in-law. The "sick role" eased the demands placed on her. In this sense, the possession had a satisfactory functional result.

Without evidence we cannot assume that the personality type of an individual who suffers possession without seeming intent would be the same as that of a medium who is possessed as part of a specialized professional role. William Lebra and I, working on Rorschach protocols obtained from Okinawan shamans, noted a wide variety of personality patterns in those assuming the role of shaman. Therefore, one cannot generalize that there is a necessary correspondence between a type of personality and a sought-after, socially accepted capacity to go into an altered state of consciousness. Schwartz's pathomimetic concept is recalled. We do not know the actual state of consciousness of all those who for religious purposes contend or pretend that they have gone into trance or have become possessed. It is very difficult for an observer to judge the genuineness of a seeming altered state of consciousness. To recognize this fact is not to go to the extreme position, which some are tempted to take, that a true dissociation of consciousness does not exist. My position would be that some people can learn to go into trance or to experience possession and by so doing release from within themselves alternate possibilities of role playing denied to them when they are too fully conscious of being themselves. Mental ill health occurs only when the individual under duress overuses that propensity for repression to such a degree that he becomes incapacitated. The capacity to repress or produce a dissociated state is a human capacity that can be utilized adaptively. Its utilization may be in the context of maladjustment in some individuals, but in others it is a type of regression in the service of the ego, as was discussed well by Heinz Hartmann (1958).

Conclusions

In utilizing the concept of psychopathology cross-culturally, one first has to make a general distinction between problems related to personality structure and problems of social adaptation. One must recognize as nonrelativistic the presence in human beings of maturational capacities to utilize higher levels of mental functioning. One must also distinguish between adaptive behavior, wherein there is occasional use of mechanisms of projection or repression, and the like, and such situations where behavior is recognized as deviant. It is a characteristic of some individuals to become psychopathological—that is, become rigidly and defensively limited to the utilization of such primitive mechanisms—to the point where they become noticeably deviant from the members of their group. Others, equally rigidified, may manifest no "maladaptability" unless faced with some crisis that socially necessitates a change of behavior. Whether rigidified, internally maladjusted individuals will manifest forms of recognizable psychopathology depends heavily on the nature of the social environment, that is, on the degree of stress and pressure put upon them.

One can find cross-culturally, in institutionalized beliefs and practices, forms of thought and behavior utilizing the same coping mechanisms found operative in psychiatric syndromes. But in some instances behavior is pathomimetic. Role playing in ritualized trance may indicate the actual utilization of a form of repression, or what one observes may simply be socially symbolic mimickry of such phenomena.

Psychological testing can be used cross-culturally. It can help us gain a glimpse into the personality structure of particular individuals, and by so doing it helps sort out the essential differences between observable role behavior and underlying personality.

REFERENCES

Bateson, G., and M. Mead. 1942. Balinese character: a photographic analysis. New York, New York Academy of Sciences.

Caudill, W. 1959. The relationship of anthropology to psychiatry in the study of culture and personality. Japanese Journal of Psychoanalysis 6:468–82.

Fanon, F. 1968. Wretched of the earth. New York, Grove Press.

Goffman, I. 1961. Asylums. Chicago, Aldine Press.

Hartmann, H. 1958. Ego psychology and the problems of adaptation. David Rapaport, trans. New York, International Universities Press.

Helm, J., G. DeVos, and T. Carterette. 1960. Variations in personality and ego identification within a Slave Indian kin-community. *In* Contributions to anthropology. National Museum of Canada Bulletin 190, pt. 2.

Honigmann, J. 1969. Middle class values and cross-cultural understanding. *In* Culture change, mental health and poverty. J.C. Finney, ed. Lexington, University of Kentucky Press.

Kluckhohn, C. 1944. Navaho witchcraft. Boston, Beacon Press.

Laing, R.D. 1967. The politics of experience. New York, Pantheon.

Laing, R.D., and D.G. Cooper. 1971. Reason and violence. New York, Pantheon.

Levy-Bruhl, L. 1926. How natives think. London, Allen and Unwin.

Malinowski, B. 1948. Magic, science and religion. Glencoe, Illinois, Free Press.

Miner, H., and G. DeVos. 1959. Oasis and casbah—a study in acculturative stress. *In* Culture and mental health. M.K. Opler, ed. New York, Macmillan.

Prince, R. 1964. Indigenous Yoruba psychiatry. *In* Magic, faith and healing. A. Kiev, ed. New York, Free Press of Glencoe.

Sarbin, T.R. 1969. The scientific status of the mental illness metaphor. *In* Changing perspectives in mental illness. S.C. Plog and R.B. Edgerton, eds. New York, Holt, Rinehart and Winston.

———. 1964. Anxiety: the reification of a metaphor. Archives of General Psychiatry 10:630–38.

Schwartz, T. n.d. A cargo cult: a Melanesian type response to change. *In* Responses to change: adjustment and adaptation in personality and culture. G.A. DeVos, ed. MS.

Scheff, T.J. 1966. Being mentally ill: a social theory. Chicago, Aldine Press.

Szasz, T.S. 1961. The myth of mental illness: foundations of a theory of personal conduct. New York, Hoeber-Harper.

Coda

The following transpired during the final moments of the conference:

      LEBRA: Any further comments? Expressions of sentiment? Disclaimers? Corrections?

      SASAKI: About Morita . . . I must speak of a work in which he could be envisioned as folk-psychiatrist. In 1915 he described invocation psychosis; that was the first work in the field of folk psychiatry in Japan. So, if he still survived, he would have been invited here. I would also like to show the relationship of shamanism and medicine. [He goes to the blackboard.] The Chinese character for medicine in ancient times was written like this:

It means shaman, two persons dancing in trance. But the character for medicine now is

So it changed from shamanism to alcohol. It is very interesting.

      DEVOS: So, we went from the shaman to the bottle.

Index